Peter J. Rodgers

CH00403420

A REGIONAL HISTORY OF
RAILWAYS

VOLUME XVI
IRELAND

OTHER TITLES IN THIS SERIES

A REGIONAL HISTORY OF RAILWAYS

Volume XVI

IRELAND

by
J. W. P. Rowledge

WITH 38 PLATES
19 MAPS
AND FOLDING MAP

TRANSPORT

Atlantic

PUBLISHERS

TO THE MEMORY
OF
BOB CLEMENTS

Rest in Peace Old Friend
You will not be Forgotten

British Library Cataloguing in Publication Data

A catalogue record for this book is available from the British Library

ISBN0 906899 63 X

First published 1995

©J. W. P. Rowledge

All rights reserved. No part of this
publication may be reproduced, stored
in a retrieval system, or transmitted,
in any form or by any means, electronic,
mechanical, photocopying, recording or
otherwise, without the prior permission
of the publisher.

Typeset by XL Publishing Services, Nairn and
printed in Great Britain by
Redwood Books, Trowbridge,
for Atlantic Transport Publishers,
Trevithick House, West End, Penryn, Cornwall TR10 8HE

Contents

Introduction

The whole of Ireland is described in this companion volume to the fifteen covering Great Britain region by region. Similarity between the railways of Ireland and Britain naturally stems from the historical fact that after 1801 and throughout the formative years of railway systems one government, at Westminster, defined the legal framework, passed the laws that regulated business and of course the Acts by which the multitude of railway companies were incorporated. Unlike the other volumes, this describes railway events in two states with consequent divergence of policies which, because of public preference for motor transport, have a common result in a reduction in mileage from its maximum in 1921 by 60 percent, large areas being entirely without railed transport – in fact the equivalent of the *Beeching Axe* was wielded rather earlier than on British Railways in both the Republic of Ireland and Northern Ireland.

The story of Ireland's railways has to be set against a situation unique in modern history – a land with an almost continuous decline in its population, being about half these days compared with the initiation of the railway age. Thus there was no railway inspired expansion of trade to compare with Britain's railway history; indeed it has been stated that the coming of the railway *aided* emigration by making the first part of the journey away from home easier. Nature denied Ireland mineral wealth and so domestic traffic was mainly the more general day by day produce from factory to shop, a great deal of it imported from England, or imported fuel, non-passenger business never having dominated receipts as in the not so long past in Britain. The largest volume of outwards traffic was livestock, mainly cattle, destined for the ever enlarging population of Britain's industrial cities. The proximity to their ports of the three populous areas with manufacturing capacity denied the railway carriage of much finished export produce, coastal shipping also serving many small places all round the coast of Ireland, often directly from Britain.

Many have used since 1921 the terms 'north' and 'south' to distinguish the two states and in the latter a number of places have reverted, or changed, to their Irish names, but with few exceptions both names happily exist together in daily use – thus the author has felt free to use either, but tending to use the better known, such as Dun Laoghaire rather than Kingstown. The renaming in 1966 of a number of stations, or rather the addition of a suffix, to commemorate several national heroes in the republic, has made life a little difficult for the railway historian in respect of Dublin's stations, for it remains easier to think of Kingsbridge rather than Heuston, but both are used. The counties in the Republic have not been altered, although two did change their names all those years ago, but in the north districts have taken over local administration – their names are not really relevant to railway history.

In the text the more important dates are given usually in full but lesser dates by year only; however, the chronology gives, with the few exceptions where information is not forthcoming, opening and closure dates in day-month-year form. There were never many sidings away from stations, either railway or private, in Ireland; some of the more important are mentioned but space forbids inclusion of others. Distances given in the text are sufficient to indicate lengths of lines and branches and the position of principal locations. Ireland is renowned for inconsistency, despite the achievements of so many Irish people in a great variety of endeavours, whether in the arts or sciences, and one form that bedevils the railway historian is the variation of station names – thus in timetables and other documents one can find Kilcoole or Kilcool, Patrick's Well or Patrickswell, Ballingrane Junction or just Ballingrane, to name but a few. A word of warning about the use of halt must be given for it has had a rather different meaning, particularly on the Great Southern Railways, to its use in Britain, indicating a station under the control of another, be it manned or just a wayside platform. Unless necessary in this text halt is not normally given as it rarely appeared on nameboards, although used in working timetables, etc. There was also a multiplicity of stops at level crossings or gates solely used by railcars and railbuses, many short-lived; they are listed for their interesting part in Irish railway operation, giving a service more in the style of a bus route.

All too often it is the case that there is far from enough space allowed by the publisher and it is the author's problem to condense, or omit, so much that is relevant. Thus so much of the text is no more than a brief sketch, even allowing for so little happening on many lines between opening and closing, they changing very little indeed. So it has been necessary to concentrate on the basic historical facts, it being impossible to give much of the company history, beyond that which bound the various routes together, most falling eventually into the two state systems that have existed in modern times.

Only brief mention is possible of industrial railways, never numerous in Ireland; Map No 18 attempts to indicate locations, ranging from the extensive Bord na Mona systems connecting the turf lifting areas and processing plants and power stations to just a few yards of track in a quarry or brickworks. As published material on locomotives is now becoming abundant it is not necessary to give more than a passing mention in this volume.

To those of us who are old enough to have travelled when a much larger proportion of Ireland's railways was in use, particularly the narrow gauge, the author hopes that the historical details will revive happy memories of railways that largely belonged to an even earlier era – to the youngsters it is hoped that this overall view of a nation's railways will help to understand the heritage of the remaining systems of Irish Rail and Northern Ireland Railways. For those who have never been to Ireland the text will show that they have missed so much in a land full of welcome and which even now with its reduced mileage still has a great deal of railway interest, showing the way in these islands with some very modern signalling and the running of very successful American built diesel locomotives.

J.W.P. Rowledge
Newton Abbot
May 1995

Abbreviations

IRISH RAILWAYS

Abbreviation	Railway	Incorporated	Gauge	Next Railway
A&EJR	Athenry & Ennis Junction Railway	1859	5–3	W&LR (1893)
ATE	Athenry & Tuam Extension to Claremorris Railway	1890	5–3	GSR (1925)
A&TR	Athenry & Tuam Railway	1858	5–3	W&LR (1893)
B&WR	Bagenalstown & Wexford Railway	1854	5–3	-
B&TJLR	Ballinascarthy & Timoleague Junction Light Railway	1888	5–3	GSR (1925)
—	Ballycastle Railway	1878	3–0	LMS(NCC) (1924)
B&LR	Ballymena & Larne Railway	1874ø	3–0	B&NCR (1889)
BBC&PJR	Ballymena, Ballymoney, Coleraine & Portrush Junction Railway	1853	5–3	B&NCR (1861)
BC&RBR	Ballymena, Cushendall & Red Bay Railway	1872	3–0	B&NCR (1884)
BER	Baltimore Extension Railway	1890	5–3	GSR (1925)
BER	Banbridge Extension Railway	1861	5–3	GNR (1877)
BJR	Banbridge Junction Railway	1856ø	5–3	GNR (1877)
BL&BR	Banbridge, Lisburn & Belfast Railway	1858	5–3	GNR (1877)
BND&BJR	Banbridge, Newry, Dublin & Belfast Junction Railway	1853	5–3	BJR (1856)ø
BBER	Bantry Bay Extension Railway	1889	5–3	GSR (1924)
BER	Bantry Extension Railway	1879	5–3	GSR (1925)
B&BR	Belfast & Ballymena Railway	1845	5–3	B&NCR (1860)ø
B&CDR	Belfast & County Down Railway	1846	5–3	UTA (1948)
B&NCR	Belfast & Northern Counties Railway	1860ø	5–3	MR(NCC) (1903)
BCR	Belfast Central Railway	1864	5–3	GNR (1885)

BH&BR	Belfast, Holywood & Bangor Railway	1860	5–3	B&CDR (1884)
B&NT	Bassbrook & Newry Tramway	1884	3–0	-
CER	Carndonagh Extension Railway	1897	3–0	-
C&LR	Carrickfergus & Larne Railway	1860	5–3	B&NCR (1890)
CHJR	Carrickfergus Harbour Junction Railway	1887	5–3	-
CK&AR	Castleblayney, Keady & Armagh Railway	1902	5–3	GNR (1912)
C&VBT	Castlederg & Victoria Bridge Tramway	1883	3–0	-
CR	Castleisland Railway	1872	5–3	GS&WR (1879)
C&LR	Cavan & Leitrim Railway	1895ø	3–0	GSR (1925)
CL&RLR&T	Cavan, Leitrim & Roscommon Light Railway & Tramway	1883	3–0	C&LR (1895)ø
CIR	Central Ireland Railway	1866	5–3	W&CIR (1877)
CDJR	City of Dublin Junction Railways	1884	5–3	GSR (1925)
C&BR	Clara & Banagher Railway	1880ø	5–3	GS&WR (1895)
CVR	Clogher Valley Railway	1894ø	3–0	-
CVT	Clogher Valley Tramway	1884	3–0	CVR (1894)ø
CER	Clonakilty Extension Railway	1881	5–3	GSR (1925)
CIE	Coras Iompair Eireann	1945	5–3 3–0	IR (1987)ø
C&BR	Cork & Bandon Railway	1845	5–3	CB&SCR (1888)ø
C&KJR	Cork & Kinsale Junction Railway	1859	5–3	C&BR (1880)
C&LDR	Cork & Limerick Direct Railway	1860	5–3	GS&WR (1871)
C&MDR	Cork & Macroom Direct Railway	1861	5–3	GSR (1925)
C&MLR	Cork & Muskerry Light Railway	1883	3–0	GSR (1925)
C&YR	Cork & Youghal Railway	1854	5–3	GS&WR (1866)
CB&SCR	Cork, Bandon & South Coast Railway	1888ø	5–3	GSR (1924)
CB&PR	Cork, Blackrock & Passage Railway	1846	5–3 3–0	GSR (1925)
CCR	Cork City Railways	1906	5–3	GSR (1925)
CDRJC	County Donegal Railways Joint Committee	1906ø	3–0	-
DCR	Derry Central Railway	1875	5–3	B&NCR (1901)
DR	Donegal Railway	1892	5–3 3–0	CDRJC (1906)ø
DRSC	Donegal Railway Station Co	1888	3–0	CDRJC (1906)
DER	Donoughmore Extension Railway	1890	3–0	GSR (1925)
DD&NR	Downpatrick, Dundrum & Newcastle Railway	1866	5–3	B&CDR (1881)
DK&ALR	Downpatrick, Killough & Ardglass Light Railway	1890	5–3	B&CDR (1893)
DR	Draperstown Railway	1878	5–3	B&NCR (1895)

D&AJR	Dublin & Antrim Junction Railway	1861	5–3	GNR (1879)
D&BJR	Dublin & Belfast Junction Railway	1845	5–3	NR (1875)
D&BST	Dublin & Blessington Steam Tramway	1885	5–3	-
D&DR	Dublin & Drogheda Railway	1836	5–3	NR (1875)
D&KR	Dublin & Kingstown Railway	1831	4–8½ 5–3	GSR (1925)
D&LER	Dublin & Lucan Electric Railway	1896ø	3–6	-
D&LST	Dublin & Lucan Steam Tramway	1880	3–0	D&LER (1896)ø
D&MR	Dublin & Meath Railway	1858	5–3	MGWR (1888)
D&SER	Dublin & South Eastern Railway	1907ø	5–3	GSR (1925)
D&WR	Dublin & Wicklow Railway	1851	5–3	DW&WR (1860)ø
DD&RR	Dublin, Dundrum & Rathfarnham Railway	1846	5–3	D&WR (1851)ø
DW&WR	Dublin, Wicklow & Wexford Railway	1860ø	5–3	D&SER (1907)ø
D&ER	Dundalk & Enniskillen Railway	1845	5–3	INWR (1862)ø
D&GR	Dundalk & Greenore Railway	1863	5–3	DN&GR (1873)ø
DN&GR	Dundalk, Newry & Greenore Railway	1873ø	5–3	-
D&CR	Dungannon & Cookstown Railway	1874	5–3	GNR (1877)
D&SR	Dunmanway & Skibbereen Railway	1870	5–3	IVR (1872)ø
E&BR	Enniskillen & Bundoran Railway	1861	5–3	EB&SR (1862)ø
EB&SR	Enniskillen, Bundoran & Sligo Railway	1862ø	5–3	GNR (1897)
F&LR	Fermoy & Lismore Railway	1869	5–3	F&RR&H (1898)
FVR	Finn Valley Railway	1860	5–3	DR (1892)
F&RR&H	Fishguard & Rosslare Railways & Harbours	1898	5–3	-
GCP& BVR&T	Giant's Causeway, Portrush & Bush Valley Railway & Tramway	1880	3–0	-
GL&MR	Grand Leinster & Munster Railway	1837	5–3	ISER (1846)ø
GN&WR	Great Northern & Western Railway	1857	5–3	MGWR (1890)
GNR	Great Northern Railway	1876	5–3	GNRB (1953)
GNRB	Great Northern Railway Board	1953	5–3	CIE & UTA (1958)
GS&WR	Great Southern & Western Railway	1844	5–3	GSR (1924)
GSR	Great Southern Railway	1924	5–3	GSR (1925)
GSR	Great Southern Railways	1925	5–3 3–0	CIE (1945)
IVR	Ilen Valley Railway	1872ø	5–3	CB&SCR (1909)
INWR	Irish North Western Railway	1862ø	5–3	NR (1876)
IR	Irish Rail	1987ø	5–3	-
IREC	Irish Railway Executive Committee	-	5–3 3–0	-
ISER	Irish South Eastern Railway	1846ø	5–3	GS&WR (1863)
K&NR	Kanturk & Newmarket Railway	1888	5–3	GS&WR (1892)

KJR	Kilkenny Junction Railway	1860	5–3	W&CIR (1896)
KJR	Killarney Junction Railway	1846	5–3	GS&WR (1860)
L&BR	Larne & Ballyclare Railway	1873	3–0	B&LR (1874)ø
L&BER	Letterkenny & Burtonport Extension Railway	1896	3–0	-
LR	Letterkenny Railway	1860	3–0	-
L&DR	Limavady & Dungiven Railway	1878	5–3	MR(NCC) (1907)
L&CR	Limerick & Castleconnell Railway	1856	5–3	W&LR (1872)
L&ER	Limerick & Ennis Railway	1853	5–3	W&LR (1893)
L&KR	Limerick & Kerry Railway	1880	5–3	GS&WR (1902)
L&BR	Listowel & Ballybunion Railway	1886	Monorail	-
LMS(NCC)	London Midland & Scottish Railway (Northern Counties Committee)	1923	5–3 3–0	RE(NCC) (1948)
L&CR	Londonderry & Coleraine Railway	1845	5–3	B&NCR (1871)
L&ER	Londonderry & Enniskillen Railway	1845	5–3	GNR (1883)
L&LSR	Londonderry & Lough Swilly Railway	1853	5–3 3–0	-
L&ALR	Loughrea & Attymon Light Railway	1885	5–3	GSR (1925)
LL&CST	Lucan, Leixlip & Celbridge Steam Tramway	1889	3–0	-
MC&SJR	Midland Counties & Shannon Junction Railway	1861	5–3	C&BR (1880)ø
MGWR	Midland Great Western Railway	1845	5–3	GSR (1924)
MR(NCC)	Midland Railway (Northern Counties Committee)	1903	5–3 3–0	LMS(NCC) (1923)
N&KR	Navan & Kingscourt Railway	1865	5–3	MGWR (1888)
NR&WER	New Ross & Waterford Extension Railway	1897	5–3	GSR (1925)
N&AR	Newry & Armagh Railway	1857ø	5–3	GNR (1879)
N&ER	Newry & Enniskillen Railway	1845	5–3	N&AR (1857)ø
N&GR	Newry & Greenore Railway	1863	5–3	DN&GR (1873)
NK&TR	Newry, Keady & Tynan Light Railway	1900	3–0	U&CLR (1903)ø
NW&RR	Newry, Warrenpoint & Rostrevor Railway	1846	5–3	GNR (1886)
NIR	Northern Ireland Railways	1967	5–3	-
NR	The Northern Railway	1875	5–3	GNR (1876)
P&PBR	Parsonstown & Portumna Bridge Railway	1861	5–3	-
P&DR	Portadown & Dungannon Railway	1853	5–3	PD&OR (1857)ø
PD&OR	Portadown, Dungannon & Omagh Railway	1857ø	5–3	UR (1876)
PT	Portstewart Tramway	1880	3–0	B&NCR (1897)
RE(NCC)	Railway Executive (Northern Counties Committee)	1948	5–3 3–0	UTA (1949)

R&NJR	Rathkeale & Newcastle Junction Railway	1861	5–3	GS&WR (1902)
R&PJR	Roscrea & Parsonstown Junction Railway	1854	5–3	GS&WR (1858)
S&SLR	Schull & Skibbereen Light Railway	1886	3–0	GSR (1925)
S&BJR	Sligo & Ballaghadereen Junction Railway	1863	3–0	MGWR (1877)
SL&NCR	Sligo, Leitrim & Northern Counties Railway	1875	5–3	-
SCR	South Clare Railways	1884	3–0	GSR (1925)
SR	Southern Railway	1865	5–3	GSR (1925)
S&LR	Strabane & Letterkenny Railway	1904ø	3–0	-
SR&CR	Strabane, Raphoe & Convoy Railway	1903	3–0	S&LR (1904)ø
T&CELR	Timoleague & Courtmacsherry Extension Light Railway	1888	5–3	GSR (1925)
T&CLR	Timoleague & Courtmacsherry Light Railway	1888	5–3	GSR (1925)
TNCR	Town of Newry Connecting Railway	1857	5–3	GNR (1886)
T&DLR	Tralee & Dingle Light Railway	1888	3–0	GSR (1925)
T&FR	Tralee & Fenit Railway	1880	5–3	GSR (1925)
T&KR	Tralee & Killarney Railway	1853	5–3	GSR (1860)
TER	Tullow Extension Railway	1884	5–3	GS&WR (1886)
UR	Ulster Railway	1839	6–2 5–3	GNR (1876)
UTA	Ulster Transport Authority	1948	5–3 3–0	UTR (1966)ø
UTR	Ulster Transport Railways	1966ø	5–3	NIR (1967)
W&CIR	Waterford & Central Ireland Railway	1868ø	5–3	GS&WR (1900)
W&KR	Waterford & Kilkenny Railway	1845	5–3	W&CIR (1868)ø
W&LR	Waterford & Limerick Railway	1845	5–3	WL&WR (1896)ø
W&TR	Waterford & Tramore Railway	1851	5–3	GSR (1925)
W&WR	Waterford & Wexford Railway	1864	5–3	F&RR&H (1898)
WD&LR	Waterford, Dungarvan & Lismore Railway	1872	5–3	F&RR&H (1898)
WL&WR	Waterford, Limerick & Western Railway	1896ø	5–3	GS&WR (1901)
WNR&WJR	Waterford, New Ross & Wexford Junction Railway	1866	5–3	DW&WR & GS&WR (1877)
WWW&DR	Waterford, Wexford, Wicklow & Dublin Railway	1846	5–3	D&WR (1851)ø
WCT&LR	West Carbery Tramways & Light Railways	1883	3–0	GSR (1925)
WCR	West Clare Railway	1884	3–0	GSR (1925)
WCR	West Cork Railways	1860	5–3	C&BR (1880)
WDR	West Donegal Railway	1879	3–0	DR (1892)ø

WC&DJR   Wexford, Carlow & Dublin Junction   1846   5–3   ISER (1846)ø
         Railway

ø = Company retitled by Act of Parliament (Westminster and Belfast) or Dail (Dublin).

OTHER ABBREVIATIONS

B&I	British & Irish Steam Packet Co
BHC	Belfast Harbour Commissioners
BOT	Board of Trade (Westminster)
BOW	Board of Works
CDSP	City of Dublin Steam Packet Co
CSE	Commlucht Suicre Eireann (Irish Sugar)
DUTC	Dublin United Tramways (1896) Co
GPO	General Post Office
GWR	Great Western Railway
IRCH	Irish Railway Clearing House
LMS	London Midland & Scottish Railway
LNWR	London & North Western Railway
LP&HC	Londonderry Port & Harbour Commissioners
MR	Midland Railway
NIRTB	Northern Ireland Road Transport Board
PWLC	Public Works Loans Commissioners
RDS	Royal Dublin Society
WTT	Working timetable

CHAPTER I

Ireland & Its Railways

History and geography have not been very kind to Ireland, lying on the western edge of Europe, isolated by the Irish Sea from Britain and largely by-passed as the centuries rolled by, the Atlantic Ocean conferring on the island a benefit in the form of a rather more equable climate than most of northern Europe although at the cost of copious rainfall which has given the land a greenness of its own, so no wonder it is the Emerald Isle. However, much of the land is barren or nearly so and therefore the benefits of modern agriculture have not had as much impact as in England. There is the advantage of scenic grandeur and coupled with sport, particularly horses and fishing in lough, river and sea, tourists have been drawn westward to sample a land that has held on to its past and is proud of it despite all that has happened in the last two centuries. Nowhere else is the welcome to the visitor quite the same.

The Irish Sea separating the east coast of Ireland from Britain varies in width from only 13 miles in the North Channel between Co Antrim and the Mull of Kintyre and 21½ miles from Donaghadee to Portpatrick in south west Scotland or the 50 miles of the St George's Channel from the south east corner in Co Wexford to the headlands of Pembrokeshire in West Wales, to the 100 miles or so midway from the coast north of Dublin to the Lancashire coast. Thus migration of early man was not hindered by a lengthy water passage so that habitation has existed since about 1500 BC. Naturally several tribes occupied the island or followed earlier settlers but the way they divided the land has survived broadly in the form of the four provinces Ulster, Munster, Leinster and Connaught. Within each province there were distinct areas, still remembered in such names as Thomond, Desmond, Dalriada, Ossory or Tyrconnell but it was not until the Anglo-Norman occupations that the counties first became recognisable. Now there are thirty-two occupying 32,588 square miles.

Geology has a great influence on the course of railway history, its main effect being the distribution of habitation and the occupations of the inhabitants. Ireland in geographical terms comprises three bands from north to south, higher ground either side of a central lowland belt. Glaciation in the successive Ice Ages has formed much of the present Ireland and left ranges of high ground, indeed mountains, valleys and many lakes, or rather loughs, with extensive drainage into large rivers. Certainly the visitor can not fail to be impressed by the size of the rivers for so relatively small a land – the principal river, the Shannon, is the longest in the British Isles, 240 miles from source to mouth, and even well inland is broad. Other effects of glaciation are the 'erratics' (a geological term) which are in fact great rocks carried far from their natural locations, the 'eskers' which are long ridges of glacial deposits to be found across the central belt and the 'drumlins', small hillocks formed by similar deposits.

A negative effect of the Ice Ages has been the stripping away of the layers which would have contained coal measures so that Ireland has been almost totally denied that source of fuel. Indeed minerals of any sort have been found only in very limited amounts so that there are few sources worthy of commercial attention. Thus there was not the geological basis for development of industry or large centres of population which occurred in Britain, making the history of the two islands so very different. Indeed some areas are virtually devoid of soil, notably the Burreen in Co Clare and the Aran Isles in Galway Bay. Inevitably in these circumstances agriculture remains the prime commercial activity in the island.

Generally railway routes lacked extremes, only one line exceeding 1,000 ft and these days the maximum is not greatly more than 350 ft. Tunnels have been few and the longest was just one yard short of a mile. There were, and still are of course, some steep sections of line, but never to the extent of areas such as South Wales. Single track predominates and many sections which were double have been reduced to one; such changes are detailed in the text.

From early days Ireland has maintained a tradition of Christianity despite events elsewhere in Europe, a beacon of enlightenment in the eyes of many, and from this have grown the fundamental political differences between Ireland and Britain. English rule over Ireland took many centuries to establish, gradually spreading from the coastal areas of the central plain following the initial invasion of 1169. The result was years of turbulence – at the time of Henry VIII it was said that 'Whoso lives by west of the Barrow, lives west of the law'. Following conquest a system of 'plantation' was imposed on lands taken over by new inhabitants from England and Scotland who were to settle and strengthen loyalty to the Crown. Although spread across Ireland the 'plantations' were especially numerous in the north in Ulster, mainly emigrants from Scotland driven out by enemies in their own country – ironically the English Government tried to drive them back to Scotland! However in 1586 they were recognised as lawful settlers and thereafter numbers increased, but they brought with them another source of difference for they were Protestants unlike the native Irish who steadfastly remained Roman Catholic.

After William III had ousted James II in 1688 he faced almost total opposition in Ireland which was reinforced by the return of James, supported by France, in 1689. The latter was defeated on 1 July 1690 at the Battle of the Boyne in Co Meath, completing the subjugation of the Roman Catholic opposition, concluded in the Treaty of Limerick, leaving some 80 per cent of the population with no say in their government. The London governments treated Ireland's commercial activities in the same manner as the many other colonies of England by imposing trade restrictions which were intended to protect England's prosperity. Thus markets for Irish products, such as livestock or wool, were denied but absent landlords took every penny they could back to England, leaving little to stimulate Irish economy. However an event far away in America, the cessation of colonies from the Crown after the War of Independence, started a process of relaxation so that in 1778 Catholics could buy land and restrictions on trade were eased. Irish nationalism was greatly stimulated by the French Revolution leading to an unsuccessful rebellion in 1798, planned to coincide with a French invasion of Ireland, the effect of which was the enforced union of Britain and Ireland in 1800.

The nineteenth century in Ireland was dominated by actions of those determined to free their homeland from English rule, there being periods of turbulence and lawlessness with campaigns against the absentee landlords and authority, represented in Ireland by the Lord Lieutenant and his staff ensconced in Dublin Castle. Despite events the population of Ireland was increasing in common with the rest of the world, having been about two million in 1700 and steadily enlarging to some five million in 1801 and so on to 8¼ million in 1841. At this time the English and Welsh population was 15 million and Scotland's 2½ million, Ireland having almost 30 per cent of the inhabitants of the British Isles. Then came a disaster when crops, particularly potato, then the staple diet of most, were blighted in the wet years of 1845 and 1946, leading to famine and starvation which continued into 1847, a stark time still spoken of with bated breath as 'The Famine'. Although there were similar crop failures in the rest of the British Isles, especially Scotland, the effect was nowhere near so devastating and historically these bad times represent more than any other the divergence of Ireland and Britain, setting in motion a long and almost uninterrupted period of emigration from Ireland so that unlike countries worldwide which have increased in population to an alarming extent the Emerald Isle has halved its numbers since the 1841 census. While England and Wales now stand at 51½ million and Scotland 5 million, Ireland is now only 4½ million, representing but 7 per cent of the total. Taking 1841 as unity, successive census figures show 1851 as 0·8, 1861 as 0·7, 1871 as 0·66, 1881 as 0·63, 1891 as 0·57, 1901 as 0·54 and 1911 as 0·53 (4⅓ million). Even now there is no real sign of an increase and officialdom remains concerned that the youth of Ireland will continue to be drawn away, as much by tradition as any other cause. Visitors to Ireland see many derelict cottages and while the foliage clad remains may look romantic they represent Ireland's lost future – when the time came to go, to America or Britain in search of food, work and a better future, the Irishman simply closed the door of his cottage behind him, always expecting to come home one day. The devastating effect of decline, partly by starvation and high average age of marriage but mostly emigration, shows in the drop in numbers in almost every Irish county; comparing 1891 with 1841 there were eleven where only about one-third remained (Kilkenny, Laois, Offaly, Longford, Meath, Clare, Tipperary, Fermanagh, Cavan, Monaghan and Roscommon) and another eleven with half or less (Carlow, Louth, Westmeath, Cork, Limerick, Waterford, Tyrone, Galway, Leitrim, Mayo and Sligo). Only three counties showed an increase, Dublin, Armagh and Antrim, the last two by more than 60 per cent, the result of the rising industrial activities of Belfast and the Lagan valley, and of course Dublin was expanding at the expense of neighbouring counties. In 1841 only ten centres were listed with more than 20,000 inhabitants (Dublin, Belfast, Cork, Limerick, Waterford, ~~Ahoghill (Co Antrim)~~, Armagh, Newry, ~~Clones~~ and Galway); in 1911 the list comprised Dublin, Belfast, ~~Monkstown~~ (Co Dublin), Kingstown, Cork, Limerick, Waterford and Londonderry. Even now such a list consists of no more than thirteen centres, Dublin, Belfast, Lisburn, Londonderry, Newtownabbey, Omagh, Cork, Drogheda, Dundalk, Dun Laoghaire, Galway, Limerick and Waterford. Thus not only has emigration emptied the rural areas but it has also prevented mass urbanisation.

Home Rule for Ireland was a thorny problem for the Westminster governments throughout the nineteenth century and nearly came about with the passing of an Act in 1914 – but as so often events elsewhere upset Ireland's aspirations when Kaiser Bill started World War I, plunging Europe into conflict until 1918 during which there was an unsuccessful rising at Easter 1916, almost totally confined to Dublin. Rail services into Dublin were suspended for a week and the city found itself in dire straits for food. The consequence was the stirring of nationalist strengths which resulted in civil strife 1920–1, followed by the passing in Westminster of an

Act which partitioned off six of the Ulster counties and set up a separate government of Northern Ireland in Belfast on 24 May 1921. Railways became targets of boycotts in the form of refusal to handle British goods or work trains with troops on board and physical damage was inflicted, resulting in the closure by military orders of many sections of line. In the meantime a provisional government was set up in Dublin until a treaty recognised the establishment of the new state with its own Parliament on 6 December 1921. The various terms of the treaty came to divide Irishmen as never before and in the ensuing civil war which started on 28 May 1922 railways became a prime target with many lines out of action for long periods, Dublin being cut off from most major centres, particularly Cork and Waterford. All this upheaval ended on 30 April 1923 and the new country, entitled the Irish Free State set about the serious business of organising itself.

Irish railways now found themselves in a new political and economic climate, as well as facing new competition from the nascent road transport. The new Free State Government seemed to have been in favour of state ownership and control but the best that could be achieved was an enforced union in 1924–5 of all the companies which lay wholly within the new state. Times were not good for the new railway company and matters were made worse when an 'Economic War' broke out in 1932 between Ireland and Britain, caused by the termination of repayment of interest on loans made many years before to Irish tenant farmers so that they could purchase their lands; Westminster retaliated by imposing a 20 per cent import duty on Irish products, Dublin introducing its own protective tariffs, the dispute not being resolved until 1938, by which time the Irish Free State had changed its status on 29 December 1938 and become Eire. However in diplomatic terms Eire was still a member of the British Commonwealth, although the 'Oath of Allegiance' no longer applied, a situation resolved on 18 April 1949 with final severance from Britain and the formation of the Republic of Ireland. The separate government of Northern Ireland, as often as not known as Ulster, remained until direct rule from Westminster took over in 1972. Unrest in the north yet again made railways a target; since 1969 there have been many cases of destruction of trains, lines and stations. Just as these words are being finalised a period of peace has settled in Ulster – long may it last and create a new prosperity for all, including Ireland's railways.

Currently in the divided island Ulster has 17 per cent of the area and 31 per cent of the total population, a slight increase from 28 per cent in 1911. In 1841 the six counties were home to 20 per cent of the total population, the change illustrating the fact that Ulster had the industrial development of the Belfast area to lessen the effects of emigration.

It is against such a historical background that Ireland's railway history has to be judged, having started at a time when there was every reason to expect increasing trade to serve an enlarging population as in the rest of Europe.

The earliest railed transport in Ireland on record was a quarry line at Ballycastle, mentioned in 1743. R.L. Edgeworth used a portable wooden track in 1786–9 during bog reclamation on his estates in Counties Westmeath and Longford, complete with tipping wagons of a rather peculiar design. Later portable iron tracks were used on bog reclamation projects at Killucan, Co Westmeath and in the Bog of Allen, Co Kildare. In 1833–4 Sir Richard Griffith used similar portable tracks (2 ft 6 in gauge) at a government backed experimental reclamation scheme in the north west corner of Co Cork.

The first Irish railway was authorised in 1826, the Limerick & Waterford Railway, but it was too early for such a long route so it was not until late 1834 that Ireland's first line, the Dublin & Kingstown Railway opened, followed by promotion of the Ulster, the Dublin & Drogheda and the Great Munster & Leinster. Then promotions were held up whilst the Government awaited the report of Commissioners appointed on 28 October 1836 to assess the island's railway needs for it was feared that unrestrained speculation could result in lines of no real value to the country. The first report of 11 March 1837 was brief and expressed the opinion that there would be no great hope of railways ever being remunerative in Ireland. At the time Cos Monaghan, Armagh, Antrim and Down were the most populous being engaged in the expanding linen trade, replacing Belfast's declining cotton industry. The report drew attention to the numerous small coal deposits in Ireland, the most important being those in Leinster in the Castlecomer area, in Ulster near Dungannon and Coalisland and in Connaught near Lough Allen; others mentioned were in Cos Tipperary, Clare, Limerick, Kerry, Cork, Monaghan and Antrim, some of which were worked in a small way. The second report issued on 13 July 1838 recommended the construction of two lines from Dublin which would open up the country in the most advantageous way, one northwards towards Ulster and the other south westerly to Limerick and Cork. The opinion was expressed that there was no need for a line westwards as two canals existed and any railway built in that direction would succeed only by taking the entire trade off the canals.

The suggested northern route (in fact the already proposed Dublin & Armagh Inland Railway of 1836) was to start from the north side of the Royal Canal, then the limit of the city area, at the then Botanic Gardens near Drumcondra, and serve Navan, Carrickmacross, Castleblayney, and Armagh (85^1/$_2$ miles) where it was expected that the line would connect with the Ulster Railway which had powers to build from Belfast; from Navan a branch would serve Cavan and Enniskillen (96 miles). Further north a route from Armagh to Portrush appeared on a map as a proposed line. The western route was to start from Barrack Bridge, $1^{1}/_{4}$ miles from the General Post Office in the centre of the city, and run by way of Maryborough, taking a course mostly a little to the north of the present railway, a $26^{1}/_{2}$ miles branch from there to Kilkenny, then on to Thurles, Holycross, Marhill, Mitchelstown, Mallow and Cork ($168^{1}/_{2}$ miles), approached by an incline plane of 1 in 15. At Marhill a line from Limerick to Waterford (the 1826 proposal) was to cross the western line but there was to be a line from Holycross to make a direct route from Dublin to Limerick. The proposals made provision for an extension from Barrack Bridge along the south side quays of the River Liffey to form a connection with the existing Dublin & Kingstown Railway; it is worth mentioning that this line was to be raised on a colonnade along the quays, with the northside columns actually standing in the river. Two other branches were considered to be advantageous, one from Limerick to Tarbert on the River Shannon ($21^{1}/_{2}$ miles), the other from Blarney to Macroom, Glengariff and Berehaven (71 miles) in the west of Co Cork. The commission expressed doubts that there could be any advantage of using a railway route through Ireland to shorten trans-Atlantic voyages, a far-sighted comment in view of several later railway promotions.

The commission thought that each route should be under single management although it doubted that anyone would be likely to build more than the first thirty miles out from Dublin, and that failing private investment there should be state assistance and perhaps local involvement by the counties and corporate towns. The public of Ireland embraced the report with enthusiasm but Westminster declined to take action. Promoters had held back whilst the report was in hand and then waited to see what the Government would do but the reality was that there were insufficient funds within Ireland and English investors viewed Irish projects with distrust even before the Famine. Lord George Bentinck attempted to get the Government to assist railway construction by advancing loans at a low rate of interest, pointing out that after a depressed market in 1841–2 in England it was railway construction that had brought about the rapid improvement that followed; the outcome was a modest allotment of £620,000 to be made available at 5 per cent (soon reduced to 4 per cent) and fully taken by 1850.

There were many generally applicable railway Acts passed by the Westminster Government but there was also a number of Acts solely for Ireland. Thus the gauge of railways was regulated by an Act of 1846. By 1843 two gauges were in use, the Dublin & Kingstown with 4ft $8^{1}/_{2}$in and the Ulster with 6ft 2in, with the Dublin & Drogheda planning to use the gauge advocated by the 1838 report, 5ft 2 in! The Board of Trade was asked to adjudicate, sending Major-General Pasley to investigate. He ignored Brunel and the Stephensons, regarding them as too committed, finding that 5ft and 5ft 6 in were most favoured so he carried out a mathematical process known as 'splitting the difference' to arrive at 5ft 3in, made compulsory by the 1846 Act. This action had lasting consequences on the other side of the world, leaving Australia with a problem of various gauges. Naturally it had been decided that the gauge in Australia would be 4ft 8^{1}/₂in but the Irish engineer of an infant New South Wales railway persuaded officaldom in London to changed the authorised gauge to 5ft 3in which of course had to be followed by Victoria and South Australia. Soon the Irishman departed and his replacement, a Scot, decided that NSW should revert to the first gauge and London agreed – it was too late for the others to change as rolling stock had already been ordered and so Australia in recent years had to build many miles of standard gauge railway to provide a basic inter-state system.

Before the railway age each town kept its own time by the sun, Dublin being 25 minutes behind London. As early as 1840 the GWR had shown the need, with its east-west axis, for a standard time, so the Dublin based companies used Dublin time throughout and others such as the W&LR as a matter of convenience for connecting trains conformed. Belfast lines had no problem as the city was just a little ahead of the capital, 1 minute 19 seconds to be precise, but the Cork lines started with local time. However by 1862 all Irish lines had adopted Dublin time well before the 1880 Time Act introduced the latter throughout the Emerald Isle. It was not until 1 October 1916 that Greenwich Mean Time was imposed on Ireland. A curious relic of the time difference was the nightly despatch from Euston of a watch, set to GMT, in the custody of the guard of the 'Irish Mail' who handed it over at Holyhead for its onward journey, to give the correct time next morning in Dublin – old habits die hard and despite the coming of radio it was not until about 1970 that this practice stopped!

Irish railways, just like Britain's, have been subject to public criticism from the first day, leading to various forms of Government and Parliamentary inquiries and laws and regulations. Many Acts were particular in application and have little impact in the overall history but some need special mention. One clause in the 1844 Railway Regulation Act gave the Government the option of purchase after 21 years of any railway subsequently authorised. In 1865 agitation began in an attempt to force the Government into applying that provision to Irish lines but the Devonshire Commission then inquiring into possible amalgamations and state involvement concluded that the railways were best left to free enterprise. A minority report in respect of Ireland advocated state purchase and that annual profits be expended on extensions into unserved areas and perhaps reductions of rates, as usual the major charge against railway management. At the time the mileage open in Ireland was 1,838 (9,251 in England) but no action was taken on either possibility. The question of state purchase was raised in many following years when Irish opinion was almost unanimously in favour and it was a widely held view that reduction to a couple of state owned systems would have been of immense value to Ireland.

The value of the Railway Clearing House in London, established in 1842, which apportioned revenue between the railway companies for through traffic, was not unnoticed in Ireland and in 1848 the Irish Railway Clearing House was set up, being incorporated by an Act of 1860, its activities covering cross-channel shipping as well. A strong lead was taken from London on methods of accountancy and generally its regulations and rules were adopted almost without change in Ireland. Even in 1926 there were affiliated to the IRCH ten Irish railways, eleven British, an Irish canal and twelve steam packet operators, but eventually there was no justification for a separate organisation and the IRCH ceased in 1971.

It became evident that several areas of Ireland would never attract railway investors but development was inhibited by lack of good communication. Elsewhere light railways had been built to meet local needs, such lines usually being of a narrow gauge. In fact just what a light railway really was has never been defined clearly but can be taken to mean a line constructed to relaxed standards, often steeply graded and worked by small locomotives, signalling and safety requirements being modified to suit. Recognition of special needs came as early as 1860 when the Tramways (Ireland) Act was passed which allowed the use of public highways and attempted to ease promotion, although any scheme still needed its own Act of Parliament. Action was effectively killed by a provision that only animal power was permitted.

It needed more specific action to encourage promotion of new lines, the Tramways and Public Companies (Ireland) Act 1883 changing requirements and extending state assistance. Promoters had to form a limited liability company and get assent for their plans from the local authorities before presenting their scheme to the Lord Lieutenant in Council in Dublin and if in order the Privy Council which hopefully would approve. Income for investors was to be supported by Baronial Guarantees whereby any deficiency of income was to be made up by local ratepayers but to ease their burden the Treasury could repay up to one-half of the amount, provided that it did not exceed 2 per cent of the capital, a total limit being set on state liability of £40,000. If a guaranteeing area had to make up deficits for two successive years the railway was to become the property of the local Grand Jury (County Council from 1898) to be worked at its expense by a committee of management. In fact this happened to four of the sixteen lines ($296\frac{1}{2}$ miles in total) constructed under the terms of this Act (nine being narrow gauge). This Act failed in that it did little to encourage new lines where they were needed most in the poorest parts of the west and south west. Investors had proved wary of a new class of stock and were then frightened by the introduction of a Home Rule Bill in 1886. Some lines had to be helped by special loans authorised by the Public Works Loans Tramways (Ireland) Act of 1886.

TABLE I

LINES PROPOSED BY ALLPORT COMMISSION 1888

1.	Downpatrick–Ardglass	Built (B&CDR)
2.	Letterkenny–Kilmacrenan–Dunfanaghy–Cross Roads	Built as L&BER
3.	Stranorlar–Glenties–Ardara–Killybegs	Built as far as Glenties (DR)
4.	Ballina–Killala–Belmullet	Built as far as Killala (MGWR)
5.	Galway–Oughterard–Clifden	Built (MGWR)
6.	Tralee–Dingle	Built (T&DLR)
7.	Killorglin–Valentia	Built (GS&WR)
8.	Skibbereen–Baltimore	Built (CB&SCR)
9.	Kinsale extension to harbour	*Not built*
10.	Bantry harbour extension	Built (CB&SCR)
11.	Dungarvan branch to harbour	*Not built*

ADDITIONAL LINES SCHEDULED IN 1889 ACT

12.	Buncrana–Carndonagh	Built (L&LSR)
13.	Stranorlar–Gweedore	*Not built*
14.	Donegal–Killybegs–Glenties	Built as far as Killybegs (DR)
15.	Westport–Belmullet	Built as Achill line (MGWR)
16.	Headford–Kenmare	Built (GS&WR)
17.	Letterkenny–Doochary Bridge–Glenties–Killybegs	*Not built*
18.	Claremorris–Clifden	Built as far as Ballinrobe (MGWR)

On 16 October 1886 a Royal Commission on Irish Public Works was appointed; chaired by Sir James Allport, General Manager of the Midland Railway, it was to inquire into fisheries, harbours, canals, drainage and rail-

ways and recommend such changes that would help trade and commerce. In respect of railways the report recommended no less than eleven new lines and that local liability should be limited to the ability to pay, that a state guarantee should be paid directly to the capitalists and that there should be strict supervision of all schemes. The limits of small new companies were recognised and therefore new lines were to be worked by existing railways under the new legislation, the Light Railways (Ireland) Act 1889. A list of seven proposed lines was drawn up (the report had recommended eleven) – see Table 1 (page 25) – but the response was poor, only three schemes being put forward, totalling but 30 miles, by railway companies. Thus the government had to create interest by introducing free grants towards construction, the entire amount for seven of the thirteen lines so built in 1892–5, totalling $238^{1}/_{2}$ miles, the procedures having been amended by the Railways (Ireland) Act of 1890. Only two lines were narrow gauge, both in Co Donegal, the railway companies in some cases having provided the extra capital to ensure uniformity with their systems.

There were still areas in need of better transport but so poor that nobody was prepared to build a railway to serve them. They were known by the curious title of Congested Districts, a political term for an area where overall population was sparse but because of the limited fertile land had pockets of high density so that the habitable land was indeed congested. It was Co Donegal which received the next form of aid when the Government paid the full cost of construction and provision of equipment, allowed by the Railways (Ireland) Act, 1896, only two lines being built and worked by the same company. However, in one respect the Act went further than hitherto by including Government supervision of construction and if needed subsequent inspection of working, which indeed happened in this case as related in Chapter 7.

In the text these Acts are known simply as the 1883 Act, etc. That so many of these lines were built to a narrower gauge than specified by the 1846 Gauges Act was largely historical accident. Three feet was chosen by a mineral line built in Co Antrim in 1873, that gauge perhaps influenced by the nearby Isle of Man Railway which also started operations that year. Certainly the next narrow gauge line, also in Co Antrim, in its Act was allowed to deviate from the laid down 5ft 3in, perhaps because it was authorised as a mineral line and no harm was foreseen in being different. However, it was the interpretation of the 1883 Act by the Lord Lieutenant in Dublin that caused so much use of the 3ft gauge; it was laid down that no guarantee should be sought on any costs arising from departure from that gauge.

In reality there was little saving by making a narrow gauge line, although attractive as a means of keeping capital expense down by purchasing very slightly less land and using a lighter rail section and because smaller locomotives would have to be used, so other structures could be cheaper in the first cost – as a matter of interest the State Government of Victoria decided that a saving of only £150 per mile was not worthwhile when tenders were received for a group of lines planned in 1872.

Against such savings there were ever present transhipment costs for the new lines were never intended to be of purely local use but make it possible to send local produce further afield – the need to change from one wagon to another so close to the originating point was not going to keep transport costs down. The folly of a narrow gauge is ideally illustrated by a small line in Co Kerry, the Castleisland Railway, which was built very lightly – needing a small engine to suit its restricted axle loading – to the wider gauge so that it could use main line stock; when the time came it was upgraded quite simply by relaying with a heavier rail. The Allport report certainly recognised that a mixture of gauges was a serious error and that great evils had resulted from it, yet narrow gauge lines continued to be built; that remark must, however, be qualified by making it clear that with one exception that no *new* narrow gauge systems came into being after the 1889 Act, all such lines being extensions.

The lack of profitability of so many Irish lines, not just narrow gauge, was as much due to extravagant and elaborate construction as misplaced traffic expectations. Years later proposals to widen the gauge of one of the major narrow gauge lines could not be sustained by the amount of traffic on offer; in fact the reverse happened in three cases as later described. Whatever the merits of the arguments, the outcome for railway enthusiasts was a handful of small endearing narrow gauge railways which helped to give the Irish railway system a charm of its own.

Public criticism, amounting almost to contempt, of Irish railways continued unabated throughout the years, the major grumble being the rates which were held by many to be a severe hindrance on cross channel trade and advancement of Irish commerce. In consequence a Viceregal Commission was set up on 18 July 1906 under the chairmanship of Sir Charles Scotter, of the London & South Western Railway; of the other members one, J.A.F. Aspinall, had direct experience of Irish railways having been an officer on the largest railway, the Great Southern & Western. They had a wide remit to look into the affairs of Irish railways which by 1906 had expanded to 3,412 miles, owned by 29 companies, having 261 directors in all. Apart from being dominated by the evidence on rates and allegations of unfair preferences, the commission looked at no less than 83 proposals for new railways or extensions (28 in Ulster, 14 in Connaught, 13 in Leinster

and 28 in Munster) but concluded that any new lines were likely to be unremunerative; only one proposal actually got as far as an Act, being authorised
in 1909 to serve the Castlecomer coalfield. The workings of the various
Tramways Acts were examined and subject to adverse comment, there
being recommendations that several lines should receive grants to overcome
deficiencies arising from the lack of capital, a direct consequence of those
Acts. The majority conclusion was that an Irish Railway Authority, headed
by twenty directors, should be formed to acquire the railways and work
them as a single system, purchase terms to be those prescribed by the 1844
Act mentioned beforehand, in effect Nationalisation. Three dissenters,
Aspinall not surprisingly being one, favoured amalgamation into a smaller
number of companies and advocated conversion of the narrow gauge lines
to broad; they held that defects in the working of Irish railways did not lie in
the management but were mainly caused by defective legislation and that
expansion of traffic had not been retarded by the companies. The majority
report was well received by the nationalist press, inspired by statesmanlike
spirit in the words of one daily, but was utterly condemned by the *Irish Times*
which sounded its death-knell when stating the 'now defunct report can be
dismissed and we can proceed to matters of importance'. Not one recommendation was ever acted upon.

On the outbreak of World War I on 4 August 1914 Irish railways were
not put under Government control, unlike those in Britain. However, as
events began to have an adverse effect Irish railway workers agitated for the
imposition of Government control so that working conditions on Irish railways would be determined in the same manner as in Britain, the Irish
Railway Executive Committee taking over on 1 January 1917 and
remaining in charge until the end of control throughout the British Isles on
15 August 1921. During this time the eight-hour day was enforced and
helped to increase working expenses to $3^1/2$ times the pre-war level –
revenue had barely doubled and all the railways found themselves in dire
straits. There was some salvation when the Irish Railways (Settlement of
Claims) Act became law in 1921, a sum of £3,000,000 being divided
amongst the controlled companies. In the midst of all this the railways found
that they were now part and parcel of two new states, the Irish Free State
and Northern Ireland.

Ireland's railways were very regional, serving their own area with little
competition from neighbouring companies; indeed very few places had
alternative routes from which to choose. Some of these routes were very
roundabout and existed only in the earlier days of inter company rivalry,
even to the extent of using river steamers in the particular case of Dublin
and Limerick traffic when almost ridiculous fares were offered. Only

between Belfast and Londonderry were there truly alternative routes in the British sense of two main lines, others such as Dublin to Athlone or Waterford being branches for the second service. Many secondary and branch lines were promoted by separate companies which were gradually absorbed into the major systems until in 1925 all those within the Irish Free State were combined into one company and ultimately only two organisations, one in the Republic, the other in Ulster, provide railway services.

Communications between Ireland and Britain have been a major influence on Irish railway history, so that inevitably lines spread inland initially from the established ports and then new ports to give a chain of connecting services. Postal requirements often decided times of both cross-channel steamers and trains, considerable capital being expended in speeding the mails, so that it became possible to post a letter in London for overnight passage to Ireland, continuing by morning mail train to Cork or Belfast where delivery and collection gave sufficient time for a businessman's reply to be in London the following morning! To a slight extent the Westminster government supported routes within Ireland which would assist rapid troop movements from garrison towns (although at times of parsimony the poor militia man found that he had to march rather than be carried by train). Britain's railway companies that entered the Irish traffic did not build their own lines in Ireland, apart from the LNWR, preferring to form associations with Irish companies, helping by granting favourable through traffic routes or subscribing to a few new lines, in one case as a joint project when the new route from west Wales to the south of Ireland was built up almost a century ago. The major case of ownership by a British railway followed purchase by the Midland Railway of the Belfast & Northern Counties Railway in 1903, serving the north east corner of Ulster.

As befits its status Dublin was the first place to have a passenger railway, its first trains running on 17 December 1834 when the Dublin & Kingstown Railway opened. Gradually the route was extended to serve the east coast south of Dublin, the Dublin & Wicklow Railway becoming in turn the Dublin, Wicklow & Wexford Railway (1860) and then Dublin & South Eastern Railway (1907) after reaching first Wexford and then Waterford. Close to Dublin, as the city and the neighbouring towns to the south expanded, two suburban services developed, that along the coast becoming Ireland's busiest route, such that today it is now an electric system. Finance had been hard to come by and initial support by Brunel and the Great Western Railway failed to materialise, delaying completion to Wexford until 1872; it needed money from the London & North Western Railway before Waterford could be served, which years later was to prove a complication for the young Irish Free State government in its amalgamation plans.

Regarding itself as Ireland's 'premier' railway the Great Southern & Western Railway of Ireland was the natural successor to the 1836 Commission's proposed route to the west and followed much of the line that had been suggested between Dublin and Cork, reached in 1849, forming the longest main line in the Emerald Isle. From the trunk line the GS&WR built, or acquired, secondary and branch lines so that the major towns of Carlow, Kilkenny, Athlone, Nenagh, Limerick, Fermoy, Killarney and Tralee were served. Extension beyond Cork was provided by the Cork & Youghal Railway which also served Cobh (formerly Queenstown) by a branch, taken over by the GS&WR in 1866.

South of the GS&WR main line the Waterford & Kilkenny Railway (later Waterford & Central Ireland Railway) had a route striking northwards from Waterford to connect with the GS&WR at Kilkenny and Maryborough, although animosity prevented the connecting up of tracks at the latter for many years. Cutting across the GS&WR the Waterford & Limerick Railway connected the two cities and served other places west and north of Limerick by originally separate companies, worked until purchased, reaching Tralee in Co Kerry and Ennis in Co Clare; the latter route was extended northwards in stages to reach Tuam in Co Galway and eventually Sligo by 1895. By then the original title was too limited and so the company became the Waterford, Limerick & Western Railway. From Limerick a short branch to the east making a connection with a GS&WR line, reached Lough Derg on the River Shannon at Killaloe.

The two Waterford companies had been heavily subsidised by the GWR which gave rebates on through traffic to England due to a closeness that had started in the earliest days when the secretary of the W&LR, W.S. Saunders, was a close relative of the GWR secretary Charles Saunders. Bristol also had close trading links with Waterford. However the GWR took a fresh interest in the south of Ireland at the end of the last century, but rather than looking towards Dublin, as Brunel had done fifty years earlier, it was Cork and the west that beckoned. Actually the stimulus was an independent attempt by two Birmingham businessmen to create a new sea crossing from Fishguard to Rosslare in opposition to the established GWR service from New Milford (now Neyland) to Waterford; when the GWR initially failed to give support the promoters turned to the LNWR, thus leading to a GWR about turn. Apart from the need for a new line to Fishguard, it was essential to improve connections in Ireland; thus an entirely new railway had to be built across south Wexford and the GWR, unwilling to bear the entire expense, found a collaborator in the GS&WR, forming the jointly-owned Fishguard & Rosslare Railways & Harbours Co in 1898. The two Waterford railways then amalgamated with the GS&WR in 1900–1, much enlarging that system (the amalgamated company then dropping Ireland from its title) and making it by far Ireland's biggest railway at the time. The new route was completed in 1906, making use west of Waterford of the Waterford, Dungarvan & Lismore Railway (dating from 1878) to join an existing GS&WR branch to reach Mallow and thereby Cork and Killarney.

The middle lowland belt across Ireland was almost entirely the preserve of the Midland Great Western of Ireland Railway, connecting Dublin with Mullingar, Sligo, Athlone, Castlebar, Ballina, Westport and Galway, initial impetus for its construction being development of the latter as a trans-Atlantic port, despite the negative view of the 1836 commissioners. The early schemes envisaged use of the GS&WR main line out of Dublin and then branching off to reach Galway and it is one of history's ironies that this is now the way to most of the places mentioned above! The MGWR also served a number of smaller places, several of the branches coming into existence after the passing of the various Tramway Acts and using substantial Government grants to reach the remoteness of the west coast in Connemara and Mayo. The 'Midland', to give its usual Irish name, has been described as the most Irish of Ireland's railways but it grew into a well-equipped system, capable of dealing with a heavy flow of cattle from the west on its way to Britain. The GS&WR had initially regarded all of western Ireland as its preserve and so quarrelled with the Midland, entering into a 'mini-war' when in 1854 the MGWR took on lease the Grand Canal which gave access to places along the GS&WR route and, by connecting with the Shannon, means of entering Limerick. Peace came in 1860 when it was accepted that each could have its own territory, the River Shannon dividing them – when the WL&WR was to be taken over by the GS&WR as described the MGWR countered by attempting to get the line itself, but had to be content with running powers to Limerick which were used for a few years.

Among the railways so far mentioned there lay a number of smaller companies, mostly light railways and many narrow gauge. The largest was that serving Co Cork west of the city, the Cork & Bandon Railway which expanded into the Cork, Bandon & South Coast Railway (1888), reaching Bantry and Skibbereen on the coast. From its Clonakilty branch a pair of small companies formed a lightly laid branch to Courtmacsherry which survived to be the last roadside line in Ireland when closed in 1961. Cork had another three railways, the Cork & Macroom Direct Railway having been one of the best paying lines in Ireland in its day, the Cork, Blackrock & Passage Railway which was converted to narrow gauge and then extended in 1900–4 to serve the west side of Cork Harbour, the other being the narrow gauge Cork & Muskerry Light Railway on the west side of the city. More remote was the small Schull & Skibbereen Light Railway, part of a grander scheme, and hopelessly badly built and equipped but it lasted until 1947. The Dingle peninsula in Co Kerry was home to the Tralee & Dingle Light Railway which crossed its mountains on a severely graded line from 1891 until 1954, latterly only for monthly cattle trains. Co Kerry was chosen by the exponents of one of the most extraordinary forms of railway ever built, the Lartigue monorail system used by the Listowel & Ballybunion Railway which worked from 1888 until 1924. Further north Co Clare was largely served by the West Clare Railway and its extension the South Clare Railways, narrow gauge lines running from Ennis to the coast to serve Kilkee and Kilrush, a system that claimed fame, or rather infamy, as the subject of a derogatory song, but later was to become a totally diesel powered narrow gauge system and indeed the last to operate in Ireland. Another narrow gauge railway served parts of Cos Cavan and Leitrim where coal and cattle were the main sources of revenue, the Cavan & Leitrim Light Railway. Dublin's streets were served first by horse and then electric trams, but extending beyond two of the termini were two steam railways. The earlier was the narrow gauge Dublin & Lucan Steam Tramway of 1881–3 which in due course changed its gauge and called itself the Dublin & Lucan Electric Railway but after abandonment in 1925 was replaced by an extension of the Dublin electric tramways on a new gauge of 5ft 3in – a second change of gauge for any line was a rare occurrence. The other tramway was always of the wider gauge, being the Dublin & Blessington Steam Tramway, climbing high into the Wicklows on the south side of the city, but it could not match competing omnibus services, closing in 1932.

When Partition occurred, all the railways and tramways so far mentioned lay entirely within the Free State. Mileages at the time were:

	NI	Free State
Companies wholly in NI	418	–
Companies wholly in Free State	–	2,219
Companies partly in both states	355 ³/₄	485 ¹/₂
	773 ³/₄	2,704 ¹/₂

The combined total was 3,478¹/₄ miles.

The Great Northern of Ireland Railway, to give its full title, became a truly international railway, complete with customs posts at border stations, connecting the two capitals, Dublin and Belfast. Unlike the GS&WR its main line was not built by a single company, originating as the Dublin & Drogheda Railway at its southern end and the Ulster Railway at the north, being connected by the Dublin & Belfast Junction Railway. The Ulster ran its first trains in 1839 and the Drogheda in 1844 but it was not until 1853 that a through journey became possible, the delay arising from the long task of completing a bridge over the River Boyne at Drogheda. The GNR was a combination of several railways, although the major companies had long intended to amalgamate. The first stage took place on 1 March 1875 when The Northern Railway (unusual in having the definite article in its title) was formed by the joining of the D&DR and D&BJR, the Irish North Western Railway being added on 1 January 1876, followed by the UR which joined the new company on 1 April 1876 to form the GNR.

An early part of the system was the struggling Dundalk & Enniskillen Railway which originated as far back as 1837 when titled Dundalk Western Railway, but it took from 1849 until 1859 to build its line. By then the Londonderry & Enniskillen Railway had completed its route and soon the former took on the working of the latter, becoming the Irish North Western Railway in 1862. The main objective of the UR was to connect Belfast with Armagh but having reached Portadown by 1842 it did not reach the former until 1848. The route was projected further south to reach Clones in 1863, connecting with the INWR which had opened a branch to Cavan in 1862; there was now an inland alternative to the main line between Dublin and Belfast, using the MGWR Cavan branch, but of no real value in practice. The UR had a second line from Portadown across to Omagh where it joined the L&ER to give a route from Belfast to Londonderry and indeed a better way of travelling from Dublin to the north west.

The GNR had a number of branches, one of the most important being that to Howth just north of Dublin on which a suburban service was provided, now being the northern part of Dublin's electric service. The important town of Newry had to be content with branch line status, its railways having been built independently by the Newry & Armagh Railway which had started as the Newry & Enniskillen Railway and the purely local Newry, Warrenpoint & Rostrevor Railway which never reached the latter resort, the two being absorbed into the GNR system in 1879 and 1886 respectively. Of the many other branches that connecting Dungannon and Cookstown was probably the busiest, serving a group of collieries and brickworks and another branch of importance reached the western seaboard at Bundoran on Donegal Bay.

The Belfast & County Down Railway, a title which precisely describes its location, came to suffer the disadvantage of so many of the towns it served having a shorter road route from Belfast, such that only the line out to Bangor has survived as a heavily used suburban route. The B&CDR was an early line having run its first trains in 1848 and expanded to reach Donaghadee in the hopes of partaking in cross channel traffic from Scotland, to Downpatrick and Newcastle. Despite its later problems with road competition the Co Down was a well run system which gave its patrons a reliable service for many years.

There was little reference in the 1836 Commission's report to serving Ireland north of Belfast but in due course the Belfast & Northern Counties Railway provided a main line between Belfast, Ballymena, Coleraine and Londonderry and the rail connection to the Larne and Stranraer sea crossing, the shortest possible between Ireland and Britain. Beginning as the Belfast & Ballymena Railway in 1848 the line was extended by the Ballymena, Ballymoney, Coleraine & Portrush Junction Railway to reach the north coast in 1855. A separate company, the Londonderry & Coleraine Railway, provided the continuation to the largest centre in the north west, being isolated until a bridge was built across the River Bann at Coleraine in 1860. When the working of these two lines was taken on the B&BR became the B&NCR, consolidating its position by taking over the Portrush company in 1861 and the L&CR in 1871. The B&NCR acquired two narrow gauge railways within its area, the oldest built as a mineral line, the Ballymena, Cushendall & Red Bay Railway, on which the B&NCR started a passenger service after purchase in 1884, the impetus being the growing number of tourists as the Victorians began to realise that the beauty of Ireland was not confined to Killarney. The other line, the Ballymena & Larne Railway, connected the two places and allowed through transit of minerals from the Cushendall line for export at Larne. Another narrow gauge acquisition, in 1897, was the Portstewart Tramway which joined the town to its station. When the Midland Railway purchased the B&NCR in 1903, it was run day to day by means of its Northern Counties Committee, a status unchanged when the London Midland & Scottish Railway took over in 1923 on the Grouping of Britain's railways. The next year the unfortunate narrow gauge Ballycastle Railway, connecting that resort with Ballymoney, closed down, the NCC being prevailed upon to take over and resume services.

Apart from the GNR there were four other systems which crossed the border. The oldest was owned by the LNWR and connected the new harbour established at Greenore in Co Louth in 1873 by means of the Dundalk, Newry & Greenore Railway with the GNR at Dundalk for traffic from the west and at Newry for Ulster traffic. However the high hopes were never realised and Euston carried a heavy financial burden until inevitable closure after the railway became the property of the nationally owned British Transport Commission in 1948. Further west the Sligo, Leitrim & Northern Counties Railway provided a link between the GNR at Enniskillen and the MGWR near Sligo from its completion in 1882; it was one of those lines that somehow maintained its independence and found an endearing niche in the minds of railway enthusiasts for its survival as a relic of a rapidly passing era when closure came in 1957. The other two systems were both narrow gauge, although the earliest portions of each had been built with 5ft 3in track, both having started in 1863 and eventually forming by far the largest system of narrow gauge lines in the British Isles. The larger started as the Finn Valley Railway, connecting Stranorlar with the L&ER at Strabane, being narrowed in 1894 to match its extension, the West Donegal Railway which struggled, in both senses, to get over the mountains of mid-Donegal and reach Donegal town in 1889. With Government help two branches were added to serve Glenties and Killybegs, by which time the company had become the Donegal Railway. Further enlargement took its trains to Londonderry itself and south to Ballyshannon, a town on the GNR Bundoran branch, but the DR soon found itself with great financial problems. However it was attractive enough for the Midland Railway to think of purchase, but the GNR (being concerned by the arrival of a far more powerful concern) joined in so that the County Donegal Railways Joint Committee was formed in 1906. A separate company, worked by the joint committee, built the Strabane & Letterkenny Railway, opened in 1909, the last new narrow gauge passenger branch in Ireland. The Donegal system had now grown to 125 miles of route.

The other cross-border company was the Londonderry & Lough Swilly Railway which originally served Farland Point and Buncrana on Lough Swilly, working the narrow gauge Letterkenny Railway from 1883 and changing to that gauge in 1885. It needed Government action to extend the system to its maximum of 99 miles, the line to Cardonagh in the Inishowen peninsula providing Ireland with its furthest north point on its railway system. The other line out from Letterkenny to Burtonport was as desolate and remote as any in Ireland, coming in for much criticism as the Government planners seem to have had only the fish traffic of its destination in mind, ignoring other places that with slight deviation could have been served. Amazingly, of all the railway *companies* that have existed in Ireland the L&LSR survives, although it has not run a train since 1953! It is still listed in the telephone book.

Lying entirely within Ulster five small lines remained independent. One was the very short Carrickfergus Harbour Junction Railway, a goods line worked by the NCC, surviving until 1957. The others were all narrow gauge with the added interest that two were electrically worked. The first was a pioneering electric line accurately described by its name, Giant's Causeway, Portrush & Bush Valley Railway & Tramway, dating from 1882 and lasting until 1949. Next was the Castlederg & Victoria Bridge Tramway of 1884 which connected the town with its nearest main line, that from Londonderry to Omagh and Enniskillen, surviving only until 1933. Geographically the Clogher Valley Tramway (Railway from 1894) of 1887 came next serving a mid Ulster farming area by means of a line from Maguiresbridge to Tynan, both termini being GNR stations. Despite the difficulties of wartime the CVR closed in 1942. The other line was the Bessbrook & Newry Tramway of 1885, a novel electric line which throughout its days up to 1948 handled passenger and goods traffic.

Apart from the railways and tramways actually built there were innumerable plans, some of which got as far as Parliament, a few getting Acts, after which nothing transpired. Many are mentioned in the text but it would become overbearing to attempt to account for all, not to mention enlarging the book beyond its permitted size; in fact it would seem that hardly a field in the land would not have a sod turned if all had succeeded! A list published by the Irish Railway Record Society (*Occasional Publications* No 2) records rather more than 700 railway names for those built, planned or merely fleetingly discussed, and includes industrial sites.

It may seem invidious to single out one man in a general history of Ireland's railway system but, just as the Stephensons and Brunel stand amongst the highest places in Britain's railway history, so does William Dargan for Ireland. His name will appear many times for he built so much of Ireland's railway mileage. As a benefactor of the nation, his name joins equally with those held in esteem through the centuries for it was not just railways that absorbed his energies and he thoroughly deserved the recognition granted, including the rare distinction of a statue, in Merrion Square, Dublin, being erected in his lifetime.

Born not far from Carlow in 1799 Dargan showed an early talent for mathematics and surveying, working under Thomas Telford on improving the London and Holyhead road, in particular gaining high esteem for the causeway at the Holy Island end, before taking his talents home. Before railway work Dargan was engaged on the Howth and North Circular Roads in Dublin and several canals and running a linen mill near Dublin, also taking a great interest in agriculture, winning prizes for his animal, floral and vegetable exhibits. He was the sole provider of finance for the Dublin Exhibition of 1853, a feat never equalled, and all too often a project came to rely almost entirely on his financial backing, he taking tremendous risks in order to mitigate, if only in part, the suffering of the times. Sadly a riding accident terminated his life in 1867.

Even now his legacy is still recognised for NIR has named the recently built railway crossing of the River Lagan in Belfast the 'William Dargan Bridge', recognition that a substantial part of the present day system in Ireland is of his construction.

The newly formed government of the Free State had many problems requiring attention but soon turned its attention to the railways, having to face the effects of the Civil War, when the situation became so precarious that the GS&WR gave notice that its trains would cease on 8 January 1923; with the Government making up losses the railway endeavoured to provide whatever services it could. As though there were not enough problems the railways then had to contend with a Railway Tribunal set up by the new Dublin government which had decided that reorganisation was imperative. The outcome was an acknowledgement that the railways had not been mismanaged in so far as they were private concerns but the future would require unification for economy of operation, the majority recommendation being purchase by the state. During this period the ruthless attacks on railways, particularly in Munster, caused five companies, CB&PR, C&MDR, CB&SCR, S&SLR and T&DLR, to stop working. To keep lines open a Railway Protection, Repair and Maintenance Corps was formed in late 1922, using many unemployed railwaymen and by use of blockhouses and armoured patrols succeeded in reopening many of the closed lines. A few steam engines were included in armoured trains and armoured Lancia cars running on the rails gave the corps much needed mobility.

During all these difficulties the November 1922 meeting of the Irish Railways General Managers' Conference recommended the formation of two groups, one southern, the other northern, the unsettled border seeming to be regarded as a purely temporary state of affairs, as the latter was to comprise the MGWR and GNR. The Dublin government soon made it clear that it favoured voluntary unification of the lines lying wholly within the Free State, setting a date of 1 March 1923, hoping that the companies would move quickly towards combination. It took rather longer, the first step being an agreement between the GS&WR and CB&SCR, circulated on 23 May 1923, to combine, other companies soon joining in, only the D&SER dissenting, wanting to join with the GNR if forced to amalgamate. It was not until 3 April 1924 a Bill was introduced into the Dail which, however, excluded the D&LER, D&BST and the L&BR (the schedule of amalgamating and absorbed companies appears in Appendix Three), the Act being passed on 23 July 1924. The Railway Tribunal was to sit if agreement had not been reached by 30 June 1924 and indeed it did so as only the amalgamation of the GS&WR, MGWR and CB&SCR had been settled. These three became the Great Southern Railway on 12 November 1924. The D&SER remained in opposition, although the leased Dublin & Kingstown Railway was most anxious to be included, the two major points of contention being:

the statutory right of the LMS (as successor to the LNWR) to a seat on the board of the D&SER, pending repayment of a loan of £100,000

made in 1902,
division of cross-channel receipts so that the Irish railway received in
effect a subsidy of £20,000 per annum.

The LNWR loan mentioned above enabled the DW&WR to build the line
from New Ross to Waterford. The only way out was to allow the LMS to
keep its representation on the new board, authorised by the Railway
(Directorate) Act of 2 December 1924. Thus on 1 January 1925 the D&SER
amalgamated with the Great Southern Railway to form the Great Southern
Railways, all the other lines being absorbed in the next few weeks, other
than that between Thurles and Clonmel as later described and three short
colliery lines, worked until taken on lease in 1929.

One consequence of the newly acquired independence was the wiser use
of the Irish language, station names and signs and tickets, etc, appearing in
both forms. Several towns adopted their Irish names, or an alternative, and
true to the endearing inconsistency that gives rise to the Irish being the butt
of stage and bar comedians, both generally remain in use. Thus the town of
Newbridge became Droichead Nua in 1925 but timetables even now show
the former on the map and the latter on the mainline timetable! Another,
Charleville, decided to become Rathluric but in recent years the former
name has come back into use – in fact in many cases both forms, Irish and
English, are used indiscriminately and everyone knows just where is meant.

In Northern Ireland a commission with a similar purpose was set up, it
recommending the continuance of working by private management
(although a minority report wanted national ownership). There was a
special proposal that the Clogher Valley Railway should be absorbed by the
GNR and that the Ballycastle Railway should become part of the
LMS(NCC), the latter in fact happening as mentioned beforehand but not
because of the report. Thus those railways outside the Free State were to
continue as before.

All of Ireland's railways found themselves facing a steadily increasing
threat from road transport, somewhat delayed in the Free State as a consequence of the civil war which resulted in many destroyed bridges and little
attention to road repairs. It is a measure of how little the threat was understood when a report, the NI commission's in fact, could dismiss motor transport as more likely to become an auxiliary than a competing factor to be
reckoned with! Some of the railways had obtained powers to run road
services at an early date, the B&NCR in 1902, but there were limitations
which prevented effective action when the spread of public carriers began to
make inroads into railway revenue. Ulster suffered particularly and in 1927
both Governments gave powers to the railways to run both passenger and

goods services on the roads. The GSR thought it advantageous to support the Irish Omnibus Co then steadily spreading throughout the Free State outside the Dublin area which had become the province of the Dublin United Tramways (1896) Company. The GNR also developed its road services, passenger and goods, and before long the NCC started to acquire competing routes. The L&LSR decided that buses were the best means of serving its remote villages and soon built up by acquisition and expansion a sizeable network serving a wider area than it could by rail, such that in 1931 the system all but closed down; however the roads were not yet capable of carrying extra traffic and trains had to run for a few more years.

GSR involvement in the IOC was totally bungled and failed to achieve any sensible coordination of services, almost wrecking both companies in the process. Where other operators were driven away fares were increased and services reduced in an attempt to force traffic back to the rails – the result was extreme public hostility to the bus company and a quick return to the 'pirate' operators as they were termed. The reality that the public no longer had to rely on the railways was wantonly disregarded. GSR affairs were now so chaotic that the Government stepped in to force the company to accept a drastic reorganisation of its capital during 1933 such that a nominal value of £26,008,707 was reduced to £12,431,739 – Debentures were reduced by 15 per cent, Guaranteed Preference Stock by 50 per cent, Preference Stock by 65 per cent and Ordinary Stock was almost wiped out, suffering a 90 per cent diminution! The same Act deprived the LMS of its right to appoint a director, totally disregarding business ethics; LMS minutes show that the company sought payment of its loan without success and record a sense of victimisation by a Left-inclined Government. The LMS also had stock which started as £2,500 invested in the D&SER which was replaced by £950 GSR stock, reduced to £95 in 1933 – when sold it fetched but £22.

In 1934 the GSR took over in its entirety the Irish Omnibus Co and with it a major road goods haulier, John Wallis & Sons, followed by a few more acquisitions so that the railway became the largest road operator in the Free State.

In Northern Ireland matters prompted a fresh Government enquiry, under the chairmanship of Sir Felix Pole, General Manager of the GWR, its outcome being the 'snatching away' and combining of all the railway's road services within Ulster into the Northern Ireland Transport Road Board. This body was supposed to coordinate its services with the railways but in practice did exactly the opposite and became a formidable competitor, to the detriment of the railways. The GNR held on to its services across the border and south of it and other cross-border operators remained independent.

The financial state of all Ireland's railways became more and more desperate, with several branches being closed and others often threatened. In the north the decline was precipitated by a long strike over wages. It may now seem curious that a combined Wages Board covered all Ireland even after Partition and since then had been applying a steady reduction in wage rates, reflecting not only the deteriorating railway position but also a quite substantial drop in the cost of living since the end of World War I. The Dublin Government gave the GSR a subsidy when the strike was threatened but Belfast would not so all but the GSR, and the County Down which had reduced its wage rates five years earlier, came to a virtual standstill on 30 January 1933. The immediate effect was the ending of some branch passenger services and in the long term a severe reduction of other services after the strike finally collapsed with a return to work on 10 April 1933. The damage was done and a road established its supremacy in the north.

A long period of stagnation set in during the decade, the GSR obtaining only 29 new locomotives in 1930–40; in fact a separate company, Transport Supplies Co Ltd, had to be formed to purchase and hire rolling stock, road and rail, to the GSR. Inevitably this lead to yet another inquiry, set up in 1938, to look into the causes of the continuing unfavourable financial position of the company and transport in general. Having acquired many of the road haulage firms in Ireland, the GSR wanted protection from those who evaded traffic regulations but the plea to restrict their working range to just 15 miles was rejected. Instead it was proposed that such operators should pay additional duties into a fund which could be used to make up losses to cover higher status stock. It was noted that while passenger receipts were well down the number travelling had increased substantially; nobody seems to have noticed that this resulted from a huge increase in excursion traffic, mainly to sporting events, which of course travelled at preferential rates! A major recommendation was the replacement of the board by two part-time shareholders' directors with a full-time Government-nominated chairman, a minority report going further, wanting state ownership. A long list of line closures (see Appendix Five) was accepted in principle but it was noted that the GSR seemed reluctant to close branches, fearing the loss of goods traffic. It was also observed that despite single ownership, buses were not really complementary to rail and ran as a separate entity. In the north there was a corresponding inquiry which recommended that the NIRTB be abolished and that a new authority should control the NCC and B&CDR and the road services, entering into a pooling arrangement with the GNR. Events elsewhere soon made it impossible to take action on either report.

It was not all gloom in the thirties. The GNR and NCC made several improvements in their services and obtained some new locomotives and rolling stock. Diesel railcars made an appearance, especially on the CDRJC and the GNR but not on the GSR which, however, made a brave attempt to use electric power in the form of battery trains in the Dublin area. A major improvement was the completion in 1934 of a new line north of Belfast as an unemployment relief project which cut out the need for reversal of main trains at Greenisland on their way to Londonderry. The GNR also added a branch to a new cement factory near Drogheda.

The effects of World War II from 1939 to 1945 could not have been in more contrast between north and south. Eire remained stoutly neutral, some holding the view that Ireland was standing up to the world, and after a period when the war seemed far away and nothing much to do with the nation it soon had drastic effects on all aspects of Irish life, interfering with trade, when shipping space was reduced to only a quarter of that normally available, making so many commodities scarce or non-existent. Food was not a problem with the exception of tea which became unobtainable at times and the quality of wheat was such that there was no white bread; the Economic War had encouraged greater home production of sugar, by growing many more acres of sugar beet, the GSR carrying much of it to the four factories set up in 1926–34, and increasing wheat acreage from 210,000 in 1932 to 230,000 in 1938, wartime demands increasing this to 640,000 acres in 1944. So it might have seemed that the Irishman at home in neutral Eire had little to suffer from what was euphemistically called The Emergency.

However the major requirement that could not be found at home was coal, turf (of which there was plenty in the numerous bogs in much of Ireland), being a far inferior substitute, although it had to be used extensively, even on locomotives in desperation. Eire needed annually some 3,000,000 tons of coal and 250,000 tons of oil, the latter reduced to less than a quarter by 1942 (a pre-World War II attempt to build a refinery in Dublin failed) so bus and lorry use became severely curtailed and private motoring impossible. Had coal been available the GSR could have benefited but it proved impossible to meet demand as coal stocks dwindled and so very little was received from Britain. Thus train services were reduced and a few branches closed as 1941 progressed, followed by even more severe restrictions in 1944 when British coastal shipping was diverted to other duties. Journeys became protracted, such that a 1939 3½ hours run from Dublin to Cork could extend to almost 24 hours – older readers will no doubt recall wartime journeys in Britain as servicemen or perhaps as children on family travel which was sometimes essential, trains being absolutely packed but even with delays they got there. They were usually far luckier than those in

Eire who suffered greatly extended journeys, more likely in old non-gangway stock. Your author was once told of a journey by an evening departure from Dublin to Kingscourt, but 52 miles, which did not get through until the morning of the third day! Goods trains sometimes took three days to complete a run, if not abandoned on the way – it was the dreadfully poor coal that was the root cause, clinking heavily and literally putting the fire out.

Appendix Six details the effects on services of coal starvation. These were the days of the 'duff', an anthracite fuel which had to be taken despite being too fine for proper combustion in a locomotive firebox, all sorts of methods of mixing and bonding to form this dust into briquettes being tried, even using cement. At times the GSR was close to total shutdown, being saved only by the release of Government coal reserves. Coal consumption increased dramatically, it being necessary to use 70,000 tons *more* coal in 1945 to run 4,000,000 miles *less* than in 1939! To keep services going frequent fire cleaning had to be carried out, trains being delayed at certain stations where gangs were stationed for that purpose, the intention being the elimination of the problem of trains stopping in the section and delaying everything else in both directions.

To many in Ireland the only possible retaliation against shortages resulting from British restrictions on shipping seemed to be the denial of that vital liquid, Guinness, Northern Ireland getting 80 per cent of its beer from south of the border!

In contrast, the inhabitants of Ulster became deeply involved in World War II and Belfast suffered terribly in two heavy devastating raids in April and May 1941 with much loss of life (Nazi bombers did indeed drop bombs on Eire, particularly in 1940–1, causing death in Dublin and at places along the east coast). Naturally the railways of Northern Ireland assisted in the war effort and handled vastly increased number of passengers (many of whom left Belfast every evening for the safety of the countryside) or workers at the Belfast shipyards and military sites such as new airfields, apart from the huge number of servicemen, many American, temporarily based in Northern Ireland. Coal supplies were not restricted to the extent of curtailing services and thus the GNR, because it was impossible to decree that engines must not carry fuel over the border, could continue to give a reasonable service in Eire. In fact, the GNR arranged many of its engine diagrams to make sure that engines crossed the border to get coal in the north. Suffering all the problems of their British counterparts the staff of the NCC, GNR and B&CDR dealt with air raids, blackout, shortages of engines and rolling stock, poor fuel, extra trains and short notice for specials – they did their job magnificently, helping to beat our European enemies.

The irony for the GSR was that the Emergency created a false prosperity but it was realised that the situation was entirely artificial and on return to normal conditions there was every likelihood that the company would collapse. Thus the Dublin government enforced the amalgamation of the GSR with Dublin United Transport, hoping that the strength of the latter would bolster the other. The second reading of the Bill resulted in defeat for the Government and promptly a general election was called, surely a railway's affairs being a most unusual reason to go to the people! The Government was returned and the Bill became law so that Coras Iompair Eireann (roughly 'Ireland's Transport Company') came into being on 1 January 1945. The new chairman, A.P. Reynolds, had in fact run both companies since 1942.

The end of hostilities in 1945 brought no comfort to Ireland's railways. In Ulster the heavy wartime traffic quickly subsided and it soon became apparent that rail services would collapse; indeed the B&CDR (then under the guidance of the GNR) announced during 1947 that it intended to close all its lines except that to Bangor. State ownership was seen as the answer and accordingly the Stormont Parliament passed in 1948 the necessary Act which included provision to *acquire or cooperate* with the GNR. In the meantime Britain's railways had been nationalised and therefore the NCC as part of the LMS became state property on 1 January 1948, being titled Railway Executive (Northern Counties Committee) but for the interim management was placed in the hands of the NIRTB! The new body, the Ulster Transport Authority, came into existence on 1 April 1948 and began by taking over the B&CDR exactly six months later, the NCC following on 1 April 1949, the GNR being left alone for the time being. With management of rail and road vested in the same body, it did not take long to carry out the earlier threat of the B&CDR so that almost all of that system was closed in 1950, followed by many NCC lines, including the last of the narrow gauge, by 1955.

The new CIE hopefully restored services in 1945–6 but trains were still limited in number on all lines. Then came disaster in January 1947 when coal supplies from Britain virtually terminated with the double effect of nationalisation of the mines and a very hard winter so that in the two months January and February several branches closed and on other lines trains were suspended on some of the weekdays, culminating with almost total shut-down of passenger services on 24 February 1947, the full details being given in Appendix Six. Nearly one hundred locomotives were altered to burn oil, being distinguished by large white circles on the smokebox and tender sides to indicate that a stop for fire cleaning was not necessary. As conditions eased, services were gradually restored from May but many branches never reopened, only livestock trains or excursions now and then being run until closure years later.

So yet another tribunal sat in judgement on Ireland's railways, chaired by Sir James Milne, the last General Manager of the GWR, presenting its report on 6 December 1948. In hindsight it is easy to see that the compilers did not, or could not, see just what was really happening in the transport world for they rejected a change to diesel traction, other than conceding that railcars might be usable on some branches, and they placed a great deal of emphasis on the contributory value of branch lines, even suggesting revival of the long abandoned Baronial Guarantee principle to keep some open, or perhaps be reopened. One part of the report produced a useful means for the historian to make a comparison between British and Irish railway traffic density when it was revealed that track between Dublin and Cork still had 50 year old rails (Euston to Crewe, for example, had a rail life of seven to ten years). Curiously, there were no worthwhile comments on Dublin suburban railway traffic. The average age of locomotives was highlighted, being 51 years, with carriages only a little less ancient at 47 years. The most radical conclusion was that a single authority should be set up to maintain railways, roads and canals and that each should make a fair contribution towards the total cost. The political result was the state ownership of CIE from 1 June 1950 but the practical result was a continuing failure to make ends meet. Slowly the little-used branches were eliminated but in contrast remaining services began to benefit from the introduction firstly of diesel railcars and then diesel locomotives, although CIE was unfortunate in its choice of manufacturer of the latter and suffered from unreliable performance.

Powers to close lines were vested in CIE, provided that a road service was substituted. Exemption Orders when granted allowed, after notice to the public (usually only a few days), termination of all services and removal of tracks, etc. Later an Abandonment Order allowed disposal of lands. In Ulster a Transport Tribunal was set up to review applications for closure and there were instances when there were *no* public objections.

The cross-border railways were left alone, the DN&GR, still owned by British Railways, closing in 1951 and then the L&LSR which dispensed with its last trains in 1953. The GNR was getting into such deep water financially that in 1949 its chairman foresaw its imminent closure but it struggled on until the company announced on 6 January 1951 that it would discontinue all services in Ulster about five weeks later, also giving one week's notice to staff. This stung the two governments into action so that a joint offer for purchase was made, becoming effective on 1 September 1953 when the Great Northern Railway Board took over. Despite all its problems the GNR had taken the pioneering step of introducing diesel railcars to its most important services, but serving two masters prevented the GNRB from achieving a real modernisation of its system by replacing steam and obsolete rolling stock and equipment. Instead the Stormont government decreed sweeping closures which took place in 1957 despite protest from Dublin and the GNRB. The poor old SL&NCR had to fall in line when services westward from Dundalk to Enniskillen and Omagh and southward from Portadown to Clones and Cavan and branches were peremptorily terminated, depriving a wide area of Ireland along the border of its railways services. Inevitably the GNRB ceased to exist as from 1 October 1958 when the remaining GNR lines were divided between CIE and UTA ownership. The sole other railway operator, the CDRJC, was not long in following the GNR into oblivion when it finally closed on the last day of 1959.

The Irish Government decided that the time had come to insist that CIE should pay its way, having received the conclusions of yet another investigation, the Beddy Report of 1957. In common with experience elsewhere ownership of motor cars was increasing rapidly in Ireland, almost threefold since 1945, but unlike most other countries the limited population of the Emerald Isle was not suffering the effects of road congestion, except of course in Dublin, because per capita there was more road space than in other lands. Statistically it was shown that CIE rolling stock was the least used in the British Isles and that there was three times the number of staff really necessary. Not for the first time it was demanded by railway management that legislation to transfer traffic to rail should be introduced in order to make more efficient use of the system for there was ample capacity, but unfortunately for CIE much of Ireland's commerce is handled and processed in port areas, somewhat limiting internal movement. Restrictions on public choice was not a political possibility and the Beddy report's main recommendations were to reduce route mileage by almost one half, to close stations so that only 57 remained, to integrate train and bus services more closely and replace much of the summer peak travel by road, so allowing a substantial reduction in the number of coaches. This resulted in a spate of line and station closures, including the last of the narrow gauge, from 1958 to 1963 but the financial objectives have never been satisfied and CIE continues to receive public funds. Implementation of the closures enabled CIE to dispense with steam in 1963, aided by the introduction of American-built diesel locomotives which have given a service far superior to those obtained from Britain. The last major closure took place in 1967 when the service between Waterford and Mallow was terminated, the through boat trains from Cork to Rosslare being diverted by way of Limerick Junction. Some lesser lines have closed since.

The names of fifteen CIE stations were changed in 1966 as part of national celebrations for the fiftieth anniversary of the 1916 Rising, giving recognition to national heroes, the changes being:

Dublin Amiens Street	Connolly
Dublin Westland Row	Pearse
Dublin Kingsbridge	Heuston
Cork	Kent
Limerick	Colbert
Dun Laoghaire	Mallin
Waterford	Plunkett
Galway	Ceannt
Dundalk	Clarke
Drogheda	MacBride
Sligo	MacDermott
Bray	Daly
Wexford	O'Hanrahan
Kilkenny	McDonagh
Tralee	Casement

In Northern Ireland there was a fresh look at the remaining railways and the Benson report of 1963 proposed the termination of non-passenger traffic and the retention only of the main line from Belfast to the border and the routes to Larne and Bangor. At the same time another learned gentleman was recommending that further expansion of Belfast should be restricted and that six towns – Derry, Omagh, Enniskillen, Warrenpoint, Newry and Coleraine – should expand as centres of population and light industry; no one in Government seemed to think it odd that all should be deprived of rail services! In the event closures were not quite so drastic, Derry retaining its NCC route through Ballymena and Coleraine, but the other lines ceased to operate in 1965 apart from that between Lisburn and Antrim, retained for the through CIE trains which carried bonded cargoes for Co Donegal to Londonderry.

Ulster's railways reached their nadir in 1965–6. The Belfast Government had to face reality, replacing its Ulster Transport Authority by a new company, Northern Ireland Transport Holding Co, with separate organisations for road passenger and road freight and selling the hotels. Rail was left in the hands of Ulster Transport Railways as a temporary expedient until Northern Ireland Railways came into being on 1 April 1968. Gradually the railways improved, despite numerous destructive terrorist attacks, leading to the building of a new central station in Belfast in 1976 and the connection of the Dublin line with that to Bangor.

In the Republic CIE shook off the traditional railway image beloved of enthusiasts with the elimination of many unremunerative lines and the end of its common-carrier status; the once staple livestock traffic ceased during 1973. In contrast mineral traffic was encouraged with the construction of a couple of special branches and is now a principal traffic, along with cement and fertiliser, other business being carried on liner trains for which most goods yards have gantries, but sugar beet carriage has been very limited in recent years. The management of CIE was divided following the passing of the Transport (Re-Organisation of Coras Iompair Eireann) Act of 1986 so that from 2 February 1987 the railway portion became *Iarnrod Eireann* (Irish Rail), the buses being divided between Dublin Bus and Irish Bus, but road freight has been placed in the railway division. CIE remains as a holding company exercising overall control.

Irish railway passenger services have become almost entirely radial in from the two centres, Dublin and Belfast, with only the line from Limerick to Rosslare Harbour being a cross-country route; there is a separate suburban service from Cork to Cobh. Generally the surviving routes have an increased number of trains compared with past years, particularly Sunday services which have become very well patronised, partly due to changing employment, many now working in Dublin and returning to their home towns at the weekends. Indeed the only line now without a Sunday service is that from Limerick Junction to Rosslare Harbour – a distinct contrast to sixty years ago, or even forty years ago, when in the Republic the GSR or CIE ran only one train between Dublin and Cork, with a Limerick connection, apart from Dublin and Cork locals, or excursions to sporting events or the seaside in the summer. The new works at Dublin and Belfast are transforming local services as described in their respective chapters.

The cross-channel railway shipping services have changed considerably over recent years. Long established as part of the through railway routes, the last three decades have seen the services in effect become part of the road system on each side as car and lorry carriage has become the major business. The Heysham to Belfast steamer crossing ceased during 1975 at a time when traffic between Britain and Northern Ireland fell substantially, leaving Holyhead to Dun Laoghaire as the primary route, with Stranraer to Larne and Fishguard to Rosslare every bit as busy. Operated as Sealink the Westminster government sold the shipping division of the British Railways Board in 1984.

Railway preservation has taken root in Ireland and steam excursions actively supported by both IR and NIR are run several times a year over the two systems. Smaller projects are gradually emerging, helping the enjoyment of Ireland's rich railway heritage by the generations who experienced steam and those too young to have known it as day-by-day normal life. These developments are referred to in the appropriate chapters; long may they grow and prosper.

History is a continuing process, and certainly not 'bunk' as once described by Henry Ford, so the story is never complete. Hence this text finishes at a time when IR has acquired new American built locomotives, Japanese built diesel railcars, added new and reopened stations in the Dublin area, and continues with the extension of modern signalling and upgrading of its track and services. Passenger traffic is holding and freight tonnages have increased. NIR has completed its new link line in Belfast whereby the isolated Larne line has been joined to the Dublin and Bangor routes. Passenger traffic remains steady at the present. However a 1993 report on the possible sale of NIR remains secret, it being clear that no early action is likely.

The railway system of the Emerald Isle now stands at 1,432 miles divided between the two operating organisations, discounting the few miles worked by preservation groups. There remains another railway organisation in Ireland, the Fishguard & Rosslare Railway & Harbours, still jointly owned by British Railways and CIE, the offices remaining at Paddington, its cross-channel services using hired vessels. Cooperation between IR and NIR is stronger than ever, the two helping each other at times of emergency and jointly using engineering equipment, such as their cranes working together at engineering jobs, or NIR locomotives receiving attention at Inchicore Works, and NIR diesel trains on loan to work local services from Dublin and between Cork and Cobh.

Thus the railway will live on in the Emerald Isle, at a time when there is greater hope for a peaceful future than ever before.

CHAPTER II

Dublin

Dublin has a long history and derives its name from the Gaelic *Dubh Linn* (the 'Black Pool') but has the alternative name *Baile Atha Cliath* (spoken something like Blaa-Cleah). Both names are derived from the earliest settlement at the lowest ford across Anna Liffey which flows through the centre of the city, the area round its mouth having been reclaimed and built up over the years to form Dublin's port area, yet curiously the international sea crossing from Britain became established six miles south east along the coast. Dublin has two other rivers, the Tolka which flows into Dublin Bay just to the north of the mouth of the Liffey and the Dodder on the south side which joins the latter at its mouth.

In 1173 King Henry II granted Dublin its charter and as the seat of government it became and remains by far the greater centre of population in the Republic. From a figure of 235,864 in 1841 the city increased to 266,700 in 1851, only to fall away to 246,326 in 1871; by 1911 the figure had reached 403,000, partly by enlargement but mainly within its central parts, such that Dublin had become infamous for the condition of its slum areas and their inhabitants. The surrounding townships on the south side also expanded so that they became hardly distinguishable; Rathmines and Rathgar jumped from 2,429 in 1841 to 20,562 in 1871 and 37,800 in 1911 and Pembroke, first counted separately in 1871 when it had 21,000, increased to 29,300 in 1911. There was less development to the north, Clontarf growing from 818 in 1841 to 3,400 in 1871 but Howth further out remained small for a long time. By incorporating some of the surrounding townships, and partly at the expense of the rest of Ireland, Dublin has steadily increased its population so that the city itself has about 600,000 persons.

To the casual visitor Dublin seems much larger because the built-up area extends as far as geography allows southward, the major towns being Dun Laoghaire and Bray; the first, Kingstown from 1821 to 1921 (so named after King George IV had departed thence) has advanced from 7,229 in 1841 to

16,378 in 1871, 17,200 in 1911, 47,803 in 1961 and is still increasing. Bray, in Co Wicklow, was fashionable long ago and so had over 3,000 persons in 1841, steadily increasing (because of the ease of travelling to Dublin and its popularity as one of Ireland's premier coastal resorts) to 6,000 in 1871, 7,700 in 1911 and about 12,000 now.

Development to the west and north of Dublin has been much slower and only in the last thirty or so years has the land been extensively taken for building. Northwards from Dublin habitation has developed along the coast so that there is a general spread as far as Drogheda. The greatest growth has been at Howth, increasing from 692 in 1841 to almost 1,000 by 1871 and now some 6,000, while Malahide has grown from about the same to half the size of Howth. Other places – Donabate, Rush, Lusk, Skerries and Balbriggan – have hardly changed in numbers. Drogheda is only slightly larger, having grown from 16,334 in 1841 to 17,000 these days. Thus population has not vastly increased above that which first attracted railway promoters, despite closeness to Dublin.

It will be clear from the above that the most attractive routes for the early railways were those along the coast to meet local needs and hence the Dublin & Kingstown Railway was incorporated in 1831 and the Dublin & Drogheda Railway followed in 1836. At the time both can be regarded as local whereas the two other railway routes out of Dublin, sought to provide communication further afield with central and western parts, being the Great Southern & Western Railway authorised in 1844 with the Midland Great Western Railway following in the next year. Each route had its own Dublin terminus and they remained unconnected for three decades; the impetus to build the connecting lines came from the need to quicken the passage of mails and facilitate cross-channel business with England rather than any desire for exchange of traffic between the companies. It was to be another fifteen years before the most important of the connecting lines was completed, so eliminating the road journey through Dublin for mails and passengers going further afield who had suffered changes of transport at Dun Laoghaire once and then twice in Dublin, all in a distance of six to eight miles!

OUT TO DUN LAOGHAIRE AND BRAY

The River Liffey offered no navigable access into Dublin itself, a bar and shoals preventing all but the smallest vessels from entering. From the mouth of the river a breakwater of no less than $2^{1}/_{2}$ miles, the Great South Wall, was built in 1748–1768, but as ships got larger it became necessary to provide a harbour elsewhere and in 1818 mail and packet vessels began to use Howth harbour. The solution seemed to be the building of a ship canal and various proposals were considered, all directed southward to the small harbour of Dun Leary; at this point the sands of Dublin Bay gave way to a granite coast with deeper water and a pier had been constructed in 1758–1768. Howth harbour offered no advantage, being liable to silt, and so Dun Leary was enlarged, work commencing in 1817 with the building of the East Pier to which a packet station was added; the likelihood of silting made it essential to add the West Pier. When the Post Office introduced new vessels on its Holyhead crossing in 1826, they were, in fact, too large to use Howth, so the service had to be diverted to Kingstown. A ship canal would have been prohibitively expensive so as early as 1825 a railway Bill was submitted to Parliament and it became a battle between those, such as the Grand Canal Company who wanted a waterway, or those who perceived a threat to their rights and properties, and the railway party. It was the imme-diate success of the Liverpool & Manchester Railway in 1830 which, demonstrating the similar purpose of connecting a centre of population with its nearest shipping point, convinced all that a railway was the answer. During the same period the Holyhead Road in England and North Wales was being improved, the Menai Bridge being finished in 1826, to further communication between London and Dublin, especially government busi-ness.

The tender of Wm. Dargan was accepted, work starting at Dun Leary on 11 April 1833, and it was hoped that trains could start on 1 June 1834 but it was not until 31 July 1834 that one line was laid throughout. The first engines were tested on the Liverpool & Manchester Railway, being of the same gauge, 4ft 8½in, and arrived in Ireland during the autumn of 1834. To the engine *Vauxhall* belongs the credit of being the first known to have run in Ireland when on 4 October 1834, a test train was hauled from Dublin as far as Williamstown, about 2½ miles. Hopes of opening on 22 October 1834 were dashed when a flood destroyed a bridge.

Dubliners opened their papers one Tuesday morning to read:

> DUBLIN AND KINGSTOWN RAILWAY
> WILL BE OPENED
> for the Conveyance of Passengers
> on to-morrow (Wednesday) the 17th instant.

Thus at nine that morning, *Hibernia* steamed out of the Dublin terminus with the first regular train, not only in Dublin but in all Ireland, the first of nine return journeys that day. To Dublin belongs the honour of being the first of the world's (present-day) capitals of having a passenger railway (London had to wait until 1836 and the London & Greenwich Railway to get its first passenger trains). The almost level line had stations at Blackrock (4) and Dun Leary (5½ miles from Dublin), served by hourly interval trains, perhaps the first such timetable anywhere. Over the years there have been numerous stations added and names changed, better summarised in Table 2.

The Dun Leary terminus lay on the west side of the harbour and therefore was not handy to the packet station, needing an extension to make the railway more suitable for cross channel travellers and the mails. Dargan built the extra half mile which opened on 13 May 1837 and immediately proved its value to travellers.

For much of the way from Dublin the line runs almost on the foreshore and at times is inundated by the sea; there is a covered way of 70 feet at Blackrock but had the original alignment been followed there would have been a tunnel of 500 yards a little further inland. At the Dublin end the line was raised on arches, including the terminus, a place that gained much notoriety for congestion and gloominess until rebuilt. When the first locomotives arrived, an 'Engine Hospital' was erected at Serpentine Avenue, about 1½ miles from the terminus, but it was clearly unsuitable for permanent use. The new workshops were established at Grand Canal Street, on the viaduct section, adapting an existing building. Acquisition came about in a curious manner; it was originally the 'Dock Distillery' and when it became unused some Dublin distillers in 1836 offered £1,000 to the railway to buy it up so that one source of competition was eliminated! The building was ready in 1839 and had the peculiarity that engines were attended to on the *first* floor at rail level. The company, far from satisfied with its engines, set about building its own and on 9 April 1841 the first, *Princess*, entered regular service, not only the first built by an Irish railway but also probably the first by any railway company in the world. Another distinctive first by D&KR engines was the addition of water tanks on two engines in 1836 so making them the earliest in the British Isles not to have a separate tender. Grand Canal Street works remained in use until 1926, having built 46 engines from 1841 until 1911.

A tramway had been laid down to carry granite quarried at Killiney to the new works at Dun Leary and its course was largely superseded by an extension of the D&KR. To get to Dalkey the D&KR leased one of the two tracks of the tramway and converted it into a passenger railway, no Act being obtained, the railway entering into possession in September 1842. It was realised that traffic would be light (Dalkey then having about 300 souls) and when an alternative to steam was offered it is not to be wondered that it was accepted – the proposal was made by the patentees of the 'Atmospheric System', Samuda and Clegg, who saw a chance to demonstrate their method

TABLE 2
SUBURBAN STATIONS HOWTH−DUBLIN−BRAY−GREYSTONES

	Station	Opened	Closed	Remarks
(a) AMIENS STREET (Connolly) - HOWTH				
0	Amiens Street	1844	OPEN	Dublin until 1854;
$0^1/_4$	Dublin	1844	1844	Temporary terminus
$1^3/_4$	Clontarf	1844	1956	Closed 1850-1898
$2^1/_4$	Killester	1845	OPEN	Closed 1847-1923
3	Harmonstown	1957	OPEN	
$3^3/_4$	Ratheny	1844	OPEN	
$4^1/_2$	Kilbarrack	1969	OPEN	
$4^3/_4$	Junction	1846	OPEN	Howth Junction from 1912
$5^3/_4$	Bayside	1973	OPEN	
$6^1/_2$	Baldoyle & Sutton	1846	OPEN	Sutton from 1901
				Sutton & Baldoyle from 1916
				Sutton from 1936
$7^1/_2$	Howth	1846	1847	Temporary terminus
$8^1/_4$	Howth	1847	OPEN	
(b) AMIENS STREET (Connolly) - GREYSTONES				
0	Amiens Street	1891	OPEN	Amalgamated with GNR
				station 1958
$0^3/_4$	Tara Street & George's Quay	1891	OPEN	Tara Street from 1921
1	Dublin	1834	OPEN	Westland Row from 1854;
				Pearse (1966)
2	Lansdowne Road &			
	Ballsbridge	1870	OPEN	Lansdowne Road from 1872
$2^1/_2$	Serpentine Avenue	1835	1835	Open only in Jan/Feb 1835
$2^3/_4$	Sandymount	1835	OPEN	Closed 1841-60, 1862-82,
				1901-28, 1960-84
$3^1/_4$	Sydney Parade	1835	OPEN	Closed 1841-62, 1960-72
$3^3/_4$	Merrion	1835	1934	Closed 1862-82, 1901-28
$4^1/_4$	Booterstown	1835	OPEN	Closed 1960-75
$4^1/_2$	Williamstown	1835	1841	
5	Blackrock	1834	OPEN	
$5^3/_4$	Seapoint	1863	OPEN	Monkstown & Seapoint from
				1964; Seapoint from 1991
$6^1/_2$	Salthill & Monkstown	1837	OPEN	Closed 1960-84; Salthill from
				1960; Salthill & Monkstown
				from 1991
$6^3/_4$	Dunleary	1834	1837	Original terminus
7	Kingstown Harbour	1837	OPEN	Kingstown from 1861; Dun
				Laoghaire from 1921; Malin
				added 1966
$7^3/_4$	Kingstown Sandycove	1855	OPEN	Sandycove from 1861;
				Sandycove & Glasthule from
				1967
$8^1/_4$	Glenageary	1867	OPEN	
$8^3/_4$	Dalkey	1844	1854	Resited
9	Dalkey	1854	OPEN	
10	Obilisk Hill	1855	1858	
$10^1/_2$	Killiney	1854	1858	Resited

Station		Opened	Closed	Remarks
10³/₄	Killiney	1858	1882	
11	Killiney & Ballybrack	1882	OPEN	Killiney from 1921
11¹/₄	Ballybrack	1863	1882	
11¹/₂	Ballybrack	1855	1863	Resited
12	Shankill	1977	OPEN	
13¹/₂	Woodbrook	1910	1960	Resited on new line in 1915
14³/₄	Bray	1854	OPEN	Bri Chualann (Bray) from 1925
15¹/₂	Bray Head Halt	1906	1907	Also known as Naylor's Cove; open for a short while in 1929
19¹/₂	Delgany	1855	OPEN	Greystones & Delgany from 1886; Greystones from 1914

(c) HARCOURT STREET - SHANGANAGH JUNCTION

0	Harcourt Street	1859	1958	
0¹/₄	Harcourt Road	1854	1859	Temporary terminus
0³/₄	Ranelagh & Rathmines	1896	1958	Ranelagh from 1921
1³/₄	Milltown	1860	1958	
3	Dundrum	1854	1958	
5¹/₄	Stillorgan	1854	1958	
6	Foxrock	1861	1958	
7¹/₄	Carrickmines	1854	1958	
9³/₄	Shankill	1854	1958	
10¹/₂	Shanganagh Junction	1861	1877	

of traction as a passenger-carrying line. This is not the place to explain *in detail* how such a railway worked, but it should be mentioned that air was exhausted by steam-driven pumps from a large pipe laid between the rails; within this pipe a piston travelled, air entering from behind being the propelling force. The piston was attached to the underside of a small carriage, the pipe having a slot along its full length, being sealed by a flap which ahead of the piston was held down by atmospheric pressure. The line was uphill to Dalkey with the pumping house at the top but trains returned by gravity. The peculiarities of the system and the persuasiveness of the patentees ensured that there were many visitors during testing and the best known outcome was Brunel's enthusiastic adoption of the principle for the South Devon Railway between Exeter and Plymouth. Opened on 29 March 1844 the line was 2 miles long and had a half hourly interval service from the start but once the novelty had worn off there were hardly enough passengers to meet costs.

With only one train on the line and independent of the main service the 'Atmospheric System' could hardly fail to impress so long as the pumps were in order, which often they were not, and so it continued until its method of operation hindered expansion southward. When the D&KR had to supply an engine in 1848–9, *Princess* no less, it was soon apparent that claims for the superiority of the atmospheric system on hills were unfounded. After the last train of 12 April 1854 the atmospheric ceased, the last in the British Isles, and work then began on conversion of the line for steam use. There is very little to show that such a method of working had been used but Atmospheric Road still exists alongside the railway at Dalkey.

The D&KR directors were men concerned with the welfare of their company and showed little enthusiasm to join with others. Hence when Brunel planned to extend the Great Western Railway across South Wales to a suitable port, establish a sea crossing to Co Wexford and build a railway northward to Dublin, he suggested that the Irish company would benefit by its ownership of the line into Dublin. That the GWR should think it worthwhile to compete for Dublin traffic needs consideration; at the time Holyhead was still not on the railway map and mail and passenger sailings used Liverpool, although calling at'the North Wales port. Furthermore the Chester & Holyhead Railway had only just obtained its Act and many doubted that it would be completed because it would be impossible to bridge the Menai Strait.

During all this posturing the D&KR, realising its importance to Brunel's plans, made the suggestion that its line should be leased by his new company, an annual rent of £34,000 duly being agreed (with also a half share of surplus revenue in excess of £55,000). The outcome was a GWR-supported Waterford, Wexford, Wicklow & Dublin Railway (the 'Three Ws' in short) and a D&KR-sponsored Kingstown & Bray Railway, both getting Acts in 1846. However, by an Act of 1847 the D&KR was to hand over its rights for the Bray extension to the 'Three Ws' once three-quarters of the latter's capital had been subscribed. Work soon started at Dalkey, Brunel paying short visits to direct activities, but everything stopped when the money ran out. In truth the LNWR was making far better progress in establishing its Irish route through Holyhead, the South Wales Railway not having any section near completion, let alone reaching Fishguard, its chosen harbour for Irish sailings. A more telling cause was the continued effect of the Famine and shortage of capital in Ireland.

In 1851 the 'Three Ws' became the Dublin & Wicklow Railway and at last Dargan built the 4 miles Dalkey and Bray section, a single line opening on 10 July 1854, joining the inland line from Dublin, opened the same day, at Shanaganh Junction (12 miles from Dublin), trains continuing over the D&WR into Bray (13¾ miles). Reconstruction and regauging to 5ft 3in of the former 'atmospheric' section was of course necessary and it reopened in 1855; the BOT inspecting officer was very critical of the manner in which it had been altered but Brunel overcame his objections with a set of working regulations which required that all carriage windows had bars, only one engine was in steam, all trains in both directions were to stop at a new station at Sandycove Road and the journey to take not less than 12 minutes. The stop was to ensure that trains would not take a severe curve at too great a speed. The D&KR was still not satisfied and so another railway farce began, passengers being prevented from alighting at Kingstown, they having to return to Dalkey; the row went on until trains ceased in early 1856, restarting later that year after further reconstruction during which a portion of the D&KR was temporarily mixed gauged through Kingstown so that Dargan could dump the extra spoil in the Old Harbour.

The lease of the D&KR by the D&WR now came into effect but until an Act of 1866 allowed a tenure of 999 yeas the D&KR section was to run as a separate line, although the gauge was altered to 5ft 3in during 1857. Doubling of the line beyond Kingstown started with the Dalkey and Ballybrack section in 1879, including the 160 yards tunnel south of the former station and from Kingstown, but not through the station, to Dalkey in 1881; the portion from Ballybrack to Shanganagh Junction remained single until 1915.

At Kingstown there were three sidings serving the harbour, of which the most important opened on 23 December 1859, allowing connecting trains to run alongside steamers at the Carlisle Pier, named after the incumbent Lord Lieutenant, being constructed by the Board of Works. The junction was in a short single track section in a cutting, partly covered, and until modern signalling arrived, trains on and off the pier had to be accompanied by a 'Packet Porter' acting as a human staff to prevent collision with trains on the main line. Two other sidings served the 'Traders' Pier' (1863) which for many years handled large tonnages of sulphur ore mined in Co Wicklow and from 1891 the old 1836 mail wharf (Victoria Wharf since 1849), paid for by the War Office in London.

The local service along the coastal line was for many years Ireland's busiest suburban timetable, growing from hourly in 1834 to half-hourly by 1888; even a couple of steam railmotors were tried (unsuccessfully) during 1907 in an attempt to combat electric tram competition. A very extensive quarter-hourly service was put on in 1922, despite the hindrance of the single line at dun Laoghaire, not to mention the civil strife of the time; the railway was the winner in its war against the trams, gaining an extra 1¹/₂ *million* passengers in 1922 and a *further million more* in 1923! A timetable of 1928 was even more ambitious, attempting to get motorists out of their cars, with six trains per hour, two for Dun Laoghaire, two for Dalkey, one for Killiney and the other for Bray. Decline began with the Emergency timetables of 1941 onwards, reaching the bottom in 1960, but have now been rejuvenated by electrification, to be described later.

Not far from Westland Row the Royal Dublin Society show grounds at

Ballsbridge were served by a siding installed in 1893 for the movement of livestock, etc to and from exhibitions. For some years special trains were run into the siding from nearby Lansdowne Road station although the inspecting officer remarked that it had been provided for livestock only. Long before lifting in 1971 traffic had ceased.

THE INLAND ROUTE TO BRAY AND BEYOND

The success of the D&KR prompted plans for another line, the Dublin, Dundrum & Enniskerry Railway, the last name being considered a place of rather more importance than Bray, despite a very much smaller population (even now there are hardly 500 souls). Before getting an Act in 1846 the route was diverted at Dundrum to reach Rathfarnham, the company being incorporated as the Dublin, Dundrum & Rathfarnham Railway. The Three Ws then arranged to use the former for access to Dublin and continue further into the city as far as St Stephen's Green. A branch was also authorised from Foxrock to Kingstown needing two tunnels through granite, which needless to say was not even started. The unbuilt DD&DR was taken over by the D&WR as successor to the 'Three Ws' and after many delays Dargan completed the 12¼ miles of line for opening on 10 July 1954 from its temporary terminus at Harcourt Road through to Bray. The former was replaced as the terminus on 7 February 1859 by Harcourt Street, an extension of 8 chains, authorised in 1857, the small station having only a single platform. Foxrock was provided with an extra platform line in 1893 to cater for race traffic to the nearby Leopardstown course.

As opened it was a single line throughout to Bray but doubling soon began when a second track was added between Bray and Shanganagh Junction in 1855, and the remainder in 1861. The final section into Bray was getting busier and in 1877 a third track was added so that the single track from Dalkey was extended into Bray as a separate line. North of Bray it was close to the sea shore but under continual attack so that eventually the D&SER was forced to move inland to a new alignment, the deviations coming into use piecemeal, the new up line for the Harcourt Street route on 4 October 1915, the corresponding down line six days later, and as a new double track from Ballybrack the Kingstown line joined the former at a new Shanganagh Junction.

Bray steadily gained popularity as a seaside resort and to some it is the 'Blackpool of Ireland' but its railway facilities lagged behind demand, having only one platform for the frequent trains on both Dublin routes and the main line service to Wexford. Long intended, it was not until 1927 that a second platform was added using land acquired with the Royal Marine

Hotel in 1900; that caught fire in 1916 and was not used until refurbished as a buffet years later. The inland route, treated as the main line for as long as Wexford trains used Harcourt Street (the October 1941 Emergency timetable finishing the custom), never had the intensive service of the coastal route. Most trains were for some years provided by the Drumm battery trains, first built in 1932; the battery, the invention of Dr James Drumm, of Monaghan, had the special feature of low internal resistance, allowing high rates of charge and discharge, but there was the penalty of weight, 15 tons per train, and they had to be recharged for every trip.

Enniskerry, three miles west of Bray, continued to expect a railway and construction actually started after the passing of the Bray & Enniskerry Light Railway Act in 1886 but only a little levelling was done before work stopped.

South of Bray the way ahead is blocked by the bulk of Bray Head (791 feet) and whatever route had been chosen there would have been severe climbing to get further south. The main road takes a course to the west of the head on its way to Delgany, the next settlement, and it is quite possible that the directors of the D&KR expected that any railway would have done so when they originally decided that their Bray extension would terminate inland rather than close to the sea and esplanade. Very probably it was the challenge of doing what others claimed to be impossible that gave Brunel the opportunity to show off his engineering prowess by choosing the difficult route, just as he did about the same time in South Devon between Dawlish and Teignmouth.

As built by Dargan and opened in 1855 the line between Bray and Greystones, the station beyond the headland, had three tunnels, all built to take a double track and five viaducts over ravines, which were miniature versions of Brunel's better known structures in Devon and Cornwall. Not surprisingly for the times there were many fearful of journeying round Bray Head where the line ran about 100 feet above the sea. A derailment in 1867 at the second viaduct certainly did not help confidence, especially when lack of management and care was shown to be a cause. The train fell from the bridge, fortunately to the landward side, for had it gone the other way it could have plunged the greater distance into the sea and there would have been many more than the two unfortunate fatalities. The geology of the head means that there have to be constant checks for rock falls which occur from time to time and the decline of the strata towards the sea always poses the threat of a slide. Storms have steadily eroded parts of the cliffs and no less than four major deviations have been necessary. Some years ago a chair lift was installed up to the head but it has been derelict for many years.

Greystones at the south end of the Bray Head section was the outer terminus for a fair proportion of suburban trains from Dublin. For the next ten miles, the longest level stretch in Ireland, the line follows the sea shore so

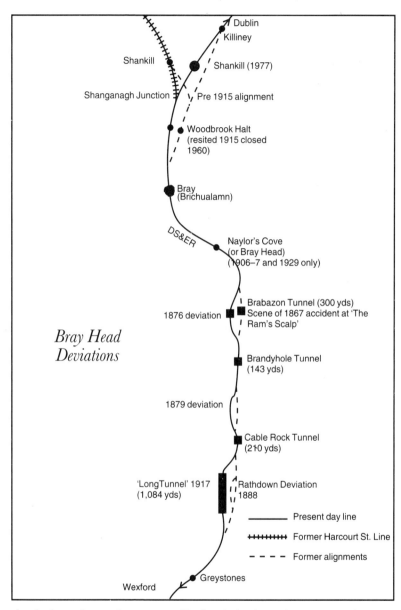

Dublin
Killiney
Shankill
Shankill (1977)
Shanganagh Junction
Pre 1915 alignment
Woodbrook Halt
(resited 1915 closed
1960)
Bray
(Brichualamn)
DS&ER
Naylor's Cove
(or Bray Head)
(1906–7 and 1929 only)
Brabazon Tunnel (300 yds)
1876 deviation
Scene of 1867 accident at 'The
Ram's Scalp'
Bray Head
Deviations
Brandyhole Tunnel
(143 yds)
1879 deviation
Cable Rock Tunnel
(210 yds)
'LongTunnel' 1917
(1,084 yds)
Rathdown Deviation
1888
Present day line
++++++++++ Former Harcourt St. Line
– – – – Former alignments
Greystones
Wexford

closely that only massive concrete blocks, chained together, prevent the track
being washed away; from 1917 until 1921 the D&SER received £40,000 in
grants from London for these defensive works and a continual watch is still
necessary along this section. In November 1971 the track was moved several

feet inland between mileposts 18 and 19 to reduce the risks. One of the original stations, Killoughter closed as early as 1867 but Kilcool, closed in 1964, reopened in 1980 with the more correct name of the nearby village of Kilcoole. In many earlier timetables this station was shown with Newtownmountkennedy added as a suffix! Wicklow (28½ miles from Harcourt Street) remained in use when the line was extended in 1861, the junction being located 27¾ miles, trains reversing until a new station was opened in 1885 on the main line; even then a solitary morning arrival from Dublin and its return used the terminus until 1893. In 1969 a weekday train for Dublin was started, using the old station reopened as Wicklow (Murrough), but lasted only until 1976. In 1877 the line was double from Newcastle to Wicklow, but was reduced to single again in 1927.

The Wicklow Tramway Co extended the line to the harbour during 1869. A further section was added at the behest of the Earl of Fitzwilliam during 1906, worked by the D&SER, but traffic was very light and ceased about 1922.

THE MAIN LINE TO THE SOUTH WEST

Dublin's third railway, the GS&WR, was to form the prime route to the west, but that company was not the first to plan this route for in 1837 the Grand Leinster & Munster Railway had been authorised to connect the city with Kilkenny, others then having ideas about extension south and west. All hopes expired when the 1836 Commission's failure to endorse the GL&MR resulted in its inevitable collapse. It was the ambitions of the London & Birmingham Railway to expand into the Irish traffic that gave fresh impetus, an Act of 1844 authorising the line to Cashel in Co Tipperary with a branch to Carlow as a first step. The choice of Cashel arose from uncertainty about the route further west; often known as the Dublin & Cashel Railway in its formative years, 'Cashels' remained the Dublin Stock Exchange name for GS&WR shares until 1925.

For their Dublin terminus the Directors chose an open space adjacent to the Kings Bridge (dated 1821) across the Liffey which, to present-day travellers, seems to be too far out of town. One hundred and fifty years ago it was on the edge of the built-up area and much of the city's business was conducted on nearby quays on each side of the river and of great importance was the relative closeness of the Smithfield cattle market on the north west side of the city to which beasts could be driven. The Government was happy with the choice because of the nearness of barracks and Phoenix Park in which extra troops could have camped had the need arisen. The station was designed in a manner befitting the company's headquarters and to this day remains one of the finest buildings in Dublin. Its position by the Liffey still gives the frontage an immense advantage over so many public places in that it is visible without hindrance from a distance. Of interest was a siding installed within the station in 1926 from the nearby route of the Dublin United Tramways Co whereby passengers off arriving trains could take a tram into central Dublin, a facility still provided by bus. A railway hotel at Kingsbridge lasted from about 1875 until 1914.

Most of the line to Carlow was built by McCormick and Dargan, some parts jointly, and the great day came on Monday 3 August 1846 when a special train ran to the Curragh, one of Ireland's premier racing grounds, in celebration. On the next day, the 4th, public services began over the 56 miles the timetable giving the journey time as 2 hours $29^{1}/_{2}$ minutes! From the start there was an unadvertised station at the Curragh for race traffic. The building of the line across the Curragh caused a measure of controversy but the presentation of a new Grand Stand placated the stewards of the course. Excursion traffic has always been heavy so in addition to the main line platforms there was a short siding (38 chains long) into the racecourse area, ready for use in 1856.

The largest railway workshops in Ireland were established by the GS&WR at Inchicore, $1^{3}/_{4}$ miles from Kingsbridge, not only building 405 steam locomotives from 1852 until 1957, and a solitary steam railcar, but also a large number of carriages and wagons, becoming one of Ireland's major engineering establishments, having employed some 1,200 at its peak. Steam locomotive repairs ceased in 1961 but diesel repairs are still carried out, the works having built forty such locomotives, including the first main line examples in Ireland, a pair dating from 1950–1.

Leaving Dublin it is necessary to climb steeply, with stretches varying form 1 in 85 to 1 in 140, as far as Clondalkin where in steam days bankers were detached. From Inchicore the 'Third Line' allows goods trains separate entry into Kingsbridge goods yard which was put down during 1847. At Inchicore a small platform on the up side was used for ticket checking and until 1877 up trains had their engines replaced by 'incline vans' so that trains ran into Kingsbridge by gravity.

Sallins was the station for one of Ireland's finest racecourses, Punchestown, some five miles to the south. Often overwhelmed by homeward bound punters the footbridge had to be fully enclosed to prevent attempts to ride home free on the carriage roofs. At Kildare the loop serving the up platform did not have a direct entry until 1891, trains running past and reversing until then.

Just west of Clondalkin station CIE proposed to build a large marshalling yard in 1947, complete with a hump. Coupled with this there was a plan to build a line across the fields to join the Cork line to the Galway line near Lucan but there was no action beyond preparing tendering drawings.

TULLOW BRANCH

West of the Wicklows and south of the GS&WR main line lies an area of good farming country but thinly inhabited; only Naas (4,500), Baltinglass (900) and Tullow (1,750) have their populations listed in gazetteers. The GS&WR considered connecting Carlow and Tullow, 10 miles apart, and continuing to Newtownbarry (nowadays Bunclody), a further 13 miles to the south east, followed by an 1864 Act for a Dublin & Baltinglass Junction Railway to run south from Sallins but it took a new Act of 1881 to get construction started, followed an 1884 Act for an extension to Tullow, the latter Baronially guaranteed. Built by Robert Worthington, the branch opened to Baltinglass in 1885 (double track Sallins to Naas, $2^{1}/_{4}$ miles, singled in 1937) and then to Tullow in 1886. For some years up to 1914 an evening coach slipped from a down express at Sallins gave a through service from Dublin.

The branch was never prosperous and in 1932 it was announced that it was to close, but it survived, with its three daily trains. After regular passenger and goods ceased in 1947, only Tullow cattle trains and Naas specials ran, the last of the latter on 21 March 1959 just before total closure.

TO THE WEST

There had been a number of schemes for lines to the west but the 1838 report considered that the Royal Canal was sufficient for the potential traffic of the area. So it was not until April 1844 that a new proposal, the Great Western Railway, was put forward, branching from the GS&WR near Sallins, to make a route through Edenderry to reach Athlone, with a branch to Mullingar. A counter-proposal to use the GS&WR as far as Lucan and then pass through more populous areas by way of Maynooth and Mullingar, adopted a new title, Midland Great Western Railway, to distinguish it from the first which was still supported by the GS&WR as the Irish Great Western Railway. Galway was the ultimate objective of both parties but wisely the MGWR sponsors limited their plans to avoid defeat in Parliament, getting powers in 1845 to build a line to Millingar and Athlone, with a branch to Longford, and to purchase the Royal Canal, complete with its hotels at Broadstone (Dublin) and Moy Valley. The canal had a line down to the docks on the north side of the Liffey at North Wall and a branch on higher ground to Broadstone on the north west edge of the city, where the railway built its Dublin terminus. The first section of railway opened on

28 June 1847 as far as Enfield (26½ miles) and continued on to Hill of Down (Kinnegad until 1853) on 6 December 1847.

Ownership of the canal assisted construction by William Jeffs as far as Enfield and Champ & Malone beyond, materials being carried on it as the works progressed – there has been a price to pay over the years where line curvature was severe in places because the canal was followed too closely and hence speed restricted. Westward the line was carried directly across the bog, a brave move by the engineer, G.W. Hemans, to avoid many curves on the canal; the inspecting officer was 'staggered' when he saw the line dipping beneath an advancing engine but eventually he was convinced that the bog would dry out and form a sound base for the track. The contractor here was Daniel Desmond (although he did not actually finish the job) and the line was completed to Mullingar on 2 October 1848.

Each section was single track when opened but the second line was added as quickly as possible, so that the Dublin to Enfield and Hill of Down to Killucan were ready in 1849, thence to Mullingar in 1850 and lastly Enfield to Hill of Down in 1851. Increasing traffic made it necessary to divide some of the longer sections by putting in five extra cabins in 1891 – some were built where there was no place to give them a name, thence three were known by their mileage, 34th, 39th and 46th! The GSR as an economy eliminated most of the double track, working up line in stages, Mullingar to Killucan in 1929 and the remainder to Clonsilla in 1930, leaving the final 7 miles double. The MGWR workshops at Broadstone also fell victim to GSR economies, having built 132 steam locomotives from 1879 to 1927, the last being repaired in 1933, after which the buildings passed to the road services of the company.

Missed by the main line, Edenderry, a cattle town of some 1,900 persons, had to wait until 1873 before a branch was proposed. Built by Bagnell, the line opened in 1877, diverging from the Galway line at Nesbitt Junction, 1¼ miles of Enfield; when the main line was singled in 1930 the former down track from Enfield became the branch, eliminating the junction. Edenderry was the destination of the earliest slip service of the MGWR, started in 1911, when a through coach from Dublin was dropped at Enfield. The branch was an early GSR closure, buses replacing trains in 1931, goods ceasing in 1932, leaving only monthly cattle trains and a few excursions until total closure in 1963.

Two major changes have been made to services over the 'Midland' from Dublin, the first being the closure of Broadstone which took place on Monday 18 January 1937 – there was no Sunday service but the last actual passenger departure was a cattlebuyers' special that day. Between 1934 and 1963 all the intermediate stations between Dublin and Mullingar closed and trains for Galway and Mayo were diverted in 1973 to run via Portarlington so that Mullingar is served only by Sligo trains. The MGWR had made a very feeble attempt to provide a suburban service as far as Enfield, running just one or two trains in addition to its main line service but in contrast CIE has made an effort to create a suburban service by resuming services on 30 November 1981 as far as Maynooth, reopening five stations in 1981–2 and adding three new in 1990. Further west Enfield reopened in 1988.

The long closed Ashtown had a special day of use in 1979 when the Pope visited Ireland. More than 250 special trains were provided, conveying some 400,000 persons, virtually all other traffic on Ireland's railways ceasing over the three days. Ashtown was used for its nearness to Phoenix Park where the meetings were held. Many years before, Sunday 26 June 1932, is claimed to have been the busiest day on Irish railways when no less than 134 specials ran into Dublin, with some 137,000 passengers bound for Phoenix Park during the 1932 Eucharistic Congress of the Roman Catholic Church.

NORTHWARDS ALONG THE COAST

Despair gripped the sponsors of the Dublin & Drogheda Railway when the 1838 report proclaimed that an inland route from Dublin was best suited for the north and north west of Ireland with Armagh and Enniskillen as destinations despite the good progress made along the coast since getting its Act in 1836. W.R. Weeks had started work between Dublin and Portmarnock before the directors suspended construction, but when it was realised that the government had no intention of acting on the commission's plans they enlisted the support of Daniel O'Connell in Parliament, getting a new Act in 1840. Jeffs took over Weeks' contract, McCormick & Dargan getting most of the remaining work on to Drogheda.

A railway was still very much a novelty and the D&DR attracted considerable interest even though the Kingstown line had been working for almost a decade, specials being run for nobility before opening. At last it was possible to start a service from the temporary terminus in Dublin to Drogheda (31¾ miles from Amiens Street) on 24 May 1844 and on the same day the Lord Lieutenant, Earl de Gray, laid the foundation stone for the permanent Dublin terminus at Amiens Street, a fine building of Wicklow granite housing the company's offices; the original plan was to carry the line into the city centre at the GPO on O'Connell Street (then Sackville Street). It was the crossing of the Royal Canal by a single wrought iron span of 144ft only half a mile to the north that had delayed use of the permanent terminus until 29 November 1844 (it was not fully ready until 1846) and made a high level line of 75 arches necessary.

Most of Drogheda town, and its quays, lies on the north side of Boyne, being some four miles upstream from its mouth. The ground on either side is well above river level, the later forming a serious obstacle to the railway builders. Hence the station has always been on the south side, away from the heart of the town and there has never been any connection with the quays.

When the line was extended northwards, it started from a temporary terminus on the north side and it took until 11 May 1853 to bridge the gap – even then it was a temporary structure of wooden scaffolding hurriedly erected so that traffic from the north would not be lost for the duration of the Dublin Exhibition that year; the permanent structure was not ready until 5 April 1855, having double track. The original terminus of the D&DR was abandoned in 1853 in favour of a new through station situation to the west and on a sharp curve which slows any non-stop trains as the route aligns itself to the river crossing. It should be borne in mind that when planned in 1844 there were not yet any of the great river crossings in Britain and so John MacNeill had to seek his own solution after consideration had been given to going somewhat further west of the town to make the crossing. In reality James Barton, MacNeill's assistant, is the man who deserves the credit for the bridge's completion, having taken over construction in addition when Evans, the contractor, failed in 1853, broken by the expense. The main girder portion comprised a centre span of 226ft, flanked either side by two spans of 141ft. Reconstruction took place in 1930–2 when axle load restrictions could no longer be tolerated. A new steel bridge was built within the original, traffic continuing on a single line which was replaced by a gauntleted double track when all was completed. The rebuilding enabled the GNR put on its best timetable between Dublin and Belfast, using its new compound 4–4–0 engines of 1932, with timings in excess of the 60mph average, though this was shortlived because of costs, the 1933 strike and the deterioration in coal supplies when the Economic War increased import costs.

Drogheda was home of one of the two private steam locomotive building works in Ireland, Thomas Grendon producing 41 known examples from 1845 until 1868 and the *only* known case of one exported, being a sub-contract to Robert Stevenson and sent in 1856 to Brazil. The works were never rail connected.

The problem of reaching the quays at Drogheda has never been solved and attempts to build a branch to a new port to be created at Mornington, at the mouth of the Boyne have always failed. Even as late as 1972 there were high hopes of building a branch, diverging south of Drogheda, of about three miles.

Although discarded in favour of Kingstown, Howth still had hopes, never realised, of regaining the Irish Sea packet boats which encouraged the

D&DR to build a branch, authorised in 1845, which however became increasingly important for residential traffic. McCormick started the branch which opened to a temporary terminus (7¼ miles from Amiens Street) in 1846, but it fell to Wm. Dargan to complete the line to Howth (8¼) in 1847. The station at the point of divergence (4¾) was simply Junction until 1912 when it became Howth Junction. Unlike the main line to Drogheda which has always been double, the Howth branch began with a single track from the junction to the 1846 terminus but was double throughout when opened to Howth. In 1892 the section from Sutton onwards was worked as a single line from the up end of the station, the second platform being kept as a bay for Baldoyle race traffic, but in 1896 double line working was resumed.

MEATH LINES

To the west of the GNR main line north of Dublin and to the north of the MGWR route to the west there lies an area of low population – less than 80 per square mile, even close to Dublin itself – a comparison might be, if the reader can imagine such, a population level of the Scottish Highlands in the area north west of London from Harrow to Northampton. The major trade of this lowland area has been cattle raising, or rather fattening those initially raised further west and moved east before export and its past gives Co Meath an important place in Irish history with its archaeological treasures, such as the Hill of Tara. West of Drogheda, Navan (An Uaimh) is the largest centre (4,000), followed by Kells a little to the west (2,200), the only other places of substance being Oldcastle (1,600) and Trim (1,350).

Two lines covered the area in the form of a cross, the horizontal arms being a branch of the GNR from Drogheda to Navan and Oldcastle and the vertical a MGWR branch from Clonsilla to Navan and Kingscourt, which represented the partially built inland route from Dublin to Belfast. It was the D&BJR which obtained authority to build a line from Drogheda to Navan in 1845 but as it was to connect with the already completed D&DR just south of the latter's terminus a clause in an Act of 1847 transferred ownership to the latter on completion. Jeffs was the contractor as far as Duleek but his use of the 'Truck' system which tied his employees to him as their sole source of food, etc, lead to his replacement by a Mrs Kelly, a most unlikely person to be a railway contractor. Moore Bros completed the 17 miles to Navan, opened in 1850, extension westward coming in 1853 when the D&DR added 9¾ miles to Kells, built by Killeen & Moore. Kells was then important enough for Parliament to stipulate that any railway building a more direct line from Dublin was to be granted running powers, which indeed happened.

There was no incentive to extend any further until an independent company proposed to continue onwards to either Cavan or Castleblayney. That resulted in the D&DR extending the branch to Oldcastle ($39^{1}/_{2}$) in 1863 but no further. So little was the habitation that the intermediate station ($33^{1}/_{4}$), shown on maps as nowhere at all, took the name Virginia Road although $6^{1}/_{2}$ miles from that town of but 500 souls laying to the north – in fact it was as close to Oldcastle on a direct road.

The MGWR branch originated as the Dublin & Meath Railway, incorporated in 1858, that company intending to have a junction with the GS&WR at Lucan, but the MGWR forced the promoters, mainly London financiers, to seek an independent terminus in Dublin at Eccles Street, abandoned when the latter granted running powers to Broadstone. Constructed by the Moore Bros the D&MR opened from Clonsilla to a temporary terminus at Navan (23 miles) in 1862; through running to Kells followed soon afterwards, using the quarter mile of connecting line which the BOT inspector had refused to pass just a few days previously (and never seems to have been sanctioned). The D&MR opened a branch from Kilmessan to Athboy (12 miles) in 1864, the contractor being Killeen. Matters between the D&MR and MGWR were far from cordial and continuing difficulties forced the former to accept working by the latter from 1 June 1869, an immediate consequence being the end of the Kells trains exactly four months later. To maintain the facility a station was built at the junction of the two railways just west of Navan, replacing the D&MR platforms; the MGWR showed this as the Navan station but the D&DR and GNR did not, regarding it solely as a place of exchange, until it appeared in GNR timetables in 1896. Continual lack of harmony came to an end when the D&MR was absorbed by the working company in 1889.

Extension north of Navan was authorised in Acts of 1865 and 1867, the Navan & Kingscourt Railway being constructed by J. Edwards and worked by the MGWR. The greater part opened in 1872 as far as Kilmainham Wood (39 miles from Clonsilla), the final stretch into Kingscourt ($43^{1}/_{2}$) following in 1875. In readiness for the extra trains the Oldcastle line was doubled from Navan Junction to Kingscourt Junction, a distance of 25 chains, but in 1911 the latter junction was removed so that the two branches ran side by side as single lines.

Attempts to divert shipment cattle away from Dublin to Drogheda resulted in the authorisation of the Mullingar & Kells Railway in 1903, supported of course by the GNR which would have benefited at the expense of the MGWR. A contractor's promotion by Rbt. Worthington, it had strong support, hopes being kept up until 1920.

Changes to the Meath lines were few; the MGWR intended to double the line throughout from Clonsilla to Navan but did so only as far as Drumree in 1889, converting it back to single from Batterstown to Drumree in 1918, the GSR competing the job in 1926. GSR passenger trains were suspended during the Emergency years and finally ceased in 1947; Athboy also closed to all but cattle traffic which lasted until 1954 and Kingscourt retained a limited goods service from North Wall which was diverted to run from Drogheda in 1961.

Oldcastle was the destination of a through coach from Dublin from 1910, slipped at Drogheda for several years. The GNR service to Oldcastle carried on until passengers ceased in 1958 and in 1963 Clonsilla to Navan Junction and thence to Oldcastle closed completely, leaving the remaining traffic, gypsum from Kingscourt, to be worked from Drogheda. In 1972 a cement factory was opened at Platin, 3 miles from Drogheda, and now zinc is extracted just west of Navan, the Tara mine being rail connected in 1977, using a half mile of the Oldcastle line from the site of the former Kingscourt Junction.

DUBLIN'S CONNECTING LINES

Many attempts were made to join together Dublin's railways and the better chances of about 1860 failed when the banking crisis of 1866, coupled with a period of unrest, deterred would-be investors. The city had not then spread out and connecting lines would have been possible through unbuilt areas. Thus four major ideas were offered being the Dublin Metropolitan Railway, the Dublin Railway, the Dublin Grand Junction Railway and the Dublin Trunk Connecting Railway. The first envisaged a high level station with connections to all existing lines, including a tunnel under the Liffey, the second planned an even larger central station, the third planned lines on both sides of the city and the last intended to circle the city with a line from Sidney Parade passing under the Liffey and Phoenix Park to reach Kingsbridge. It was the last which succeeded at Westminster, getting an Act in 1864; there were to be stations at Irishtown, North Strand, Drumcondra, Phibsborough, Cattle Market and Phoenix Park and work started to the extent of digging a shaft at each end of the Liffey tunnel but by May 1866 everything stopped and the London-based Dublin Trunk Connecting Railway was no more.

A key part of the railways which formed Dublin's connecting system was not built for that purpose at all, the MGWR soon finding that access to shipping at North Wall was essential. The unused 1846 powers were revived in 1859 and the four miles of double track alongside the Royal Canal, with a short tunnel of 292 yards, built by the Moore Bros, opened for goods traffic on 1 March 1864, diverging from the main line at Liffey Junction, 1¼ miles from Broadstone, which from then on had only cattle trains for the nearby Smithfield Market. North Wall had become the Dublin terminus for LNWR steamers from Holyhead in 1859, well used for they offered third class (unlike the CDSP mail boats which were first and second only) and cheaper fares. The LNWR called North Wall a station and had a few sidings which connected with the MGWR. The Liffey Branch was steeply graded and called for special operating instructions, all goods trains being restricted to 8mph on descending the incline and had to be banked when the load exceeded specified limits. When the Spencer Dock opened in 1873, at the junction of the Royal Canal and Anna Liffey, a short branch was built to serve it, having sidings into the CDSP premises.

So far Dublin's railways were not connected and most goods had to be carted to and from the docks. The next move came in 1869 when the D&DR was authorised to build the 'Drogheda Curve', sharing the expense with the LNWR; it was to diverge from the Drogheda line at East Wall Junction and drop down alongside the MGWR line, but not connect with it, to join the LNWR sidings – it was built as a joint line but in May 1878 was equally divided at Church Road between them. East Wall Junction, 1 mile north of Amiens Street, has the geographical peculiarity of being some ¾ mile to the north of North Wall; it also has the rare distinction of a non-passenger location appearing in Bradshaw's timetables when in 1918 it was given, with times, as a footnote in the table of steamer connecting services.

The GS&WR put forward its proposal in 1872 to build a line from Island Bridge Junction (¾ mile from Kingsbridge) which would pass below Phoenix Park by a tunnel (757 yards) and join the MGWR Liffey Branch at Glasnevin, a distance of 2¾ miles. Using 1¾ miles of the MGWR, a second part was to diverge at West Road Junction to join the LNWR at Church Road (a length of 12 chains). T.W. Chester had the contract for both the D&DR and GS&WR lines and they were finally ready in 1877, having relied so heavily on the support of the LNWR; the GS&WR trains were the first to run into North Wall LNWR station on 3 September 1977, MGWR and GNR trains following on 1 December 1877; the former added exchange platforms in 1881 at Liffey Junction, unlike the other two which took their through passengers to Kingsbridge and Amiens Street. Early passenger returns must have caused no little dismay to LNWR directors after spending so much, successive months showing 110, 204, 425, 329, 305 from GS&WR trains and 106, 151, 425, 284 and 204 leaving by GS&WR trains. The first month of MGWR and GNR trains showed 60 and 7 arrivals and 327 and 9 departures! The next month was little better, the figures being 115 and 9 inwards and 215 and 12 out. However, there had been a mass of harvestmen coming home to Ireland, 9,870 passing through from September to November, the MGWR providing trains before their own passenger service commenced. The vessels were, however, well used and obviously most passengers travelled to and from Dublin itself. The GS&WR provided cattle sidings at Cabra, north of Phoenix Park tunnel, and later its own goods depot and cattle yard were opened at 'The Point', further along the North Wall, in 1886. The LNWR opened a hotel in 1885 at North Wall which lasted until 1923, its gardens being described as a green oasis in a desert of docks and warehouses; the buildings still exist as offices.

The Mails were still handled at Kingstown and the road journey from Westland Row remained. Opposition to filling the gap between the latter and Amiens Street or Kingsbridge was kept up by the LNWR, its efforts being directed at getting the Mail contract and so making a greater use of North Wall. The virtual isolation of the DW&WR is nicely illustrated by the movement of two engines sent on loan to the Waterford, Dungarvan & Lismore Railway in 1878; they left the former's Grand Canal Street works for Macmine Junction, where they then worked to Bagenalstown and Kildare, being only 30 miles away after travelling 154$^{1}/_{2}$ miles to get that far on their way to Waterford (South) via Mallow, a further 189 miles (the proverbial crow would have had an easy 100 miles flight and doubtless arrive there long beforehand).

It took a rare display of unity by Irish members at Westminster to defeat the LNWR in Parliament when the mail contract was very nearly taken from the CDSP in 1883. The price of their success was a commitment to support a connecting line and the DW&WR revived a plan of 1872, getting the immediate support of the GNR and CDSP, the MGWR joining some- what reluctantly but the GS&WR after initial interest withdrew, it being generally held that the L&NWR had exerted pressure on the former. However, in 1884 the City of Dublin Junction Railways was authorised, having overcome opposition to its plans for a high level line and a bridge across the Liffey, many fearing the aesthetic effect – it is no wonder that a rival plan to build a line directly across south Dublin from Blackrock to Kingsbridge attracted more than its fair share of attention. Built by a Dublin contractor, M. Mead & Sons, the one mile of line between Westland Row and Amiens Street became known as the 'Loop Line', being partially opened on 12 December 1890 so that the mails could go through to the GNR, followed by full opening on 1 May 1891. At Amiens Street a new set of platforms was built alongside the GNR terminus, the connection between the two railways being 11 chains further on.

There remained to build a connecting line to the MGWR Liffey Branch which, as authorised by the 1884 Act, would join the latter at Newcomen

Bridge Junction. The MGWR and GS&WR both held that a junction at that point would be unsafe for passengers and mails, due to the steep gradient and the crossing of the Royal Canal. There then followed the 'Battle of Newcomen Bridge' when contractors attempted to build the junction; first the wall was knocked down, then rebuilt by the opposition, events giving Dubliners and their papers plenty to talk and write about. Suddenly the MGWR withdrew its opposition so that the double track curve from Amiens Street came into use in 1892, but the GS&WR still refused to accept the junction which forced the DW&WR to work the through carriages destined for the former all the way to Islandbridge Junction; the latter had to acquire new engines for this work, being three large 4–4–2T engines supplied by Sharp, Stewart in 1893.

The expansion of the built-up area on the north side of Dublin encouraged the incorporation in 1894 of the Drumcondra & North Dublin Link Railway. The GS&WR appeared uninterested but behind the scenes was comparing the merits of the line and the already-mentioned Kingstown & Kingsbridge Junction Railway, taking action in an Act of 1896 to purchase the north side line. It was entirely a duplication but when completed provided an easier route and has been of great value to the GSR and CIE. Originally T.H. Falkiner was to have built the line but he died before starting, leaving it to his representatives to get it ready for opening in 1901. However, it was not actually of immediate benefit, although giving access to North Wall from which a none-too-useful local service to Kingsbridge ran

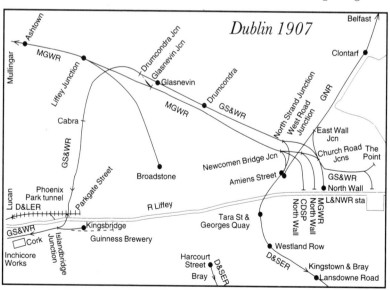

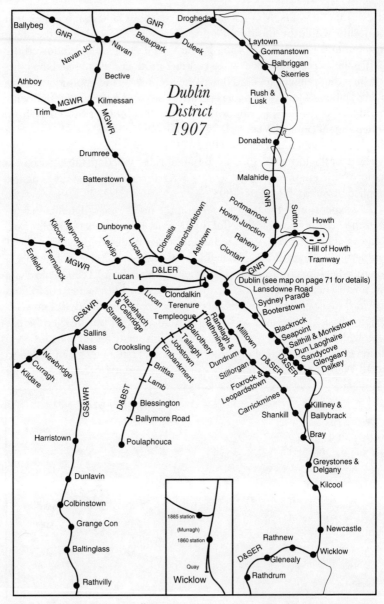

calling at Drumcondra and Glasnevin. A period of disagreement and inac-
tion of no credit to businesses who purported to serve the public followed, it
taking until the end of 1906 to complete the direct access into Amiens Street
from North Strand Road Junction, a line of no more than 36 chains, the

quarrel arising from the relocation of some sidings at Amiens Street, with the line itself ready since August 1903. At last GS&WR trains could avoid Newcomen Bridge and engine changing then took place at Amiens Street; the local service was diverted as well but it was far too late, for Dublin's electric trams served both suburbs with frequent services on direct roads. Thus the local service ceased as soon as 1 October 1907, a steam railmotor having been used.

Just to confuse everyone, the GS&WR called its 1901 junction for the new line Drumcondra; the other end of what now became a short connecting line (15 chains long) the MGWR called Glasnevin but both were total misnomers – the latter lies in Phibsborough and the former was in opposite direction to its namesake! Once the direct GS&WR line into Amiens Street opened, the two junctions had no purpose but they were retained for the exchange of Guinness traffic bound for the west; even this stopped within six months when it transferred to North Wall but it was not until 1921 that the MGWR agreed to its removal. Apart from North Wall traffic, the two lines were used by boat train connections to the latter and Kingstown but the former ceased during November 1921. North Wall had been in decline for years, the LNWR moving its best services to Dun Laoghaire in 1909, completing the move on replacing the CDSP vessels in 1920; after 1921 a once per week sailing lingered on until 1926.

The GSR made no changes until 1 October 1929 when trains to the Meath line and Cavan were diverted from Broadstone to Amiens Street, but were caught out during the GNR strike of 1933 because that company's cabin controlled the north end of the GSR station there, forcing a temporary return to Broadstone. The GSR undertook extensive resignalling of the Dublin area using electric signals, one consequence being at last full use of the GS&WR line into Amiens Street, following the closure of Broadstone. The first of the new cabins was Amiens Street which freed the GSR of dependence on the GNR cabin in 1934 (the connecting line between the two railways was reduced to a single line), followed by Westland Row in 1936 (its area being extended almost to Dun Laoghaire in 1937). The next cabin heralded in a small way the now common remote control of lines and junctions; it was called West Road, a new location just north of Amiens Street on the line to North Strand Junction, but it also controlled the lines out of North Wall running at a lower level and the new junction at Glasnevin, two miles away. A new connection between the two lines at Glasnevin was installed in the opposite direction to the 1877 and 1901 junctions which allowed use of the better graded former GS&WR route and was ready on 22 November 1936, being put into full use when trains were diverted from Broadstone a few weeks later. At last the expenditure of

1901–6 had been fully justified; the line had nearly 'died' when in June 1926 the 'Economy Committee' of the GSR referred a proposal to revert to the pre-1901 arrangement to the Chief Engineer (all that happened was the singling in 1928 of the curve from Amiens Street to Newcomen Junction). The Dublin area resignalling was completed in 1938 when a new cabin at Kingsbridge covered the station and Islandbridge, being extended to include Cabra in 1939.

For the trains diverted from Broadstone there was the curiosity that those for Kingscourt and Cavan used only Amiens Street but for other destinations Westland Row was the terminus, calling at Amiens Street only on the up journey. The old MGWR line had a booked passenger train again from 1961, but only until the next major development in the area. So that the former GNR platforms at Connolly could be used by trains from the west a new junction was installed, known as Ossory Road, where the main line and the 'Loop Line' ran side by side, north of West Road cabin, coming into use in 1973. Former GNR platforms at Connolly were rearranged so that there was an extra one in the area formerly occupied by sidings between the arrival and departure sides and a second connection was installed between the Loop Line and the GNR down main, effectively restoring the second track discarded in 1934. In the North Wall docks area the Dublin Port & Docks Board extended the tracks eastward along Alexandra Road during 1971 for a half mile to serve a new ferry port laid out by B&I.

A TRAMWAY TO LUCAN

Lucan, nine miles to the west of Dublin, lies between two main lines but stations on each were about a mile away and few trains stopped. The village grew around a cloth factory and flour mills, while sulphur springs nearby encouraged the building of the Spa Hotel, offering relief to Victorian rheumatics. So in 1880 a tramway was proposed using the direct road to Dublin and curiously the gauge chosen was 3ft despite the use of 5ft 3in by Dublin's horse tramway along the north side quays of the Liffey as far as the entrance to Phoenix Park. Incorporated by special order of the Privy Council in 1880, the contractor Alexander Ward made such progress that the D&LST was opened as far as Palmerstown in 1881, but a Public Works loan had to be obtained before the company could complete the tracks through to Lucan in 1883. Steam power was used and an early vehicle given a trial was a double decker railcar built by Manlove, Alliot & Fryer of Nottingham but the company chose to use Kitson tram engines.

Celbridge, which lies four miles beyond Lucan, and Leixlip, a couple of miles away on another main road, were both objectives of an extension company, the Lucan, Leixlip & Celbridge Steam Tramway which gained the necessary Orders-in-Council in 1889. The section from Lucan to Leixlip was opened by June 1890, Ward having laid it down, but that to Celbridge never materialised. The Leixlip line proved to be other than remunerative and had a period of closure in 1893; working by the D&LST ceased in 1896, a contractor providing a service until final closure in October 1897.

The line now entered the second stage of its life for an abrupt change of plan brought about regauging to 3ft 6in and reopening as the Dublin & Lucan Electric Railway in 1900, using both single and double deck open top cars providing first and third class accommodation and one old steam carriage was rebuilt to carry the post, marked with the royal cypher and lettered 'Royal Mail'. There was also an electric locomotive to haul the limited goods traffic. A short extension was opened in 1909, restoring that part of the former Leixlip line from the Lucan terminus to the Spa Hotel at Dodsborough, but it was a separate concern, the Lucan & Leixlip Electric Railway, one of the shortest in the world, being barely half a mile in length. Early enthusiasm for electrification prompted plans for extension as the Celbridge, Clane and Donadea Light Railway, places further west also calling for a line to reach Prosperous and Robertstown, ideas likened to plans to build a railway across the Sahara Desert, or nearer home, over the Bog of Allen.

By 1925 the company had fallen into a critical condition but closure raised such a public outcry so that pressure by both politicians and Dublin Corporation forced a second rebuilding of the line. In its third phase the line became 5ft 3in gauge electric tramway, operated as part of the DUTC, reopening in 1928, trams running right into Dublin, terminating at the O'Connell Bridge until closure in 1940.

So ended a route with such a chequered history but now the area it served is entirely built over as the western most suburbs of Dublin, complete with a motorway style approach from Leixlip almost as far as Heuston station.

UP INTO THE HILLS

Apart from the Tullow branch, there was almost no public transport to the south west of Dublin and west of the Wicklows; quarries near Embankment provided much of Dublin's building material and Blessington had been a place of little or no importance but was in severe decline after the Famine. An early plan of 1864 proposed a line from central Dublin to Rathcoole (to the west of Embankment) with an 1865 extension to Ballymore Eustace and a narrow gauge line was put forward in 1880, also to start in central Dublin, falling through when Dublin Corporation objected to steam traction in the city area. This plan was revised that year as a 5ft 3in line to start at Terenure, the connection with the city being an existing horse tramway of that gauge (the reason for the change from narrow), and run $15^1/_2$ miles to Blessington, eventually getting approval in 1887, coupled with a Baronial Guarantee, as the Dublin & Blessington Steam Tramway. Built by Ward, the tramway opened in 1888, its trains consisting of locomotive hauled double deck tramcars, the engines having very tall chimneys and a cab at each end and the cars top deck roofs. Goods traffic was also handled, cattle wagons being worked over the DUTC to Ringsend Dock for export or to the cattle market. Coal was worked similarly from Dublin onto the steam tramway.

The road to Blessington is steeply graded as it climbs the western face of the Wicklows and the line reached 700ft at Crooksling, giving views across Dublin and central Ireland, even the Mountains of Mourne being visible in the best conditions. This summit was exceeded in Ireland only by that of the BC&RBR in Co Antrim. An extension of $4^1/_2$ miles was built by the Blessington & Poulaphouca Steam Tramway, incorporated in 1889 but not opened until 1895, to serve a well-known beauty spot where the River Liffey falls 150ft in a gorge. The service on this section was sparse and indeed in some years ran only on Sundays. In 1897 an ambitious plan was published showing an extension from Poulaphouca through the Wicklow Mountains to Glendalough and Rathdrum (but no connection with the DW&WR was planned), a highly scenic route reaching some 1,600ft, costly to build and operate with no prospect of traffic other than tourists – in fact a route more unsuited to a railway would be hard to find!

With aged and underpowered engines the tramway became decrepit, the slowness of the journey and frequent breakdowns attracting an adverse press, the tram being called 'The Scrap Iron Express' at one time. Ambitious plans to electrify as far as Crooksling were announced in 1911, allowing through running by the DUTC; to get beyond Crooksling trams were to attach a petrol-engine generator wagon. The only effect was the use of petrol-electric cars, partially successful, but steam remained in use to the end which was a long time in coming, there being much public resentment over the Baronial Guarantee still payable because the line had not been included in the GSR amalgamation. The Poulaphouca extension had outlived its usefulness by 1927, the D&BST itself lingering on until its trams stopped on the last day of 1932.

The north side of Dublin Bay is dominated by the Hill of Howth, a rocky prominence of 560ft in distinct contrast to the very low flat area on the north side of Dublin. The hill had become popular with homeowners and tourists, a plan of 1883 advocating a line with very steep gradients, followed in 1894 by a Clontarf & Howth Head Tramways as a continuation of a Dublin horse tram route from its Dollymount terminus to Howth west pier, with a steeply graded branch to the summit. This achieved part fruition in the form of the Clontarf & Hill of Howth Tramroad in 1900, operated as part of Dublin's street tramways. Hence the GNR itself decided in 1896 to build and work a line over the hill connecting Sutton and Howth by a circuitous route, opening in 1901. Interestingly the line had in common with the D&LST and the D&BST the contractor, Alexander Ward.

At Sutton the line had its own power station and depot, being connected with the Howth branch. Nearby the DUTC Howth tramway was crossed on the level but without connections. In fact what appeared to be a tramway was really an electric railway, its traffic being worked by tramcars which did not have Public Service licence plates and nor did the drivers and conductors wear PSV badges. Of doubtful profitability, dependent so largely on tourists, the line was closed during the 1933 strike and did not restart afterwards until the company bowed to political pressure. The tramway put the GNR in the unique position of operating simultaneously steam and diesel trains, electric tramcars, a horse tramcar, buses and lorries. The ten bogie trams were all open-top double-deckers, the line becoming the last in the British Isles so worked and the end came, after passing to CIE ownership in 1958, during 1959 when buses took over. Thus Dubliners lost one of their favourite places for outings for the journey provided on a fine day a pleasant trip, especially on the top deck, with wide views over both Dublin Bay and the coast to the north. The replacing bus service could not provide the same public facility because of the steep roads and did not last beyond 1964.

THE PRESENT DAY SYSTEM

Apart from a few months in 1941–2 when the GNR assisted by working trains through Amiens Street onto the GSR Dun Laoghaire line Dublin's railways had remained largely independent even after being connected by the Loop Line, through working mainly benefiting cross-channel passengers. It was not until 8 December 1958 that a train from Dun Laoghaire to Amiens Street was extended to Howth and back, just a week after the management of the GNR and GSR station had been amalgamated, to establish the present route from Bray to Howth. Within a few years the suburban service out to Dun Laoghaire, Bray and Greystones declined so much that it became no more than a rush hour provision.

Curiously it was not until 1957 that the single track-bottle neck of Dun Laoghaire station was eliminated when a second platform and track were provided. Suburban passenger carrying had dropped staggeringly since 1938, by almost 3,000,000, and the reason lay in the closure of the Dalkey tram service in 1949, modern replacement buses being more comfortable than the trains and Dublin's traffic had not reached saturation. Hence CIE terminated the inland suburban line from Harcourt Street on 1 January 1959, having shown that there was annual loss of £53,000. Even so, losses continued to mount and in 1960 it was claimed that suburban traffic revenue was but £71,000 compared with costs of £241,000 (the latter excluding track costs which were charged against the main line trains to Wexford). So a new timetable of 1960 reduced the number of trains to but 15, a sad comparison with the days of as many as six departures each hour from Westland Row to Dun Laoghaire, Dalkey or Bray and Greystones. With the reduced service stations at Sandymount, Sydney Parade, Booterstown and Salthill closed but doubts were expressed about the legality of this action in respect of the first two mentioned, notice being too short, so they re-opened after a week, lasting only until the statutory two month's notice expired in September 1960 – it is not unfair to remark that rail transport had been virtually written out of Dublin's transport planning. Limited improvements came when more extensive through running at Connolly started on 13 March 1967.

As traffic congestion within the city worsened attempts to attract drivers showed some success so that by 1970 small annual increases became evident, giving sufficient confidence to reopen some stations and add new. Thus to

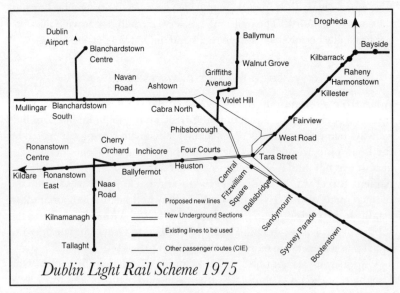

Dublin Light Rail Scheme 1975

the north Kilbarrack on the main line and Bayside on the Howth branch opened in 1969 and 1972; on the south side Sydney Parade reopened in 1972 and Booterstown in 1975. Nobody seems to agree on the spelling of the former for even recent timetables show Sydney Parade on the map and Sidney Parade on the timesheets. A new station was built at Shankill in 1977, serving much the same area as the earlier Shankill on the Harcourt Street line but a more drastic solution to Dublin's traffic difficulties than just 'tinkering' with the coastal railway service was needed. As an interim measure, very much 'make do and mend', diesel train power cars were converted for locomotive powered push-pull workings, but as they and the locomotives were worn out these trains, coming into use in 1973, offered little comfort or improvement in journey times. The number of daily passengers had almost doubled since 1968 and overcrowding was unavoidable.

A 1970 plan showed no interest in rail transport but a 1975 Dublin Rapid Rail Transit Study produced a scheme which proposed new links across the city area and three new out of town lines, as shown on the map. Over the years three 'new towns' – Tallaght, Clondalkin and Blanchardstown – had been developed to the west of the city and their entire needs had been thrown on the roads as the population of the whole area approached one million. Irrespective of other plans the bold decision was taken in 1979 to electrify the coast line from Bray to Howth, using a 1,500v DC overhead conductor, sensible enough for the Dublin area, which avoided excessive raising of structures and once all the civil engineering work and resignalling was completed, electric trains manufactured in Germany, but with British equipment, started to run on 23 July 1984; two stations, Sandymount and Salthill reopened that day and services were transformed.

A major casualty was the loss of boat trains to Carlisle Pier, due to the 'impossibility' of retaining the junction at Dun Laoghaire, which ceased on 10 October 1980; by then relatively few steamer passengers used the rail connection. At the north end of Connolly the track layout was remodelled to give a new double line connection in place of Ossory Road Junction, but facing in the other direction, Sligo trains using a new connection closer to the platforms; named Suburban Junction the new layout came into use on 9 August 1981.

For the greater part of the day a fifteen-minute (half hourly on Sundays) interval service is provided by two-car trains, doubled at peak times, giving the world's oldest commuter route a thoroughly modern image. As part of the system, buses connect at some stations to form integrated journeys to and from the suburbs, the whole being operated as the Dublin Area Rapid Transit. Stations are equipped with ticket-operated turnstiles and have full public address controlled from Connolly, the 'nerve centre' of the DART

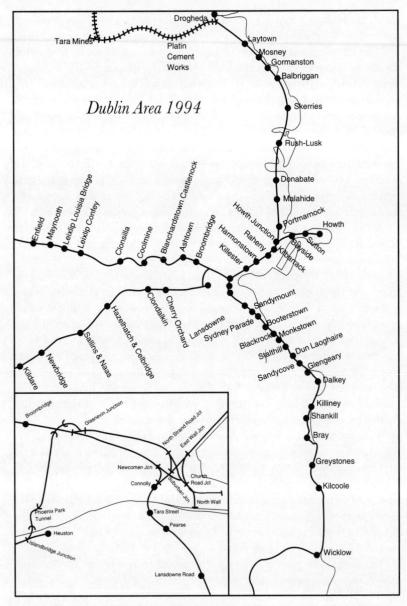

Dublin Area 1994

trains. Drivers are in radio communication with the central control and are aided by an automatic train protection system, so that speeds are governed by line conditions, there being in-cab signal indication; in fact the system is more advanced than any suburban section of British Railways. The former

GNR diesel depot at Fairview, just north of East Wall Junction, was converted to maintain the electric stock and on the main line a small halt for staff has been provided. Tara Street, between Pearse and Connolly, is now the busiest station in Ireland with more than 20,000 passenger per diem.

In 1992 it was announced that for the first time a suburban service was to be provided on the GS&WR main line as far as Droichead Nua and Kildare, using a bus link from Heuston into the city centre, Clondalkin, Hazlehatch & Celbridge and Sallins stations reopening with a new station at Cherry Orchard to serve Ballyfermot. Railcars were ordered from Japan and the weekday Arrow service started on 16 May 1994.

A further announcement of 1992 introduced the Dublin Transport Initiative, a mixed road, bus and light railway plan designed to serve Tallaght, Cabinteely (using in part the old Harcourt Street line) and Ballymun, with a possible extension to Dublin Airport and Swords, and perhaps Finglas, with sections of street running in the central area. Also involved are plans to extend electric trains to Greystones and perhaps northwards to Malahide and add two stations to the DART service, one at Barrow Street just south of Pearse and another at Fairview, north of Connolly; a branch leaving the GNR mainline north of Howth Junction could serve Dublin Airport. To allow a more frequent service to Maynooth it is planned to double the line from Clonsilla. In the longer term, it could be possible for local services from Kildare and Maynooth to run through to Tara Street and Pearse. In 1994 plans were published for the enlargement of Heuston to no less than *ten* platforms, doubling the present number and so many more than the three which existed until 1972. The hopes were expressed that, subject to finance and technical resources, the Tallaght and Cabinteely lines would be completed as the first phase by 1997 – it remains to be seen if after all the talk anything is done at all!

INDUSTRIAL AND CONSTRUCTION LINES

When an aerodrome was built by the British Government about 1917 near Tallaght, a branch from the D&BST carried workmen and construction materials to the site, about one mile towards Clondalkin, trams possibly working through from Terenure; in fact goods were carried over the DUTC system all the way from the RDS siding at Ballsbridge, apparently hauled by a DBST engine throughout. At the aerodrome a contractor's 2ft gauge line was laid down and worked by a couple of British War Department locomotives. Not far away there was another airfield construction line connecting Lucan (GS&WR) with its site at Baldonnel $2^{1}/_{2}$ miles to the south. Like the Tallaght line it carried materials and personnel from 1918 to 1919 and was no more permanent; Baldonnel aerodrome is now the headquarters of Ireland's air defence force.

Perhaps the best-known commercial enterprise in Dublin is that of Arthur Guinness, the brewers of porter established in 1759 who, by 1825, had extended into the English market. The brewery site had two working levels and transport between them became a problem, the 1ft 10in gauge system (initiated about 1874) with its miniature locomotives hardly able to cope as the connection was made by a hydraulic lift, a severe impediment to the increasing output as only one wagon at a time could be handled. To overcome this, a novel method, unique in Ireland, was used, installing a spiral incline in a tunnel with 2·65 turns and a length of 865ft. The miniature engines proved quite unsuitable and the company's engineer, Samuel Georghehan, solved the difficulty by designing one of the most extraordinary locomotive types ever to exist. No less than 18 were built from 1887 to 1921 in Dublin by Wm. Spence, having to fit into a loading gauge of 5ft by 6ft high, pass round many sharp curves and haul wagons up inclines as steep as 1 in 40; this was done by placing the boiler between the frame plates and fitting the cylinders above. Authority for a 5ft 3in tramway connection to the GS&WR at Kingsbridge was contained in an Act of 1874 obtained by the railway, the line being 31 chains long from its junction just west of Kingsbridge station, using St Johns Road alongside the departure side of the station and then the quayside for entry into the Guinness yard. Completed about 1878, it was horse worked until 1893; in that year Georghehan showed his ingenuity yet again by devising a 'haulage wagon' into which a narrow gauge engine could be placed to drive it on the broader-gauged line. However about 1903 a broad gauge petrol-engined locomotive was obtained, one of the earliest non-steam industrial locomotives in the British Isles, followed by a couple of ordinary saddle tanks and then a diesel in 1949. With ever increasing road traffic and the diversion of Guinness output from rail despatch, the tramway was taken out of use on 15 May 1965. The narrow gauge system continued, diesel gradually replacing steam, until it too was discarded on 5 August 1975.

South of Dublin two reservoir projects in Co Wicklow both used contractors' railways. That at Roundwood was started in 1908, using a 3ft gauge system and took until 1925 to complete, there being a succession of firms involved, Dublin Corporation having to take over for a while in 1912–13. The other near Poulaphouca on the other side of the Wicklows took from 1937 until 1942, Cementation Co using 2ft and 1ft 10in gauge systems and a mixture of steam and diesel locomotives.

CHAPTER III

Waterford and the South East

South of the Dublin area centres of population are small with only Waterford and Wexford having any size, there being a scattering of small towns. The area is dominated by the major rivers of the Slaney, Barrow, Nore and Suir, the last three having a common estuary. There is much high ground and mountain ranges divide the rivers but there are good fertile areas. The major settlement is Waterford, on the south side of River Suir, with some 28,000 persons, having increased from about 23,000 in pre-Famine days. Other places of size are Wexford (10,000), Enniscorthy (6,000), Carlow (7,700), Kilkenny (10,000), New Ross (5,000), Arklow (5,400), Carrick-on-Suir (4,700) and Dungarvan (5,200). Only Arklow has shown an increase from 3,500, since the Famine, everywhere else diminishing, drastically in the case of Kilkenny, by almost half, and about a third for most of the remainder. The two Munster counties (Waterford and Tipperary) have some of the least populated areas of Ireland with much the same density as Co Wicklow at barely 80 per square mile; the rest of the area does not exceed 100 per square mile.

It is perhaps an accident of history that the very first railway in Ireland to be authorised by Parliament, in 1826, was the Limerick & Waterford Railway; proposed by Limerick businessmen, its purpose was to quicken the passage of exports from that fertile area of Ireland but there was insufficient capital and the scheme foundered. The whole area was largely ignored by the 1836 Commission and although there were early plans for a Dublin and Waterford route it was a piecemeal process that established the area's system. Apart from the navigable portions of the rivers, the only canal is the Barrow line of the Grand Canal which serves Athy, Carlow and Bagenalstown, joining the river a few miles north of New Ross.

Waterford has been the port of entry from South Wales and Bristol since medieval times but in the railway age the desire to shorten sea passages created an entirely new port on the south east corner of Co Wexford, that town's harbour not being suitable for development. The new crossing from

Fishguard to Rosslare Harbour was much later than that from Holyhead and Dun Laoghaire and resulted in the laying down of a new railway across south Wexford, with two of the finest bridges in Ireland, as late as 1906. The coast of this area is generally low and lacks the grandeur of headlands and inlets but that is compensated for by the fine estuaries of the Slaney at Wexford Harbour and the combined Barrow, Nore and Suir at Waterford Harbour.

SLOWLY DOWN THE EAST COAST

Southward from Wicklow the DW&WR touched the coast only at Arklow, being mostly inland on its route to Enniscorthy and Wexford, both the latter towns lying on the River Slaney. Edwards had the contract to build the line as far as Enniscorthy, completing the first portion to a temporary station at Kilcommon on 20 August 1861, a large viaduct slowing progress before the next opening on 18 July 1963 when trains reached Avoca (Ovoca until 1911). In this stretch there are three tunnels at Rathdrum, Nos 1, 2 and 3 of 190, 25 and 90 yards respectively. A longer section to Enniscorthy followed on 16 July 1863 and that was the end of the line for the next nine years. A Wexford & Enniscorthy Railway had been proposed in 1863 and briefly the DW&WR flirted with the idea of obtaining running powers before opposing the interloper.

The area around Avoca is one of the prettiest in Ireland and the destination of many tourists who visit places such as Glendalough with its lakes and round tower or the *Meeting of the Waters* near Avoca. The DW&WR built a hotel at Rathdrum about 1893 in an attempt to boost the tourist trade but it closed after a couple of decades. Like so many areas of beauty there are minerals and there were sidings to serve a limestone quarry and mines from which copper, iron and sulphur ores were shipped by the DW&WR to Kingstown for export. Two mining companies were active in the area, the Wicklow Copper Mine Co and the Hibernian Mining Co which had powers to take over and improve Arklow harbour and to build a canal up to Avoca and Glendalough as early as 1780. Ores had to be carted some eight miles to Arklow until one owner, Henry Hodgson, put down a tramway, using a gauge of 3ft 6in; little of its history is to hand but it was taken over by the DW&WR in 1861 and used until July 1874. A chemical industry has developed out of the mining company, producing fertilisers, although in World War I the plant was used by Kynoch, well known explosives manufacturers, to provide large quantities of cordite for the war effort, using a 2ft gauge system. In 1964 new sidings came into use, known as Shelton Abbey, at Arklow to serve the present-day chemical plant run by Nitrigin Eireann Teoranta which produces fertilisers, ammonia and sulphuric and nitric acids, providing heavy traffic for Dublin and beyond, the first load being despatched on 26 July 1965.

After crossing the River Slaney at Enniscorthy the line on to Wexford, built by Edwards, passes immediately through a tunnel of 405 yards; nearer Wexford there are two more tunnels, 89 yards at Killurin and 296 yards at Ferrycraig, making the journey from Dublin the route with the most tunnels in Ireland. Trains reached a temporary terminus at Wexford on 17 August 1872, a half mile extension to the permanent site opening during August 1874, using in part a goods line of 1873 to a yard beside the River Slaney. During November 1875 a horse worked tramway onto Wexford quays came into use.

When the DW&WR was at last joined to other Irish railways in 1873 a station was built at Macmine, junction with the line from Bagenalstown, to be described soon, which originally was no more than an exchange platform with the main line on one side, the branch on the other, the connection being through a siding between them at the Dublin end. In 1905 the Junction was remodelled following the opening of the DW&WR service to Waterford, having three platforms and a main line loop.

South of Wicklow the stations have been much reduced in number, most closures taking place in 1964, but Avoca may still be used by excursions. The route's passenger service has since 1925 worked beyond Wexford to Rosslare Harbour, but freight is now restricted to the Shelton Abbey traffic and cement and fertiliser to Wexford.

Shillelagh means to many a stick used by an Irishman and it seems quite probably that it is derived from the very small town of that name in the extreme south of Co Wicklow, shown with but 186 inhabitants before the Famine and only 118 in 1961, yet it was a branch terminus. Following its Act of 1863 Lord Fitzwilliam helped considerably by giving land, so much so that it was often called the 'Fitzwilliam Railway', his Lordship having a private waiting room at the terminus. Edwards was again the contractor, the 16½ miles branch from Woodenbridge Junction opening in 1865. In 1892 there was an attempt to extend the branch onwards to Newtownbarry (twenty years earlier, an objective of the GS&WR) and down the Slaney valley to Scarawalsh on the DW&WR main line north of Enniscorthy. For years the branch was a busy line, both Aughrim and Tinahealy having rather greater populations than Shillelagh, some 500 and 400 respectively, but all services were suspended in 1944 with total closure in 1945, the tracks beyond Aughrim being lifted for use elsewhere on CIE. A mill at Aughrim continued to be served by an occasional train until 1947 and then the only traffic until total closure in 1953 was stone for coast protection works beyond Greystones and Wicklow.

THE GS&WR MAIN LINE

West of Cherryville Junction the next important places on the Cork main line are Portarlington and Maryborough, reached on 26 June 1847, two contractors building this section, the first an unidentified firm, the second Killeen & Moore. Portarlington, notable for its original buildings, some of the best surviving GS&WR architecture, is the junction of the branch to Athlone, the eventual outcome of one of the early schemes for a line across the middle counties to Galway. Maryborough, now Portlaoise and the county town of Laois, is perhaps better known these days for its gaol. The population remains at just over 3,000, much the same as pre-Famine days, having recovered from a decline to but 2,000 in 1851. The next section of the main line opened as far as Ballybrophy on 1 September 1847. Contracts were shared out to Jeffs who built as far as Mountrath and Dargan who continued on through Ballybrophy to about the 74th mile.

There was a junction at Maryborough, or rather a place to change trains, when the line from Kilkenny was completed in 1867; the GS&WR refused to allow the completion of a connection and it was thus impossible to exchange rolling stock or run through passenger trains. All that the W&CIR was allowed was a single track into a bay alongside the down main platform. However, once the Waterford railway had amalgamated with the GS&WR a full junction was installed in late 1901 and then an alternative route to Kilkenny and Waterford was available. The greater part of Maryborough's railway layout belongs to the Kilkenny line and it is more appropriate to describe it later.

The GS&WR main line remains double track and both Portarlington and Portlaoise are open, getting a good service for their size.

TO CARLOW AND KILKENNY

Turning southwards from Cherryville Junction the town of Carlow (56 miles from Kingsbridge) was the first destination of GS&WR trains when the initial section opened on 4 August 1846, a double line constructed by McCormick & Dargan. There was an immediate change to the pattern of travel in the south, Carlow becoming the starting point for coaches to Kilkenny, Waterford and Clonmel; the down evening train had an overnight road connection to Cork which could be reached at five the next morning.

The major change to the route was the recovery of the second road for use on the nearby colliery lines during World War I, the line being singled from Kildangan to Athy and Mageny to Carlow in 1918 and the remainder

in 1919. This action was to have international repercussions after the formation of the Free State; as London had undertaken to pay the cost of restoration the GS&WR sent a demand in April 1922 for the sum required to put
back the second line, to be told that this had become a matter for Dublin.
The company took action in London, lost, won an appeal which had the
proviso that liability commenced only when the work had been done and
therefore the cost known and then lost in the House of Lords.

The first of Ireland's sugar beet factories opened just north of Carlow in
December 1926, being a private company until the state took over during
1934.

South of Carlow the line was extended by the Irish South Eastern
Railway, a protégé of the GS&WR; its origins lay in two earlier schemes, the
Grand Leinster & Munster of 1837 and the Wexford, Carlow & Dublin
Junction of 1846, backed originally by the GWR as an alternative to the
coastal route to Wexford. A Dargan line, trains provided by the GS&WR
ran as far as Bagenalstown on 24 July 1848, continuing through to Kilkenny
(80³/₄ miles from Kingsbridge) on 12 November 1850. Kilkenny was already
served by trains of the W&KR and the GS&WR service approached the
town over 2¹/₄ miles of the former's track. However there was no junction
where the two railways met at Lavistown, the W&KR providing an independent track for the newcomer (the inspecting officer was very specific in
his report about this arrangement, for it had been usual to state that the
second track did not exist until about 1867). Athy, Carlow and
Bagenalstown remain open, other intermediate stations having closed in
1963, and with the closure of the Kilkenny and Maryborough section at the
end of 1962 this now forms the only route from Dublin to Waterford.

FROM WATERFORD TO THE MIDLANDS

As an established port, it was inevitable that a railway would be proposed to
run northwards from Waterford to the centre of Ireland with the intention
of drawing traffic away from Dublin, starting with the incorporation of the
Waterford & Kilkenny Railway in 1845. It took a long time for completion,
an authorised branch to Kells, some five miles west of Thomastown, not
being started at all; what attracted promoters to such a small place (about
400 in 1851 but only 100 now) is difficult to see, unless they hoped for tourist
traffic to the site of the largest Irish monastery, long since ruined. The
W&KR, which became the Waterford & Central Ireland Railway on 13
July 1868, had an unfortunate history, never paying a dividend, suffering
remote management from London and its engineer, Captain Moorsom,
saddled the company with a contract to use Prosser's Patent Guide Wheel

system and wooden rails. Prosser demonstrated his invention on Wimbledon Common and, apart from the Irish railway, persuaded the Guildford & Woking Railway to take up his patent; both paid dearly for release from their contracts. Before long the railway press was to state that the concern had been driven almost to bankruptcy by mismanagement, jobbery, engineering blunders and reckless expenditure; Moorsom had been paid £12,883 for only 11¹/₂ miles of railway in 1849!

Wright & O'Toole built the W&KR as far as Bennett's Bridge and Hammond, Murray & Patterson did so to Thomastown, opening taking place on 12 May 1848. Progress southward was slowed by work on the viaduct over the River Nore, two miles south of Thomastown, so the next extension took trains only as far as a temporary station, Jerpoint Hill, on the north side on 29 May 1850. The next five miles were built by J. Burke and the remainder to Dunkitt (28³/₄ miles from Kilkenny), near Waterford, by Heusler & Ellis, the line being the first to reach Waterford, albeit to a temporary terminus, opening on 23 August 1853, leaving passengers a journey of two miles into the city.

In endless difficulties the W&KR sought an agreement with any other railway as a solution, succeeding when the W&LR worked the line from 8 January 1861 to 1 June 1867. To get further north a new company, the Kilkenny Junction, was formed in 1860, successor of the planned Galway & Kilkenny Railway of 1845 which by Act of 1846 became the Kilkenny & Great Southern & Western Railway, intending to join the GS&WR main line west of Maryborough. The first contractor was Alexander Gordon, replaced by W. Oughterson who built the line through sparsely-inhabited bog country, opened from Kilkenny to Abbeyleix in 1865, worked by the W&LR but there was so little traffic that the service was suspended in 1866, restarting when the whole 28¹/₂ miles was ready for opening to Maryborough in 1867. An Act of 1866 allowed extension northwards to Mullingar, superseded by an Act of 1873 for a shorter line to Geashill, the Central Ireland Railways, which became part of the W&CIR in 1877. Constructed by Oughterson from Conibery Junction, ³/₄ mile south of Maryborough, the branch opened as far as Mountmellick, 6³/₄ miles, and no further, in 1885. The GWR had subscribed a sizeable portion of the capital and when the W&CIR amalgamated with the GS&WR that stock was bought out, the sum then appearing as 'Geashill Extension Stock' in GS&WR accounts until 1924. Following the 1900 amalgamation and the provision of a junction at Maryborough, it became the practice for Dublin and Waterford trains to split at Kildare and, one part travel via Carlow, the other through Maryborough, joining again at Kilkenny and vice versa.

From Kilkenny northwards to Maryborough total closure took place at the end of 1962, together with the Moutmellick branch, the latter having lost its passenger trains in 1947. Subsequently a length of $2^1/4$ miles from Maryborough was returned to use as a siding to serve a milled peat factory at Coolnamona during 1965, and now the site of Conibery Junction has become a concrete sleeper plant. South of Kilkenny only Thomastown remains open, other stations closing on the first day of 1963. The two separate lines into Kilkenny were abolished by installing a junction at Lavistown on 9 June 1979, controlled from Kilkenny. The lack of a curve to give a direct run to Waterford has hindered efficient working of liner trains and in late 1994 work started on a cut-off at Lavistown which will save some 20 minutes in running time.

TWO COLLIERY LINES

The largest coalfield in Ireland lies in Co Kilkenny, centred on the small town of Castlecomer, a place that has declined sharply since 1841 when its population was some 1,700 but is now only 700. The coal is a poor quality anthracite and the field has never been able to compete with imported coal which was always far cheaper. Public agitation for a line between Athy and Kilkenny was expressed very strongly before the 1906 Vice Regal Commission, resulting in an Act of 1909 for the Kilkenny, Castlecomer & Athy Railway ($26^3/4$ miles) but no construction was undertaken. It was wartime scarcity of fuel that caused the British Government to use powers contained in the 1871 Defence of the Realm Act to build two branches, one from Athy to the Wolfhill area, the other from the Maryborough–Kilkenny line to Castlecomer both worked by the GS&WR. Perry was the contractor for the latter and perhaps the former as well.

Wolfhill line traffic commenced in 1918 and was apparently substantial for a few months. Lightly built and laid, the 10 miles gave access to pits at Gracefield and Modubeagh. The Castlecomer line, the last branch built in Ireland (except for short cement factory and mineral branches), commenced at Castlecomer Junction ($24^1/2$ miles from Maryborough) and was stiffly graded with sections of 1 in 41, the steepest on any 5ft 3in gauge line in Ireland. Coal trains started on the $7^1/4$ miles to Castlecomer in 1919 and were extended for another $2^1/2$ miles to Deerpark colliery in 1920. The two lines are interesting in that they were the last to be checked in Ireland by inspectors from London, both being seen in October 1920, when it was noted that there was little likelihood of traffic on the Wolfhill line, there being only about one mineral train per week and the future was very uncertain – the war had ended and British coal was becoming plentiful again. A passenger service to Castlecomer ran from 1921 only until 1931.

In 1921 the new Free State found itself the owner of these two lines, handing both over to the GSR in 1929 on lease. The Wolfhill line was cut back to a beet loading bank at Ballylinan (4½ miles) in 1930 and all remaining use of both lines ceased in 1963, apart from just 26 chains, including a bridge over the River Barrow, retained as a headshunt for a cement products factory at Athy.

MAIN LINE FROM LIMERICK

Dargan continued the building of the W&LR main line eastwards from Clonmel, opening as far as Fiddown & Portlaw (67¼ miles from Limerick) on 15 April 1853, and on to a temporary station at Dunkitt (75½) on 23 August 1853. In his report the inspecting officer expressed considerable concern over the working of the single line when he found that an earlier guarantee by the W&LR engineer that a pilotman would be used for each section had been over-ruled by the directors – he questioned whether in future *any* section of single line could be sanctioned.

To approach Waterford north or south of the River Suir took some resolving, and when the former was selected Parliament required that Portlaw, a place of some industry on the south bank, should have good access to a station. Thus the W&LR had to build a wooden road bridge, charging tolls that were not abolished until recently; after sale in 1984 a new bridge was built. Following station closures in 1963 the line was upgraded three years later by installing two-way signalling for faster running through extended loops in readiness for traffic diverted by the closure of the Mallow and Waterford in the next year.

Part of the price paid by the GS&WR to keep the DW&WR quiet at the 1901 amalgamation with the WL&WR was the granting of running powers for all traffic from Waterford to Limerick. The GS&WR refused to grant through rates and therefore the DW&WR started to use their powers, but only for goods as far as Limerick Junction from 2 May 1904 until the end of June 1908. For a time traders did well out of the rebates given by the rivals until the GS&WR, after arbitration, conceded the through rates.

MALLOW TO WATERFORD

An 1845 attempt to build the Cork & Waterford Railway along a coastal route failed so far as the latter city was concerned, the western part materialising as the Cork & Youghal Railway (see Chapter 5). Subsequently a less direct line was completed, piecemeal and inland, between Mallow and Waterford, starting with the westernmost portion. To the east of Mallow the

Co Cork town of Fermoy was an important garrison, but now is a shadow of its former size, population having increased to 8,700 in 1861, falling away to only 3,200 these days. The military connection ensured that there was a scheme to build a branch from the GS&WR main line as early as 1845 but it was not until 1854 that the Mallow & Fermoy Railway was incorporated. Dargan built the line of 16¾ miles which, by opening in 1860, had become GS&WR property. To continue eastwards a separate concern, the Fermoy & Lismore Railway, was formed and, being almost totally funded by the Duke of Devonshire of Lismore Castle, was known as the 'Duke's Line'. His desire was to improve transport to his estates and the local people, the towns of Lismore and Tallow having suffered severely, falling from almost 3,000 and 2,000 respectively in 1841 to just over 800 each. Lismore is a town of antiquity and was noted for scholarship – Alfred the Great is said to have been a pupil. The 15¾ miles of railway, authorised in 1869 and built by Bagnell, opened in 1872, being worked as a continuation of service from Mallow by the GS&WR. However on 1 March 1893 the WD&LR took over and trains then ran from Waterford.

The 1898 Act of the F&RR&H gave approval for a shorter line between Fermoy and Cork, joining the Youghal line at Dunkettle, but a shortage of funds forced abandonment during 1901. The railway had to concede that fares would reflect the shorter distance of the non-existent line which would have saved about 16 miles.

Mitchelstown on the main Dublin to Cork highway would have been on the recommended south and west trunk line had the 1838 plans been implemented, but since then it has lost some 40 per cent of its population, now down to about 2,600. Efforts to build a line from Cahir to Fermoy through Mitchelstown failed because the W&LR and GS&WR would not give support so the town had to wait a half century before getting its branch line from Fermoy, making its railway distance from Dublin 173¼ miles compared with 128¼ miles by the main road. Built by W.M. Murphy, the Baronially guaranteed line of 11¾ miles opened in 1891; there was still worthwhile military traffic and a halt, Brigown, built to serve a camp was so close to the terminus that it lay within the distant signal for Mitchelstown – the camp lay some 2½ miles to the south on the main road from Fermoy. Lightly laid, it was necessary for the GS&WR to build a couple of special small tank engines for the early years, relaying due course allowing heavier locomotives to work its traffic, which was never great, so the branch lost all but its cattle trains in 1947, the latter lasting until complete closure in 1953.

The Waterford end of the route remained a void on the Irish railway map when attempts in 1865 to build both the Waterford, Lismore & Fermoy Railway and the Clonmel, Lismore & Dungarvan Railway failed.

Success followed the passing of the Waterford, Dungarvan & Lismore Railway's Act in 1872, but only after a 35 years Baronial guarantee was secured. Construction was shared between Smith & Finlayson who built as far as Dungarvan and J.W. Stanford thence to Lismore. During the initial inspection of the line in June 1878, the inspecting officer obviously enquired about the engines the company had on order; he strongly condemned the design as far too heavy at 36 tons and this may be the *real* reason for their refusal. Tradition has it that the company refused to take them as they were late, but in fact these Avonside 0–6–0 were advertised for sale in October 1878, the MGWR purchasing all four in 1880 and getting a bargain for they were to work the heaviest of main line goods, much rebuilt of course, for well over sixty years.

The 42½ miles of the WD&LR opened in 1878 from a terminus on the south side of the Suir, some half a mile west of the toll bridge, known as Waterford South from 1900. It was a stiffly graded line having many ups and downs, with a tunnel (418 yards) and a major viaduct at Ballyvoile, both west of Durrow. There was little traffic to be gained and journey times lengthy so the route offered little advantage to the through traveller who would have to change twice, at Lismore or later Fermoy and Mallow on his way to Cork – it was as quick, or quicker, to go via Limerick Junction with a single change. The company enjoyed the support of the GWR to the extent of a special division of through receipts in its favour so that they received 16 per cent rather than the 10 per cent due on a strict mileage basis for traffic to London.

On 12 August 1898 the WD&LR was merged into the F&RR&H Company, the GS&WR taking over the working on 1 November 1898; in addition to purchase costs the new owner had to repay £43,000 of the £93,000 loan from the Treasury, obtained when building the line. Apart from new railways in the Waterford area the former WD&LR line had to be improved but it never really achieved a first class state for a major route, nothing being done to ease curves or gradients other than a deviation at Carroll's Cross in 1909. The first through service between Waterford and Cork started in May 1899, connecting with the morning arrival of the GWR steamer from New Milford and the evening departure. This was replaced by a new express service on 30 August 1906 connecting the enlarged port of Rosslare with Cork and continued with interruptions until total closure of the line between Waterford and Mallow on 27 March 1967 when the boat trains were diverted to run via Limerick Junction. The major interruptions were due to wartime events, when the steamers were suspended and the Ballyvoile viaduct destroyed on 8 August 1922, the line not fully reopening until 1 July 1924 (Dungarvan to Durrow being the last of the war damaged

THE IRISH SCENE

1. CIE 4–6–0 No 401 departs over the down crossover from the single main-line platform at Limerick Junction for Cork in June 1955. The layout was altered in 1957 so that down trains ran first onto the up main and then over to the down main. (*P.W. Gray*)

2. Cavan & Leitrim Railway narrow-gauge 2–6–0T No 10L arrives at Ballinamore from Belturbet with a mixed train in June 1955. The carriage was made up of two former bus bodies! (*P.W. Gray*)

STEAM-HAULED PASSENGER TRAINS

3. The 'Tourist Express' with through coaches to Dublin ready to leave Clifden, c. 1906. MGWR 2–4–0 No 33 *Arrow* was built at Broadstone in 1898. (*Author's collection*)

4. B&CDR 4–4–2T No 30 departs from Belfast Queen's Quay with a Newcastle train. (*H.C. Casserley*)

5. CIE 4–6–0 No 800 *Maedhbh* clears Clondalkin on the 10.30am down express to Cork, August 1954. (*D. Murray*)

6. Up Mail leaving Cork (Glanmire Road) at 3.15pm on 1 July 1955. The assisting engine is 0–6–0 No 195 and the train engine 4–6–0 No 401. (*P.W. Gray*)

7. Typical CIE Dublin suburban train near the end of steam days – 2–6–2T No 850 on a down service at Seapoint in 1953. (*D. Murray*)

FREIGHT TRAFFIC

8. 'A' class CIE diesel No 022 leaves Mullingar with empty cement wagons from Longford to Dublin in 1989. (*J.M. Allen*)

9. Cork and Youghal goods at Midleton, May 1978, with General Motors diesel No 168. (*J.M. Allen*)

10. NIR had a contract to carry infill from Magheramorne to Clogham Point, near Whitehead, for an oil terminal in 1974–5. No 102 *Falcon* approaches Ballycarry in May 1975. (*J.M. Allen*)

11. A modern train on a turf bog railway of Bord na Mona with a 'Wagonmaster' diesel LM237. (*Lensimen, Dublin*)

12. Shannonvale mill siding in Co Cork, the horse drawing the empty wagons back to the junction with the Clonakilty branch. (*W. McGrath*)

STATIONS GREAT AND SMALL

13. Belfast Queen's Quay frontage just before closure in 1976. (*J.M. Allen*)

14. Frontage of Heuston station, Dublin (formerly Kingsbridge) in 1987. (*J.N. Faulkner*)

15. A 'Midland (MGWR) country branch terminus – Ballaghaderreen in September 1960. The engine is ex-MGWR 2–4–0 No 655. (*D. Murray*)

16. Tramore station in July 1950 with ex-MGWR 0–6–0T No 560 ready to work an evening train to Waterford. (*T.J. Edgington*)

17. Courtmacsherry, c. 1905. 2–6–0T *Argadeen* prepares a mixed train. (*Real Photographs*)

A PAIR OF BRIDGES
18. Chetwynd viaduct between Cork and Waterfall, Bandon section of GSR, built for the opening of the line in 1850. (*J.N. Faulkner*)
19. Bridge over the River Suir, west of Waterford, under construction in 1906 as part of the F&RR&H new works. (*H. Fayle – IRRS*)

lines to reopen), boat trains having been diverted to Limerick.

After closure a new source of traffic presented itself when an American firm began mineral processing at Ballinacourty, east of Dungarvan, CIE laying down a 1½ miles branch. Trains commenced during 1970, the closed line having been renovated. Dolomite came from Bennett's Bridge on the Kilkenny line and oil from Cork, the products then being taken to another factory at Tivoli, near Cork. Suddenly all production ceased after twelve years and the line closed; at the time of writing both F&RR&H and IR intend to abandon the line, having converted it into a siding in 1993.

A LINE ON ITS OWN

Tramore some seven miles south of Waterford has become one of Ireland's most fashionable seaside holiday resorts, having a fine strand and a race-course, its population rising from a mere 1,000 in 1841 to some 3,000 nowadays, many residents of course travelling daily into Waterford. When it was clear that a short branch line from the abortive 1845 Cork & Waterford Railway would not be built the Waterford & Tramore Railway was incorporated in 1851, the 7¼ miles built by Dargan opening on 7 September 1853 (the official opening had taken place two days earlier) and it remained totally isolated from the remainder of Ireland's railways. Excursion traffic immediately engulfed the W&TR and it is recorded that only two days after opening some 5,000 travelled; from a newspaper report it would seem that railway had only *four* carriages! From the start the railway was a paying proposition and for a great many years there were more trains on Sundays than weekdays each summer. There were even 'late night' specials, or rather trains in the wee small hours in latter years, one in 1952 leaving Tramore at four in the morning.

The line was exceedingly economically worked and never had more than four engines at any time; in 1925 these included two single tanks dating from 1855. One was still in use in 1935, coming to grief when derailed whilst hauling a train; until that day, 24 August 1935, the Tramore was the last place anywhere that one could travel behind a single driver on a public railway (the LMS having retired its celebrated Caledonian single the year before). The coaching stock was an amazing collection and some of the originals lasted until 1933, even a few with no glazing on one side (including a First). Being so short the line was exempt from the legal requirement to use a continuous automatic brake and it was not until 1933 that the GSR transferred stock so fitted to the line; some of that stock had been supplied as steam railcars in 1928 by Clayton Wagons of Lincoln and having failed to perform satisfactorily, became locomotive hauled coaches.

Rumours and threats of closure abounded over the years but the line was not listed for closure in the Milne Report. Diesel railcars began to replace steam in November 1954 but even this could not avert closure and all services terminated on 1 January 1961. So ended a small railway that had done its job well, serving in isolation a purely local need.

INLAND ROUTE TO WEXFORD AND WATERFORD

The ISER reviewed plans for an inland line from Bagenalstown to Wexford, 44 miles – yet the rivals, the coastal line from Bray with 80 miles to go, completed their line first! Thus in 1854 the Bagenalstown & Wexford Railway was incorporated to pass through totally unremunerative wild and inaccessible country, the prospect of through traffic beguiling promoters. Despite almost no capital, work started in 1855, Bagnell building to main line standards, the 8 miles to Borris opening in 1858, the GS&WR working the line. The next section was completed by Bagnell, opening to Ballywilliam in 1862. Two features were noteworthy, a 16 arch viaduct just south of Borris, followed by a tremendous rock cutting. Some work had been done nearer Wexford, including the entrance to a tunnel near Ferrycarrig (but not the present tunnel). So far the company had been supported by the ISER but when the latter amalgamated with the GS&WR in 1863 disaster befell the B&WR, the latter being very hostile, and the DW&WR had reached Enniscorthy; the B&WR was now out in the hills with neither friends nor funds. So the line closed in 1864.

There next followed more ambitious plans, an Act of 1866 authorising the Waterford, New Ross & Wexford Junction Railway to purchase the B&WR and extend to New Ross and Waterford and to a junction with the DW&WR at Macmine (13¾ miles). Edgeworth & Stanford gained the contract to revive the original line and build a new, reopening to Ballywilliam and extending to a temporary station at Macmine in 1870. Because the DW&WR had not yet opened between Enniscorthy and Wexford the WNR&WJR was in fact closer to Wexford and advertised a road service from Sparrowsland. At Macmine the half-mile gap between the two railways was closed in 1873 but trouble was not long in coming, the GS&WR withdrawing its trains later that year because the 'line is not safe for traffic,… being out of gauge,… sleepers rotten, ballast wanted,… and milesmen off the line' according to the latter's engineer.

It is surprising that the railway had lasted as long, for it was earning the least in Ireland. At the time the average per mile per annum was around £1,200, the lowest being the L&LSR with £513 and the Thurles–Clonmel line (Southern Railway) with £495, but the poor old WNR&WJR could get no more than £85 per mile in 1872! Fresh efforts got the line into a fair state, sufficient for the GS&WR to resume a service in 1874, but receipts were only a little better meeting hardly half the expenses. Therefore the inevitable sale followed, being initially purchased by the GS&WR for £40,000 in January 1876, the DW&WR honouring its agreement to purchase the portion south of Ballywilliam pro rata to the mileage. However the line was worked as one, the DW&WR providing all trains from 1 March 1876; in 1885 the service was split at Ballywilliam when the GS&WR resumed the working of its portion.

The DW&WR decided to make a branch from Palace East to New Ross, getting powers in 1877. Far bigger ideas took hold in 1878 it being decided to extend to Waterford and make connections with the W&CIR and WD&LR lines. It needed a new Act in 1882 for the 8¼ miles to New Ross, Rbt. Worthington completing the line for its opening in 1887. At New Ross there was a major bridge of 590ft across the Barrow (with an opening span) preceded immediately by Mount Elliott tunnel (720 yards). The DW&WR continued to work the 3¼ miles from Palace East to Ballywilliam, having tried since 1887 to get the GS&WR to take over, succeeding only when on 1 October 1902 the latter became leasee in perpetuity.

DW&WR finances were too weak to continue beyond New Ross so an independent attempt was made in 1895 to promote a New Ross & Waterford Junction Railway, forcing the DW&WR to get a fresh Act in 1897 for a separate undertaking to which both the WL&WR and F&RR&H could subscribe. Suddenly in 1898 that support was withdrawn because of the purchase of the F&RR&H by the GWR and the promotion of the South Wexford line. Undaunted, work was started in 1899 by S. Pearson, but progress was slow until the LNWR realising that it would be facing new competition from the GWR, came to the rescue, granting a loan of £100,000 and giving other help in 1902, an action that was to have interesting consequences twenty years later as described in Chapter 1.

Traffic into Waterford on 13½ miles of new railway began during 1904 and on 1 June 1904 a through Dublin and Waterford service commenced, having dining facilities for all three classes for the first time in Ireland. It was a direct consequence of this line that the DW&WR became the D&SER on 1 January 1907. The Bagenalstown and Palace East line declined seriously, becoming the first route of the GSR to lose its passenger service when it ceased in 1931 but goods, restricted in later years, continued until complete closure in 1963. That year all services were terminated between Macmine Junction and New Ross and passengers through to Waterford; from 1976 traffic to New Ross was restricted to fertiliser, interrupted during 1993, the line closing 'until further notice' to allow reconstruction of a road bridge, traffic resuming in 1994. In 1995 construction of a short spur into a timber processing plant was in hand, its junction being close to Waterford – the position of the factory made it impossible to lay a siding directly from the South Wexford line.

New Ross remains a quite busy port with as many as five vessels daily making passage along the River Barrow. The branch has regained a substantial traffic in fertilisers after a lull in recent years and its future seems secure.

WATERFORD STATIONS AND DEVELOPMENTS

The first two railways to arrive at Waterford, the W&KR and the W&LR, soon extended from their temporary termini at Dunkitt, over the 1½ miles to a permanent station on 11 September 1854. At the time the only means of crossing the River Suir was by means of the toll bridge, 830ft long with 39 arches, dating from 1793 so the W&LR put on a free ferry, having to cease when the Bridge Commissioners objected. The next extension of 19 chains took the railway to the north end of the road bridge on 28 June 1964; both railways used this as an excuse to raise fares and even in those days called it a 'revision'. The land available being so limited by the road to Clonmel and Mount Misery made extensive piling necessary to provide a base for the new jointly owned station. When the W&KR resumed its own working in 1867 a row broke out over station charges and Kilkenny trains then reverted to the 1854 terminus on 1 October 1867, only to be blocked by the W&LR. So the W&KR then used a hurriedly-erected station one mile out, calling it Newrath Common, within a few days where trains terminated until returning to the 1854 terminus on 1 April 1868. Eventually terms were agreed and to the relief of all the 'Battle of Newrath' ended when the W&CIR trains reverted to the 1864 terminus on 1 July 1869.

Ambitious plans to bridge the Suir and connect Waterford's railways were put forward in 1873 and 1874. The Waterford Free Bridge, Railway Bridge & Tramways envisaged tramways along both banks of the River Suir, a new bridge well west of the town to join the W&LR, a tramway across a replacement of the toll bridge and a short branch into the town area. A rival favoured by the W&LR, the Waterford Railways Junction & Tramways, planned a railway from the W&LR nearly one mile west of its terminus which would cross the river to join the WD&LR and then pass under part of the town through a tunnel of 870 yards to reach the eastern end of the city and the W&TR. It was left to the W&LR to build its own extension to the wharves on the north bank, involving heavy works along the base of Mount Misery, a single line opening in 1883, being doubled at the beginning of 1884.

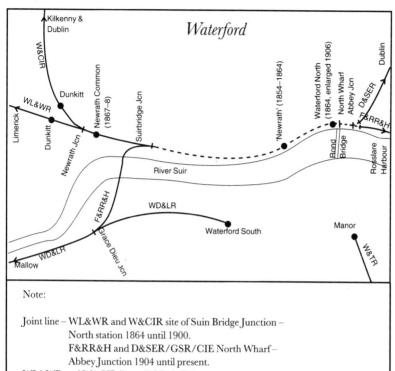

Note:

Joint line – WL&WR and W&CIR site of Suin Bridge Junction –
  North station 1864 until 1900.
  F&RR&H and D&SER/GSR/CIE North Wharf –
  Abbey Junction 1904 until present.
WL&WR and W&CIR lines all GS&WR from 1900–1.
WD&LR line F&RR&H from 1898.
Limerick and Kilkenny lines had separate tracks between Newrath Junction and site of
  Suir Bridge Junction until 1883 and again from 1929.

Originally there was only a single line from the junction of the railways at
Dunkitt and it soon became necessary to provide separate tracks, but when
the W&LR doubled its line as far as Fiddown in 1883 a new junction was
established at Newrath. This junction was abolished in 1929 when the
double line was singled, the junction between the Limerick and Kilkenny
lines reverting to its pre-1883 site.

When the DW&WR reached Waterford in 1904 it had to make use of as
a temporary arrangement the former WL&WR goods extension to reach
the 1864 station, having to pass it and then back in to an extra platform on
the north side. The new line from Rosslare entered Waterford from the east,
joining the DW&WR at Abbey Junction, and passed through the
completely rebuilt station, Waterford North from 1900, and continued
westward to bridge the Suir to join the former WD&LR at Grace Dieu
Junction. The bridge consists of nine spans, being 1,205ft long, with a

Scherzer lifting span and was built by Sir William Arroll of Glasgow. All was completed for the boat trains to start on 30 August 1906.

The old toll bridge was purchased by Waterford council in 1906 and immediately work was started on its replacement; the tolls were abolished on 19 December 1907 and Waterford South closed in early 1908. The new station at Waterford North was the first major work in Ireland to use ferro-concrete, a noticeable feature being the diversion of the main road to Clonmel out over the river. The single main platform at 1,210ft was the longest in Ireland and has a central crossover to the parallel through lines. Now all Waterford routes lie to the north of the Suir – in fact the station is in Co Kilkenny and Co Waterford itself is utterly devoid of working railways. The principal service is now that to Kilkenny and Dublin, with the Limerick and Rosslare lines having only a limited timetable and perhaps a none too secure future.

THE SOUTH WEXFORD LINE AND ROSSLARE HARBOUR

After the South Wales Railway completed its line to Haverford West and Neyland on the Welsh side of St Georges Channel in 1856 (Neyland immediately became New Milford and Neyland again in 1906) a steamer service to Waterford was started, operated in conjunction with Ford & Jackson (the GWR taking over in 1872), a crossing of some eight hours; a second service to Cork was started later and for some years operated by the City of Cork Steam Packet Co. A shorter sea passage was still the objective and Greenore Point on the extreme south east corner of Co Wexford was selected to be the Irish port. No doubt because of the Greenore further north in Co Louth, already established as a cross-channel port, another name had to be used. So eventually Rosslare Harbour came into being, the village of that name being three miles further north. The rail connection in Ireland was to be provided by the Waterford & Wexford Railway, authorised in 1865 to build $26^3/4$ miles of line from Wexford to Ballyhack, with a branch to Greenore. The route to the east bank of Waterford Harbour was chosen to avoid a long bridge at Waterford, using another company formed in 1862, to connect the city with Passage East, the Waterford & Passage Railway planning to use the Manor terminus of the W&TR. Another Act of 1863 authorised piers for the ferry crossing at both Arthurstown and Passage at a point where Waterford Harbour narrows and passes through a gap in the hills, almost a gorge in fact. To connect with the other Waterford railways the W&WR planned a separate line which was to join the W&TR to the W&KR at Newrath on the north side of the river.

The only line completed was that between Wexford and Rosslare and that took long enough, Barnett & Gale starting work in 1875, giving way to Watson, Smith & Watson and then W.M. Murphy who eventually had the 9¹/₂ miles ready for opening in 1882. Being connected to the DW&WR at Wexford the line was worked by that company but only until 1889 when services ceased, other than a few cattle specials and an occasional goods train. At Rosslare trains ran on to the pier when necessary to connect with ships. The pier was not railway owned, having been provided by the Rosslare Harbour Commissioners, being open to any shipping as a general harbour. South of Wexford much of the land has been reclaimed from Wexford harbour and is now fertile but on the old coast line lie the remnants of quarries. One was worked by H.J. Cooper from about 1885 and he connected his quarry and a small cement works at Drinnagh to the W&WR (2³/₄ miles from Wexford DW&WR); the gauge within the quarry and works area was 3ft 7in. While the W&WR was closed Cooper took to working his own traffic to Wexford and Rosslare, using his own engine, a vertical boiler 'coffee pot', so valuable was the rail connection to his trade.

Efforts on the Welsh side to create a new and shorter crossing were prolonged and involved, the GWR not taking much interest until it seemed that the LNWR might become involved. As part of the activities two Birmingham businessmen, Rowlands and Carter, agreed to purchase the pier at Rosslare and the near-derelict W&WR, obtaining an Act in 1894 to vest both in their Fishguard Bay Railway and Pier Co, authorised in 1893 to build a line of just one mile to extend the GWR Fishguard branch to deep water. The whole concern was now retitled Fishguard & Rosslare Railways & Harbours Co. Another Act of 1895 authorised the company to operate steamships between the two ports, with not less than one sailing daily in each direction. The size of the enterprise made it necessary to seek wider assistance and both the GWR and GS&WR were approached in 1897, the latter making a condition that it must have access to Waterford. A joint Bill of 1898 proposed that the GS&WR and GWR would acquire the WD&LR as well as the F&RR&H; the latter wanted to build a new line from Rosslare to Waterford and attempted to get the GWR to take over entirely. However the latter felt quite unable to incur so much expense in Ireland, drawing in the GS&WR, both taking over the Bill and getting powers in 1898.

Having been taken over by the F&RR&H, the Wexford & Rosslare line reopened during 1894 but only as far as Rosslare Harbour (better known as Kilrane), the final mile to Rosslare Pier not getting trains until June 1895. The latter was described as a platform at the landing stage and a ticket platform on land. As agents for the GS&WR the DW&WR worked the line from 12 February 1898, the former taking full control on 1 November 1898. The major contract for the new lines went to McAlpine of Glasgow who built the section from a junction at Rosslare to Abbey Junction, Waterford, a spur from this line at Killinick to the W&WR line at Felthouse Junction and the new section across the River Suir at Waterford. East of Waterford a new bridge of 2,131ft across the River Barrow is Ireland's longest river crossing (and when built only the Forth and Tay Bridges were longer), there being 13 fixed spans and a centrally-pivoted opening span. Just west of this bridge there is a short tunnel of 217 yards at Snow Hill.

The new line was opened on 1 August 1906 for a local service from Waterford to Wexford, joining the old line at Felthouse Junction; in 1910 this service was altered to run by way of Rosslare Strand and the direct line was taken out of use during 1911. At Rosslare the pier was completely rebuilt and extended by 15 chains, the contractor being C. Brand of Glasgow. Now up to four vessels could lie on the inner side and loading of livestock was separated from the passenger platform. A new cabin and sidings at the landward end, known as Ballygeary, took the place of the earlier Rosslare Pier platform and the original Rosslare Harbour became Kilrane. The new steamers and boat trains started on 30 August 1906, using a new three mile section of line from Rosslare Strand to Killinick. A new township was built at Rosslare Harbour for local railwaymen, including drivers and firemen at the new engine shed, comprising 44 company-owned houses in four streets named after F&RR&H directors.

The GWR made great use of its new service for excursions, a popular destination being Killarney, Friday night departures and Sunday arrivals at Paddington allowing a whole day in Kerry. Services were interrupted when the steamers were suspended during 1917, not being resumed until 17 September 1923. By that time the line between Rosslare and Waterford was out of action because Taylorstown Viaduct west of Wellington Bridge was blown up in July 1922 and the Barrow Viaduct rendered unusable in February 1923, achieved so simply by doing no more than opening the bridge, removing a vital crown wheel in the control mechanism and dropping it into the river below. Despite military presence a young man had coolly rowed out in darkness to perform a so simple but devastating act, with not a shot fired nor explosive used. When the steamers resumed it was necessary to run the boat trains through Wexford and Macmine Junction to reach Waterford, the South Wexford line not fully reopening until 1 January 1924. After the tragic loss of SS St Patrick on 13 June 1941 there was a long period of suspension from November 1941 until 23 May 1947, other than temporary restorations for the Christmas periods of 1941 and 1943. The Waterford steamers ceased on 14 January 1944, not being restored until 16 July 1945, apart from the Christmas 1944 period. The restored service of 1947 comprised three weekly crossings each way in the winter timetable, doubled each summer. Expansion of the service to cater for motor car traffic commenced in 1962 and soon made it necessary to remodel Rosslare Harbour because the existing method of unloading motors had become archaic - they had to be lifted off by crane to be carried on flat trucks to an unloading ramp at Ballygeary. The alterations allowed cars to be driven on or off, the first sailing doing so being the arrival on the evening of 23 May 1965. Since then traffic has changed out of all recognition and the railway activities of Rosslare Harbour have steadily lost importance, to the extent that the timetables of Irish Rail do not even mention cross-channel services. To cater for ever-expanding demand, a new passenger terminal was built in 1989, its railway platforms replacing the two stations at the harbour.

On the South Wexford line a small temporary platform was provided at Kilmokea, at the east end of the Barrow Viaduct, 6 miles from Waterford, in 1966 for use by workers building the nearby Great Island power station, closing when construction had ceased; to carry them CIE used a small Walker-built diesel railcar which had been purchased from the SL&NCR. Some stations have closed and from 1970 there were two platforms at Rosslare. One, Ballygeary was renamed in 1977 as the rather prosaic Rosslare Harbour Mainland, clearly defining its location; the station at the end of the pier then became Rosslare Harbour Pier, but both have been replaced as described above.

Waterford continues as a port with Bellferry container traffic having used sidings near Abbey Junction since 1969. These have now been replaced by new sidings four miles east of Waterford station known as Belview, coming into use during 1993. The South Wexford line suffered a more recent temporary closure during 1986 when the Barrow Bridge was damaged by a ship on 7 April 1986, buses having to run in place of trains for three months. Such vulnerability and its rather limited traffic suggests that the future remains somewhat precarious for the line between the new sidings and Rosslare Strand, notwithstanding beet traffic from Wellington Bridge. Ultimately renewal of the Barrow viaduct may well be the deciding factor.

OTHER LINES

There were few small lines in the south east corner of Ireland. The oldest, abandoned about 1880, served copper mines near Bonmahon on the coast of Co Waterford, midway between Tramore and Dungarvan, the metal being exported to Swansea and Liverpool. Copper had been extracted in the area for a great many years and sometime about 1870 the Mining Company of Ireland established its horse-worked lines – there have always been strong denials by locals that any locomotives were used. Further round the east coast the Courtown Brick & Tile Co had a small quarry and works about one mile from Courtown harbour, four miles from Gorey. A line of 1ft 8in gauge connected the quarry with the works and until 1948 when a small diesel was acquired it was horse-worked; the diesel pushed its load up from the quarry. Around the works itself there were tracks of 2ft gauge used in the manufacture of clay pipes. All came to an end in 1971 when plastic products ousted the traditional pipes.

Preservation is represented by the small circular 3ft gauge line of the Irish Steam Preservation Society at Stradbally Hall, seven miles east of Port Laoise, established in 1969. The site these days hosts one of the great annual steam fairs of the British Isles – long may both line and fair survive. At Carrick-on-Suir the old goods shed is now used by the Irish Traction Group to house its growing collection of former CIE diesel locomotives, it being the intention to acquire an example of each type as far as practicable and restore them to working order. Just how large the collection will become remains to be seen and whether IR will eventually allow operation on rail tours remains problematical.

CHAPTER IV

Limerick and the Golden Vale

Limerick, the third city of the Republic, grew up at the lowest fordable place on the River Shannon and indeed remains the nearest road crossing to the mouth of the river which has another fifty miles to flow. The population of the city has steadily increased in recent years after a long decline since the Famine before which there were almost 50,000 inhabitants, falling steadily to the turn-of-the century figure of 38,000, increasing again to about 60,000. The greatest change has been the development of Shannon Airport, which being the nearest in western Europe to North America, offered the shortest air route when flight range was still rather limited. It was in 1934 that Ireland, Britain, USA and Canada agreed to cooperate in a trans-Atlantic air service and in 1936 Rineanna in Co Clare was chosen to be a combined land and marine airport. Situated some 15 miles west of Limerick, it lies at the confluence of the Shannon and Fergus rivers and its importance has not declined even with longer range aircraft which now fly non-stop from London westward. The airport is a duty-free area and coupled with it a duty free industrial estate has enabled Ireland to enter export markets. However the railway has not benefited, other than through the increase in Limerick city's population.

On the north bank of the Shannon Co Clare tends to be poor land with a smaller population, Ennis being the only town of size, having halved its number since 1841 to 5,000 in 1911 and only now increasing, being about 6,000. Kilrush, near the mouth of the Shannon, has little more than half its pre-Famine total of 5,100. On the south bank Co Limerick and part of Co Tipperary, the North Riding, there are some of the most fertile pastures of Ireland, famous for their dairy products and a prime reason for early attempts to build a railway from Limerick to Waterford to give access to English markets.

Probably better known as a song title, Tipperary has lost a third of its former number of 7,500 before the Famine and now thrives on horses, their breeding and hunting. The remaining areas are poorly populated with

centres such as Listowel, (2,900) and Newcastle West (2,600) to the west, and
Clonmel (10,000), Nenagh (4,300), Thurles (6,400), Cashel (2,700),
Templemore (1,800) and Roscrea (3,400) to the east. Some of these places
have suffered heavily since 1841 when Clonmel had some 12,500, Nenagh
8,600, Thurles 7,200, Cashel over 7,000 and Roscrea 5,300 – it is little
wonder that the eastern side of Co Tipperary is one of the lowest-populated
parts of Ireland. The highest ground forms the Galtee Mountains, Galtee
More standing at 3,018ft.

A VERY PECULIAR JUNCTION

The main line from Dublin to Cork continues in a south westerly direction
from Ballybrophy to Charleville (now Rathluirc) and then turns southwards
towards Cork. Ballybrophy to Thurles (86½ miles from Dublin) opened on
13 March 1848 as a double line, one of the Moore brothers continuing from
the 74th mile for a few more miles and Hammond & Murray the rest of the
way to Thurles. Ballybrophy was Borris & Roscrea until 1857 when it
became a junction for the latter town, being renamed Roscrea &
Parsonstown Junction, changing to Ballybrophy in 1870. Lisduff, a late
addition to the stations, had been a private flag station known as
Knockahaw for use by Lord Castleton. A large quarry on the down side
adjacent to the station has been for many years the major source of ballast
for the GS&WR, GSR, CIE and IR. Thurles became a junction in 1880
when the Southern Railway from Clonmel was completed, the point of
divergence, Thurles Junction, being at 87¾ miles. In 1934 a large beet
processing factory was established close to Thurles Junction, having extensive sidings for the beet which mostly came from the South Wexford during
the season, October to January.

From Thurles onwards the GS&WR main line opened as a single track,
the second coming into use a little later. Such was the hurry to get to Cork in
order to placate the people of Munster that the GS&WR directors awarded
a single contract to Dargan for the entire 78 miles from Thurles, opening to
the spot where the main line crossed the rails of the W&LR on 3 July 1848,
the second track being added later that year. Here an exchange station was
built – for the want of a local name it became Limerick Junction, 107 miles
from Dublin, although in fact just inside Co Tipperary. As the W&LR had
opened its first section two months earlier, Limerick now had rail communication with Dublin.

Limerick Junction has been famous throughout the years for the antics of
arriving and departing trains; in fact it is a very peculiar junction. In the
original layout trains had to run past and clear of a central crossover and

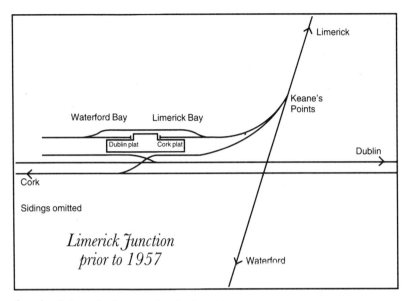

then back into the long main platform (see sketch), done to avoid facing
points on the main line and to make it easier for passengers to transfer, the
other faces of the platforms serving Waterford and Limerick bound trains.
The footbridge was the only way to and from the platform. W&LR trains
gained entry by a curve opened the same day as the GS&WR line from a

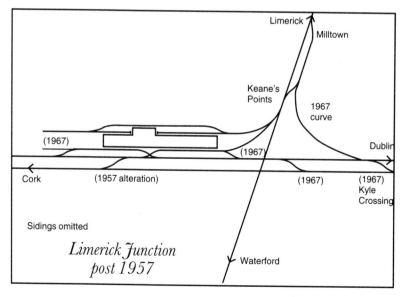

junction $^1/_4$ mile to the north, known for ever more as Keane's Points $(21^3/_4$ miles from Limerick) after the railwayman first responsible for their operation. A Waterford train's movements round the back of the station buildings into the bay, departing by backing out all the way to Keane's Points, before resuming its journey, and a Limerick train's, are also evident from the sketch. Thus all trains stopping at the junction had to back into their respective platforms. As a point of exchange the junction was important enough to justify a small commercial hotel which lasted from 1849 until 1927.

As early as 1849 it was decided that a second platform was 'indispensable'. The GS&WR produced a plan in 1855 but the W&LR protested on grounds of expense. The W&LR, as tenant, was often in conflict with the GS&WR, as owner, and at times threatened to cease using the station. In 1866 there seems to have been a temporary platform for use by W&LR trains not stopping at the junction, but after a major quarrel the GS&WR gave notice to the W&LR so that the latter's trains ceased to run into the station after 20 July 1880, using instead platforms erected at Keane's Points in the vee of the direct line and the curve to the GS&WR station. The BOT picked this up and sent an inspector post haste who was horrified to find that there was no shelter nor any facilities and no path at all, passengers having to make their way as best they could for 330 yards alongside the tracks, there being no lighting for night use! After that there must have been a very quick return to the GS&WR station.

In 1905 there was a plan to put in direct connections off the main lines, to reposition the Waterford platform and build a direct curve to allow Dublin and Limerick goods trains to work through without reversal – nothing happened. The post-war plans of CIE included the reconstruction of Limerick Junction, including loops from the main line to give direct running to both Limerick and Waterford, but the Milne Report, admitting the inconvenience of the layout, held that any resultant economies would be too small to justify the alterations. So far the layout had remained virtually unchanged since 1848, but in 1957 new connections were put in to allow Limerick cement traffic to work directly onto the main line (see sketches).

Ambition knew no bounds when a new plan was prepared in 1962. There was to be an entirely new down island platform with a connection from the Limerick line and an extra down goods line from a point well east of the crossing so that three tracks would have crossed the single Waterford and Limerick line. From the goods loop there was to be a direct curve to the Waterford line which would have been useful for beet traffic from South Wexford destined for Thurles, but the more necessary curve to give direct Dublin to Limerick running was not included. The whole area was to have been resignalled, mostly with three-aspect colour lights, complete with direction indicators. Again nothing happened and five years later a much simpler plan was adopted in preparation for the diversion of the Rosslare boat trains from the Waterford and Mallow route. The main platform was considerably lengthened, to 1,598ft, with the central crossovers resited to suit and new connections put in at each end to allow direct running into the platform. That from the Mallow direction came into use on 1 March 1967 and that from Dublin eight days later, bringing to an end a method of operating that had defied change for 118 years. At the same time, at long last, the much-needed direct curve ($\frac{1}{2}$ mile long) for Limerick was installed from a junction at Kyle Crossing, joining the Limerick line at Milltown Crossing. The curve came into use for goods during 1967 and for passengers the next year; a special on 8 August 1968 was hailed as the first to run non-stop from Dublin to Limerick.

Westward from Limerick Junction the GS&WR main line entered somewhat rougher country, the single line extension opening through to Charleville (and Mallow) on 19 March 1849, the second track coming into use eight months later. An economy considered by the GSR in 1930 but not pursued was to single the whole section from Limerick Junction to Mallow; had it been done it was to have been controlled by automatic signalling, not Electric Train Staff. Ballybrophy, Templemore (by virtue of the establishment of the Garda training college in the town), Thurles, Limerick Junction and Charleville remain open, the other stations being closed in 1963–77.

CLONMEL & CASHEL BRANCHES

Two branches diverged southwards from the GS&WR main line between Ballybrophy and Charleville, the longer and older being the Southern Railway of Ireland, connecting Thurles and Clonmel, getting an Act in 1865, but failing to get powers to continue on to Youghal and a branch to Dungarvan. Thomas White gained the contract and started work in 1866 but trouble came almost immediately when financial backers collapsed; fresh contractors, F. Appleby and then J.P. Ronayne, could to little to speed construction which did not start until a Baronial Guarantee of £63,000 for 30 years was arranged. Eventually in 1879 the first part opened, $8\frac{1}{2}$ miles from Clonmel to Fethard, followed by the remaining $15\frac{3}{4}$ miles to Thurles Junction in 1880, worked by the W&LR.

There were coal mines in the Killenaule area, a couple of miles east of the line near Laffan's Bridge; indeed, stretching eastwards there were several small mines along the Slieveardagh Hills (in alignment with the Castlcomer coalfield), 1866 authority to build a branch of $8\frac{1}{2}$ miles to the Ballingarry area not being used. An unpaid debt of £55,000 left the Board of Works no choice but to take possession, leaving the W&LR and then the GS&WR to provide the trains. The company itself faded out of existence and no shareholders were traceable so that in 1925 there was no one to give the necessary legal consent to absorption into the GSR. Advertising failed to locate any proprietor and so it was not until 17 November 1925 that the SR was vested, the last company to be taken into the new GSR.

Little changed on the branch over the years, a platform being provided at Powerstown in 1916 for the racecourse, about a half-mile from Clonmel. Attempts to reduce costs saw trial use by CIE of a bus converted to run on rails during 1954; when sent down from Inchicore it could not serve every platform as it has only one entrance – a hurried alteration was needed to make it accessible from either side! Passenger trains were taken off in 1963, but specials ran, including some making use of Powerstown platform, until all traffic ceased in 1967.

Cashel was to have been served by a branch from the projected Limerick & Waterford Railway of 1826 and again by a Cashel Junction Railway of 1886 as a branch of the Southern Railway. It was not until late 1904 that a 5¾ mile branch to Cashel from Goolds Cross, having been authorised in 1901 and built by Fisher & LeFanu, became a reality. Inchicore built a steam railmotor (having obtained drawings of Drummond's design for the London & South Western Railway) in 1904, but it was soon replaced by an engine and carriage. Water was always a problem at Cashel and in 1928 the GSR put a Drewry petrol railcar to work, based at Thurles, one train each day running through, but a couple of years later it was replaced; a Sentinel steam railcar was also tried. After suffering the suspensions of 1944–5 the branch closed in 1947, only cattle specials and a few excursions using the line until closure in 1954.

LIMERICK TO CLONMEL

Limerick lies too far off any direct route between Dublin and Cork but was important enough to be included in all early plans. In due course Parliament authorised in 1844 both the GS&WR and W&LR to serve Limerick, but only by one line with the proviso that if the latter failed to build it the former could then do so. This ensured that the businessmen of Limerick began construction as quickly as possible and just when money was scarcest had their line built by William Dargan to the highest standards, clearly expecting through traffic from Dublin. Helped by a large government loan, Dargan had the gently rising line as far as Tipperary (24¾ miles) ready for traffic in 1848, W&LR trains subsequently running in and out of Limerick Junction station soon afterwards. At first only a single line was in use, the second track from Limerick to Pallas was being added in late 1848, followed by the second track on to Keane's Points during 1849 but the curve into the junction station remained single.

The W&LR was notorious for the short time in office of so many of its officials in the earlier years and one of its most unusual characters was chief engineer in 1845–8, Richard Boyse Osborne, born in London of Irish descent, who had worked in Canada and the USA. He persuaded the directors to adopt 'systematic management… without confusion' (unsuccessfully for subsequent history of the company indicates anything but that) and he introduced American-pattern rolling stock, the first to run on bogies in the British Isles. After Osborne's return to America the 'Yankee' vehicles immediately fell out of favour and most were cut in two, some still being in use nearly thirty years later.

The line was worked by Dargan from August 1851 until May 1853 as one of his 'haulage contracts' and during this time he completed the section from Tipperary to Clonmel (47½ miles from Limerick) in 1852.

In 1929 the double line from Killonan to Limerick Junction was singled, all stations becoming crossing places and in 1931 the junction at Killonan was abolished, the two tracks from Limerick becoming separate single lines for Limerick Junction and Ballybrophy; however in 1947 double line working to Killonan was restored. Most of the smaller intermediate stations were closed in 1963, leaving Limerick Junction, Tipperary, Cahir and Clonmel in business and signalling was modified in 1966 to take trains diverted from the Waterford and Mallow line.

LIMERICK STATION AND JUNCTIONS

Four routes converged on Limerick where the first trains of 1848 used a temporary terminus, 25 chains south of the permanent buildings; by October 1856 it was minuted that the terminal buildings were approved but it is not clear just when trains first ran into the present station. When the Castleconnell line from its junction at Killonan was inspected in August 1858, it was discovered by the BOT inspector that the extension had not been sanctioned. The railway claimed that the new platforms were in use in July 1856 when the first part of the Foynes line was checked and protested that they were merely alterations of the arrangements passed in 1847. However the BOT decreed otherwise and therefore the new works were inspected in September 1858.

A direct entry into Limerick station by the Foynes line would have needed a steep up grade so to avoid it the new line joined the W&LR main line a half mile to the south with the junction facing Waterford. This made it necessary for Foynes trains to back out of the station along a separate third line to the junction and then proceed westwards, an arrangement which displeased the inspecting officer, especially as engines also had to use it to reach the engine shed. By this time the tracks out of the station, east to west, were a siding, down main line, arrival line, the Foynes down line and a goods line; at the junction there was a ticket-checking platform on the up line, destined to remain in use until 15 June 1963 (for an arrival from the Ennis line), being the *last* in the British Isles of a once-common feature. Later the platform gave its name to Limerick Check Cabin. The Ennis line diverged at Ennis Junction, one mile out, having a conventional double line junction with the main line. There was also a $^3/_4$-mile long tramway, authorised in 1860 and opened in 1864, serving Limerick market to the east of the station and a factory, the latter part falling out of use about 1931 and the rest about 1940 (apart from a short section which served the GSR bus depot until 1950).

In contrast to the L&FR, the C&LDR decided that it would build a direct curve into Limerick station which diverged from the Foynes line $^1/_2$ miles from Limerick Check, being completed in 1862. At first the inspecting officer refused to sanction the new double line curve and the new platform built alongside the W&LR station – he used the name Nelson Street – because it was intended that trains would be propelled in from a check platform outside; only when the layout was changed so that the second track became a siding and trains were to run directly into the platform did he give his consent, GS&WR trains working in from Charleville first using it in 1863, having had to reverse like the W&LR trains in the meantime. In the station there was no connection between the two companies' tracks.

Limerick now had its basic layout with six cabins as shown on the sketch. However it was not 'all change' in 1901; the reversal of Foynes and Tralee line trains at Limerick Check continued although the C&LDR platform could easily have handled extra trains. The engine shed, locomotive and wagon works were becoming progressively more cramped, despite enlargement in 1896, and extra sidings were needed.

The locomotive works built six engines in 1888–99 and many of the carriages and wagons of the WL&WR despite its smallness. It was not until August 1910 that a number of changes were completed:

(a) Access from the Foynes direction to the three western-side platforms Nos 2, 3 and 4; all trains from this direction now ran directly into the station and the line from Foynes Junction to Check Cabin was no longer to be used for passenger trains.

(b) Abolition of Ennis Junction by continuing the single line alongside the main line to a new junction at the Check Cabin.

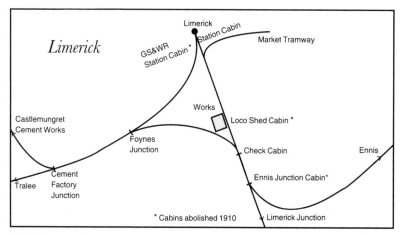

(c) Closure of Loco Shed, Ennis Junction and former GS&WR Station
cabins; a new Check cabin replaced the original, coming into use in July
1910.

Track changes now made it possible to run off the Ennis line into the original Foynes line. The main line still had a check platform and three new
check platforms were added, one each on the curves from the Foynes route
into platforms 2, 3 and 4 (being used until 1920). Years later, in 1931, the
Foynes Junction cabin was closed, being replaced by power points for the
station and loop divergence, worked from the Check Cabin.

For some years a cement factory at Casltemungret, west of Limerick, sent
its products by road to Limerick before going on by rail. In 1953 it was
decided to serve the factory by its own branch of 3 miles, built by Murphy
Bros of Cork and opened in 1957. It diverges from the Foynes line at
Cement Factory Junction (1¼ miles from Limerick station) and handles a
considerable tonnage for distribution throughout Ireland, but such was the
volume of traffic that it was necessary to alter the layout so that on 11
August 1968 a separate track was provided all the way from Limerick Check
cabin, alongside the Foynes line which was busy with oil and minerals. After
the termination of the Foynes and Tralee passenger trains in 1963 the direct
curve into the station lasted only until 1975.

BRANCHES WESTWARD FROM LIMERICK

The L&FR, authorised in 1853, another Dargan line, opened as far as
Rathkeale (Ballingrane Junction from 1867), 16¾ miles in 1856, being
extended to Askeaton in 1857 and Foynes (26¼) in 1858. Foynes was a
place that thought itself the ideal trans-Atlantic port but all it got was a river

steamer which crossed to Kildysart and another downstream to Kilrush, operated as an extension of the railway service. Many years later the trans-Atlantic dream came true in another way when Foynes was chosen in 1936 as an interim airport for flying boats pending completion of Shannon, the first PanAm 'clipper' touching down on 28 June 1939. During the World War II years the base was manned by British Overseas Airways staff and for a while was one of the world's busiest airports – and in a neutral country! In October 1945 all activities passed to the new Shannon airport.

A short line, the Rathkeale & Newcastle Junction Railway, authorised in 1861 and built by J. Hargreaves (of Cork) took the route on to Newcastle West (27½ miles from Limerick) but the W&LR which worked the line demanded extra works, delaying opening until 1867. The two branches were anything but a gold mine and in an attempt to work them economically some of their trains were combined; in early timetables the up morning train from Foynes waited for 80 minutes at Ballingrane whilst its engine went down to Newcastle West, collected another train and then combined them for the journey into Limerick, the reverse happening in the evening. A viaduct at Robertstown near Foynes in a low-lying marshy area was condemned as dangerous by 1878 and filled in to form an embankment.

An 1865 attempt to extend further west was authorised as the Limerick & North Kerry Railway but succumbed in the money crisis of 1866 so it was left to the Limerick & Kerry Railway, which shared its chairman, the Earl of Devon, with the R&NJR, to fill the gap to Tralee. Completed by J.W. Stanford the line opened throughout to Tralee (70½ miles) in 1880. Newcastle West remained a terminus, all through trains having to reverse there; each company had its own track on either side of a central platform and each had its own turntable. In later years railway enthusiasts enjoyed the delay when their engine left the train at the platform to leisurely turn and then come back, about a quarter hour being allowed, but others over the years must have cursed the arrangement. Out of Newcastle West westbound trains faced a stiff six-mile climb to Barnagh, passing through a tunnel of 100 yards at a summit of 538ft, which after other closures was the highest in Ireland for many years. Worked by the W&LR, both the R&NJR and L&KR remained independent companies until absorbed by the GS&WR in 1902.

The line from Limerick terminated a little to the north of the GS&WR station at Tralee (see Chapter 5) and connecting tracks were not ready until 1882, not being used for passenger trains until 1901. Only small vessels could reach Tralee, the nearest deep water being at Fenit, to the north west. Tancred & Falkiner built the Baronially Guaranteed line of 8 miles, worked by the W&LR from opening in 1887. Fish traffic was the objective and the line was continued on to a pier, the property of the Tralee and Fenit Pier and Harbour Commissioners, which consisted of a half-mile causeway, the Earl of Listowel meeting most of its cost. Despite all efforts, the branch remained a purely local affair but did well with Sunday excursions. Soon in receivership, the company remained independent until 1925. Fenit branch trains, which continued to use the old W&LR station at Tralee until 1914 when the junction was altered so that they could run into the main station, ceased in 1934, although excursions continued. Goods traffic was very limited from 1947, hopes raised in 1955 that Fenit would reopen as a port soon being dashed, beet traffic lasting until 1978.

Foynes passenger trains survived closure threats in 1940 and 1952; for many years they consisted of a tank engine, a six-wheeler coach and the odd wagon – the rare passenger would have been a railway enthusiast for would anyone want to spend 140 minutes to travel $26^{3}/_{4}$ miles, walk around Foynes (700 persons) for nearly three hours, and then take 155 minutes to get back to Limerick at 7.00pm? The Foynes and Tralee passenger trains ceased in 1963 and afterwards the Tralee line steadily 'disintegrated' as first the middle section from Newcastle West to Listowel was trainless, followed by closure from Ballingrane Junction to Listowel in 1975, the westernmost part lingering on for beet traffic, being cut back to Abeydorney in 1977 followed by the remainder in 1978. In contrast Foynes developed as never before, handling oil for some years and busy with minerals from Silvermines on the Nenagh line for shipment until late 1993; at the time of writing traffic is limited to variable quantities of grain, coal and oil.

A DIRECT LINE TO CORK

The GS&WR needed its own access to Limerick, one attraction being cattle traffic to Dublin. A plan of 1845 fell through and it was not until 1860 that an Act established its replacement, the C&LDR, J. Trowsdale & Sons building a line from GS&WR main line 1 mile north of Charleville to join the Foynes line at Patrickswell ($17^{3}/_{4}$ miles), opening in 1862. Originally many of the trains ran through from Cork to Limerick but when the company was absorbed by the working company, the GS&WR, in 1871 they simply became 'Croom' branch trains terminating at Charleville. In order to improve the running of up cattle trains the GS&WR added a north curve at Charleville in 1897 but it was extraordinary in that it was signalled in one direction only! Thus an up cattle train could run without reversal but down empties had to work to Charleville and then reverse for Limerick – a one way railway has been distinctly unusual – but the curve closed about 1906. In 1923 the branch junction at Charleville became the first to be remotely worked when the power points controlled from the station cabin were installed. Passenger trains ceased in 1934 but an overnight goods service between Limerick and Cork used this route until 1967.

THE MONORAIL CURIOSITY

One of the finest railway curiosities of the British isles served the small town of Ballybunion in Co Kerry for thirty-six years, catering for the local populace and day trippers and carrying inland sea sand, much in demand by farmers. Agitation for a narrow gauge tramway from Listowel, began in 1883, being expanded into the Munster Steam Tramways and serve Ballylongford and Tarbert as well: a competitor, the Limerick & Kerry Light Railways, planned a 5ft 3in gauge line between the two Kerry towns. Both failed because of local opposition to the proposed guarantees, it being all too obvious that ratepayers would face perpetual support.

A Frenchman, C. Lartigue, now entered the scene with a proposal to build the Ballybunion line using his monorail system, then being strongly advocated as the ideal for areas where gradients were steep and curves sharp and traffic potentially light – the last certainly applied but neither of the first or second were applicable in this case. The track was to consist of a single elevated load-bearing rail supported by trestles, there being guide rails at a lower level, with rolling stock designed to suit; thus each locomotive, carriage and wagon was of a duplicated pattern, riding astride the rail. Such an arrangement made points quite impossible, so it was necessary to use turntables to gain access to sidings for shunting, etc, a prolonged and complicated affair. Level crossings were impossible so that for major roads a drawbridge arrangement was used while at farm crossings a section of track was swung aside like a gate. Another complication was access to carriage portions on the further side of the rail – this could be done only by adding an external set of steps to some of the vehicles, one of which had to be within each train. Carriages were not comfortable, passengers facing outwards and the noise of the wheels on the elevated rail, almost at head height of a seated person, was unbearable to many – early complaints were laughed off, it being said that it was due to the newness and would soon disappear.

Unusually the Listowel & Ballybunion Railway, 9¼ miles long and authorised in 1886, was not Baronially guaranteed; it may be that the Lartigue Railway Co which had approached the original promoters did *not* know of the system, but on the other hand they may have been so confident of financial success that one was not sought (*or* the wily locals kept quiet, knowing that such a request would ensure that no railway was built!). When the company sought later in 1886 to make the Tarbert line they did indeed seek a Baronial guarantee – needless to say this branch was not built. Construction proved two points of the Lartigue system, that it was easy to lay down, being completed in five months, and that it was cheap, costing little more than £3,000 per mile. Formal opening took place on 29 February 1888, with public services starting six days later. At Ballybunion a short extension continued on to the beach for sand traffic. Losing more and more over the years, this curiosity attracted little technical attention once opened. Being in receivership since 1897, its form of construction ensured that in 1924 the company would be excluded from the general amalgamation. Thus on 14 October 1924, following High Court direction, the line closed, the manager no longer having funds to continue operation. Ballybunion, despite having no trains, has developed into a holiday resort with about 1,200 souls, compared with but 300 in 1841 and barely 200 when railway communication was first proposed.

THE MOUNTAIN RAILWAY

Dingle, the 'most westerly town in Europe' (not really true as Iceland is much further west) lies on the south side of the Dingle, or Coraguiney, Peninsula at the head of a virtually landlocked harbour and of course survives on fishing. The whole area has been heavily depopulated since the Famine, when Dingle had some 3,400 persons, down to 2,000 when the railway came and now less than 1,500. The narrow peninsula has a backbone of high mountains, the Slieve Mish range towering above the bays on either side, Mount Brandon being the highest at 3,172ft. It was the difficulty of getting fish and cattle to the nearest railhead, Tralee, that encouraged the sponsors of the Tralee & Dingle Light Railway.

The railway was sanctioned in 1884, using the Tramway Acts, raising high hopes in the area guaranteeing £120,000 out of its £150,000 capital. Robert Worthington, the contractor, wanted to lay down 5ft 3in gauge track, apparently hoping that the GS&WR would work the line, but had to accept the 3ft gauge. After a fairly easy ten miles as far as Castlegregory Junction (Camp Junction until 1895), the line climbed steeply, much of the way at 1 in 30, for 4 miles to a summit at 680ft followed by parts as steep as 1 in 29 on the descent to Dingle, the whole line being truly a 'Mountain Railway'. The 6¼ miles Castlegregory branch served such a small place, which however has a fine strand, that it is difficult to see why it was built, there being less than 300 in later railway days, although there had been over 800 in 1851.

The whole system, including goods extensions at each end, through the streets of Tralee to the GS&WR station and for a further ½ mile down to

Dingle pier, opened in 1891. Inevitably the line did not pay and Kerry County Council had to take over its management in 1896; the Treasury then paid £80,000 to redeem its liability to make up interest, the sum being used to reduce the guarantee capital and give some relief to the ratepayers of a still poor area. With its fearsome grades accidents had to happen, the most serious in 1893 on Glengalt bank, just above the junction, a train running away and killing three employees, including the locomotive superintendent, when derailed on a curve of 3 chains radius across a viaduct. Eventually the company obtained a grant which was used to build a deviation on a slightly lesser grade and ease the curve to 8 chains, the new line being 72 chains long and coming into use at the end of July 1910, adding about a half mile to the journey.

Slowly the roads in the Dingle peninsula were improved to take motor traffic but it was not until 1939 that the GSR could terminate all passenger trains and close the branch entirely – the replacing bus did the journey to Dingle in 45 minutes less time. A daily goods remained until withdrawn in the 1947 coal famine, after which there was but a monthly cattle special (or two if required) from Dingle and for which the line became well known. It was a real battle, a great demonstration and triumph of enginemanship, but despite all the misadventures that could befall a very run-down line these trains did get through, the final working being on 26/27 June 1953.

So ended what had been one of the finest railway trips in the British Isles.

LIMERICK TO THE NORTH

Ennis as a town of size was expecting a railway at an early date, the Limerick, Ennis & Killaloe Railway being authorised in 1846 to connect the two towns with Limerick. The first part was revived as the Limerick & Ennis Railway in 1853 and soon a contract was awarded to Johnson & Kinder (of Bromsgrove) to build and work the line but in 1856 they were replaced by Dargan. The line failed early inspections because the long bridge over the Shannon was found to be very unsafe; the report showed it to be one of the worst bridges ever built with confusion compounded – the inspector deciding that the bridge would be unsafe according to the drawings, the contractor, Kinnaird, stated that it was built to another plan, but when checked it conformed to neither! The inspector regarded it essential that the bridge be completely reconstructed but all that seems to have been done was to insert more props; somehow it did get sanction in November 1858 and amazingly was not rebuilt until 1909.

The delays resulted in the line of 24½ miles being opened in sections during 1859, the first from Longpavement to Clarecastle, then into Limerick, followed by the last section into Ennis, the W&LR providing the trains. The L&ER decided to work itself as from 14 November 1859, following many complaints about its services – no doubt the W&LR used engines and stock no longer suitable for its main line – and much to the chagrin of the latter the Ennis company made a reasonable success of its services. However the W&LR took over again on 22 April 1861, absorbing the L&ER in 1893. Always a secondary line, all the intermediate stations were closed in 1963 and then the passenger service terminated in 1976. Use by excursions and goods continued and in more recent years there has been a revival of passenger traffic from Ennis to Limerick with an unadvertised morning train to the city and an evening return, connecting with Dublin trains; however the summer 1993 public timetable shows a morning departure for Dublin and an evening return for three days. Earlier that year (19 February) a down Dublin train was extended on Friday evenings to Ennis, with an up return on Sunday to give a weekend service. Even so a bus may be substituted if passengers are few for the evening trip. During the winter of 1994–5 the line became unusable for several months due to flooding, a frequent occurrence over the years at Ballycar – when diesel trains were first used over the line a steam locomotive was retained at Limerick for some years to run as a substitute at such times.

NARROW GAUGE TO THE SEASIDE

The narrow gauge West Clare Railway is better known for the ridicule heaped upon it by a well loved songster, Percy French, than its years of useful, if sometimes erratic, service to the people of Co Clare. He missed a performance at Kilkee in 1896 because of a delayed train, and no doubt hearing more about its misdeeds, produced the song *Are Ye Right There Michael?* describing delay and frustration when 'railling from Ennis to Kilkee' – your author went so one day in 1955 but by then it had become something of a model 3ft gauge line.

The first line promoted in the south part of Co Clare was to connect the two towns in its title Kilrush & Kilkee Railway & Poulnasherry Embankment Co, coupled with reclamation of the bay, all authorised in 1860. The line (8½ miles, 5ft 3in gauge) was to have started at Cappa Pier and run through Kilrush to follow an almost straight line between the two towns; in 1864 the contractor, T. Bourke of Howth, made a start and before long the embankment was taking shape, but all was abandoned in 1866, leaving the bay to return to nature.

As early as 1862 a tramway from Ennis westward to Lahinch was surveyed, the W&LR agreeing to work the line at cost. More than twenty years were to pass before the West Clare Railway was formed in December

1883 and this time the narrow gauge was chosen and of course the local Baronies were involved, guaranteeing £163,500, only £16,500 being raised in ordinary shares. W.M. Murphy was the contractor and made such progress that in May 1887 the first engine steamed into the coastal terminus of Milltown Malbay (27 miles from Ennis). Early timetables show that the three passenger trains were worked from the outer end, services having started on 2 July 1887 (a Saturday); it was on the next day that the public tried the line when an excursion took them to the seaside. There were problems from the beginning and usually the 0–6–0T engines supplied by Bagnall have been blamed but they were of much the same power as other Irish narrow gauge engines of the time; in fact it was the parsimonious action of the Clare Grand Jury which reduced the capital so that there was insufficient to build adequate workshops and there was ample evidence to show that trackwork was very soon defective.

Kilrush was still in need of a railway and in 1884 the South Clare Railways Co Ltd was formed, Baronially Guaranteed, to continue the West Clare southward. Work was delayed because the Grand Jury would not give up its demand that the abandoned embankment should be revived; there was a rival scheme for a Kilrush Extension Steam Tramway and a proposed Kilrush & Kilkee Light Railway which may have reflected local frustration with the delay in starting work, Murphy again being the contractor. In the summer of 1892 the 8¼ miles between Kilrush and Kilkee was passed by the BOT, regular trains starting that August (there had been specials as early as 3 July 1892). It took until 23 December 1892 to get passenger trains running south from Milltown Malbay to Moyasta Junction (16 miles), although goods had been running since the summer. At Moyasta Junction there was a direct line, completing a triangle, which allowed through running from Kilrush to Kilkee, used by trains which connected with Shannon steamers until 1916.

The 1906 Vice Regal report stated that it was generally expected that the GS&WR would take over the West Clare in 1901–2, failing only because of the MGWR running powers to Limerick. It was pointed out the line was extravagantly worked at almost double the cost of the Donegal Railway. There was also a demand that the gauge be widened to allow through running.

Despite the low population the West Clare system was always well used by the locals and the companies did not miss the chance to encourage tourist traffic, building a five-vehicle train of tourist stock in 1905–6 at Ennis. The exposed western coast left trains vulnerable to high winds and not only was stock ballasted by extra weights but an anemometer was installed at Quilty in 1911. When winds exceeded 60 mph any non-ballasted vehicles were prohibited from trains and at 80 mph all trains had to stop.

The GSR gave an early trial to petrol engined railcars when two Drewry cars, seating 30, were put to work but the gradients were too much so they were soon confined to a Kilrush and Kilkee service, lasting about six years. The West Clare had built for itself a small Ford powered inspection car in 1922 which the GSR found useful, moving it to other narrow gauge lines as necessary. Always there was the threat of closure, countered by demands to widen the gauge to allow through running, but distance was always a handicap, the rail journey from Limerick to Kilkee being $72^{1/2}$ miles compared with 57 by road. However CIE undertook a programme of modernisation and put four diesel railcars to work in 1952, adding several wayside stopping places. Three small diesel mechanical locomotives took over the goods trains in 1955 but the inevitable closure came all too soon when all traffic ceased in 1961. Ironically a line that seemed too often not to have a future became the very last of the public Irish narrow gauge railways.

ANOTHER WAY TO LIMERICK

There was a proposal as early as 1838 for a Dublin & Limerick Railway as an offshoot of the Grand Munster & Leinster Railway which would have taken a course through Maryborough and Roscrea, followed by another plan in 1846 to make a branch from the GS&WR at Ballybrophy to serve Roscrea and Nenagh and join the proposed Killaloe branch of the LE&KR. It was not until 1854 that the first part was sanctioned as the Roscrea & Parsonstown Junction Railway, the contractors Bagnell & Edwards completing the $10^{1/4}$ miles from a junction at Ballybrophy to Roscrea in 1857 and the final 11 miles to Parsonstown next year. The change from Parsonstown to the better known Birr was made in 1900 at local request; the old name was that of the family of the Earls of Rosse of Birr Castle where one of them built a huge astronomical telescope in 1845, the largest in the world at the time. Birr, its population having halved to 3,200 since the Famine, is generally regarded as the geographical centre of Ireland.

Roscrea was chosen as the junction for the next section, authorised in 1861, to run westward to Nenagh and meet the L&CR at Birdhill. Bagnell was the contractor and the course across fairly level farming country was completed to Nenagh in 1863 and onwards to Birdhill ($42^{1/2}$ miles from Ballybrophy) in 1864. Thus a second route to Limerick was completed but no through trains were provided, being worked as separate services from Nenagh, eastward to Ballybrophy and westward to Limerick, engines being changed at Birdhill, carriages being provided in alternate months by the GS&WR and W&LR. However, from May 1901 through trains were put on from Dublin to Limerick.

The remainder of the route was built by the Limerick & Castleconnell Railway, incorporated in 1856 and worked by the W&LR until absorbed in 1872. The contractors were Bagnell & Smith who built the line through to Killaloe, opened from Killonan to Castleconnell in 1858, on to Birdhill (14¹/₄) in 1860 and finally Killaloe (17 miles from Limerick) in 1862.

The attraction of Killaloe is its location at the south end of Lough Derg where the Shannon commences its last real inland part to the sea beyond Limerick. Connecting steamers were put on to serve other localities around the lough and further afield to Athlone, continuing until 1914; the GS&WR tried hard to develop excursions from Dublin, offering round trips in either direction via Killaloe and Banagher, and earlier the area had been one where the GS&WR and MGWR were in conflict, the latter having invested in the Killaloe extension of the L&CR, its holding being transferred to the GS&WR in 1860. From 1864 Killaloe was the terminus of a short branch, but for several years its trains were run from Limerick with those for Nenagh. The original station at Killaloe (not actually in Killaloe, which is on the opposite shore of the River Shannon in Co Clare, but at Ballina in Co Tipperary) was well short of the road bridge to the town and the steamer berths. There was also a quay on the east bank of Lough Derg further north and an Act of 1866 permitted the building of a ³/₄ mile extension; it progressed very slowly and was recorded as only partly finished in 1874 but seems to have been in use by 1883. By then the W&LR was running a steamer as a subsidiary company, the Shannon & Inland Navigation Co, on Lough Derg. The inconvenient passenger terminus was replaced by a new station in 1894, 34 chains to the north and just beyond the road bridge, making it more suitable for the lough steamers.

From May 1901 the Killaloe service worked only from Birdhill. It must have been one of the last regular public services worked by a four-wheeled engine, a Sharp Stewart 0–4–0ST, which was derailed in 1914, attracting severe comments from the inspecting officer. The branch lost its passenger service in 1931 and its goods train in 1944, closing in 1953. The Birr branch was totally closed at the end of 1962 and the lesser stations between Roscrea and Limerick closed during 1963; one however, Castleconnell reopened in 1989.

At the western end of the route mineral traffic developed with the building of a branch of 1¹/₄ miles to Silvermines, diverging at Silvermines Junction, 35¹/₄ miles from Ballybrophy, opened at the end of 1966. Its products, barytes, lead and zinc, used to run in block trains to Foynes, coming to an end in 1993; there are hopes that mining will resume. Further west at 40³/₄ miles a siding was added at Kilmustulla in 1982 for shale destined for

Limerick cement works.

Services on the line always suffered from the disadvantage that the junction at Ballybrophy trailed for trains from Dublin, making reversal necessary. The station existed solely for railway purposes for there is hardly even a hamlet nearby. In 1986 the full junction was removed, leaving access to the branch through a siding connection, a reversion to layouts so often used more than a century ago. Thus it has become just about impossible for a through train to be provided by the Nenagh route.

THE STOLEN RAILWAY

Portumna is a small town just in Co Galway at the head of Lough Derg, its population of 800 being only half of that in 1841; the area about is thinly inhabited, being low lying land on each side of the Shannon. One man, the Earl of Clanricade of Portumna Castle, strove for a connection with the GS&WR at Birr, an Act of 1861 authorising 12 miles of the Parsonstown & Portumna Bridge Railway. It terminated at a lonely spot on the east side of the Shannon, near the bridge well over one mile east of the town. The first contractor was E. Bond of London who not surprisingly suffered bankruptcy when work done could not be paid for, succeeded by H.P. Bradley of Liverpool who soon gave up, leaving Bagnall to complete the line from a junction just outside Birr station. Worked by the GS&WR the branch opened in 1868; at Portumna the line continued for 29 chains beyond the passenger station to reach a small pier at the north end of Lough Derg.

Complaints about the service were continual, trains running at times of little use to most, but the traffic just was not there, so when the ten year working arrangement came to an end in 1878 the GS&WR withdrew, the company being in receivership and in debt to the PWLC as mortgagee, the latter attempting to get the GS&WR to purchase it. The railway indicated that they would accept the line for nothing 'free from all encumbrances', but the idea of giving it away was too much for a government body. After closure the line was kept in order and patrolled until 1883 after which it was left to itself – then various creditors moved in and took everything portable so that soon there was nothing but a few stone bridges and the girder bridge over the River Brosna, and that is reputed to have remained only because a patrolling policeman interrupted a 'contractor' who had started to remove it with a steam crane! Agitation continued for several years but the GS&WR always replied that the line must be restored to working order by the state who abandoned it – they were on pretty safe ground knowing that it was very unlikely that the line would be rebuilt. Now only a few earthworks show that the 'Stolen Railway' had ever existed.

ARDNACRUSHA

Just north of the bridge over the Shannon near Longpavement on the Ennis line there was a branch of $1^3/_4$ miles to the Electricity Supply Board's Ardnacrusha hydro electric power station, built under the direction of the Ministry of Industry & Commerce in 1928 and transferred to ESB ownership on 1 June 1930, being used as necessary for the transport of machinery; now only a short siding remains.

During the building of the hydro electric plant and the various works on the River Shannon the contractors, the German firm of Siemens-Bauunion laid down extensive narrow gauge railways and imported all the engines and rolling stock needed, sending everything back on completion. The system, laid down in 1925, started on the north side of Limerick, materials having been unloaded at Limerick docks and carted by road thus far, and ran through to Ardnacrusha and beyond as far as O'Briensbridge (8 miles), one section being electrically worked; on the way there was a level crossing, fully signalled, with the Ennis line near Longpavement. During the construction period the line to the power house was of mixed gauge. There were many subsidiary branches of 1ft $11^1/_2$in gauge, the main line being 2ft $11^1/_2$in, with subsidiary works further up the Shannon, particularly near Meelick and Banagher where a few engines of the narrower gauge worked. By 1931 everything had gone.

The Shannon scheme was the greatest industrial undertaking in Ireland and the new Free State Government was very proud of the whole project, issuing special stamps on completion. From March to October 1929 the GSR issued return tickets at single fares valid for three days to Limerick for excursionists to visit the new works.

The lack of a rail connection to Limerick docks and the use of heavy lorries through the streets of the city prompted the corporation to suggest the building of a line, first proposed about 1880. In May 1928 they voted to abandon the project, alleging that the Government had failed in its promise to build it as part of the Shannon scheme. Late in 1929 the corporation gave permission to Limerick Harbour Commissioners to built a link line from the GSR goods store. Hopes were high that work would start in late 1930 and that it would be electrically worked, but nothing materialised and Limerick docks remain without rail communication.

OTHER LINES

Bord na Mona has a system serving bogs in Co Tipperary, a 3ft gauge route completed in 1982 connecting several sites south of Thurles near the course of the former Clonmel branch. The most southerly is at Killeen, close to the former Horse & Jockey station, and a series of workings stretches north eastwards for about ten miles, the oldest part at Littleton dating form 1950, to reach Templetuohy bog, first cut in 1955, serving other smaller bogs on the way. There are processing plants at Littleton and Templetuohy.

There were four 'industrial' lines in Co Clare. Many attempts had been made to reclaim lands in the estuary of the River Fergus south of Clarecastle where several thousand acres of fertile land were tidal mudlands little more than a century ago. In 1846 the PWLC allocated funds and from 1860 there were several attempts, including that of the River Fergus Reclamation Co of 1870, promoted by H.C. Drinkwater, a London financier, which started work on a massive sea wall, on which a 2ft 6in gauge (most unusual in Ireland) railway was built later. In 1881 a small Hunslet 0–4–0ST *Fergus* was at work and it was probably this engine which had a 'ducking' when a train was derailed and fell into the river, fortunately without injury to the men who were on the train. Violent storms in the winter of 1802–3 finished Drinkwater's activities, the PWLC continuing on a reduced scale until the Fergus Reclamation Syndicate Ltd, a group of Limerick businessmen, took over in 1892. They laid down a 2ft gauge line, steam worked for a few years and later a section of horse-worked line on a farm seems to have been the sole remnant, extent until about 1930 or so.

At a remote quarry on the coast of Co Clare G.A. Watson & Co used a small 4ft 8½in gauge saddle tank from 1903 until 1908 – it must have been some under taking to get the engine, and other machinery, and later remove it, to Donnagore which lies a little to the north of the great Cliffs of Moher, one of the sights of Ireland, being 700ft straight up from the water. One of the most extraordinary 'private' railways ever to have existed was situated on the farm of Mr John Bianconi at Lacknashannagh near Kildysart in Co Clare on the north bank of the Shannon estuary. Bianconi was the grandson of Charles Bianconi, an Italian who made his fortune as the pioneer of Irish stage coach travel before railways came, and had large estates in Cos Clare and Tipperary. The 2ft gauge railway was not large, being only one mile in length, but it was remarkable in having a full signalling system, uniformed staff, a pony-hauled coach and a remarkable oil-burning steam powered lorry on rails which dated from 1912. Built in 1910, this system connected the farmhouse with a small quay, from which Bianconi ran a shipping service to Limerick and Kilrush, the various farm buildings and some of the fields, carrying both produce and incoming supplies. Everything was sold off in 1929 following Bianconi's death; all that remains is the plate 'J.B. No 1, 1912' taken from the steam lorry and retained at the farmhouse.

PRESERVATION

At Tralee two preservation projects are in hand. The Great Southern Railway Preservation Society started with a depot at Mallow but moved to Tralee and has hopes of reviving the Fenit branch. More recently a part of the former Tralee and Dingle has been rebuilt, starting form the outskirts of the town to Blennerville, $1\frac{1}{2}$ miles, with hopes of further extension. In contrast with other preservation projects the first $\frac{1}{4}$ mile from Ballyard (on the west side of Tralee) is an entirely new railway. The engine used is former T&DLR 2–6–2T No 5 which has returned from the United States, having been there for nearly thirty years. Regular running began on 1 April 1993 and the 1994 season must be judged successful with no less than 45,000 passengers having enjoyed the line.

CHAPTER V

Cork & the South West

County Cork is the largest local government area in Ireland and the city of Cork the Republic's second centre of population. The present day total of almost 130,000, rather more than its previous 88,000 in 1851, is housed in a much-expanded city. Standing astride the River Lee the city centre lies mainly on an island within the river and derives its name from the former marshy state of the area, much of it not properly drained until the eighteenth century. Ease of navigation allowed vessels of the time to reach the city and it has several quays on the four banks of the river, those further upstream no longer accessible once a pair of lifting bridges was fixed in 1977. Industry developed mainly around distilling, brewing, hosiery and clothing, being joined by motor car production and tyre making. Shipbuilding became established, particularly at Rushbrooke and Passage West, but has not survived the recent years of change. It was not until 1961 that an airport was established, some four miles to the south west. Cork was the destination of the 'Innisfallen Way', a direct steamship route between Fishguard and the south west of Ireland, operated by the CDSP Co until 1969 when B&I took over, soon moving the service to run from Swansea.

Cork Harbour gives protection to Cobh, formerly Queenstown, which for many years was the last port of call for America-bound ocean liners, or the first on the homeward passage, the importance for Ireland's railways being the carriage of mails and passengers who could take advantage of the shortened sea passage. This was advertised in GS&WR timetables, times of ocean liners being included, complete with a map of the North Atlantic showing 'The Overland Route Between Europe and America' giving the impression that the only railway of importance was its own main line between Dublin and Cork! The lower Lee which flows into Lough Mahon and then Cork Harbour was a highway for the citizens of Cork and the townships on their shores, served by very competitive steamboats, some railway operated, but that mode of transport largely ceased a lifetime ago.

Geographically the area includes much of the highest ground in Ireland, particularly around Killarney in Co Kerry where Ireland's highest mountain stands. The western coast line comprises long sea inlets with mountain ridges forming the peninsulas between, making them into deep drowned valleys and the southern coast line, mainly further west, is broken up into a multitude of small bays and islands, mostly remote and thinly populated. A major purpose in building railways to their small ports was to improve the carriage of fish to markets further away, particularly England, but they did not entirely replace coastal shipping which could avoid some of the transhipment of cargoes; another reason was the contentious rates, railways usually being accused of charging excessively. Inland there are good farming areas with a scattering of towns which had attracted railway promoters but for many places it needed government investment before railway communication was established with the aim of promoting trade and improving the prospects for those remaining in what had become 'depressed areas'. Although furthest away from Britain the local railways made huge efforts to tempt tourists and the issue of guides and brochures was not neglected. Killarney was the major draw but the great beauty of the area encouraged the GS&WR to build several hotels.

All that now remain of the lines described in this chapter are the Dublin and Cork main line, its suburban continuation to Cobh, the Kerry line to Killarney and Tralee and, presently moribund, the branch to Youghal.

MAIN LINE TO CORK

At Charleville (Rathluirc) the GS&WR main line finally turns southwards to serve Mallow and Cork. From Limerick Junction to Mallow a single track opened on 19 March 1849 and thence to a temporary terminus (164 miles from Dublin) to the north of Cork on 29 October 1849. A second track was completed as far as Buttevant later in 1849, extended on to Mallow and then Cork during 1850. Immediately after Mallow the River Blackwater was crossed by a fine stone viaduct of ten arches; there was another, even higher, of eight arches, at Monard in very much the roughest country encountered between Dublin and Cork.

Mallow, 21 miles up line from Cork, became a junction in 1854 with the opening of the Killarney Junction Railway and then acquired a second junction in 1860 when the branch to Fermoy came into use. Mallow's population has not changed much over the years, being almost 6,000 in 1841, 4,100 in 1871 and around 5,500 at the present. Lying astride the River Blackwater it is the heart of an agricultural area but more than a century ago the town gained a measure of favour as a spa, the 'Irish Bath', and was visited by Sir Walter Scott among others. Better known to railway enthusiasts is the beet processing factory established in 1934 by CSE. Mallow is still busy as the junction for Killarney and Tralee but all the other intermediate stations have closed.

Buttevant, between Charleville and Mallow, will haunt railway safety experts for many years for on 1 August 1980 a serious derailment took place in a manner which really belonged to the railways of more than a century ago. The 10am down Cork express was derailed in what became the worst railway accident in the Republic, eighteen lives being lost. Unbelievably a facing turnout to a ballast siding was hand worked and not connected to the signal cabin even though it had been installed six months earlier. As the express was approaching, the points were unlocked to allow a light engine, then standing on the up line, to enter the siding – the lack of cooperation with the signalman who had control of the crossover and would have told of the accepted express had his permission been sought was utterly incredible. Several departments were held at fault for lack of coordination and their working methods, rules and notices were severely criticised.

The temporary Cork terminus was situated just outside the northern edge of the city and on high ground. The official title was Victoria but the local area name, Blackpool was that normally used. The station was well built as it was clear that it would take Dargan a long time to complete the steeply-inclined (1 in 60) 1,355 yards tunnel, now the longest in Ireland, and it was not until 1855 that the permanent terminus adjacent to Penrose Quay was completed. Even then it was necessary to make use of what was to be the goods depot from 3 December 1855 until the adjacent station on a very cramped site between the tunnel mouth and the north bank of the River Lee was ready on 28 July 1856 (165½ miles from Dublin).

Because of the incline it became the practice to marshal up goods trains at Rathpeacon sidings, 4 miles out from Cork, working timetables showed 'Runs of Goods' separately from the main timetable, 20 minutes being allowed for the up trip and 15 for the return to Cork goods yard, a practice which continued until liner trains replaced traditional loose-coupled wagons.

The station, which had Glanmire added by 1871, could not be enlarged and the GS&WR had no alternative but to build a new station. To the east of the terminus the only railway development had been the laying down of the connecting line to the Queenstown and Youghal line in 1868, much of the area between it and the nearby Lower Glanmire Road being marshy. Work started in 1890, the whole area being filled in and the connecting line rebuilt to form the platform lines of a sharply-curved station. The greater part of these platforms is covered by an overall roof and today it looks much the same as the day trains started to use it on 1 February 1893, although the hotel on the down platform closed about 1946. A pair of goods avoiding

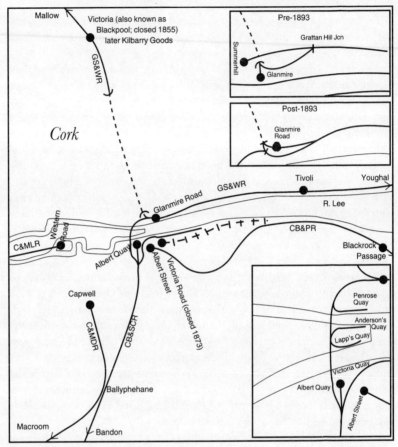

lines pass round the south side of the station and to complete the 1893 alterations a new goods yard was built to serve the warehouse which was in effect
turned by ninety degrees.

Two relics of the earliest days of railway travel in Ireland are now on
display in the main concourse, GS&WR Bury single No 36 dating from
1847 which stands on a length of original GS&WR 90 lbs per yard bridge
rails, having been placed there in November 1950.

As the main line of the GS&WR the Dublin and Cork service enjoyed
the greatest number of trains on the system, usually five or six and steadily
accelerated over the years, from the seven hours of 1849 (twelve hours for
the lowest class passenger) to about four hours by 1884 which remained in
force for many years. During the winter of 1879–80 a sleeping car was
included in the Up Night Mail which did not last; in fact there was only one
other attempt in Ireland to provide this facility, on the GNR. Ireland's first

Travelling Post Office started on 1 January 1855 between the two cities and lasted until 1994. The departure time of the Down Day Mail steadily became earlier as the London to Dublin journey time shortened so that the 10am start of 1849 became 6.40am by 1897. For trans-Atlantic passengers the American Mails first ran on 6 November 1859 and continued until 1914. At first there was just a weekly train (on Sunday) for the Cunard line, a second (on Thursday) being added in 1892 for the White Star line, by then running through to Queenstown. The corresponding up service could not be fixed and so mail vans were attached to the next convenient train and a special would run if there were at least six first fare passengers. The main line service suffered severe interruptions in 1921 and 1922–3 when the Mallow viaduct was blown up in August 1922. To keep a service of sorts going a temporary station was put up at the south end and connecting trains completed the journey, 45–50 minutes being allowed for the road transfer. The new Irish government required a resumption of services as quickly as possible and therefore a steel girder viaduct was substituted for the original stone. Work had to be done with military protection and the new bridge was opened by President Cosgrave on 16 October 1923. One of the best ever steam runs over the main line was made in March 1934 when a special of but 93 tons trailing whisked the new American ambassador up from Cork to Dublin in 2 hours 27 minutes. It was the introduction of the new and magnificent 800 Class 4–6–0 express engines in 1939–40 that permitted a final steam era acceleration whereby trains of more than 300 tons could make the trip, with six stops, in 3 hours 33 minutes. The timings were made with ease and, but for World War II, further improvements may have resulted – we shall never know.

During 1932 the signalling was centralised at one cabin which had the largest mechanical frame in Ireland with 110 levers, replacing the two 1893 cabins. The nearby engine shed received much of its coal at a quay on the River Lee which was then hauled along an overhead gantry, 1,140ft long, to a dump by the 'Loco Yard'. It dated from 1885 and was worked by an Inchicore built vertical boiler steam engine, universally known as 'Loco Pat', there being six hoppers to carry the coal. Although 5ft 3in gauge, the tracks were connected to the rest of the railway. The gantry and the engine lasted until 1963.

A TRUNCATED MAIN LINE

As early as 1846 an Act authorised the Cork & Waterford Railway, supported by the GWR, which was to have run along the south coast of Ireland passing through Youghal; the eastern part eventually materialised as the WD&LR (Chapter 3), the westerly end was built between Cork and Youghal, but the middle section between that town and Dungarvan was never undertaken. It took until 1854 to get new powers as the Cork & Youghal Railway, with additional powers to build a branch to Queenstown in the next year. Construction was started by the Moore Brothers but soon stopped, to be started again by R.T. Carlisle of Canterbury who made such slow progress that the company decided to finish the job with its own labour and enough was done to allow opening between Dunkettle and Midleton in 1859. The line was extended during 1860 to Killeagh and then Youghal (26³/4 miles), a seaside resort, but all efforts to develop the town have failed to maintain the population, which has halved from 10,000 since 1841. Attempts by a spectator, Leopold Lewis, to create 'The Brighton of Ireland' after he purchased the entire town in 1861 from the Duke of Devonshire were doomed because of his other financial involvements, which included the C&YR, he becoming bankrupt for the *third* time a few years later with debts of £850,000 (say in excess of £50,000,000 nowadays).

Entry into Cork was difficult, having to pass along the base of cliffs; Brunel had surveyed this section but it did not rival Dawlish to Teignmouth in South Devon. Dunkettle to Tivoli was opened in 1860 and in order to get its trains into Cork the company resorted to horse haulage over temporary tracks to what was advertised as 'Cork Temporary Terminus' (otherwise known as Bruin Lodge) from 1 October 1860; at Tivoli six horses replaced engines to draw three coaches, the need ceasing when the line closed in May 1861 for completion with permanent track and reopened on 30 December 1861, being extended a short way towards but never reaching the intended terminus at King Street (now McCurtain Street). The C&YR terminus was normally referred to as Summerhill and from 1871 this suffix appeared in timetables.

The branch to Queenstown, or Cobh to give the modern name, turned southwards on diverging form the Youghal line at Queenstown Junction to cross the Fota estuary on a six-span viaduct and then the Belvelly viaduct to get onto Great Island (the largest in Cork harbour) to serve the shipbuilding centre of Rushbrooke and the harbour town of Queenstown which became a port of call for trans-Atlantic liners (served by tender) from 1859. Historically Cobh was the starting point for the *Sirius*, the first steamship to cross the Atlantic solely under power as long ago as 1838. The town has suffered quite a dramatic change in population, from 5,100 in 1841 to 11,400 in 1851, 10,300 in 1871 and now 5,200. The branch (5³/4 miles), constructed by J.P. Ronayne of Cork, opened in 1862. Fota on the Cohb branch is a private station without road access serving Fota Island Estate but available to the public. Queenstown was extensively rebuilt in 1889 with a slight lengthening of the line and has been altered several times since to improve transfer between ships and trains. Originally all single line the route was doubled from Cork to Tivoli in 1862, on to Dunkettle in 1867, to Queenstown Junction in 1868 and thence to Queenstown in 1882, but the Youghal branch remained single. The GS&WR commenced the working of the C&YR on 1 April 1865 and acquired the concern on 1 July 1866, paying £310,000, a matter which angered some shareholders who held that it had been over valued, one calling the deal a 'marriage to a bankruptcy'. A considerable amount had to be spent to build a connecting line at Cork, a difficult project which led to conflict with the BOT over signalling. Because of the closeness of the GS&WR tunnel to the terminus, it was necessary to put a single line junction and crossover within the tunnel – the Inspecting Officer made it very clear that such a junction was far too dangerous and could never be sanctioned; he required a full double track junction outside the tunnel. The new line was 38 chains of double line, other than the junction, joining the Youghal route at Grattan Hill Junction. Mails were sent through as from 3 January 1869 and goods was diverted from Summerhill during December 1868 but it was not until May 1873 that a satisfactory junction was approved. The through running of passenger trains, began with the Day Mail as from 1 January 1876, followed by the American Mails exactly one year later.

In 1893 Queenstown and Youghal trains ceased to use Summerhill, the junction line having been realigned so that they joined the original route a little further east than the 1868 connection; an annual 'train' ran until 1927 to maintain the right of way to the old terminus and it was not until 1971 that formal abandonment took place. The Cork and Queenstown (Cobh) service was the only one of a suburban nature outside Dublin and Belfast. In 1896 Queenstown Junction was realigned to make what had been the branch to Queenstown into the main line and allow faster running. Through trains from Dublin, which were hauled by the largest express locomotives, were abruptly terminated on 8 August 1922 when the viaducts to Great Island were blown up; restoration afterwards did not allow use of such large engines though in fact the need for the Mails to run to Cobh had disappeared as post from Britain no longer passed through Ireland on its way to America.

Throughout the difficult forties only the fuel famine of 1947 stopped trains to Youghal, Cobh retaining its trains. Youghal passenger trains were taken off in 1963, but Cobh continues to have its service with a dozen each weekday and seven on Sundays. Regular goods trains to both Cobh and Youghal ceased during 1978 and seasonal traffic and seaside trains on the

Youghal branch were terminated as from 30 August 1982; since then some of the track has been lifted but the line has not been formally closed.

East of Cork the line has developed as Cork's freight area, oil sidings being built at Tivoli in 1973 and a container depot at North Esk (3¼ miles out) was established in 1975, followed in 1980 by sidings for an ammonia plant at Marino Point (7½ miles) between Fota and Carrigaloe. Beyond this plant there is now to all intents no non-passenger traffic, scrap metal being the last a few years ago. During 1994 IR announced that upgrading of the Cobh service was intended, with a new Cork terminus at the Brian Boru Bridge on the course of the old Cork City Railways route, and possible restoration of services to Midleton and through local trains from Mallow, calling at a reopened Blarney and a new station at Kilbarry – however no dates have been announced. A small change has taken place – Cobh Junction became Glounthaune in late 1994.

CORK HARBOUR BY TRAIN AND STEAMER

Proud of the fact that its line was the first within the city, the Cork, Blackrock & Passage Railway connected the three places by a line of 6¼ miles which followed an almost level course downstream along the south bank of the River Lee. Opened in 1850, after completion partly by one of the Moore brothers, the rest near Passage by Dargan, the Cork terminus lay at Victoria Road, about a ½ mile east of the centre, close to the City Park (that name being used locally rather than its official title). For many years Passage had been connected to Cork by a fleet of paddle steamers taking an hour over the journey; as early as 1832 a railway was proposed to quicken communication, followed by an Act in 1837 but no railway was built until powers were revived in 1848. The easy ground attracted the attention of the Cork & Bandon Railway which considered a level but lengthy route through Passage and then Monkstown before turning west towards Bandon, while the Cork & Waterford Railway promoters considered a line to Passage and a ferry across to Great Island as an alternative to a more direct course along the north bank of the Lee. Monkstown with only about 500 persons was attractive enough to seek a two mile extension Act, obtained in 1847, but the line was not built at the time.

The service started with ten trains daily at hourly intervals, worked by a fleet of three Sharp, Stewart single driver tank engines, and had to face the rivalry of the established steam boats which had the advantage of berthing well up the river close to the centre of the city. Within a year the railway directors found it necessary to participate in the river traffic, forming a company in 1852, the CB&PR not having such powers, to run vessels as an

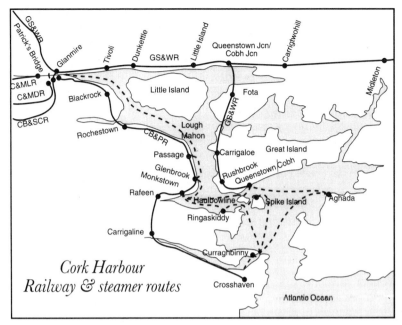

Cork Harbour
Railway & steamer routes

extension of the railway, beginning with a service from Passage to Monkstown and Queenstown and of course the inevitable fares war, not settled until 1856. By this time several places around Cork Harbour were served by both passenger and goods sailings, leaving the railway with virtually no goods traffic, there being no sense in transhipping for the short railway journey. The CB&PR obtained its own powers in 1881 to run the boats and continued the competition with the major rival, the Citizens River Steamers Co Ltd, until the latter succumbed in 1890, leaving the railway as the sole operator.

Cork Corporation plans to develop the river front and the Admiralty plans for a dock involved in the CB&PR in a major deviation, the necessary powers being obtained by the Corporation as part of the Cork Improvement Act of 1868. Financed almost entirely by the council, a new line of about 1½ miles was built to the south of the original route to a new terminus a little nearer the city centre. Thus on 5 February 1873 trains last used Victoria Road and next day ran out of Albert Street. Although well-run and serving its part of the Cork area with frequent trains, the company suffered heavily from the seasonal nature of its business, but managed a reasonable profit. So it was expected that extension beyond Passage would be beneficial, especially if all-the-year-round residential traffic could be encouraged, but it would be costly as the terrain was more difficult. A change from the 5ft 3in gauge of the existing line to the narrow 3ft would allow sharper curves and somewhat steeper gradients and hopefully reduce expenses. Powers to extend to Crosshaven were gained in 1896 and work began late in 1897.

The new line proved more difficult to build than expected and there was constant friction between the company and John Best of Edinburgh, the contractor, but conversion between Cork and Passage was completed so that the new narrow gauge trains commenced on 29 October 1900, the last of the old trains having run two days previously; the change was made by adding an inner third rail, leaving the surplus rails for removal later. Such was the growth of traffic that it was necessary to double the line from Albert Street to Blackrock, not with the gauge conversion but during 1902, and by this time there was a new from of competition, the Cork Electric Tramways & Lighting Co Ltd having extended out to Blackrock in April 1901, the railway losing a substantial number of passengers as a result. It is on record that the railway had given consideration during 1899 to electrification.

The Crosshaven extension took much longer than planned, the railway having to obtain a large BOW loan and issue debentures as well as en extension of time. It was possible to open as far as Monkstown in 1902, with a new station at Passage adjacent to the original terminus and a tunnel, unique on Irish narrow gauge railways, of 585 yards. Then in 1903 trains were extended to Carrigaline and at long last the extension was completed to Crosshaven (16 miles) in 1904. Such was the demand that all four engines and all coaches (extra having been obtained) had to be used on summer Sundays when a half-hourly service was provided. The steam boat services were altered to work to and from Monkstown and served Ringaskiddy, Haulbowline, Queenstown, Currabinny and Aghada (where there was a goods tramway along the pier) and also Crosshaven in the summer.

The extension became profitable in itself but the company was hampered by the immense debt raised for its construction. World War I created military traffic and workmen's trains to Passage for the dockyards and Haulbowline Island were necessary and, to help out, the railway borrowed at the direction of the Irish Railway Executive Committee a 2-4-0T engine from the CDRJC and coaches from the L&LSR, the company having to make small alterations to some of the platforms to give clearance for the latter. Valuable extra traffic was generated when Fords opened a motor car factory near Albert Street station.

A branch was considered during 1912 and revived and enlarged in 1922 as part of an ambitious plan to create a port on Spike Island where Cork Harbour was deep enough to take the largest of ocean liners – Independence and the Civil War put an end to any real hope for an Irish trans-Atlantic port, apart form the fact that Queenstown was already well established for that purpose. The GSR soon made economies, stopping the steam boats and singling the line to Blackrock in 1927. Increasing bus competition soon reduced the number of trains and the end came early compared with other narrow gauge lines, the services finishing in two stages in the summer of 1932, only five days' notice of closure being given for the first and three for the second. All four engines and the 34 wagons were soon transferred to the C&LR section of the GSR, thus giving the more numerous railway enthusiasts of the fifties a chance to see something from the CB&PR. Since then the area south east of Cork has developed into a fairly dense residential district, although the dockyard at Passage has long since gone, but surprisingly much of the course of the line remains, enough to encourage publication of a plan for a modern style rapid transit line from Cork to Blackrock and Passage, mostly as a railway with a couple of sections of street running.

TO BANDON AND THE WEST

The Cork & Bandon Railway was a miserable concern with a parsimonious directorship which tolerated frequent breakdowns of ancient engines until the reality had to be faced that railway equipment does wear out and needs renewal. With just over 6,000 persons in 1841 Bandon (then a cotton and woollen centre) was the largest town west of Cork city and after the failure to build a line through the area based on the 1836 Commission proposals maintained a strong interest in connecting the town by rail to Cork. By 1844 a direct line of 20 miles had been agreed but it had the disadvantage of a long steep climb out of Cork – several years later it was claimed that it had been expensively built and the route had been chosen to show the prowess of the engineer, Edmund Leahy. The western part, built by four small contractors (Bolton, Henright, Jones & Parrett and Condor) was ready first, having a tunnel of 170 yards at Kilpatrick, the first in Ireland through which trains passed, trains running from Brandon to Ballinhassig from 1849, horse-drawn omnibuses providing a connection to Cork.

The remainder of the line between Cork and Ballinhassig involved the building of a large viaduct at Chetwynd, four miles out of Cork with four spans of 110ft and a headroom of 83ft, and a tunnel of 900 yards at Gogginshill, just east of Ballinhassig, which at the insistence of the PWLC had to be wide enough for a double track. The years of construction had not been without drama, leading to a quarrel with the contractors, Fox & Henderson, due to lack of finance and the means to pay them, although outwardly all appeared fine, *Herepath's Journal* having described company in glowing terms during 1851, blissfully unaware of the reality. The directors announced that the service would start on 7 August 1851, but the contractors decided otherwise and there followed one of the most bizarre incidents in the history of the railways in the British Isles – men were sent out and systematically set about making the line unusable! Rails were ripped out, sleepers removed and rocks and earth covered the track and, of course, there were no trains the next day. Naturally the matter came to Court and worthy of comment was the engagement of Isaac Butt as chief counsel for the defence, he later taking a major part in Ireland's history when he fostered the Home Rule Movement. The contractors were found not guilty and the line was soon put into working order, allowing a ceremonial opening on 6 December 1851, the public service beginning two days later over the full 20 miles to Bandon.

West of Bandon the most important centres are Dunmanway, Bantry and Skibbereen, all of which have suffered a severe loss of population since 1841, the first two halving, the last now well under half. It was the West Cork Railways that gained an Act in 1860 to build onwards from Bandon to Skibbereen but for all the effort expended the line was completed only as far as Dunmanway (37³/₄), although some work had been done in the Skibbereen area. The junction with the C&BR was installed a little to the Cork side of their Bandon terminus having an exchange platform known as West Cork Junction. Despite problems with a contractor, Wheatley & Kirk, who went bankrupt, the line was almost ready by early 1865 but there was a hold up at Bandon where a ¹/₂ mile deviation had to be authorised in 1865 to overcome objections from Lord Bandon. Opening took place in 1866, the company having to manage with but two engines, which they did not own. Having cost £20,000 per mile the railway was burdened with the consequences of extremely dubious methods of raising capital, most payments being made by issue of Lloyds Bonds and continual disputes with the C&BR.

Prior to railway expansion beyond Dunmanway the Irish Tramways Co Ltd was formed in 1872 with an ambitious plan to lay down roadside tramways with a gauge of 2ft 9in, strongly recommended by no less a personage than Charles Spooner, and expected to cost no more than £1,400 per mile, the anticipated traffic being capable of yielding 20 per cent. However nothing came of plans to connect such places as Clonakilty, Crookhaven, Bantry, Drimoleague, Rosscarbery and Castletown Berehaven although Grand Jury approval had been obtained.

It was not until a new company was formed, the Ilen Valley Railway, in 1872, that Skibbereen had any hope of getting its railway, the failure of the first contractor, Nixon & Gordon, delaying matters until J.B. Crawley completed the line. Opened in 1877 with great enthusiasm, the line was worked by the West Cork; it was now obvious that unified control of the whole route was desirable and so in 1880 the C&BR and the West Cork amalgamated, leaving the Ilen Valley as a worked company until taken over in 1909.

Bantry town stands at the head of the 21 miles long inlet Bantry Bay and twice it was the landing place for attempted invasions by the French, in 1689 and 1796. The harbour, well protected by Whiddy Island which years after the railway had gone became an oil terminal, was home to a fishing fleet and the small boats which provided a passenger and goods service to places around the bay. It was the Ilen Valley that obtained the necessary Act, in 1878, which authorised the Bantry Extension Railway, complete with a 35 years Baronial Guarantee. Thomas Dowling had the contract and completed the line to a terminus up above the town and harbour in less than two years so that trains started during 1881, being worked by the C&BR. Bantry was approached by a fall of 1 in 60 and on 7 July 1887 became the scene of a runaway when the down early morning mail train hit the buffers, killing the driver. Drimoleague had a very simple layout for a junction, merely a set of points with the platforms in the vee formed by the Skibbereen and Bantry lines, quite adequate for dividing or combining trains; a larger layout with a passing loop and platforms on the Cork side of the junction was installed in 1899.

Having expanded far beyond Bandon the C&BR changed its title in 1888 to Cork, Bandon & South Coast railway. The system by then had two more branches, both reaching towns on the south coast of the county, Kinsale and Clonakilty. The older was built as the Cork & Kinsale Junction Railway, authorised in 1858, completed by J. Trowsdale & Sons and opened in 1863. The junction was at a new station 13½ miles from Cork, rejoicing in the short but accurate title of Junction, becoming Kinsale Junction in 1888. Like Bantry, the terminus was high above the town and the branch did little to attract the fish traffic upon which so much hope had been placed by the promoters; Kinsale was another town that had suffered severe depopulation, dropping from 6,918 in 1841 to only 1,500 in 1962.

The second branch was laid down by the Clonakilty Extension Railway following an Act of 1881, the remnant of ideas originating in 1864 for a line from Gaggin, (the later Clonakilty Junction) 4 miles west of Bandon, to Clonakilty and then westwards to Roscarbery, about halfway along the coast to Skibbereen; the 8¼ miles branch opened in 1886, the contractor being J.W. Dorman.

Efforts to promote tourism using the CB&SCR made a great deal of a visit of the Prince of Wales to the area in 1858, when he travelled west to Bantry Bay and Glengariff before continuing through Kenmare to Parknasilla and Killarney. To draw attention to the route and its beauties the company marked it on its maps and titled it 'The Prince of Wales Route'; indeed the title continued to be used by the GSR well after independence. Through bookings from Paddington and other major stations in

Britain were a feature of the special fares and inclusive holiday schemes on offer for a great many years.

The CB&SCR saw no reason to expand its system but the Allport Commission in 1888 recommended three new lines, their prime purpose being the encouragement of fish traffic. One, an extension to Kinsale harbour, was ignored by the railway, but the other two were soon constructed, W.M. Murphy building both. The company submitted plans for the Bantry Bay Extension Railway to the Government and received a grant. A line of two miles diverged from the existing branch just outside the old terminus and ran round the back of the town right down to the harbour and a new terminus at $57^3/_4$ miles, replacing the original, and a $^1/_4$ mile continuation onto the pier, opening in 1892. The other line was also constituted as the separate Baltimore Extension Railway. Because the area was so severely distressed, the CB&SCR declined to contribute and it had to be funded entirely by the Treasury in London, apart from a nominal capital of £70 to enable individuals to act as directors. Opened in 1893 as a continuation of the Skibbereen line, its terminus was at Baltimore ($61^1/_4$ miles). Much later when a substantial traffic in fish had built up a short extension was built onto the pier by 1917, the CB&SCR having agreed in 1912 to contribute £1,000, the remainder coming from other public bodies. Baltimore and the pier became the most southerly point of the entire Irish railway system. Nowadays the town has importance as a tourist centre in rugged underdeveloped country but its population remains at a mere 200. By the time that the 1925 Amalgamation was in hand the company had become something of a ghost concern with no records of meetings after May 1921 and it is worth naming the directors at the time, if only for the confusion of their names, William Martin Murphy, James William Lombard and William Lombard Murphy! No secretary could be located when it came to signing transfer and share cancellation documents and absorption by the GSR became legal only when one of the directors appended his signature.

Under GSR ownership the 'Bandon' section lost only the Kinsale branch which closed during 1931, the first on the amalgamated company to lose all its traffic. The other lines lasted until 1961 when the remaining West Cork railways were closed to all traffic, the introduction of diesel trains and locomotives in 1954–6 not being sufficient to prolong existence.

Two private sidings connected to the CB&SCR have interesting histories. A major activity at Bandon was distilling, Allman's business employing some 300 men and exporting its products worldwide. A siding was provided in 1874, being extended during 1876 as a roadside tramway into the factory about a $^1/_2$ mile from the station but production ceased in 1925 and distribution in 1930. The Cork Milling Co had a mill connected by a $^1/_2$ mile siding to the Clonakilty branch two miles south of Ballinascarthy, dating from about 1890. Its falling gradient allowed inwards loaded wagons to run down by gravity to the mill but a horse pulled the empties back up and so far as is known no locomotive ever worked over the siding. When in the 1958–9 season grain was too poor to be milled, it had to be taken away for use as fodder, distributed locally at Timoleague – the eight mile journey involved horse on the siding, a diesel locomotive to Ballinascarthy and steam for the remainder.

THE ROADSIDE TRAMWAY TO COURTMACSHERRY

The 1883 Tramways Act prompted ideas for a line from Bandon southwards to Timoleague (9 miles) but it was a shorter Baronially Guaranteed railway diverging from the Clonakilty branch that was approved in 1884. Unlike other lines built to the same Act, this one adopted 5ft 3in for its gauge, the argument, put forward very strongly by the contractor Robert Worthington, that it would assist through traffic being accepted. Eventually the Ballinascarthy & Timoleague Light Railway was formed in 1888, to be extended by another Baronially-supported company, the Timoleague and Courtmacsherry Extension Light Railway, also dating from 1888. The 6 miles to Timoleague opened in 1890, followed by the other 2³⁄₄ miles to Courtmacsherry in 1891. A siding onto Courtmacsherry pier was added during 1893, handling a variety of goods such as coal and fish. Lightweight locomotives, originally complete with bells and skirting (but not duplicate controls at the front) had to be used, a requirement that ensured a long life for several small GSR and CIE engines, until modest-sized diesel locomotives made their appearance in 1957.

From the start, and almost until closure, excursion traffic flourished, the citizens of Cork enjoying the fine sands around Courtmacsherry on many a summer Sunday, travelling in special short bogie stock provided by the CB&SCR for the trip from Cork. In many years one of the little line's trains would run through to Clonakilty Junction to connect with Cork trains and in 1941 the solitary train ran to and from Clonakilty. There was virtually no chance of even meeting working expenses and under the terms of the Baronial Guarantee Cork County Council soon took over the management of the line. Receipts and expenditure in just two years show just how much was lost by the local ratepayers:

	Receipts	Expenditure
1913	£1,830	£2,669
1919	£2,538	£5,674

When a Light Railway Commission sent out a questionnaire to railways in Britain and Ireland during 1920, the T&CLR stressed the unfairness of national wage rates and the new eight hour day, instancing the two sets of enginemen now needed who did but a single trip each but earned as much as those on the mighty LNWR! No wonder so much had to be paid out to keep the line going. Earlier, in 1897, the staff of the line had caused quite a sensation when they were the first in the British Isles to press their management for implementation of the new national wages demanded by the Amalgamated Society of Railway Servants – a curious way to assail the mighty portals of Euston by starting with a line quite unable to pay its way, thundered a Dublin daily editorial.

The new owners of 1925 found that the Courtmacsherry branch was unsafe and closed the line on 1 June 1925; no doubt they hoped that it could stay closed but the Ministry of Industry & Commerce in Dublin ordered that repairs be done and trains resumed on 1 September 1925, lasting until the 1947 crisis which finished all but wagon-load traffic, meaning winter beet, continuing as did Sunday excursions, until total closure in 1961.

NARROW GAUGE TO SCHULL

West of Skibbereen lay a remote area, the Mizen Peninsula, where there were modest sources of copper and barytes and, more important, fishing. The Clyde Shipping Co included Schull in its west coast services and was the only way to send out local produce. First plans envisaged a narrow gauge tramway from Skibbereen right though to Mizen Head with hopes that Crookhaven would develop as a port for American mails, saving several hours of their passage. With other ideas of serving Rosscarbery to the east of Skibbereen, the West Carbery Tramways & Light Railways Ltd was incorporated in 1883 but only the western line was approved as far as Schull; much to the dismay of those living to the east of Skibbereen the Baronial Guarantee was a liability for all the local areas. The West Carbery title remained but throughout it was usual to call the line the Schull & Skibbereen Light Railway.

Built by McKeon, Robinson & d'Avigdor the line followed the road contours for most of the way, apart from a long deviation near Ballydehob with a large viaduct across an inlet of Roaring Water Bay, the greatest work on the line. At Skibbereen the station was added to that of the CB&SCR, its layout making it necessary for trains to back out into a siding before proceeding to Schull. A special for pigs from Ballydehob two days before the official opening enabled farmers to get better prices and all seemed set for a rosy future.

For motive power Dick, Kerr of Kilmarnock had supplied three special enclosed tram engines, their most interesting feature being the fitting of 'superheaters' in the firebox through which the exhaust passed, the makers claiming that they had to be used instead of roof-mounted condensers which would make the engines top-heavy. The failure of the superheaters, and the inability to haul the rated load of 30 tons up 1 in 30, caused immediate disorder, such that within one month of opening during 1886 trains ceased for ten days; worse was to come with total cessation of services in 1887 so that the engines could be modified, the BOT enquiring into the matter. A new larger engine was ordered and has its place in Irish locomotive history, being the first with a Belpaire boiler to work in the British Isles. It then became possible to restore services at the beginning of 1888.

A small addition was made to the line when a ¹/₂ mile extension from Schull station to the pier was completed in 1893. Inevitably losses resulted in Cork County Council appointing a Management Committee in 1892 but the line continued quietly to serve the locality, managing as best it could without any capital for improvement. It was the local lack of good roads that kept services going until they were suspended in 1944 (the pier branch had fallen out of use some years earlier). Resumption in 1945 proved to be a short reprieve for total closure came with the 1947 coal famine, the line and rolling stock lying idle until abandonment was permitted in 1954.

THE PLUM OF IRISH RAILWAYS

Macroom lies 24 miles west of Cork close to the upper reaches of the River Lee in a fertile area but typically has lost considerably in population, having 4,800 in 1841, down to 2,700 in 1871 and some 2,200 these days. It was not until 1860 that real interest in a railway emerged, three proposals being debated – a northerly line through Coachford, a middle line to follow the Lee, and that actually built, a more southerly course, having easy gradients. Taking the title Cork & Macroom Direct Railway, it was ready in 1866, its 23¹/₂ miles having been built by J.P. Ronayne, making use of one mile of the C&BR and its terminus at Albert Quay; thus these two railways were the first in Cork to be joined. However friction over hindrance to traffic caused the C&MDR to seek an independent terminus, achieved during 1879 with the opening of Capwell station on the south west side of the City. The junction was immediately removed and the line isolated from the C&BR. The extension was built by B. Mullen.

A thoroughly local concern, the CM&DR achieved a level of prosperity envied by many other companies but complacency allowed the line to fall into a poor state, such that a derailment of a down train on 8 September

1878 (there being five fatalities) was directly due to the state of the track. It was some time before prosperity was regained, another blow being the opening of the C&MLR Coachford line but when the amalgamation came it was a justifiable claim that the little railway was the 'plum' of Irish railways during arbitration sessions of the Railway Tribunal.

The small town of Ballincollig was a British military garrison and in peaceful times the line's isolation was not a problem, but war made it imperative to have through facilities. Thus the Admiralty in London insisted that a junction siding was installed at Ballyphehane, completed during April 1918; in 1920 the junction was declared unnecessary and it was offered to both railways; surprisingly the C&MDR offered £115 for its portion, the CB&SCR showing no interest until 1922 when both made offers, the former £15, the latter £200, although the British Government expected £500 and would accept £400. After purchase the junction was removed. The first act of the GSR was to close Capwell in 1925 after the junction had been restored, power points controlled from Albert Quay being installed, making it the most remote controlled junction in Ireland at the time (and possibly worldwide). Passenger trains to Macroom ceased in 1935, goods lasting until 1947, after which only monthly cattle trains ran until 1953, when the Lee near Macroom was dammed to create large reservoirs for a hydro electric scheme.

SERVING THE MUSKERRY

Immediately to the west of Cork city lies a well-developed farming area, the Barony of Muskerry with its small towns of Coachford (361 in 1841, 128 in 1871 and 267 in 1961) and Donoughmore (224 in 1961) unlikely to entice any railway promoter but for Blarney with its world-famous 'Blarney Stone' at the castle. Noted for its tweeds, the town was still small in railway days (253 in 1841 and 346 in 1871) but grew with the tourist trade and the spread of Cork, six miles distant by direct road; although not yet a suburb, it now numbers some 1,000 souls. The 3ft gauge Cork & Muskerry Light Railway needed a Parliamentary Act because of local opposition with delayed incorporation until 1886. Worthington was the contractor and the first section ran from a terminus just off the Western Road in Cork to Blarney (8¾ miles) opened in 1887, the branch from Coachford Junction (6¼) to Coachford (15½) opening in 1888. The extra distance to Blarney over the direct road from Cork was no disadvantage in pre-motor days when there was substantial excursion traffic but the hoped-for residential traffic out of Cork never materialised.

The wisdom of not including a branch of 8½ miles to Donoughmore in the original scheme was to be demonstrated by the independent but worked Donoughmore Extension Railway, approved by the Privy Council in 1891, Alexander Ward getting the contract, and opened in 1893 from a junction at St Anne's (7¼). It was not long before this branch passed into the hands of Cork County Council.

The choice of the narrow gauge by the C&MLR had an interesting consequence. Being isolated from all the other Cork railways and anxious to reach the quays, the directors of the light railway persuaded the newly-authorised Cork Electric Tramways & Lighting Co Ltd to build its street tramways to a gauge ½in narrower which would allow railway vehicles to run along its tracks (the tramway having the narrowest gauge of any electric system in the British Isles), flanges running in the tram rail grooves. The only result was the spectacle of electric trams and steam trains running side by side along Western Road from 1898 to 1931.

After the amalgamation, it was not long before motor traffic took both passengers and goods away, such that Blarney was left without trains in some timetables after 1925. Losses became considerable and when the government grant which replaced Baronial Guarantees in 1925 ceased, the GSR announced that all services would finish at the end of 1934.

CONNECTING CORK'S RAILWAYS TOGETHER

From as early as 1850 there was much talk about how to overcome the isolation of the lines on the south side of the city and connect them to the GS&WR. The problem was Cork's quays, it being feared that any bridges would interfere with shipping. The first link to exist was a horse tramway opened in 1872, lasting only three years, to run from the GS&WR to the CB&SCR but of course it did not help with West Cork goods traffic which was often sent by road directly to and from Glanmire rather than by rail to avoid double transhipment.

Planners chose routes around the west side of the city, one of 1888 intending to connect Waterfall on the Bandon line to the new CM&LR, adding a third rail as far as Blarney and then continuing on to join the GS&WR main line. The new direct line from Fermoy (see Chapter 3) intended to enter the city from the north east and pass all round the west side to a terminus on the south side of the Lee close to the City Park, such a route being necessary to overcome the difference in levels; the sketch shows the route and its connections. Later plans for tunnels under the river and high level bridges also failed and it was not until 1906 that the simplest method was approved, an Act of that year incorporating the Cork City Railways. The major subscriber was the GWR which was allowed to have

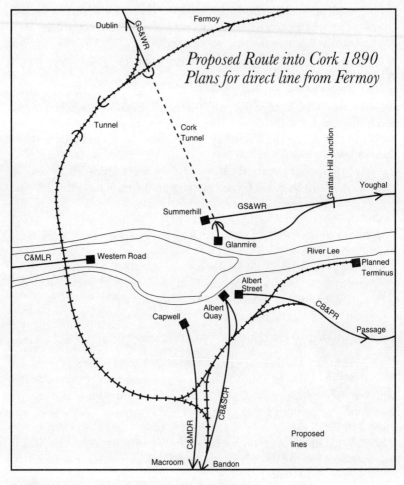

Proposed Route into Cork 1890
Plans for direct line from Fermoy

three directors. Using the streets the line was opened in 1912 with permission to work mixed trains, provided that no shunting was done by such
workings. Actually at each end, Glanmire GS&WR and Albert Quay
CB&SCR, any passenger trains would have had to reverse in and out of the
platforms, it not being possible to run directly into either station. Apart from
running in the middle of the road there was the interesting feature of *two*
lifting bridges, erected in the vertical position, over the two parts of the Lee
and there were sidings to adjacent quays. Another feature was the level
crossing over the Cork electric tram tracks outside Albert Quay station.

The GS&WR worked the through goods and the CB&SCR to some of
the quays. Just for a while in the summer of 1914 there was a solitary

through coach each way over the line. Trains had to be accompanied by the ringing of bells, some engines being fitted, but for others a handbell had to be used! The line was far from profitable and by 1923 losses amounted to almost £20,000 so it is not surprising that closure was attempted, although nothing came to public notice. The GWR made it clear that enough was enough and transferred its interest to the GS&WR, literally giving away its investment. When losses reached an annual sum of £4,000 the GSR announced in 1927 that it would apply for abandonment and removal of the bridges, causing uproar. One line put forward by the City Commissioner was that if abandonment was permitted because it did not pay, the whole purpose of the recent amalgamation would be defeated and he could not support a grant from city finances as it would set a precedent – little did he or others realise that the dilemma over the Cork City line was in truth the emerging pattern leading to extensive closures and the present-day need for massive external support to ensure continuation of railway services. Ironically the line outlived the closure of the West Cork lines in 1961, fertiliser and oil traffic to Albert Quay continuing until 1976. Since then the bridges have been fixed and today few, if any, of Cork's motorists know or care that they have to thank the railway companies for an alternative river crossing to the much older St Patrick's Bridge, all now part of a mammoth one-way traffic system.

THE KERRY LINE

Prior to the amalgamation of 1900–1, Killarney was second only to Cork in importance to the GS&WR, much effort being expended on tourist traffic, including some of the best trains on the line. The area was well-known for its beauty long before the railway came and was visited by almost everyone of note. The fame was, and is, worldwide and the appeal of the town, the lakes and the mountains (Macgillicuddy's Reeks which include the highest in Ireland, Carrantuohill, 3,414ft), is undeniable. The population of Killarney after falling is now about the same as 1841 (7,000) whilst Tralee, the county town of Kerry, has remained fairly constant at little more than 10,000.

It is therefore no surprise that the area attracted early promoters, the Killarney Junction Railway being authorised in 1846 to build a line of 40 miles from Mallow. Built by Dargan, after a delayed start following the worst of the Famine years, the line was one of the first to have its associated telegraph line from the start. The local company was the owner of Ireland's first railway-operated hotel, opened on 11 July 1854 and still in business as the Great Southern Hotel although not owned by CIE since 1984. For the less well off the GS&WR built a more mundane establishment, the New

Hotel in 1907, now also sold.

Completion through from Mallow to Killarney was delayed by a problem viaduct near Headford, the line opening initially to Mill Street and then Freemount, a temporary station, and then throughout to Killarney during 1853. The junction with the Cork main line was made immediately south of the Mallow Viaduct at 145¼ miles from Kingsbridge, being known as Killarney Junction. There was an early siding just west of Killarney Junction serving Webb's grain mills at Quarterstown, being about a half mile long; a goods train was maliciously diverted along it on 8 February 1864. It lasted until 1970, seeing very little traffic in the latter years. At 1¼ miles from the junction the CSE beet factory sidings of 1934 lay adjacent to the Kerry line, but it had no rail deliveries from 1974 until 1989.

Like the Killarney Junction, the Tralee & Killarney Railway, sanctioned in 1853, was a separate promotion, although in reality a subsidiary of the GS&WR, both being absorbed in 1860. Dargan was again the contractor and with a Government grant of £50,000 finished the line in three years so that it opened in 1859. Killarney station remained a terminus and trains continuing to Tralee had to back out into a siding at a point called Tralee Junction and then run forward to complete the journey, likewise running into the siding and then backing into the platform on an up journey. Inspecting Officers were critical of this arrangement but it survived until 1976 when a crossover was put in to give a direct run onto the main line before backing in. Killarney was important enough to have through trains or coaches from Dublin at an early date; indeed the 'Killarney Express', inaugurated in the summer of 1898 was a 'shop window' train for the GS&WR, aimed at Americans, the down service making the Kerry town in 4 hours, despite 40 miles of single line.

Despite the importance of the branch the GSR remodelled the junction with the main line by closing the cabin in 1926, replacing the double line junction by remote-controlled points in the up line; from then on Kerry line trains used the up line from and to Mallow station, much to the puzzlement of so seasoned a traveller as T.R. Perkins who noted that he could obtain no 'intelligible' explanation from station staff of 'this exceedingly curious working' when compiling his diary record of a 1932 visit to the Emerald Isle.

Several of the wayside stations closed in 1963, leaving Killarney and Tralee as the major railheads. A popular annual television event had an unexpected effect on the Kerry line when Ireland found itself host for the Eurovision Song Contest of 1993 – a local businessman persuaded the promoters to hold the show at Millstreet rather than as customary at the host nation's capital. To cater for the influx of visitors, the platform was lengthened to no less than 765ft, making it one of the longest in Ireland.

In 1967 the chance of a grand tourist attraction at Killarney was lost when a proposal by Summit Cableways Ltd to install a telfer route from the Windy Gap road out of Killarney up to the summit of Mangerton Mountain (2,756ft) failed due to massive local opposition. There would have been marvellous views, especially northwards over the lakes and Killarney and the mountains all around.

NEWMARKET BRANCH

1,900

Newmarket in the north of Co Cork has lost population heavily, declining from 4,200 in 1841 to 765 in 1871 and remaining about that figure. George Francis Train, the American tramway pioneer, was behind a scheme of 1865 to build a roadside horse tramway from Newmarket to the nearest station on the Kerry line at Kanturk (later Banteer) and the same route was part of the 1872 scheme put forward by the Irish Tramways Co Ltd. The project was revived in 1884 but instead the Baronial-guaranteed Kanturk & Newmarket Railway was registered in 1888, local landowners being behind the scheme. The contractor Robert Worthington provided much of the capital and seems to have manipulated events to cause an early quarrel with the GS&WR which worked the line from opening in 1889. From the junction at Banteer, the line served Kanturk (another town that rapidly lost population from 4,400 in 1841 to but 2,000 at present) and Newmarket (8½ miles). About a year later the K&NR rid itself of the working company and Worthington worked the service, but after twelve months the GS&WR returned, acquiring the line in 1892. The end for most traffic came in 1947, only monthly livestock trains, mostly from Kanturk, continuing. However the Transport Tribunal declined to grant an Abandonment Order in 1955 so CIE decided to restore goods trains, using a small diesel locomotive. Following trials, services resumed in 1956 to considerable rejoicing in the district. The branch now seemed to be 'safe' but the end came very suddenly on the first day of 1963.

THROUGH DEEP VALLEYS TO KENMARE

Kenmare town lies at the head of an estuary known as the Kenmare River at about the midpoint of the erstwhile 'Prince of Wales' tourist route. Unusually for Ireland the population increased from 1,300 in 1841 to 1,500 in 1851, but is now about 1,000. Set amongst some of the finest scenery in the British Isles and with a most equable climate, Kenmare is an ideal centre for touring but in the past had been prosperous with sea fishing and iron smelting, a woollen mill giving extra employment. In 1880 two schemes were put forward, one for a branch from the Kerry Line, the other an extension from the C&MDR which actually got an Act, but it was the 1889 plan for a line from Headford, with a Government grant of £45,984 and £60,000 4 per cent Baronial Guarantee stock (which was not a charge on the locality), that materialised in 1893. The route chosen made use of the tortuous valleys of the Roughty and Loo Rivers and included sections of 1 in 60 with mountains towering over the line, the contractor T.K. Falkiner having a difficult enough task. Intermediate traffic was just about non-existent and the anticipated fish trains never materialised, but there were some tourists to Kenmare. Tank engines were used at first but they were soon replaced by small 4-4-0 engines and then the ubiquitous 101 Class 0-6-0 locomotives until the line closed in 1960. The GS&WR had four hotels in the Kenmare area, three called Great Southern, one in Kenmare opened in 1897 and sold in 1977, another at Parknasilla, one of the best-known hotels in Ireland, dating from 1897 and now in the hands of the CIE hotel subsidiary (*Ostlanna Iompair Eireann*) and the other at Waterville, leased in 1895 and disposed of in 1932, all lying on the highly scenic 'Ring of Kerry' tourist route between Bantry and Valentia. There was also a smaller hotel at Parknasilla, the Bishops House, opened in 1905 and closed a few years later. Kenmare still benefits from the tourist trade as a centre for fishing (both sea and river) and its scenic beauty.

AS FAR WEST AS YOU COULD GO

As far west as you could go took one to Valentia Harbour, once the most westerly railway station in the British Isles (but only just,as Dingle on the other side of Dingle Bay is as far west) after travelling over one of Ireland's finest branches, scenically and operationally. It was a late branch for there was no commercial attraction in reaching Valentia, better known for the fact that the original trans-Atlantic telegraph cable came ashore at that point, completed after many difficulties in 1866. Actually Valentia is an island, connected by ferry in railway days and more recently by a long bridge. Valentia had been the objective of railway planners as early as 1835 for a line from Dublin and the maps attached to the 1836 Commission showed both Valentia and Berehaven as potential ocean packet ports. In 1847 an Act was passed for a Killarney to Valentia line and another in 1860 for a branch to Ballybrack, but nothing was done until the GS&WR took action in 1881, using powers dating from 1871, to build a branch as far as Killorglin.

The 12½ miles branch, laid down by Falkiner & Frazer and opened in 1885, ran over fairly level ground, diverging from the Tralee line at

Farranfore, the junction facing the former. Of interest is the fact that this branch was the first in Ireland to have the electric train staff from opening. The Allport Commission revived plans to continue the line for 27 miles to Valentia and the Government soon agreed to finance construction, provided that the GS&WR built it, work starting in 1890, the company using direct labour. Opened in 1893, it was heavily engineered due to the nature of the country, costing no less than £8,800 per mile. Capital came from three sources, the grant of £75,000 from the Government, a Baronial Guarantee of £70,000 (but the 4 per cent interest was not a charge on the district) and £65,000 found by the GS&WR which of course worked the line. It was hardly a 'light' railway with two major viaducts, one over the Glinsk River being on a curve of 10 chains radius and 70ft above the stream, the other a long girder viaduct over the Valentia River just east of Cahirciveen, a section running along a narrow ledge 270ft up on the cliff face of Drung Hill overlooking Dingle Bay and complete with two very short tunnels and a covered way, long grades and heavy earthworks. The curvature was such that bogie stock was not permitted for many years, in fact not until those with elliptical or larger circular buffers could be spared about sixty years ago. Unusually there was no engine shed at the end of the branch; the depot was at Cahirciveen, the only town in the area, and the otherwise empty trains between the two places were shown in the public timetables. Initially tank engines were used but soon the ever-present 101 Class 0-6-0 engines took over and remained until replaced by diesels in 1957-8, the final motive power on the line for it closed in 1960. The replacing bus service was a single weekday journey from Cahiciveen to Killarney, with a Friday-only connection to Tralee, Valentia no longer having any public transport, compared with better times when there were three trains over the branch.

Another Great Southern Hotel was established at Caragh Lake when purchased about 1894; despite being enlarged by the railway company it was sold in 1933.

THE CASTLEISLAND RAILWAY

Castleisland, with a consistent 1,600 or so persons through the railway age, was noted for its red marble quarries, their products finding much favour for interior decor. To keep costs down, the Castleisland Railway of 1872 obtained BOT authority to use a 40 lbs per yard rail which restricted speed to 20 mph and axle loading to 6 tons, but the GS&WR declined to work the line when it was opened in 1875. However Inchicore Works built a light six-coupled locomotive with a carriage portion over a rear bogie. This 0–6–4T exceeded the permitted axle loading so the BOT had to sanction an amending order to permit 6½ tons. Built by Collins & Crosby, the branch ran from Gortalea for 4½ miles across a level area to the town. It is on record that the combined engine and carriage removed a rake of 29 laden cattle wagons from the Castleisland Fair in September 1875, quite a feat for so small a locomotive of but 26½ tons.

After the GS&WR purchased the company in 1879, traffic became too much for small locomotives and so new rails of 74 lbs per yard were laid in 1897, allowing the use of larger engines and greater speeds. In 1947 regular services ceased, only cattle specials and a few excursions running until a goods service was restored in 1957, using a small four-wheeled diesel-mechanical locomotive. However total closure took place in 1977; the surprise is that the service lasted for so long.

OTHER LINES

There were few users of small lines in this area, some having been mentioned above. In 1875 when the British Government was building a dock (started in 1865) and naval stores on Haulbowline Island in Cork Harbour, a 3ft 6in gauge system was laid to serve the area. After handover to the new Irish Government the establishment fell out of use and by 1933 all plant and machinery was disposed of, although most of the track remained there for some twenty years or so. The British Government also had a munitions store at Fort Camden at the very mouth of Cork Harbour, its storage tunnels being cut into Ram's Head. It is only recently that the 18in gauge system has come to wider notice, having connected two deep-water wharves with the storage areas on one level and a short section at a higher level with what is reputed to have been an engine shed – nothing has come to light to confirm that an engine was ever used – manpower seems to have done most of the moving of the small trucks, the line being used from about 1870–80 until about 1920. There was also a big underground munitions store on Rocky Island near Haulbowline; for obvious reasons its small trucks were hand propelled and its rails were of brass. West of Cork explosives had been manufactured at Ballincollig for many years from 1794 and in the latter quarter of last century a small tramway was put down by the owner, but in 1898 the factory was sold, closing about 1903.

Henry Ford, the motor car builder, established a plant in 1920 at Cork on the south bank of the Lee, becoming one of the major employers in the city. In 1929 a short 2ft gauge line was installed to take coal from vessels at the quay to the bunkers, nearly 200 yards away – what was unusual was its position on the *roof* of the factory! Small petrol engines were used, one built by the company itself. During World War II the plant was nearly at a standstill and the railway and many of the staff were moved out of town to work a turf bog at Nad (between Donoughmore and Banteer) during 1941, being restored in 1945 on the roof, lasting only until 1949. In more recent years the former naval establishment on Haulbowline was transferred to the semi-state Irish Steel Co which now has a small 4ft 8^{1}/$_{2}$in gauge line connecting a jetty with the plant. For motive power it uses Unilokomotives, an ingenious unit which can use either rails or the road, and manufactured in Galway. Bord na Mona also had a bog railway in Co Cork, started in 1960 at Barna near Ballydesmond, on the western border of the county on a road from Banteer to Castleisland but it has ceased cutting.

CHAPTER VI

The Midlands and Far West

The existing Royal Canal, considered in 1838 to be sufficient for the transport needs of the midland counties of Ireland, climbed steeply out of Dublin to cross the extensive bogs to Mullingar and beyond to join the River Shannon at Termonbarry, just west of Longford town, a total of 90 miles. Derided as unnecessary even when planned, traditionally because of a quarrel on the board of the Grand Canal, it was exceptionally difficult to build and then failed because it did not draw traffic away from the latter as it was too close for much of its distance.

The great natural feature of the western counties is the River Shannon, even in its upper reaches, being navigable northwards from Athlone across Lough Ree and having short stretches of canal to avoid unnavigable parts, almost to its source in Co Cavan. Further north there is high ground with one of Ireland's sources of coal and further west, bordering the Atlantic, there are mountainous areas with many peaks exceeding 2,000ft; loughs are numerous, large or small, and with the rivers attract many fishermen. The coast line is deeply indented with bays and inlets, one, Killary Harbour, being more like a Norwegian fiord. Islands are numerous and Achill Island, Co Mayo, is the largest off the coast of Ireland.

The whole area has its beauty, rugged to the west or open to the east, but it does not sustain industry or population, having lost heavily from its peak about 1840–5. The largest centre is the city of Galway, situated at the head of Galway Bay, made famous in song, at the boundary of the open east and the heights of the west. The city's population totals are rather erratic, being:

1841	17,600
1851	24,200
1871	15,600
1911	13,000
1961	22,000

Other sizeable places are Sligo, Athlone, Ballinasloe, Ballina, Westport, Castlebar and Boyle, all still railway-served, but only the first name exceeds ten thousand. Tuam, a place that exceeded 6,000 in 1841 and now with 3,500, has lost its passenger trains, although Westport, now with under 3,000 is still served; the explanation lies in the fact that the latter is the end of a radial route from Dublin, whereas the former lay on a cross-country line. Historically the proprietors of the GS&WR sought to serve the area but were thwarted by the MGWR which gained access almost throughout, the one major line not in its control being that from south to north, connecting Limerick to Sligo. Ironically the passenger from Dublin now uses the GS&WR route for the start of his westward journey, track capacity enhanced by modern signalling making it possible for Irish Rail to use only one major line in that direction out of Dublin; only Sligo is served by its original route and is effectively the terminus of a very long branch of 133¼ miles.

ACROSS THE MIDLANDS

Early schemes for trunk lines across the midlands envisaged such railways as the Grand Atlantic (to reach Blacksod Bay), Irish Western (to Galway) or the Irish East & West in 1835–6, followed by the Great Central Irish Railway, proposed by Charles Vignoles in 1837, the latter getting as far as Parliament. Acts of 1846 and 1847 settled that the MGWR would build westward beyond Mullingar to Athlone and then Galway but fate intervened as the Famine worsened and capital became scarce so that contracts lapsed. A special Act of 1849 authorised the PWLC to advance £500,000 at 3½ per cent interest with repayment of the capital, deferred for ten years, at 1½ per cent per annum; any deficiency in repayment of the 3½ per cent not realised by working profits was to be made good by a rate levied on baronies on Cos Roscommon and Galway along the route – seemingly the first Baronial guarantee and making it necessary to keep a separate account for the Athlone and Galway section.

Built through relatively easy country, work started in July 1849, the whole distance (76¼ miles) covered in one contract, awarded to William Dargan who made such good progress that he completed the work five months early. All was ready for opening throughout from Mullingar to Galway (126¾ miles from Broadstone) on 1 August 1851, double track as far as Streamstown, the rest single, apart from one mile at Athlone and ¾ mile at Ballinasloe; later in 1851 a second track was added between Athlone and Ballinasloe and from Oranmore to Galway, with Streamstown to Athlone being doubled in 1852. In 1912 a little more was doubled, Attymon Junction to Athenry.

There are two major bridges, the longest the crossing of the Shannon at Athlone, needing five spans, one opening, the other a three-span bridge across Lough Atalia, just outside Galway; at the insistence of the Admiralty it had to have a swinging span, 157ft long on a central column – its greater claim to fame is the fact that after being opened for the Inspecting Officer it never opened again! After 38 years of disuse even the Admiralty had to concede that opening was not necessary and so it was fixed in 1890. There had been no need for a tunnel but there was one just after the 53rd mile – it existed only because a cutting would have removed the garden of the house almost above.

The population of Athlone has increased dramatically from 6,400 in 1841 to almost 10,000 now and Ballinasloe has grown from 1,000 to some 6,000, so uncharacteristic of most Irish places, but many of the other towns have diminished substantially. The directors of the MGWR supported a number of schemes to make Galway a point of departure for North America, but the company itself did not put money into any scheme, which was fortunate for the railway as all attempts were dogged by misfortune and loss. The first steam vessel, the *Viceroy*, sailed on 1 June 1850 but was lost on the homeward passage, and despite the Trans-Atlantic Packet Station Commissioners' verdict in 1852 against the use of any Irish port, a Manchester merchant, James Lever, established in 1858 the Atlantic Steam Navigation Company to run from Galway although it lasted only until 1864. At Galway the MGWR laid down in 1858 a ¼ mile goods branch into the docks, diverging from the main line just outside the station (with various periods out of use the line lasted until about 1960). The company built a fine hotel at Galway, the Railway Hotel, completed in 1851 but unlike the GS&WR at Killarney did not run it, leasing it to a series of managers until taking over its management in 1924; it was renamed the Great Southern Hotel and remains in CIE control. The use of funds by the MGWR backed by the Baronial Guarantee to build the hotel was a source of controversy until an Act of 1854 removed that amount from the guarantors' liabilities.

Livestock, particularly cattle, became a major source of revenue for the MGWR; giving evidence to a House of Commons Select Committee the general manager, Tatlow, stated that in 1892 the company had run 1,723 cattle specials conveying 835,018 head from no less than 1,150 fairs. Empty stock was sent out the day before and moved off as soon as loaded, Dublin being the destination for a great many trains but some went to Belfast as well for export and others ran to stations on the Meath line. The greatest fair of all was held at Ballinasloe, so important that not only did the senior managers attend but also some of the directors, entertaining the more important of the cattle traders. Originating about 1800, or even earlier, the fair attracted all sorts, honest traders, those with other than honest intent and others who had nothing better to do; not only livestock changed hands for there were stalls for almost anything and the fourth and last day became known as the 'poor man's fair' when all and sundry from a wide area attended. In 1861 *Saunders Newsletter* quoted some figures for Ballinasloe:

	Sheep	Cattle
1800	70,386	7,749
1815	94,764	8,149
1860	81,861	17,474

All this trade has been lost to the railway, being a road haulage preserve these days.

Four daily trains between Dublin and Galway taking nearly six hours soon proved to be too generous and MGWR services became sparse and slow with trains stopping at all stations. An agreement in 1889 with the GPO introduced a faster limited mail service but it was not until 1902 that accelerations gave a main line service comparable with elsewhere in Ireland. A tourist express started in 1903 ran to Galway in 3 hours 10 minutes, continuing to Clifden in Connemara, leaving an Achill portion at Athlone, both destinations to suit patrons of the company's hotels at Recess and Mullarany. When tourists returned to Ireland after World War II CIE took the novel step in 1950 with the introduction of a 'Radio Train', running from Dublin, the popular destinations being Galway and Killarney. A studio coach was included in the train from which a commentary on the route was relayed to all carriages with music and radio programmes as well. Lunch was served on the outward journey and high tea when returning, enlivened by amateur performances from the studio coach. The train remained popular for some twenty years but ceased in 1980 after a steady decline in the number of tourists.

The greatest change to the 'Galway Road' was the elimination of the second track by the GSR as an economy, starting with the westernmost portions, Oranmore to Galway in 1926 and Attymon Junction to Athenry in 1927. Then the public was informed in 1928 that the remainder of the route was to be singled, causing an immediate outburst, the matter being raised in the Dail, the GSR countering that with the most modern equipment it had become a practical proposition to make the change. Crossing loops were aligned for fast through running, the main track being straight, with both lines fully signalled in each direction, the route being equipped with the Webb Thompson Electric Train Staff system and mechanical staff changing. Conversion started at Ballinasloe and continued eastwards in stages to reach Athlone in 1928 and Mullingar during 1929. Ironically an Irish railway invention, the Bretland track layer, was used to lift the surplus track panels; A.W. Bretland was the last Chief Engineer of the MGWR when the device was first used in 1924 and it was built in collaboration with Herbert Morris of Loughborough (the London & North Eastern Railway also used the system). The horizontal jib of the relayer would lift out a 60ft length of track, stow it on a trailing wagon, bring forward a new section and lay it, then move on to the next section. Electrically powered, GSR notices described its work as 'electric relaying'.

The diversion of most Galway and Mayo trains away from their traditional route in 1973 finished the process of 'downgrading' the MGWR route, forecast when the singling took place, but with the passing years has proved in the main to be an improvement. The most recent change has been the replacement of Athlone MGWR station by the reopened former GS&WR station on 14 January 1985; then it became necessary for trains using the former main line through Mullingar to reverse at Athlone to reach the new station. Inevitably the use of that line became limited, timetabled trains ceasing in 1987, but there is the rare train.

ATHLONE BRANCH

Ambitions of the GS&WR to serve the west were curbed when the MGWR obtained its founding Acts, the former being confined to a branch from Portarlington to Tullamore in 1847. All through these years relations between the two railways and a third party, the Grand Canal, were strained. The GS&WR and the canal had a traffic agreement which the MGWR claimed was being used unfairly against it but to complicate matters the canal was anxious to sell. The outcome in 1853 was a seven year lease of the canal by the MGWR. An attempt by the two railways to buy the canal jointly in 1857 was barred by the BOT in London and then the MGWR went on the offensive, competing for Dublin and Limerick traffic, by rail to Athlone, Shannon steamers to Killaloe and a coach thence to Limerick, a journey of $10\frac{1}{2}$ hours but at half the GS&WR fare! Before long it was imperative that their differences be settled and so two arbitrators were appointed, Huish of the LNWR and Watkin of the Manchester, Sheffield & Lincolnshire Railway, hardly a pair to agree on anything, making it necessary to engage Leeman of the North Eastern Railway as umpire. No doubt it was Leeman who actually decided the outcome in 1860, the main result being a dividing line defining territories, from Dublin through Edenderry to Athlone, down the Shannon to Lough Derg and across to Ennis and the mouth of the Shannon. The canal was handed back to its reluctant owners.

The 1857 Act for extension to Athlone resulted from GS&WR support of Lord Lucan's plans for the Great Northern & Western Railway but the town was an important military depot and Government support ensured an easy passage through Parliament. Built by Dargan throughout, the first part of the line from Portarlington reached Tullamore (15½ miles) in 1854 and then Athlone (38¾ miles) in 1859 with an important intermediate station at Clara (22¾); the extension diverged from the original branch just outside Tullamore station and until resited in 1865 trains ran in and out of the original terminus, the new station being 16¼ miles from Portarlington. At Athlone the GS&WR station was built on the east side of the Shannon and reasonably close to the town centre, unlike the MGWR station which was on the other side of the river. There was no connection between the two railways at Athlone until October 1860 when exchange of wagons commenced, followed by passengers soon afterwards; the few through passengers were taken by a GS&WR train to the MGWR station, the train returning empty and vice versa.

A long time in building, the Midland Counties & Shannon Junction Railway, a long name for a short line, was authorised in 1861 to build a branch from the GS&WR Athlone route to Banagher and over the River Shannon to Meelick. French & Cheyne began in 1862 but work stopped in 1864 when the money ran out. Nothing happened until an Act of 1880 revived the line as the Clara & Banagher Railway but it needed a BOW loan and a Baronial guarantee to enable W.M. Murphy to build the 17½ miles from Clara to Banagher Junction (1½ miles north of Clara). Opened in 1884, extension to Meelick was not possible as the working company, the GS&WR, would have infringed the 1860 agreement by crossing the river; the local concern was absorbed by the GS&WR in 1895. Banagher, where the station was often inundated by the Shannon, now has but a thousand inhabitants, a third of the pre-Famine number. Passenger trains ceased in 1947 but goods continued until total closure at the end of 1962.

The Athlone branch of the GS&WR did not achieve any real importance until the 1973 changes made by CIE. In 1941 a siding diverging at 1½ miles from Portarlington was laid down to serve a new power station at Clonsast but it lasted only until 1965. A change to the destination of a train using the branch was a portent of things to come when during the summer 1950 timetable a morning train was extended to Galway and back. Then in 1953 one daily Galway train began to run via this route, although still using its usual Dublin terminus, Westland Row. It was twenty years before any more trains were diverted, being the majority for Galway and the Mayo line from 1973, using Heuston as their Dublin terminus. To cater for them an extra crossing place was put in between Clara and Athlone at Clonydonnin, 31 miles from Portarlington, coming into use in 1974. Reopening of the old GS&WR station at Athlone, closed in 1925, in place of the MGWR in 1985 has been described.

'A BLOT ON THE RAILWAY MAP OF IRELAND'

So stated Captain Mark Huish of the LNWR whilst giving Parliamentary evidence on behalf of the MGWR during 1860 when the company sought abandonment of powers for construction of the Streamstown and Clara branch, the consequence of attempts to prevent expansion of the GS&WR beyond Tullamore. In 1857 the MGWR had to be content with a shortened branch, but in reality there was no need for it; however there were demands from the mill owners in Clara that it be built, it being completed by J. Bagnell and opened in 1863.

This unwanted branch with its two daily trains, which usually ran through from Mullingar, lingered on. An early action by the GSR was the closure in 1925 of the exchange platforms at Clara and revision of timetables so that one engine could work both the Banagher and Streamstown lines, still working through to Mullingar. Despite its obvious lack of profitability, the line escaped listing for closure but its charmed life could not prevent suspension of its trains from 1941, only valuable spirits traffic from Horseleap remaining; even this had to stop in 1944. Goods resumed in late 1945 and passengers a year later for what proved to be a short-lived revival. All services were suspended in 1947, and afterwards this unwanted line lingered on with just a few trains until taken out of use in 1965 – a curious life of just a century from the time that the MGWR did not want it at all!

LOUGHREA BRANCH

Loughrea had expected to have a railway at an early date for it lay on the projected route of the Irish Great Western Railway at a time when it was a sizeable place with almost 5,500 inhabitants (down to 2,800 by 1962). The MGWR showing little enthusiasm for a branch but did serve the town with a cartage service from Woodlawn and appointed a local agent. Further attempts to get a branch were hampered by the opening of the A&EJR from Ennis to Athenry in 1869 with a station seven miles to the west of the town. In 1883 active promotion began, succeeding in 1885 when the MGWR agreed to work a Baronial Guaranteed line from a junction at Attymon. Worthington was the contractor and the Loughrea & Attymon Light

Railway opened its 9 miles in 1890. Galway County Council's auditor, in his check of the company's 1917 accounts when assessing the amount due as the Baronial Guarantee, found that the line had actually been in funds and so demanded the return of the sum paid by the council; that the money had been paid arose from the suspension of accounting during the war and was based on the 1913 results. The Government declined to make a refund, the matter went to Court and in 1919 the Irish Railway Executive Committee was empowered to settle with the local authority. Nominal independence was maintained until the company was absorbed into the GSR in 1925.

Threatened with closure at times, the branch had a longer life than its contemporaries, steam being replaced by small 160 hp diesel locomotives in 1962; the heating of the solitary passenger coach of each train was novel, storage heaters being installed and charged when standing at Loughrea. The service was doubled to four trains daily and the future seemed assured, having become the last rural branch in Ireland, but all trains ceased in late 1975.

OUT TO WILDEST CONNEMARA

The major Balfour line worked by the MGWR served Connemara but it took attempts over several years to get it built. Most schemes, one as early as 1866, favoured the direct inland road despite its lack of habitation, although one of 1872 planned a 3ft 6in gauge line along the coastal road on the north side of Galway Bay through Spiddal and Costello, even obtaining an Act. In an attempt to serve a greater population, a circuitous route was proposed from Galway through Headford, Cong, Leenane and Letterfrack to Clifden, 77 miles against the 50 of the direct road, but of course it was quite impracticable. The MGWR let it be known that it would work whichever route was chosen and in November 1890 the direct was selected. Tradition has it that Balfour, having enjoyed fishing in lakes close to the route, would hear of no other plan and so the opportunity was lost to build a coastal line, not much longer, that would have benefited many more people.

Robert Worthington had the initial contract to get the project started but the main contractor was Charles Braddock, well known in England, but within a year his company had collapsed. T.H. Falkiner completed the branch which opened during 1895 in two stages, firstly from Galway to Oughterard (17 miles) and thence to Clifden (49¼ miles). Apart from the problems of laying the line in boggy areas, it was necessary to cross the River Corrib just outside Galway, the bridge having three spans of 150ft and a Bascule lifting span of 21ft, with a small five lever cabin, interlocked with Galway, at the Clifden end. At Prospect Hill, Galway, there was a 240 yards long tunnel, on a 12 chains curve.

Connemara was much visited by the Victorians, Clifden (1,500 in 1851 but presently about 1,000) being the major centre. Before the branch was built, the MGWR subsidised car services from Galway and Westport for through travellers. The area is dominated by the Twelve Pins, a range with peaks in excess of 2,000ft, and has many loughs and sea inlets, all making it an area of great natural beauty. The MGWR purchased a hotel at Recess in 1895, fully rebuilding the place by 1898 and adding a platform (35³⁄₄ miles) to serve it in 1902; however closure came at the end of 1922 after the hotel had been burnt down maliciously.

Once the motor bus was established the Clifden line had no chance and all services ceased during 1935.

A PORT FOR GALWAY?

In 1911 a line of 1¹⁄₂ miles was laid from a junction with the Clifden branch just west of its crossing of the River Corrib to quarries at Shantalla to carry both granite and marble, built after a contract placed by the MGWR for ballast ensured sufficient traffic. There were still those who envisaged a future for Galway as a major trans-Atlantic port, but it would need a much larger harbour for ocean liners; those that did call had to stand off and use tenders to ferry passengers and luggage to and from Galway harbour. Worthington and 'others' were behind a 1912 scheme for the Galway (Barna) Railways & Harbours which intended to extend the quarry line for 3 miles to reach high water at Rushee Point, near Barna, and provide massive piers, necessary because of the shallowness of the bay, one of about 1¹⁄₄ miles to the east and another nearly as long one mile to the west. All this was to cost £1,500,000 but no Act was obtained and the Shantalla branch continued to carry the quarry products for a few more years, after which the track bed was incorporated into a major new road.

LORD LUCAN'S RAILWAY

Apart from the Grand Canal the GS&WR and MGWR were in conflict over a railway to serve the west coast north of Galway. Lord Lucan (of Crimean War fame) proposed in 1856 to continue the GS&WR northwards from Tullamore to serve Athlone, Roscommon, Castlerea and Sligo, a plan detrimental to the MGWR which would loose traffic from Athlone and greatly reduce the potential of its intended extension from Longford to Sligo. It was a revival of a planned Grand Junction Railway of Ireland promoted by the GS&WR in 1854. When Lucan obtained an Act in 1858

for the Great Northern & Western Railway he had to concede the
Tullamore and Athlone portion to the GS&WR and give up the Castlerea
to Sligo section to placate the MGWR. Lucan ran his railway from London
but it was worked by the MGWR; years of friction between the two companies followed, not resolved until they were amalgamated on 1 July 1890.
Constructed by Smith & Knight, the first portion (18¼ miles) opened to
Roscommon in 1860 and a considerable livestock traffic was soon established. Castlerea (34¾ miles), reached later in 1860, was the limit of the
1858 Act and the line continued to Castlebar (72 miles) under 1859 powers,
reaching Ballyhaunis (46) in 1861, and then Claremorris (56¾) and
Castlebar during 1862. Further extension was permitted by Acts of 1861
(Westport Quay) and 1862 (Ballina) but lack of capital and disagreements
delayed the works. Work on the Westport line had begun in 1962 (John
Rummens was the contractor) but suspended until J.W. Kelly of Belfast
resumed construction in 1865 so that Westport (83 miles) was reached early
in 1866. Kelly also made a start on the Ballina branch which opened from
Manulla Junction to Foxford (11 miles) in 1868, but further work stopped
when the money again ran out, trains not reaching Ballina (20¼) or
Westport Quay (84¾) until 1873. The latter soon came to the attention of
the BOT when the railway removed the signal interlocking as imperfect,
accepted by the inspecting officer when he was told during his visit in April
1875 that there was only a single passenger train daily.

Increasing traffic, especially cattle, made it necessary to double the line
from Athlone as far as Roscommon in 1879 and Claremorris expanded
considerably in 1892–5. There was just a single platform until 1892 but in
readiness for the Ballinrobe branch a loop and sidings were added, being
further enlarged in 1894 to accommodate the W&LR extension northwards
to Sligo. Thus a wayside station had expanded into a railway crossroads
with the addition of a branch.

The new branch served Ballinrobe, a small town with less than half of its
pre-Famine 2,700 persons, laying on the main road from Galway to
Castlebar; it had been on the course of the Connaught Junction Railway of
1844–5 from Loughrea to Ballina and Sligo. In 1862 the South Mayo
Railway planned a line from Claremorris through the town to Cong, with
steamers on Lough Corrib reaching Galway. The Baronially Guaranteed
Ballinrobe & Claremorris Light Railway was formed in 1884, backed by
Robert Worthington who built the line but it was not until 1890 that a
working agreement was made with the MGWR, the 12½ miles branch
opening in 1892; the local company remained independent until 1925.

All that materialised of plans to build railways along the northern coast of
Mayo was the 8 miles extension of the Ballina line to the severely-depopu-

lated village of Killala (1,446 in 1841, 970 in 1851, 654 in 1881 and 359 in 1962). T.H. Falkiner was the contractor and the line opened at the beginning of 1893. Traffic was light, trains being mixed and passenger traffic ceased in 1931, followed by complete closure in 1934.

Once in MGWR hands, becoming known as the 'Mayo Lines' the service, considering the population, was generally good but it was the cattle traffic that kept the line busy – for many years there was an interesting working between Castlerea and Cavan in each direction. Trains to Westport Quay were seasonal from 1889 and ceased at the end of the summer service of 1912, *Bradshaw* informing its users that there would be no more trains on and from 14 September. The GSR eliminated the double line from Athlone West Junction to Knockcroghery during 1930 and thence to Roscommon in 1931. Claremorris had built up a very substantial traffic in pilgrims from all over Ireland who used it as the railhead for the final seven miles of their journey to Knock, revered as a holy place since 1879. For many years pilgrims were mainly local, but sixty years ago travellers from further afield made it necessary to provide special trains, using Ballyhaunis initially. In 1936 Claremorris became the rail destination and the number of trains began to increase, bringing Sunday traffic to the area. From 1948 there was a rapid increase in the number of special trains and pilgrims, to the extent of some Sundays seeing a dozen or more from almost anywhere in the Emerald isle, including places on branches closed to passenger traffic. On such days Claremorris took on the role of major railway centre with such tasks as servicing trains, including restaurant cars, with water (and at one time gas) and turning and watering engines in steam days. In 1952 it was necessary to make changes which gave an extra platform by converting the down main platform into an island and at times even the cattle bank had to be pressed into use, accessible from either Sligo or Westport.

Surviving a closure threat in 1930 and the later suspensions, the Ballinrobe branch was the subject of an unusual experiment in its final years when CIE ran parallel road services at train times to assess public reaction – in retrospect it seems to have been a futile exercise, not delaying closure in 1960. Most of the smaller stations on the Mayo line closed in 1963 and from that year the Limerick and Sligo service was diverted to Ballina, causing much resentment as it was the solitary train to the town for many years.

THE ACHILL LINE

The area north and west of Westport offered nothing to railway promoters but its inhabitants who had become some of the poorest in Ireland needed better contact with the outside world, especially for fish, their main product. Belmullet is one of the most remote places within the British Isles and to visit it really does seem like a trip to the edge of the world; its population has surprisingly risen from 637 in 1841 to 935 in 1851 (but was down to 742 by 1962). In January 1884 the MGWR took notice of a planned Ballina and Belmullet Light Railway but it needed the 1889 and 1890 Acts to make a railway possible. Thus in January 1890 William Barrington's plans for a Westport and North Mayo Railway to build a 44 miles line to Belmullet were put before the MGWR Board and the Light Railway Commissioners who endorsed the project only from Westport to Mallarany, to be 5ft 3in gauge if worked by the railway company, otherwise narrow gauge. This arose from the uncertainty about the destination, Belmullet or Achill, as there were still plans for a line westwards from Ballina, either direct through Crossmolina (40 miles) or around the northern coast through Killala and Ballycastle (47 miles). The whole district, being steadily depopulated, rated high in the list of congested areas and needed Government intervention to get a railway built. A.J. Balfour, M.P. (Chief Secretary for Ireland), visited the area in the autumn of 1889 and very quickly made the decision to extend to Achill; tradition has it that when he arrived at Achill there was a large public demonstration wholly in favour of a line, a sharp contrast to his visit to Belmullet where he got a hostile reception at the hands of those who saw the railway as a threat to their livelihood as jarvies and carters (although the *Connaught Telegraph* stated that there was no demonstration of any kind, either friendly or hostile, at Belmullet, but did describe the Achill welcome).

As usual with Government-funded lines, each project was separately organised so that the Westport & Mullarany Railway came into being with Robert Worthington as contractor. As soon as Achill became the destination, Balfour brushed aside the red tape and within a month Worthington started the job. In fact many provisions of the relevant Acts seem to have been ignored, especially the requirement that an existing company was to promote or undertake the working, so it is just as well that the MGWR did come to an agreement with the BOW, which was entirely responsible for the Achill Extension Railway, handing it over on completion. Achill Island (population 5,260 in 1962), is separated from Co Mayo by Achill Sound, bridged in 1888 by a swivel bridge.

The line opened first to Newport ($7^3/4$ miles) and then Mallarany ($18^1/2$ miles) during 1894 but as no agreement had been reached over a junction between the two projects Worthington had to provide a temporary platform on the connection between his two contracts, replaced by a new station when the line opened through to Achill ($26^1/2$ miles) in 1895. It was not an easy line, requiring viaducts at Westport and Newport and a tunnel (133 yards) just north of Newport viaduct. It was soon necessary to divert the route just south of Newport for 35 chains where there had been a sharp curve round the side of a hill which was then pierced by a tunnel of 88 yards. It is probably not unfair to say that the line was too substantial and over-equipped for the traffic potential, with a service of three each way, some through connections with Dublin. The branch experienced non-steam traction at an early date when a petrol-engined railcar was provided to work the mail service, starting in November 1911 and lasting until 1916 – it as the first such vehicle in Ireland to carry passengers.

Like the other Balfour lines the branch to Achill was an early closure, losing its trains in 1935; however, the local roads were not yet in a fit state for buses and so the trains resumed during 1936 lasting only until total closure during 1937. The railway retained a connection with Mulrany (as Mallarany had become known) by running the Great Southern Hotel which had been opened by the MGWR during 1897 but it was sold by CIE in 1977.

A SECOND MAIN LINE

Sligo was a town of some importance before the Famine with over 12,000 inhabitants (then seventh in Ireland) but suffered heavily during the Famine to become fifteenth when the railway arrived in 1862, but has now recovered its population. The very earliest proposals envisaged serving the town by a route from Mullingar closely similar to that eventually built but the only early Act (1846) empowered a short line, never built, the Sligo & Shannon Junction Railway which intended to connect the Arigna coal mines with Lough Gill just to the east of Sligo, a distance of 13 miles. There were several grandiose schemes but it was never doubted that the MGWR would eventually reach the town, even after a Bill of 1846 had been withdrawn and a subsequent Act of 1852 granted powers only from Mullingar to Longford and Cavan; serving the latter was not expected to be profitable, its purpose being to gain traffic between Belfast and Galway. Originally it was intended to diverge from the Galway line at Belmont, three miles west of Mullingar, with the Cavan branch junction at Rathaspick (about two miles south west of the later Street & Rathown station) but by adopting a more easterly course the branch was shortened.

Wm Dargan built both lines, completing that to Longford (26 miles from Mullingar) first so that it opened in 1855. A platform was provided at Clonhugh for the Earl of Granard who had the right to stop any train – years later in 1873–4 his successor, Lord Granville, argued the point, wanting to use the evening train, but the railway had its way by taking the service out of the timetable! The Cavan branch (24³/₄ miles) was ready soon after the Longford line, opening in 1856; an exchange station was provided at the junction, 10³/₄ miles from Mullingar, called Cavan Junction until 1878 when it became the better known Inny Junction, nor did it appear consistently in timetables until 1882. On the Cavan line Float derived its name from a ferry across the River Inny some two miles away on the Castlepollard road, the nearest place of any consequence. The line from Mullingar as far as Cavan Junction was doubled in 1858 and thence to Longford in 1878.

The 1856 plans to build the North Western Railway of Ireland (initially styled as the Grand Junction Railway of Ireland) from Longford through Ballaghaderreen to Castlebar and Ballina failed despite MGWR support, largely due to the plans of the GN&WR already mentioned. Compromise in 1857 gave the MGWR powers to build from Longford to Strokestown, Boyle and Sligo, but once the GN&WR had shown its intentions the MGWR realised that it was more sensible to avoid mid-Roscommon and take its line through Carrick-on-Shannon, obtaining a deviation Act in 1859, the reason for quite an abrupt change of direction just after leaving Longford for Sligo.

Smith & Knight built the line, the whole section of 58 miles opening in late 1862 to a temporary terminus at Sligo (84 miles from Mullingar). The permanent station at Sligo did not get approval until early 1864 and presumably came into use immediately. At the same time the second track from Ballysodare to Sligo came into use. For goods traffic there was a separate goods depot on a branch of one mile down to the quays west of the station. A bridge across the River Shannon a mile south of Drumsna was interesting, having an opening span, described as 'telescopic', being drawn back rather than swivelling.

Ballaghadereen (1,400 persons) in the north west corner of Co Roscommon and an important market town agitated for a line as soon as the Sligo route was working, the Sligo & Ballaghadereen Junction Railway getting Acts in 1863 and 1866. The company was based in London and in common with others so managed had great difficulty in raising capital. Eventually the 9¹/₂ miles branch from Kilfree Junction, built by Nowell, opened in 1874, worked by the MGWR on a one year term. This was a wise move as the service was suspended entirely for three months in 1876 due to lack of traffic, resuming when a guarantee against loss had been negotiated. The owners were more than happy to sell their line to the MGWR in 1879.

Several times a proposal had been put forward for a line from the Cavan branch to go through to Enniskillen and eventually the MGWR agreed to work the portion authorised in 1883. Thus the 7 mile line from Crossdoney to Killeshandra, built by Walter Scott, opened in 1886 but there was never much traffic, despite which there were repeated calls for extension to Enniskillen by continuing the line through Swanlinbar to meet the SL&NCR at Florencecourt, traversing difficult almost uninhabited country.

When the SL&NCR completed its final section from its station at Collooney to a junction with the MGWR at Carrignagat (78½ miles from Mullingar) in 1882 the MGWR extended the double line southwards from Ballysodare. Running powers allowed the SL&NCR to enter Sligo and use the quay branch and now the town had direct rail communication with Ulster. The third approach to Sligo gave the W&LR entry in 1895, the junction also being at Collooney, but further south; the short section of 24 chains from the MGWR station to the new junction was doubled in 1897, but the next 62 chains to Carrignagat Junction remained single.

Sligo station was maliciously destroyed in 1922 and its rebuilding not being completed until 1928, when The Great Southern Hotel was opened; it was sold in 1977 and renamed the Southern. The MGWR singled the section between Inny Junction and Longford in 1924 and the GSR the remainder to Mullingar in 1929. In 1930 Carrignagat Junction was eliminated, the old up line from Ballysodare being retained solely for SL&NCR trains; later that year the short doubled section from Collooney to Collooney North Junction was singled and power points at the latter, controlled from Ballysodare, replaced the cabin. When Inny Junction was closed in 1931, passengers changing between Cavan and Sligo line trains had to do so at Multyfarnham (3½ miles nearer Mullingar at no extra fare!) and the cabin was replaced by power points. Afterwards the only users of Inny Junction were railway families who could use solitary up and down trains on Thursdays and Saturdays – in fact they had no other means of transport as there had never been a road of any description to the site of the junction.

The Sligo route was regarded as the second main line of the MGWR and services have continued throughout, other than that 1947 coal famine suspension, although in recent years there has been much concern over the state of the route, only now getting attention to upgrade its track. Many of the lesser stations were closed in 1963 and more recently the number of block posts has been severely reduced, there now being only five between Mullingar and Sligo, the last section from Boyle being no less than 27¾ miles. The last section of double line, Ballysodare to Sligo, was singled in 1959 after the closure of the SL&NCR in 1957.

The Killeshandra branch lost its regular trains in the 1947 coal famine, making do with a few cattle workings and excursions until complete closure in 1955. The Cavan line always had limited traffic levels, although most of its trains ran separately from Dublin. During 1918 a down Sligo train slipped a Cavan coach at Inny Junction – the curiosity was that a light engine to collect it had run ahead from Mullingar! Passenger trains were suspended during World War II years and permanently in 1947; even goods trains ceased for a while that year. However the CIE station at Cavan remained in use until trains on the GNR line from Clones were terminated in 1957. Complete closure to Cavan followed in 1960. The Ballaghadereen branch retained its trains until closure in 1963; from 1947 there were only trains during the morning and early afternoon, the last working finishing at Ballaghadereen at 2pm.

COAL BY NARROW GAUGE

Ireland's best known source of coal lies in Co Leitrim in the Arigna area close to Lough Allen but it was not coal that subsequently attracted railway promoters for there were numerous livestock fairs at the towns of Ballyconnell, Ballinamore, Drumshambo and Mohill. An attempt to cater for general trade was made by the opening of the Ballinamore & Ballyconnell Canal in 1860 but it was a dismal failure, tradition having it that only *eight* boats used it before it fell into disuse in 1869. In 1872 the MGWR was asked to build a branch from Dromod to Ballinamore but was not interested at the time; a decade later a similar line was proposed, coming to fruition when the 1883 Act encouraged local formation of the Cavan, Leitrim & Roscommon Light Railway & Tramway Co Ltd which gained approval and Baronial Guarantees for a line from Dromod to Ballinamore and Belturbet, which was to become the terminus of a GNR branch in 1885, with a branch from Ballinamore to Arigna and on to Boyle in Co Roscommon; a short 2 miles extension from Dromod to Roosky on the Shannon was not approved. In 1895 the title was shortened to Cavan & Leitrim Railway Co Ltd as little of the mileage authorised in Co Roscommon had been built. The local population as small, Mohill falling from 1,600 in 1841 to under 1,000 in 1961 and Belturbet dropping from 2,000 to 1,100; nowhere else had remotely near a thousand inhabitants. Collen Bros constructed the system which opened from Dromod to Belturbet in 1887 and Ballinamore to Arigna in 1888, the latter a roadside tramway. Arigna and the last 1½ miles were in Co Roscommon but after that county withdrew its support the ratepayers of Co Leitrim became responsible for the guarantee.

From the start the railway was a liability, partly because of the failure to built the Arigna to Boyle line and the Roosky extension which deprived the line of worthwhile cattle traffic. The coal mines were three miles beyond

Arigna; mining had been long established and an ironworks was started in 1830 but was not a success. A tramway connected the two but was little used, its formation surviving to be incorporated into a mineral extension in due course. There were attempts to build an extension in 1901–5, the latter making some progress until local hostility towards the Arigna Mining Co and its close relationship to the railway erupted into anger and stopped all activities. Then came the Sligo & Arigna Railway, authorised in 1908 to construct a line to Sligo Quay, having a mixed gauge portion at the Arigna end and to be worked by the MGWR, all endeavours coming to an end in 1914 when Leitrim County Council killed any hope of progress.

It took a war to get a railway built to the Arigna mines, the Government using powers incorporated in the Defence of the Realm Act, 1871. The GNR was put in charge of construction and the line followed the winding Arigna River and then the old tramway course, being constructed in 1918–9 but it was too late for the real war effort, not opening until 1920, the C&LR borrowing two NCC 0-4-2ST engines and forty wagons to augment its own stock. The extension to Aughabehy was $4^{1}/_{4}$ miles long, serving Derreenavoggy coal pits at $1^{1}/_{2}$ miles; at Aughabehy there was an inclined plane (2ft gauge) to the Arigna Mining Co pit but output was small, five wagons a day being usual. At the amalgamation the extension remained the property of the BOW, worked by the GSR until leased at one shilling per annum from 1 January 1929.

The C&LR had over many years covered its operating costs but there was never enough to cover interest and by 1924 losses were becoming alarming. The line continued much as before under the GSR, its staff showing a healthy independence and rather contemptuous of HQ staff; during 1930 the Arigna Valley line was cut back to Derreenavoggy and in 1931 the whole tramway section was threatened when the GSR board ordered closure in a minute dated 1 May that year, but in fact there is nothing to show that it did close. The GSR and later CIE transferred engines and rolling stock so that the line became a mecca for enthusiasts, who in its later years, could see locomotives originating from three of the six narrow gauge railways taken over by the GSR. Coal traffic was heavy at times, requiring its own trains and in 1956 an assured future seemed possible when Arigna coal started flowing to Drogheda for the cement works, CIE transferring a former T&DLR engine from the West Clare to help. The pace slowed in 1958 and the end came soon enough for on 1 April 1959 services were no more. Thus it was no longer possible to travel on a roadside line, steam hauled and sometimes in one of the original 1887 coaches with access from open end platforms. No more would there be collisions with motor vehicles at any of the many places where trains seemed suddenly to jump from one side to the other of the highway, nor would enthusiasts make their way to a remote and quiet part of Ireland to see the past in action.

Very recently, on 2 June 1993, the Cavan & Leitrim Railway was re-incorporated in order to rebuild part of the line. Work quickly started on the first half mile at Dromod with the hope of reaching Mohill. It will be some time before trains run again.

FROM SOUTH TO NORTH

The continuation of the Limerick and Ennis line to the north involved five separate companies and took 35 years to complete. Other than Ennis and Sligo there were no places of much size, Tuam being the largest, on the route of 145½ miles from Limerick, nor was the country much better than the poorest in Ireland, being mostly unsuitable for agriculture. On completion in 1895 the entire route was worked by the Waterford & Limerick Railway which then changed its title to Waterford, Limerick & Western Railway on 1 January 1896; a proposed name Irish Great Western Railway had raised protests from the MGWR.

The line from Ennis to Athenry and Tuam was built by two closely associated railways, worked by the W&LR from 1872 until absorbed in 1893. The older was the Athenry & Tuam Railway, authorised in 1858, built by Dargan and opened in 1860, the MGWR agreeing to work the line for ten years. Looses were heavy and new terms could not be agreed so in 1870 the A&TR had to find its own means of working. The Galway & Ennis Grand Junction Railway was proposed in 1845 but nothing transpired until 1859 when the Athenry & Ennis Junction Railway was formed, getting an Act in 1860; Athenry was chosen as the northern junction, rather than Oranmore which would have bee more suitable for Galway, in order to join the Tuam line. The W&LR agreed working terms in 1863 soon after W. Munroe of London began construction, but everything came to a stand when he could not be paid. After work resumed in 1865 Munroe became bankrupt and his successor Chambers soon dropped out, leaving Edgeworth and Stanford of Dublin to resume work in 1867. The A&EJR then cancelled the W&LR agreement and tried the MGWR, but failed as it could not repay the £6,000 advanced by the W&LR in 1863. This left the A&EJR to find its own means of working, having to purchase or borrow old engines and rolling stock, before it could open its 34¾ miles of line in 1869.

Neither of the Athenry companies had much success at working, their engines being so decrepit that frequent breakdowns made it necessary to borrow other engines, and they were continually harassed by creditors – on 10 November 1870 the Co Clare sheriff took possession of a train but allowed it to proceed with a posse of bailiffs on the footplate who in turn were put off by the Co Galway sheriff at Gort four days later, the train being impounded. The problem went back to Munroe's bankruptcy but it was found the coaches still belonged to a finance company, only the engine belonging to the A&EJR; when it was put up for sale only the railway made a bid and so found itself buying its own engine back! No wonder working was handed to the W&LR in 1872, the latter finding itself the reluctant custodian of six old engines, 14 carriages and 57 other vehicles, all very run down.

The W&LR integrated the services so that they became through workings from Limerick to Tuam. In November 1874 only four engines were required to work the entire service north of Limerick:

1. 2.30am   Limerick–Tuam (2.45pm) pass & goods,
    3.45pm   Tuam–Limerick (9.40pm) pass & goods,
2. 7.45am   Ennis–Limerick (9.10am) pass,
    9.55am   Limerick–Athenry (1.40pm) pass,
    4.40pm   Athenry–Tuam (5.25pm) pass,
3. 6.15am   Tuam–Limerick (11.20am) pass,
    3.20pm   Limerick–Tuam (7.40pm) pass,
4. 8.45am   Tuam–Athenry (9.25am) pass,
    10.0am   Athenry–Tuam (10.35am) pass,
    11.35am Tuam–Athenry (12.10pm) pass,
    2.0pm   Athenry–Limerick (6.15pm) pass,
    6.55pm   Limerick–Ennis (8.20pm) pass.

At a time when railwaymen worked long hours, the W&LR had the reputation of working its staff to excess and it is very probably that the enginemen worked the same duties as those shown above for the engines, including the three-day cycle from Ennis.

Naturally the MGWR was keen to prevent any further extension by the W&LR and attempted to purchase both the Athenry railways, very nearly succeeding in 1892; had the MGWR done so the chances of a line running north from Tuam would have been very slight although the clumsily but accurately-named Athenry & Tuam Extension to Claremorris Railway (usually Athenry & Tuam Extension Railway) had already been authorised in 1890. With no likelihood of being in the least remunerative it required a Baronial Guarantee before W.M. Murphy could build the line which opened in 1894 to a temporary terminus at Claremorris (93 miles from Limerick). Worked by the W&LR and then the GS&WR the railway remained an independent concern until 1925.

The Light Railways Acts of 1889 and 1890 were used to construct the final portion of the Limerick and Sligo route. Two companies were formed, the Claremorris & Swinford Railway and the Collooney & Swinford Railway, necessary as the first was in Co Mayo and the second in Co Sligo which guaranteed interest on £40,000 and £80,000 respectively, but in reality the companies seem never to have existed. Even with these guarantees the Government had to make a free grant of £146,042, some of it for engines and rolling stock which were, however part of the ordinary stock of the W&LR. The Grand Juries had initiated the project as relief works but the real originator was Henry Tottenham of the SL&NCR; he wanted that railway to work the line but failing to get its interest he persuaded the W&LR to step in. Robert Worthington started the job but had to hand over to Fisher & LeFanu due to bankruptcy, the 46½ miles of line opening in 1895 from the 1894 terminus to the MGWR station at Claremorris and then on to the latter at Collooney. There was a connecting line, 46 chains long, which passed under the MGWR line to join the SL&NCR at its Collooney station; it was available for goods traffic from the opening of the Claremorris line but was not passed for passenger trains until July 1896. The route north from Claremorris offered only meagre traffic, despite which the stations were all subsequently built – after all the Government was providing the money! The route became valuable as a through line for livestock which passed onto the SL&NCR and then the GNR for export from Belfast.

The events leading to the amalgamation of the WL&WR and the GS&WR in 1901 have been alluded to but the necessary Act was not obtained without counter moves by the MGWR; while tolerant of the weaker company it certainly did not want the far more powerful company in its area. Both the MGWR and GS&WR put up Bills in 1900 but Parliament decided in favour of the latter, a move generally welcomed by local interests which believed that they would benefit from competition, much regretted a few years later when complaints were voiced to the 1906 Vice-Regal Commission. All that the MGWR obtained was the granting of running powers from Athenry to Limerick. The passenger service, a single Limerick to Athenry train and back started on 1 June 1902, but lasted for only a few months. The goods also ran from Limerick to Athenry and back and lasted until January 1910, cattle specials continuing until the end of 1911. The MGWR thus kept a couple of engines at Limerick for these trains.

Little changed through the years but in 1934 a beet factory was established at Tuam, having three tank engines of German make. With a reduced service after 1947, trains continued to connect Limerick and Sligo until the passenger service ceased between Claremorris and Sligo in 1963, several of the other intermediate stations closing at the same time. Goods trains continued to run to Sligo until the section closed completely in 1975. From 1976 the entire route was without daily passenger trains but continued in use for Sunday specials to Claremorris and for limited through freight workings. More recently the passenger specials have ceased and Tuam beet factory closed in June 1985. The route was downgraded in 1991, closing for a while so that the better condition rails could be recovered for use elsewhere, traffic resuming between Ennis and Athenry during 1992 and on to Claremorris two years later. Its future relies on continued cement and fertiliser trains.

PLANS AND MORE PLANS

Several proposals have been mentioned but there were numerous other schemes, some extremely ambitious and really beyond realism. The Roscommon Central Light Railway planned in 1884 to continue the C&LR from Dromod to Roosky, with a crossing of the Shannon, and Strokestown, where a branch from Carrick-on-Shannon would join, continuing to Roscommon, 25 miles of main line and 15 miles of branch. In the same year there were plans to connect Longford and Strokestown and Roscommon and Woodlawn, the Roscommon & Mount Bellaw Steam Tramway and the Woodlawn, Mount Bellow & Mount Talbot Tramway competing for promotion. Roosky continued to beckon the C&LR directors who decided to try again in 1898 and 1901 but by 1908 all chance of the extension had died.

An ambitious scheme to extend the planned Newry, Keady & Tynan Railway even further west than empowered (see Chapter Seven) was launched so that there would be a *narrow gauge* railway all the way across Ireland from Greenore to Clifden by way of Roscommon, Tuam, Cong and Leenane after crossing the Shannon, with branches to Ballinrobe and Galway from a junction at Shrule in Co Galway. The Ulster & Connaught Light Railway, first mentioned in 1888, lay dormant until 1905 but in the meantime the C&LR and the CVR had discussed a connecting line, the Bawnboy & Maguiresbridge Railway, before the idea was adopted by the Ulster & Connaught when it obtained its Act in 1906. By 1910 this grandiose plan had been put aside – the reader is left to imagine for himself a journey of 234 miles across Ireland in a narrow gauge train, taking ten or more hours, and very likely the solitary passenger at times for there were few to be gained from most of the route through thinly-populated counties.

Other schemes of these years, using the 1889 Light Railways Act, envisaged a line from Ballaghaderreen to Castlerea which the MGWR supported in opposition to the Claremorris and Collooney line. The MGWR also agreed to work two planned branches from the Achill line, the first in 1897 for a goods line to a proposed pier on Achill Sound, the second in 1903–4 from just north of Westport to an intended pier at Inishlyre. Belmullet again became the objective of a railway along the north coast of Sligo and Mayo when in 1908 the Collooncy, Ballina & Belmullet Railways & Pier Co obtained an Act. As with schemes half a century before, the attraction was a shorter crossing of the North Atlantic but this time the promoters were more ambitious, dreaming of an 'All-Red' route between Britain and Australia via Canada, using Belmullet as its port. The final madness of the schemers was the hope of laying down a third rail over the SL&NCR and GNR through to Belfast, connecting with Britain's railways by a tunnel under the North Channel. Despite further Acts in 1911 and 1912, the whole idea fell through – would there really have been a worthwhile saving in time when a passage across the Atlantic would begin with a train journey of almost 700 miles from London, not much shorter than going to the extreme north of Scotland?

NON-PUBLIC RAILWAYS

The narrow gauge is not dead in Ireland! There is still an extensive mileage, mostly 3ft gauge, but some of 2ft as well, serving the turf bogs of Bord na Mona, most of which lie in the midlands, and carrying cut turf to factories and power stations. Apart from these lines there were others to be mentioned. There was an early line in Co Galway, certainly being there in 1864, connecting quarries of the Marble & Stone Co of Ireland with a wharf on Lough Corrib at Anglingham, four miles north of Galway city.

A 2ft gauge line existed from 1906 until 1922 in Connemara near Clifden to serve the wireless station of the Marconi Wireless Telegraph Co Ltd. Only 1¼ miles long, it crossed a bog to connect the station with a road, being used to carry construction materials and then supplies for the station. The place has its niche in the history books for its was from here in 1907 that the first trans-Atlantic radio messages were exchanged with Canada. In 1919 the line again enjoyed a historical event when the aviation pioneers Alcock and Brown made their landfall close by at the end of the first powered flight across the Atlantic and were helped out of their damaged plane by Marconi staff. Use came to an end when the station was totally wrecked in the Civil War; what plant could be salvaged was taken to a site in Wales, including the little Dick, Kerr 0–4-0ST.

On Achill Island whitestone was quarried in the hills on the north side and the Irish Industrial Minerals Co laid down a 2ft gauge line to carry the stone to a quay at Keel, much of the produce being sent to the Potteries of

Staffordshire. It lasted from 1910 to 1916. In the extremes of Co Mayo there were two small lines at whaling stations owned by Norwegians, one at Rusheen on Inishea South Island to west of the end of the Mullet peninsula stretching southward from Belmullet and the other at Elly Point on the other side of the peninsula; the former was in use from 1910 until 1914, the latter from 1908 to 1913. Propelled by hand, coal, etc was received and oil, fertiliser and other products taken to waiting vessels; the gauge is not on record. At Blacksod Point, the very tip of the Mullet peninsula, an English company worked granite quarries and in 1887 set about laying down a tramway to a pier near the lighthouse. The route crossed land owned by the Commissioners of Irish Lights but had to be abandoned in 1891 when they wanted it back. In 1900 the quarries reopened and a new tramway was built, the Commissioners allowing passage across their estates, but by 1907 the quarry had ceased production. Wagons were manhandled apart from being hauled up into the quarry by a winch. Part of the course is still visible, the rest having been washed away by the sea. It would appear that some of the track was moved to a site at Pickle Point close to Belmullet but whether it was used has not been ascertained.

One of the earliest attempts to process turf was started in 1860 some three miles north of Monasterevan when Charles Hodgson set up the Derrylea Peat Works. He not only built a tramway (5ft 3in gauge) to carry the produce to a wharf on the Grand Canal's Athy branch but used tracks to carry a patent turf cutting machine, driven by a six horse-power portable engine. However, the price of imported coal deterred the use of turf and the works closed down about 1867, but it had shown that mechanical rather than hand cutting was feasible. A list of plant for sale in 1870 indicates that there was a locomotive, an adapted Robey traction engine.

The greater part of Bord na Mona's bog railways lie east of the Shannon, north of the Dublin and Cork main line in Cos Offaly, Roscommon and Longford, with outposts in Galway and Mayo. It was in Co Offaly that a cutting machine was first used successfully in 1924, the bog supplying a small power station near Ferbane. Greater Government interest was shown in 1934 by setting up the Turf Development Board and demand was huge when domestic coal supplies were virtually non-existent during World War II after which Bord na Mona was established in 1946. Large areas are now being cut and the only way to move the turf from the cutting beds is by rail, conveyers being far too expensive and roads impossible to establish without affecting the bog underneath. The bulk of production is taken to power stations built adjacent to the major bogs by the permanent tracks, tempo-rary lines being used as needed in the working areas; as tracks extended, several of these systems have been joined together. Power stations are situated at Portarlington, Ferbane, Rhode and Shannonbridge (Co Offaly), Lanesborough at the north end of Lough Ree (Cos Longford and Roscommon) and Bellacoorick (Co Mayo, west of Ballina). The first-named is the oldest, dating from 1941, others date from 1957–62 and the most recent is Shannonbridge (1968), all operated by Bord Solathair an Leictreachais (Electricity Supply Board). Bord na Mona attempted to use steam locomotives, built by Barclay in 1949, having fireboxes designed for turf burning, but they were not very successful on tracks over a bog, diesels proving much more versatile and able to cope with the temporary tracks. Several makes were tried and then Bord na Mona, with the help of Hunslet of Leeds, designed the very capable 'Wagonmaster' locomotives, nearly one hundred being produced. The total fleet has been as many as 250 locomotives and well in excess of 3,000 wagons and a few coaches and small railcars for staff use. Two major features are bridges across the River Shannon, the oldest at Kilnacarrow (near Lanesborough) being 386ft long, built in 1958, the other more recently (1968) at Shannonbridge being 525ft long; this bridge gives access to bogs in Cos Roscommon and Galway. The Grand Canal is crossed at Rhode by a lifting span, installed in 1960 (there is another at Allenwood in Co Kildare, dating from 1952).

Other uses of turf are for briquettes and moss peat for gardeners, the latter being an export industry. Smaller bogs in the Attymon area met some of the latter needs and had a small railway system. A decade ago a new area in Cos Roscommon and Galway lying to the west of Athlone and north of Ballinasloe came under development, serving a plant at Ballyforan, some 15 miles west of Athlone; its system is now connected to those in Co Offaly. Part of the newest area took over an earlier farming area which produced animal feed stock, run by CSE until 1978, having used a 2ft gauge system to carry cut grass to the factory. There is a limited life for turf removal and it is likely that use at power stations may well cease in the first decade of the twenty-first century.

PRESERVATION

Bord na Mona now has a visitor centre at the Blackwater workings near Shannonbridge in Co Offaly and associated with it there is a 45 minutes tour of some five miles over the bog lines, a diesel hauling a coach with the legend *Clonmacnoise & West Offaly Railway*. Westrail is a group based at Tuam station and in 1989 commenced a summertime steam service to Athenry, using the former Castleisland engine mentioned in Chapter Five. From 1991 the service was altered to run between Athenry and Galway.

CHAPTER VII

Dundalk to Donegal

The railway connecting the two political centres of Ireland runs northward close to the east coast and is now the only one left of all described in this chapter, broadly the south and west side of the province of Ulster. Northern Ireland Government policy of forty years ago ensured that none of the others would survive; perhaps those last to close in 1965, to Londonderry and to Newry and Warrenpoint, might have had a future, but it is difficult to see how the others could have lasted much longer than they did. The towns in the area are not large other than Londonderry (more usually Derry) with little more than 31,000 at the present, a drastic fall from 53,000 only thirty years ago or 40,000 at the turn of the century, although greater than the 15,000 before the Famine. Other towns are Dundalk (22,000), Newry (11,000), Armagh (10,000), Enniskillen (6,500), Omagh (28,000), Ballyshannon (2,500), Donegal (1,500), Strabane (7,800) and Letterkenny (5,000). Of these Dundalk has doubled in size since 1841, becoming a manufacturing town associated with footwear, brewing and tobacco (and a railway works), Armagh has recovered from a slump to 7,400 in 1911, Newry has only a little fewer than 1841, although rather down on its 13,400 of 1871, Strabane has nearly doubled in size since 1841 and so has Letterkenny, other being much the same, apart from Omagh where growth has been spectacular in recent years, a mere 3,000 in 1841, some 8,000 in 1961 and now the 28,000 given above. The failure of Newry to expand is a direct consequence of the success of the Ulster Railway which assisted Belfast's industrial growth and its domination of the north.

The east coast north from Dublin Bay to Dundalk is low lying, bordered on the north side by the Carlingford Mountains which form a barrier between Leinster and Ulster. Inland there are areas of higher ground and broader valleys with many loughs in the Cavan and Enniskillen vicinity, leading to the extensive Lough Erne north west of the latter town. To the north west the 'Donegal Highlands' have several peaks in an area which for years was as poor as any in Ireland. Londonderry stands astride the River

Foyle and has seen considerable importance as a British naval base at times of conflict. West of the lough the Inishowen peninsula nowadays provides the geographical curiosity that the 'furthest north' point of Ireland lies in the 'South'.

Before the railways, canals gave some service to the area; Newry has a long history as a port, an Act of 1755 establishing the original ship canal, enlarged in 1850 and still in use. From this port the Newry Canal, completed in 1742 and which carried trade until 1949, traversed the gap between the high ground of Cos Armagh and Down to join the Upper Bann near Portadown. The Upper Bann flows into Lough Neagh, the largest tract of freshwater (150 square miles) in the British Isles, and from its south western corner two other short canals, the Tyrone Navigation and Ducart's Canal, served collieries in the Coalisland area; the latter used three incline planes instead of locks. The much longer Ulster Canal was started in 1825 and by 1841 had connected Lough Neagh with Clones and Upper Lough Erne, making navigation possible from Newry or Belfast to Enniskillen and Belleek at the far end of Lower Lough Erne. Strabane, even then a prosperous market town, was connected by a short canal northwards to join the River Foyle; finished in 1796, it held its own against the Londonderry & Enniskillen Railway for many years and continued in business until 1962.

A feature of several lines in this area was the provision of numerous wayside stopping places, often at road level crossings, at which small railcars and railbuses could stop once diesel traction became an economical means of running local trains. The long route from Dundalk to Enniskillen and Omagh had at various times no less than 37 such stops and there were twelve between Portadown and Omagh; the CDRJC had as many as 32 such stops and there were several on the Clogher Valley, other GNR branches and the DN&GR also having some. Few were advertised and even fewer were mentioned in the timetables, being provided as necessary to meet a purely local requirement. One on the GNR main line, Aughteranter between Coraghwood and Scarva, lasted until 1965. Such stops were to be found elsewhere in Ireland to a lesser extent.

NORTHWARDS INTO ULSTER

The gap between the Dublin & Drogheda Railway and the Ulster Railway was 55¼ miles and it took eight years from incorporation in 1845 to achieve unbroken travel by rail, the last section being the completion of the crossing of the Boyne as described in Chapter Two. From the temporary terminus at Newfoundwell, a quarter-mile north of the viaduct, it was comparatively easy for Hammond, Murray & Patterson to build the line as far as the White

River, just north of Dunleer, and Killeen & Moore the rest of the way to Dundalk Junction (53³/₄ miles from Amiens Street), opened on 15 February 1849. On the same day the D&ER opened as far as Castleblayney, and with a road journey of 18 miles to Armagh, cut the overall journey from Dublin to Belfast to about eight hours. A little to the north of the Boyne viaduct a cement works was connected to the main line at 32¹/₂ miles by a branch (1¹/₄ miles) in 1938 but production ceased about twenty years ago.

Ardee, a small town of some 2,700, lies to the west of the GNR main line and remained without a railway until the 4³/₄ miles branch from Dromin Junction opened in 1896, having been authorised in 1892. In fact it was a plan of 1884 to lay down a roadside steam tramway from Dundalk that prompted GNR action. The branch was a typical short spur and survived the 1933 strike but not for long as passenger trains ceased during 1934, its goods service continuing until 1975, the line having been worked latterly as a siding.

North of Dundalk the promoters chose the direct course using the Moyry Gap instead of diverting round the coast through Carlingford and Newry to avoid the mountains of the peninsula. This left the important centre of Newry off the line, a situation that had drastic implications for both the town and the local railways. Northward the line shadowed the course of the Newry Canal for most of the way to Portadown and a junction with the Ulster Railway, although some shareholders wanted a more direct route towards Belfast through Banbridge and Dromore. Construction of the route from Dundalk through South Armagh (an area these days known as 'bandit country' where trains in the last twenty years have been attacked far too often – the GNR main line has probably been disrupted more than any other in history) was shared by the Moore brothers who built 9¹/₄ miles to Meigh, and Killeen & Moor who continued for 7³/₄ miles to Mullaglass; they built the great Craigmore viaduct, the largest masonry structure on Ireland's railways with its eighteen arches of 60ft span, the highest being as much as 140ft above the valley floor and the cause of delayed opening. From Dundalk trains were extended as far as Wellington Inn (1¹/₂ miles north of Meigh), a temporary station, on 31 July 1850, road coaches then ran to Portadown to make the Belfast connection. Once the Craigmore viaduct was ready, trains ran on to Mullaglass (70¹/₂) as from 10 June 1852 and through to Portadown (87¹/₄) as that section had already opened on 6 January 1852, being constructed by Dargan & McCormick. Mullaglass was the station for Newry, two miles down the road, but it was replaced by Newry Main Line in 1855, a mile from the town but up a steeper road, a move intended to

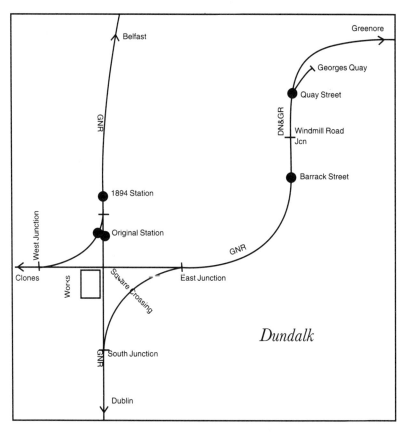

divert Newry traffic away from the newly-opened N&ER when the two companies were in bitter conflict. Later called Bessbrook, the station fell out of general use in 1933, retaining only Sunday trains which had bus connections for Newry and for customs purposes, and one each way on the third Monday of each month! Wartime conditions finished Bessbrook as a station in 1942, but the 1984 revival in Ulster ensured its reconstruction and reopening as Newry – in fact such had been considered in 1965. Other intermediate stations all closed in 1965 but Poyntzpass and Scarva also reopened in 1984.

Apart from the permanent Boyne viaduct, the entire line from Drogheda to Portadown Junction was single line at first but traffic increased quite considerably at an early date and so doubling had to be started; from the viaduct the second track came into use in 1860 to Dunleer, 1858 to Castlebellingham, 1854 to Dundalk and on to Mountpleasant, 1858 to Adavoyle, 1860 to Goraghwood, 1861 to Scarva and 1862 to Portadown Junction.

Dundalk became the mechanical headquarters of the GNR, the works being established in 1882 and building 39 locomotives between 1887 and 1937 as well as carriages, diesel power cars and wagons. On the division of the GNR, the works was separated as the Dundalk Engineering Works and left to make its own way, gaining some non-railway work. It was not a successful venture, closing when the Dublin government decided in 1966 that it could no longer provide aid. The original junction station lying in the vee between the D&BJR and D&ER lines was replaced by a modern new station, a half mile to the north, in 1894.

The great scare for the Dublin and Belfast main line came in 1967 when the NI Government announced that the line would be singled from the border ($59^1/2$ miles from Dublin) to Portadown. Planning was detailed and envisaged a single line starting at Adavoyle ($62^1/2$), loops at Summit ($65^3/4$), Poyntzpass (77) and at 81 miles, double track resuming at $83^3/4$ miles. Fortunately for all the idea was shelved at the end of the year and now improvements and major upgrading to allow a line speed of 90 mph are in hand.

A SPRAWLING LINE

The second railway at Dundalk formed part of a route to the far north west, familiarly the 'Irish North', originating in two companies, both incorporated in 1845 and taking an extraordinary time to complete, Enniskillen being their meeting point. The eastern part was first sanctioned in 1837 as the Dundalk & Western Railway which never built an inch of the way, being followed by the D&ER authorised as far as Clones with the intention of using the N&ER onwards. However the latter failed to get anywhere near Clones so its powers passed to the D&ER. Work on the D&ER was started by McCormick & Dargan in 1845, the latter working the line under a haulage contract from the opening of the first 22 miles to Castleblayney in 1849. One of the places on the route, Culloville, after Partition found itself in one country, Northern Ireland, and its station in another, the Free State, the border being the local river. At Dundalk the D&ER chose to build its terminus on the east side of the town at Barrack Street and pass round the south side, crossing the D&BJR on the *level* at the *Square Crossing* before joining the curve from the latter's Dundalk Junction station; although passed for passenger trains in 1849, when the inspecting officer understood that they would start from Barrack Street and call, with a reversal, at the junction, there is no evidence whatsoever that the former was actually used by D&ER passenger services. The square crossing was the scene of a number of incidents and collisions, a cause of concern to BOT inspectors for many years.

Beyond Castleblayney the D&ER had some doubts about its destination after opening the next stretch as far as Ballybay during 1854 and to Newbliss in the next year, constructed by Killeen & Moore. A plan to divert northwards to Armagh gained no support but a branch to serve Cootehill and Cavan, making a connection with the MGWR, was authorised in 1855. When work resumed McCormick, Green & Smith built westwards to reach Clones and Lisbellaw in 1858 and finally Enniskillen (62¼) in 1859, where the D&ER station was not ready until 1860 so in the meantime the existing L&ER station was used, reached by a sharp connecting curve. Later the D&ER station was enlarged by extending along the curve, reputedly the sharpest on any line in Ireland, the old L&ER station then closing. The curve from Dundalk Junction to Dundalk West cabin was double track, the remainder of the line to Omagh single. Passenger services from Dundalk to Clones ceased on 14 October 1957 and goods lingered on until total closure on 1 January 1960. From Clones to Enniskillen all services terminated on 1 October 1957

Two branches diverged to the south of the Dundalk and Clones section, the oldest being that to Cootehill from Shantona Junction (26½ miles from Dundalk) where there was no station although the inspecting thought one desirable. Laid down by Greene & King, the 7½ miles branch was opened in late 1860 but the extension to Cavan was dropped as it was becoming clear that the Ulster would soon reach Clones and continue to Cavan as quickly as possible. The other branch was nearer Dundalk, diverging at Inniskeen to run for 6¾ miles to Carrickmacross, built by Collen Bros and opened in 1886. Both branches lost their passenger services in 1947, the former seeing mainly cattle specials until 1955 but the latter was served by goods trains until 1960. Cootehill was a good example of the integrated rail and road working of the GNR, the station not ceasing public business until 1 August 1957 when the remaining staff were withdrawn.

The 'Irish North' continued beyond Enniskillen to Omagh. It gained its popular name from the post-1862 Irish North-Western Railway title of the former D&ER, following the 1860 lease of the L&ER. Making slow progress southwards from Derry the portion north of Omagh will be described later as it more naturally fitted in with services from Belfast and Portadown. From Omagh (87¾ miles from Dundalk) McCormick made reasonable progress, getting the line ready in stages, to Fintona in 1853, to Dromore Road and then Enniskillen the next year, where the original station later became the goods yard. Fintona itself was left at the end of a 55 chains branch when the line was pushed on; it became famous for the use of a horse-drawn tramcar for 104 years, although of course the small amount of merchandise traffic was steam-worked. At Fintona Junction the horse would be put into a shed when steam trains were about. The long-surviving car (built 1883) took first and second in its saloon and third on the open top deck – at least that was the intention but all too often passengers stood with the driver!

That the D&ER leased the L&ER arose from fear, the latter having offered itself to *any* railway; had it fallen to the Ulster it would probably have been worked in two parts, north and south of Omagh, which years later happened, and so despite disadvantages the D&ER took the line over. The L&ER remained a separate company until amalgamated with the GNR in 1883. In the widespread closures of 1 October 1957 the entire line from Enniskillen to Omagh, including the Fintona tram, closed – thus ended the situation of a railway working steam, diesel and horse-powered trains, an electric tramway and both buses and lorries on the road simultaneously.

A branch from the 'Irish North' built by Brassey & Field and opened in 1866 reached the coast of Co Donegal, being incorporated in 1861 as the Enniskillen & Bundoran Railway and altered in 1862 to the Enniskillen, Bundoran & Sligo Railway; the latter portion was never built despite many attempts. The junction station had a succession of names, starting as Lowtherstown, before the change to Bundoran Junction when the branch opened; in 1894 a direct curve from north to west was added to enable trains from the Omagh direction to avoid reversal, Bundoran attracting much excursion traffic. The branch eventually gained a through train from Dublin, the Bundoran Express which started about 1943 and ran in the summer months. Its real purpose was to make it easier for pilgrims to reach Lough Derg, north of Pettigo in Co Donegal, but the seaside resort became the main destination. To avoid customs the trains ran non-stop between Clones and Pettigo. Bundoran became a popular resort making it worth the purchase of a hotel in 1899, renaming it Great Northern Hotel; post 1958 it became another Great Southern Hotel but was sold in 1977.

After 1921 the branch illustrated the complexities of an international railway with three border crossings; in 1941 Double Summer Time was introduced in the North but the South remained on Summer Time producing extraordinary timings. A couple of morning trains will show the consequences:

Bundoran Jct 9.12, Kesh, 9.35, Pettigo 8.47, Castlecaldwell, 10.02, Belleek 10.12, Ballyshannon 9.20 and Bundoran 9.30am,

and

Bundoran 10.25am, Ballyshannon 10.43, Belleek 11.53, Castlecaldwell 12.03pm, Pettigo 11.17am, Kesh 12.27pm, Bundoran Jct 12.50pm. Thank goodness Double Summer Time finished in 1947! Like so much of the GNR, the Bundoran branch was totally closed on 1 October 1957.

SLIGO LEITRIM

One of the most endearing lines in Ireland remained independent throughout its 78 years. A local engineer, Henry Tottenham, was the driving force behind the 1875 incorporation of the little line with the big name, Sligo, Leitrim & Northern Counties Railway, its inland route to Enniskillen chosen in preference to the coastal line to join the Bundoran branch. Cheaply built by Tottenham, capital being scarce, with constant changes in grade and in perpetual trouble with slips because cutting sides were too steep, it provided an outlet from Sligo to the east and north, the inhabitants giving strong support as it would break the Dublin monopoly on transport. The first section opened during 1879 from Enniskillen to Belcoo and included the major engineering work on the line just outside Enniskillen, the Weir Bridge of eight spans across the River Erne which imposed a maximum axle load of 15 tons throughout. The line was extended to Glenfarne and then on to Manorhamilton during 1880, the latter becoming the mechanical engineering centre of the railway. During 1881 the line was carried on to Collooney, not far from the objective and a junction with the MGWR, but it took until late 1882 to achieve a connection at Carringnagat Junction, 42¾ miles from Enniskillen. In addition to the stations there were several halts, some having very restricted services on specified fair days. The company sought passengers from afar, such as describing Florencecourt in timetables as the station for Swanlinbar and Bawnboy, 5¾ and 9¾ miles to the south, or Ballintogher as the stop for Ballyfarnan 10 miles (and only four miles from Arigna). Originally the Sligo Leitrim did not enter the GNR station at Enniskillen, using a temporary platform outside until a bay was provided in the rebuilt GNR station in 1883.

Never a financial success and in receivership from 1890 until 1897, the company was nearly forcibly sold by the Treasury in London to the MGWR and GNR which would have resulted in division at Manorhamilton. Partition in 1921 prevented absorption by the GSR, the border having a devastating effect on the traffic the line was built for by diverting it away from the more natural course to Belfast, such that grants from both Governments were needed. Help was given by the GNR, particularly with the provision of railbuses to replace most of the steam passenger trains.

There was no alternative to closure when the Stormont government announced the end of GNR services so the Sligo Leitrim finished that same day, 1 October 1957.

The Sligo Leitrim was the last *privately*-owned and operated line in the British Isles and had survived because its staff managed with the minimum of mostly old equipment, maintained by craftsmen unequalled for their versatility; the oldest equipment was the signalling, almost entirely the original of 1879–82, and white *was* still the clear indication at level crossing signals, nor were distants ever changed from red to yellow. So ended a railway that depended so much on the dedication and capabilities of its staff.

A RAILWAY PORT AND ITS LINES

Barrack Street yard, with its container facilities, and reached from the main line at Dundalk South Junction by means of a curve to the Irish North tracks laid down in 1874, served Dundalk until 1995, being replaced by a siding at Dundalk station. The town had a quay near Barrack Street served by the Dundalk & Newry Steam Packet Co Ltd and in communication with Liverpool, but without a railway for many years, powers of 1862 lapsing, until the DN&GR built a siding in 1873 close to Quay Street station. After that railway closed, a short section to the quay was vested in the Ministry of Industry & Commerce, Dublin, and worked by the GNR for a few more years.

With the intention of diverting traffic, particularly livestock, from the midlands and north west away from Dublin the LNWR backed plans for a deep water port at Greenore and the Dundalk, Carlingford & Greenore Harbour & Railway. A report to LNWR shareholders in 1863 told them that existing steam packet companies would run the vessels to Holyhead and that the new line did not involve any outlay by their company – events proved this to be extremely wide of the mark. Conflict with Newry interests resulted in a change of route so that two companies, the Dundalk & Greenore Railway and the Newry & Greenore Railway, were authorised in 1863. Soon the English company found it necessary to provide most of the capital and it took until 1869 to get the contractors Connor & Olley started on both the railway and harbour. The LNWR also had to provide all the rolling stock so that the Dundalk line could open in 1873; running powers allowed trains to start from the D&BJR Dundalk station, back out to the West Junction and then run along the Barrack Street line to the company's own metals at Windmill Road Junction in their 14³⁄₄ miles journey.

The Newry & Greenore Railway could not raise any capital, so in 1873 the powers were vested in the renamed Dundalk, Newry & Greenore Railway. Constructed by Connor & Mannisty (earlier Olley had the misfortune to be killed during construction) the northwards line was opened in mid-1876 as far as Newry Bridge Strcct (14 miles from Greenore); passenger trains were extended in 1880 over a goods extension of 1877 into the main Newry station at Edward Street, adding ³/₄ mile to the journey.

The system was purely LNWR in all appearances, Quay Street station being described as better placed in an English mining town, with its trains in purple-brown and spilt milk, hauled by pure Crewe saddle tanks. Officers at Euston held the corresponding post on the DN&GR with operation in the hands of the Divisional Superintendent, Crewe, and engineering under the District Engineer, Bangor, North Wales. The LNWR had to provide the vessels for the 75 miles crossing to Holyhead and despite all the promises and not for the want of traffic the line instantly became a heavy burden for its English owners, rarely covering the working expenses, never yielding any return on its share value, all of which came to be owned by Euston. Apart from the lines and harbour, the LNWR built the entire town of Greenore.

Ferries which lasted until 1920-1 were started by the LNWR across Carlingford Lough to Greencastle, Rostrevor and Warrenpoint in Co Down and until 1876 the company ran an office at the latter. Support was given to the Greencastle & Kilkeel Railway & Pier Co, incorporated in 1876, a line of 5¹/₂ miles, empowered to use the 3ft gauge but all that was done was the building of a pier at Greencastle in 1880, the LNWR having acquired the powers through the DN&GR in 1878. Partition aggravated the ever-mounting losses and the passenger steamer facilities ceased during the British General Strike of 1926 but goods remained until the last sailing of 29 December 1951. The service had never bettered times via Dublin despite a direct Belfast train from 1903 worked by the GNR, and travellers did not take kindly to 'mixed' boats which handled cattle and merchandise.

In 1933 agreement was reached so that the GNR took over the day-to-day operation of the DN&GR; thus no longer did the LMS send men from its Wolverton carriage works to attend to the coaches. Losses could not continue and in 1950 the British Transport Commission, as owner, announced that the line and hotel would close after trains last ran on the final day of 1951 – that year expenses were four times receipts! Winding up took until 1957 and the net proceeds of the disposal of assets were £70,000, all that was saved from a capital of nearly £600,000, arrears of interest then amounting to £420,000.

THE NEWRY RAILWAYS

For the reasons given,Newry had to be content with branch line status. In that respect and due to ineptitude by one of the town's early railways Newry has not been as well served by the railway as it deserved. The two watering places of Warrenpoint and Rostrevor attracted three groups in 1845, at a time when they were the major resorts in the north, sheltered by the Mountains of Mourne. Two were purely local, the other more ambitious with a proposed line from Belfast to Downpatrick to Rathfriland, Newry and Warrenpoint, grandly titled The Great County Down, Belfast, Newry & Warrenpoint Railway. The other two were the Newry, Warrenpoint & Rostrevor Railway and the Newry & Warrenpoint Railway, combining in 1845 to build a purely local railway along the north shore of Carlingford Lough. Dargan was the builder of the short level line of 6 miles authorised in 1846 and opened in 1849 between Kilmorey Street in Newry and Warrenpoint; the remaining $2^{1}/_{2}$ miles to Rostrevor were never built. Dargan took on the working of the line in 1850 for five years in an effort to make it more profitable but the company, managed from Liverpool, was never prosperous, suffering from ever-mounting debts despite the dock at Warrenpoint to which Dargan ran a steamer service bringing in a fair amount of goods traffic from Liverpool. In 1878 a BOT inspector described a railway which can only be considered as a decrepit run-down concern with track in a poor state and only two of its four engines working. When the PWLC attempted to enforce repayment of an 1866 loan, the NW&RR directors retaliated by successfully seeking a sale to the GNR which took place in 1886 – the reward to shareholders was but 8·8 per cent of their nominal investment.

Rostrevor eventually had a rail connection, in the form of a $2^{1}/_{2}$ miles roadside horse tramway of 3ft gauge (some state 2ft 10in) which opened in July 1877, and continued for goods a further $^{3}/_{4}$ mile to Rostrevor quay. There were through bookings and goods rates with the NW&RR and the Warrenpoint & Rostrevor Tramway Co was quite successful until early motor charabancs captured its passengers. A terrific gale in 1915 washed away a stretch of track and the trams never resumed.

The popularity of the area round Warrenpoint encouraged the GNR to take over three hotels in 1899, the Beach Hotel at Warrenpoint (sold in 1922), the Great Northern Hotel (sold in 1966) and the Woodside Hotel (sold in 1906), both the latter being at Rostrevor.

Plans to connect Newry with Armagh and Enniskillen ($71^{3}/_{4}$ miles) seemed sound enough but Parliament laid down that the Clones and Enniskillen section was to be built first and shared with the D&ER; in the event the latter built the section as earlier described. The London-based company had extreme difficulty in financing the work, such that it took Moore, the contractor, until 1853 to complete but $3^1/2$ miles up the bank from Newry to a junction with the D&BJR at Goraghwood and it was expensive, costing twice the average per mile at the time. Although planned to open on 7 January 1854, there was no rolling stock and it took until March to get trains started. The Newry station was soon known as Edward Street and from there a $3/4$ mile goods extension was built to the Albert Basin, opened during 1854. Goraghwood station on the main line was actually provided by the N&ER for junction purposes, the D&BJR paying rent. Relations with the latter were poor, with many obstacles placed in the way of traffic exchange despite the concurrent passing of Cardwell's Act which required that railways cooperated over through traffic and rates – such was the antagonism between the two companies that goods unloaded at Warrenpoint and taken by the NW&RR to Newry was *carted* to the D&BJR Newry station rather than being reloaded at Edward Street. Prosperity eluded the company and extension was seen to be the solution, so in 1857 the company recognised that it was to get no further than Armagh and became the Newry & Armagh Railway, remaining independent until absorbed by the GNR in 1879.

Early timetables suggest that the line to Albert Basin was used for passenger trains, apparently confirmed by a BOT report of 1877 in which was stated that this line was originally passed for passenger use, but was long disused for that purpose and not likely to be used again.

In 1857 the Town of Newry Connecting Railway was authorised to build a short stretch through the town; Greene & King converted 29 chains of the Albert Basin line for passenger use and laid down a further 57 chains from King Street Junction to join the NW&RR 10 chains beyond its terminus. NW&RR trains used the line as far as Dublin Bridge during 1861, its Kilmorley Street station then closing but opening of the rest was delayed until a working arrangement was agreed. Later in 1861 the line opened to Edward Street and when common sense prevailed trains ran through from Warrenpoint to Goraghwood and eventually, after the GNR took over, to Portadown and Belfast. The 1877 line connecting the DN&GR to the N&AR paralleled the existing single track but in 1907 the two were made into a double line to King Street Junction. Newry had several private sidings, sources of coal traffic for a wide area of Ulster and the midland counties, exceeding the tonnages of Belfast, contributing towards Newry's status as a first class station on the GNR. In 1963 the short section of double line mentioned above reverted to single track. Now all this has gone, all trains from Goraghwood to Warrenpoint ceasing at the beginning of 1965.

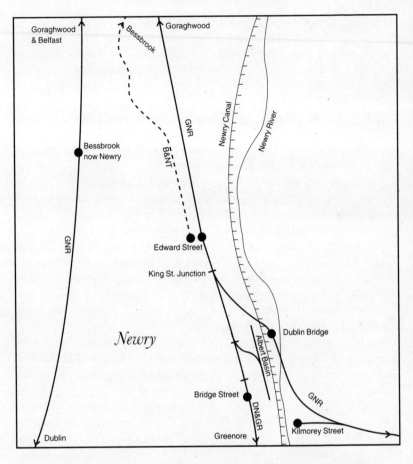

However Newry remains a major coal importer, much of it in containers.

Newry also had a 3ft gauge line, the Bessbrook & Newry Tramway, its 3 miles built to serve the Bessbrook Spinning Company, one of Ireland's largest linen mills, and its staff, many of whom lived at the 'Model Village' and others at Newry. The company was set up in 1884 and decided to use electric power, although no specific permission seems to have been granted. An electrical engineer, Dr Edward Hopkinson, was responsible for construction, Mather & Platt supplying the electrical equipment so that services started on 1 October 1885, having the distinction of being the first all year round electric service in the British Isles. A live centre rail supplied the power, except at a major level crossing at Millvale when a short length of overhead line was installed, the cars having a bow collector as well as shoes. Wagons carried coal and raw materials to the mill and linen back and so

TWO SIGNAL CABINS
20. LMS (NCC) style cabin at Limavady Junction just before closure in 1976. (*J.M. Allen*)
21. Waterford Central cabin on 1906 built for the new works of the South Wexford line. (*H. Fayle – IRRS*)

ON THE NARROW GAUGE

22. Clogher Valley Railway 0–4–2T No 6 *Erne*, built by Sharp Stewart in 1887. (*Real Photographs*)

23. Castlegregory branch terminus on the Tralee & Dingle Railway, complete with engine shed and goods store. (*H.C. Casserley*)

24. Narrow gauge compound (von Borries system). MR (NCC) 2–4–2T No 101 at Larne in 1924. (*LCGB Ken Nunn collection*)

25. 2–6–0T No 5T shunts at the Arigna mines, Cavan & Leitrim Railway, in June 1955. (*P.W. Gray*)

26. Cork & Muskerry Light Railway 4–4–0T No 7 *Peake* at Blarney when quite new. (*L&GRP*)

IRISH ODDITIES

27. Fintona station GNR with horse tram in August 1950. The tram dates from 1883 and is now preserved. (*J.N. Faulkner*)

28. The line through the streets of Cork in 1958, with CIE diesel No C232 crossing the Clontarf lifting bridge adjacent to Albert Quay station. (*T.J. Edgington*)

29. A 1924 view of a train on the Dublin & Blessington Steam Tramway at Embankment; the engine is 2–4–2T No 10. (*LCGB Ken Nunn collection*)

30. 1ft 10in gauge Guinness Brewery locomotive in place on a haulage truck, enabling it to work trains on the 5ft 3in gauge. It has just entered GS&WR property at Kingsbridge. (*L&GRP*)

31. The Lartigue monorail system at Ballybunion, showing a turntable and double-sided carriages and wagons. (*H. Fayle – IRRS*)

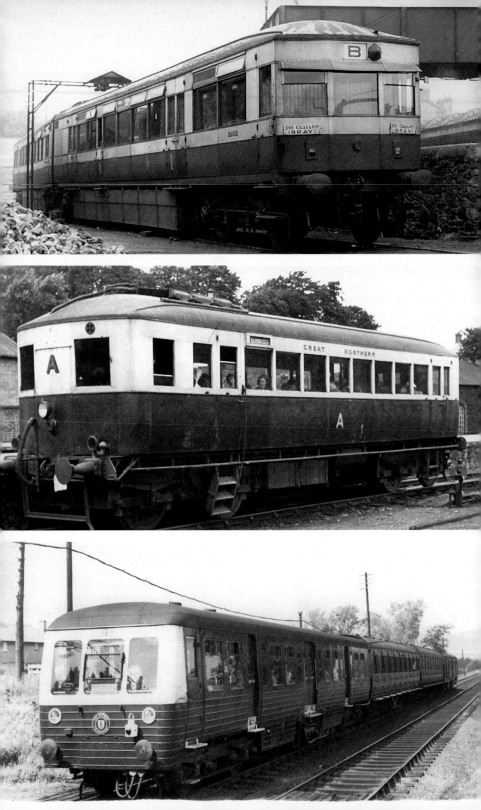

RAILCARS AND RELATED VEHICLES

32. GSR Drumm battery train 'B' standing at the recharging gantry at Bray, July 1934. (*H.C. Casserley*)

33. GNR railcar 'A' at Scarva, c. 1950, when working the Banbridge service. (*J.N. Faulkner*)

34. UTA multi-engined diesel train on the Bangor line, c. 1955, with power car No 35 nearest; the intermediate coaches are adapted steam stock. (*J.N. Faulkner*)

35. Sligo Leitrim railbus No 2A stalls on the bank between Glenfarne and Kilmackerril Halt, June 1955. (*P.W. Gray*)

36. County Donegal railar No 14 after arrival at Letterkenny from Strabane in August 1959. (*D. Murray*)

THE MODERN RAILWAY
37. A four-car DART train pauses at Dublin Pearse (formerly Westland Row) on its way from Howth to Bray in October 1987. (*J.M. Allen*)
38. A three-car 450 class diesel train of NIR enters Whiteabbey on 4 June 1988. (*J.M. Allen*)

that they could be hauled along the public roads they had flangeless wheels; when on rail they were guided by outside raised rails. The line, starting close to Edward Street station in Newry, was steeply graded and climbed no less than 190ft, passing under the GNR Craigmore viaduct and its services appeared in public timetables published in Ireland. The inevitable competing bus route of the NIRTB ensured the tramway's demise early in 1948, bringing to an end one of the pioneers of electric traction.

OVER THE HILLS TO ARMAGH

That unfortunate concern, the N&AR, obtained a fresh Act in 1857 to continue its line on to Armagh, involving no less than four firms in the construction of 16¾ miles from Goraghwood. McCormick, Greene & King started work on the western end from Loughgilly to Armagh but stopped when the money ran out. A new contract for the whole line went to A T. Gordon in 1860, replaced in 1861 by R.S. North, replaced by Watson & Overend in 1862 who completed the line for opening in 1864 to a temporary terminus 1 miles short of Armagh, trains entering the city's station in 1865 when the junction was completed. Watson & Overend accepted Lloyds Bonds in payment from the company and became almost sole owners which soon led to disaster after they joined with the Contracts Corporation of London in 1865, crashing in 1866 with the failure of Overend's bank that year.

The line was single and quite hilly so that there were two tunnels, that at Lissummon being the longest in Ireland at 1,759 yards, the other near Loughgilly being 365 yards; the latter partly fell in on 25 January 1914 and trains were not restored until 1 May 1914, none having run between Goraghwood and Markethill. The 1933 strike finished the passenger service throughout and goods from Markethill to Armagh, the remainder lingering on until 1955.

If one event on any railway in the British Isles did more than any other to change the course of history, it has to be the devastating accident that occurred on 12 June 1889 just a couple of miles up the 1 in 75 out of Armagh. On that Sunday a grossly-overloaded excursion bound for Warrenpoint set out in a train of 15 coaches but it stalled only a ¾ mile short of the summit, having declined banking assistance. In an attempt to clear the section, the official in charge decided to divide the train, after which the rear part, now unsecured and without any brake power, ran back to meet the following booked train, time interval working being in force. The action which set the coaches off is regarded to be a momentary reversal of the engine, having stopped on dead-centre – the consequence was a collision in which the death toll reached 88, a quarter of them children.

This is not the place to analyse events and apportion blame, whatever actually started the vehicles off on their course to destruction. The law makers responded immediately, having by-and-large in previous years been reluctant to enforce any standards despite the frequent entreaties of the BOT inspecting officers who campaigned year after year for requirements which now became compulsory with the passing of the Regulation of Railways Act to become law on 30 August 1889. Thus a continuous automatic brake on passenger trains became compulsory, together with block signalling and interlocking of points and signals on all lines carrying passengers. All this started unprecedented activity by railways throughout the British Isles which had until 1893 to comply and laid the foundation for a transformation in railway equipment and working methods – in fact, it can be said quite fairly that it made possible faster and heavier trains more usually associated in historians' minds with improvements in locomotive capacity.

A novelty encountered on the journey from Goraghwood to Armagh was a horse tramway (1ft 10in gauge) which started from Loughgilly station yard and ran for $2^1/2$ miles southwards to three linen factories at the town of Glen Anne from 1897 until wartime difficulties brought about the end of this little tramway around 1917. The owners provided a carriage, which they named *Carew*, for their staff and others in addition to using the line for coal deliveries and linen outwards.

THROUGH MID ULSTER

Having 'rested' at Portadown, the Ulster Railway needed a fresh Act in 1845 to revive powers and continue as first intended on to Armagh ($35^3/4$ miles from Belfast) and Dargan was soon at work. Generally rising from Portadown, the line was ready for use during 1848; at first only one track was sanctioned, the second following later that year. A succession of small towns, many engaged in the linen trade beckoned and so Acts of 1855 and 1856 authorised extension to Monaghan and then Clones, Dargan completing the first for opening in 1858, but Edwards Bros built the extension. This diverged from the original course at Monaghan just north of the 1858 station which was replaced by a new one nearer the town and opened in 1863 as a double line to a junction with the INWR just east of Clones ($64^1/2$ miles from Belfast).

The gap between Clones and Cavan was closed in 1862, trains running into the MGWR station at the latter ($79^3/4$ miles from Belfast). This line was constructed by Greene & King and its Act of 1859 allowed contributions by the UR, D&DR and D&BJR, the D&ER providing the rest and working it from opening; the GNR altered services so that trains ran through from Belfast to Cavan. In 1930 a small platform was built to serve Loreto College (2 miles north of Cavan); normally a conditional stop, it was served for many years by special school trains, that from Cavan in the morning having to reverse back empty with the opposite procedure in the afternoon. Somewhat perversely the only original intermediate station was named Belturbet Junction long before it was in fact a junction. When the branch to Belturbet (4¼ miles), built by Collen Bros, opened in 1885 the station became Ballyhaise, without a Junction suffix. The branch provided a connection with the C&LR narrow gauge, its main traffic being cattle and later coal, transhipped by hand until the very end. A feature of the Cavan line was its frequent crossing of the political border between Clones and Redhills, six times in fact but as the area was virtually uninhabited and marshy it was treated as entirely in the south.

Partition dealt a heavy blow to the line as its natural flow to Belfast was broken. Economies made it necessary to eliminate most of the double line, singling from Monaghan to Clones taking place in 1932 and from Richhill to Armagh in 1934. On the remaining double line a factory opened at Brownstown Crossing (1 mile south of Portadown Junction) about 1942 and after the entire closure of the route from the junction to Glaslough in 1957 its traffic was retained, being worked as a siding until it also finished in 1965. South of Glaslough the remaining passenger trains, including the Belturbet branch, lasted only for a couple of weeks after above closure. Goods trains ceased to serve Glaslough in 1958 and Belturbet at the same time as the narrow gauge Cavan & Leitrim section of CIE closed in 1959, lasting only until the beginning of 1960 for the remnants north and south of Clones to Monaghan and Cavan.

A SHORT-LIVED LINE

Extension northwards from the MGWR Meath lines terminus at Kingscourt was viewed as a continual threat by the GNR, possibly becoming reality in 1894. When in 1900 the Kingscourt, Keady & Armagh Railway, with MGWR backing, obtained an Act, the GNR came to terms with the promoters so that in 1902 the scheme was retitled the Castleblayney, Keady & Armagh Railway. Progress by Robert Worthington was so slow that in 1908 the railway took over the job. Built over bogs and through rock cuttings, needing three major viaducts, the line reached the highest point on the GNR at 613ft at about the half way mark but the area had little to offer, although Milford and Keady had a number of linen mills which produced a fair amount of traffic. Despite the order of its title the line was built from Armagh, sensibly as this was the busier section, so that the 8 miles to Keady opened in 1909, the remaining ten miles to Caslteblayney following a year later. At Castleblayney the connection with the Irish North was by means of a siding, accepted by the inspecting officer due to the light traffic expected. The creation of the Border in 1921 finished the line off south of Keady and all trains ceased in 1923; it seems that the cost of providing customs facilities was too much for the meagre traffic. Passengers to Keady lost their trains in 1933 but a full goods service remained until the 1957 closures.

CLOGHER VALLEY

The Clogher Valley is a well-farmed area with a certain amount of small town industry, brewing, milling, linen and woollen mills, and of course the fairs but there has been steady depopulation and the later presence of the frontier nearby did not help. Of proposals for a railway there were plenty, beginning with a plan to link Fintona to Armagh through Clogher, put forward in 1853 and discarded when the direct line from Portadown to Dungannon and then Omagh began to make progress. In 1861 the PD&OR obtained an Act for a branch from Dungannon to Aughnacloy which failed to materialise, followed by ideas for a narrow gauge line, the Armagh, Tyrone & Fermanagh Railway of 1872 being one of the first 3ft gauge lines planned in Ireland; the 1875 plan for a line from Florencecourt on the SL&NCR, 5ft 3in, would have taken the course eventually used. Finally it was the 1883 Act which gave rise to the Clogher Valley Tramway late that year, defeating a rival Tyrone Steam Tramways aiming to build a line northwards to Dungannon and Moy; the CVT changed its title to Clogher Valley Railway in 1894.

With a Baronial Guarantee arranged, McCrea & McFarland built the line in 1885–7, opening taking place during 1887 although some goods had been carried from late 1886. At each end of the 37 miles line, which ran for much of its way alongside the county road, the GNR stations at Tynan and Maguiresbridge were used. The headquarters and largest station was Aughnacloy with the interesting facility of a coaling gantry at the platforms, the whole being described as more suitable to a large prosperous railway than an impecunious rural tramway! At Fivemiletown the railway became famous for the passage of trains along the main street. Ever-mounting losses lead to a Government investigation in 1927 and the imposition of a committee of management in 1928; the latter included the energetic Henry Forbes of the County Donegal and resulted in the use of a diesel railcar and a tractor from 1932–3 but neither could stem the loss of traffic which gave the Northern Ireland Government no choice but to close the line, the last trains running on the final day of 1941; by then the company was almost wholly owned by the Government, most shareholders having accepted £6 for their £10 shares in 1930 – they should have counted themselves very lucky.

A GRANDIOSE IDEA

There was no stopping the enthusiasm of the late Victorian and Edwardian promoters when they hit upon the idea of linking together three narrow gauge lines and laying down a third rail on other sections so that a through route from an Irish Sea port was created, reaching into the midland counties. They started with the Newry, Keady and Tynan Railway of 1899 which was to connect the CVR at Tynan to the B&NT at Bessbrook (25¼ miles), passing Keady on the way, use the tramway into Newry, build a connection (70 chains) to Albert Basin and make a junction with the DN&GR so that they had access to Greenore. Getting an Act in 1900, this intrepid bunch formed an even more remarkable plan by seeking powers to push westward from the Maguiresbridge terminus of the CVR to reach the C&LR at Bawnboy Road. Their new Act, of 1903, changed the name to the all-embracing Ulster & Connaught Light Railway and their ideas of reaching all the way across Ireland to Galway and Clifden have been described in Chapter 6. Needless to say, nothing happened, although the scheme was kept in being until 1910, even though in 1905 a measure of reality prevailed when the original name was restored. In expectation of its construction, the builders of the CK&AR had to leave a short tunnel through an embankment at Keady.

THE DERRY ROAD

Effectively the second main line of the GNR, the railway west of Portadown to Omagh and then Londonderry was the outcome of two railways. The older was the L&ER which struck southward from the 'Maiden City' to Omagh and then Enniskillen, the latter already part described, and for many years services were based on the two historical routes, it not being until after Partition that timetables were altered to show Portadown to Derry rather than Dundalk to Derry, although through coaches from Dublin had been routed via Portadown for many years. From 1908 until about 1918 the GNR advertised First Class sleeping accommodation on the Night Mails from Dublin to both Londonderry and Belfast but only from the latter for the up journey to Dublin.

Dungannon was the first objective when the Portadown & Dungannon Railway was authorised in 1847, backed by the UR, but its 14 miles to a temporary terminus from a junction a ¹/₂ mile west of Portadown station, started by Fox & Henderson and finished in default by Dargan, did not open until 5 April 1858. Use of the junction at Portadown was delayed until approved on 4 July following, a temporary platform being used meanwhile. In 1857 the concern became the Portadown, Dungannon & Omagh Railway and was extended westwards by A.T. Gordon who finished the line for opening on 2 September 1861. At Dungannon the new line started with a tunnel (a half mile), forced on the builders by Lord Northland who would not tolerate the sight of smoke from trains, followed by the permanent station. At the other end of the line the L&ER station was used, there being a ¹/₂ mile branch to serve Omagh market, opened in 1862, on the east side of the town. There was a steady climb from Portadown to a summit 52 miles (from Belfast), for most of its existence the highest point (561ft) on the GNR.

The impecunious L&ER took a long time to build its 33³/₄ miles southward from Londonderry to Omagh; it was surveyed as early as 1837 by George Stephenson but no Act was obtained until 1845. Leishamn built the first section from a temporary terminus at Derry to Strabane which opened on 19 April 1847 but it struggled against the existing river and canal traffic. The 1847 terminus was some way upstream from the city's river bridge and to overcome its inconvenience the line was extended on 18 April 1850 by a half-mile to a new site just north of the bridge (becoming Foyle Road from 1906), 100¹/₂ miles from Belfast.

Disheartened, the proprietors considered abandoning the rest of the project but efforts by the Duke of Abercorn resulted in the awarding of a contract to McCormick for the remainder to Omagh and Enniskillen, being completed as far as Newtownstewart on 9 May 1852 and on to Omagh on 13 September 1852 where the station was resited at the junction of the Irish North and Portadown lines in 1883. In 1853 the section from Newtownstewart to Omagh was doubled, only to be singled in 1883, otherwise the line was single throughout in those days.

Cookstown, to the north of Dungannon had been served from Belfast since 1856 by the B&NCR, but in 1874 the Dungannon & Cookstown Railway was promoted by the UR and PD&OR, their interest being in part the output of collieries around Coalisland. Oughterson was the contractor and the line was completed by the GNR who had purchased the concern in 1877; opened in 1879, the branch started from Dungannon Junction, a ¹/₂ mile west of the station and ran 14 miles to a

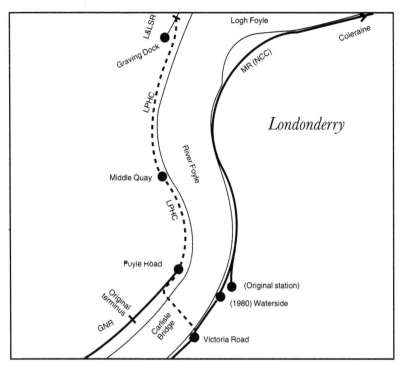

station adjacent to the B&NCR at Cookstown where each railway had its own facilities, although from 1923 a single station master had charge of both. More than any other line in Ireland this branch had an 'industrial' atmosphere with its sidings to half a dozen collieries and brickworks (and much later a bacon factory near Cookstown) around the two intermediate stations. A new colliery was sunk just north of Coalisland (6½ miles) in 1924 and opened with great ceremony but it never produced the anticipated 100,000 tons per annum, failing to find coal of quality.

The GNR started a programme of track doubling west of Portadown, as far as Annaghmore in 1902, on to Trew & Moy in 1903 and Dungannon to Donaghmore in 1906 (the section between remained single because of Dungannon tunnel). At the Derry end from St Johnstown to Derry was doubled as far as the Locomotive Yard (subsequently Londonderry South Cabin) in 1904 but the remaining ½ mile into the station had to wait until 1906. The need to economise resulted in removal of the second road in stages, St Johnstown to Derry South cabin in 1932, Dungannon Junction to Donaghmore in 1936 and the remainder in 1959.

The Cookstown branch lost its passenger service during 1956 and was cut back to Coalisland in 1959, the rest being worked as a siding from

Dungannon for sand traffic, the junction being abolished so that main line traffic was restricted to the old down road and the siding used the old up line. The Derry road remained substantially busy but closure came on 15 February 1965, being deferred from 4 January 1965, the day on which the Coalisland siding closed. Traffic from Dublin bound for County Donegal under sealed transit was diverted to run by way of the remaining route through Coleraine to Londonderry.

THE CASTLEDERG TRAM

Castlederg lies in the north west corner of Co Tyrone, a woollen town of but 750, well to the west when the L&ER opened its line from Strabane to Newtownstewart, its nearest station Victoria Bridge, by a river bridge of about 1840 and named after the queen. Eventually an Act was obtained in 1883, a little prematurely for the Baronial guarantors as it was just too soon to qualify for Treasury indemnities; in fact the Castlederg & Victoria Bridge Tramway, $7^{1}/_{4}$ miles of 3ft gauge and built by T.I. Dixon, was quite prosperous for several years. Opened in 1884, the automatic air brake was adopted from the beginning, following pressure from the BOT well before automatic brakes became compulsory, being one of only two users in steam days in Ireland.

Latterly the line struggled on, getting more and more into debt and not getting any help from the Stormont Government; when the Northern Ireland railway strike of 1933 ended the company decided not to restore its trains and formal winding up took place at the end of September 1933.

A DIESEL PIONEER

Penetration of Co Donegal by railways was slow and was not achieved fully until narrow gauge tracks were laid down, aided by the Tramway Acts. In the whole county only the portions of the Derry and Strabane and of the Bundoran branch within it were 5ft 3in gauge, although two narrow gauge sections had originated on that gauge. The more southerly of the two 3ft gauge companies, the Co Donegal, became the largest narrow gauge system in the British Isles with 125 miles of route, having begun as the Finn Valley Railway in 1860 to connect Stranorlar with Strabane on the L&ER. Moore Bros completed the line in 1863 from a junction just south of Strabane and the company entered into a working arrangement with the INWR, successor to the L&ER, although from 1872 the FVR had its own rolling stock, relying on the INWR and then the GNR for engines until conversion to narrow gauge on 30 June 1894;

at the same time a short extension took the line into a new separate station at Strabane, alongside that of the GNR for easy interchange.

Donegal town had not shown much interest in being connected to Stranorlar, 18 miles away over mountains, when Ballyshannon lay only 11 easier miles to the south. However the West Donegal Railway was formed in 1879 to build a narrow gauge line along the only possible route from Stranorlar through the Blue Stack Mountains to Donegal but it took a long time to get there. Dixon gained the contract and completed the line as far as Drumminin (Lough Eske from 1889), four miles short of Donegal, when the money ran out. Trains, which started in 1882, faced a 12 miles climb from Stranorlar to the summit of the Barnesmore Gap at 591ft and at the height of a gale a train could be halted, or, worse its carriages derailed on occasion. To close the four miles gap, more capital was raised in 1886 with a Baronial Guarantee, but even that was not enough for the station at Donegal was financed by another concern, the Donegal Railway Station Co; both were built by John Hegarty of Larne and trains eventually ran into Donegal in 1889.

Before any expansion took place, the FVR and WDR amalgamated in 1892 as the Donegal Railway which opened four new lines from 1893 to 1905. The first two were 'government lines', the outcome of the many routes proposed by the Allport Commission and the 1889 Act (see Table 1) and paid for by grants of £121,436 and £123,886, having guaranteed capital of but £1,000 in each case. The Killybegs line continued westward along the coast for 19 miles from Donegal and was built by Dixon, being opened in 1893. The Glenties branch of 24¹/₂ miles, laid down by McCrea & McFarland of Derry and opened during 1895, climbed up the Finn Valley to open sparse country. Further expansion came without Government help; the railway relied on transhipment from the GNR for its Derry traffic and not surprisingly planned its own line. Authority was obtained in 1896 for such an extension and for a line from Donegal southwards to Ballyshannon, both of course opposed by the GNR. The 14¹/₂ miles of the Derry line was soon built, Topham, Jones & Railton having the contract, and passed through Co Londonderry on the east bank of the River Foyle after crossing over the GNR a little to the north of Strabane, opening in 1900. New powers had to be obtained in 1902 for the Ballyshannon line, the same Act authorising purchase of the separate Donegal Station company, and Dixon soon began its building so that 15¹/₂ miles of line was ready in 1905. The junction at Donegal trailed so that excursions from Stranorlar, etc had to reverse on their way to the popular strand at Rossnowlagh, a favourite Sunday destination right up to closure.

The DR had not prospered with its enlargements and when the Midland

Railway, fresh from its entry into Irish railway management, looked further afield it seemed probable that it would buy up the narrow gauge company. The GNR, alarmed by such a possibility, reached agreement with the MR for a joint purchase, duly sanctioned by Parliament in 1906 which set up the County Donegal Railways Joint Committee to manage the system, including the Strabane to Derry line excluded by the lawmakers. As the GNR already had a route from Strabane to Londonderry, Parliament, fearing a GNR monopoly, decreed that the narrow gauge line be passed to exclusive Midland ownership – hence the anomaly of a major English company owning a 3ft line in another country worked by another party which later had its headquarters in what was to become a foreign country at the time that the MR became the LMS. The British Transport Commission continued the 'foreign' representation on the committee and when the GNR was replaced by the jointly-owned board in 1953, its participation passed to CIE and UTA representatives.

This extensive system was completed by the opening of the Strabane & Letterkenny Railway (19^{1}/$_{4}$ miles) at the beginning of 1909, the last new narrow gauge passenger railway in Ireland. It started as the Strabane, Raphoe & Convoy Railway in 1903, the two small towns considering themselves important enough to need public transport, the latter being engaged in the woollen trade. Support from the GNR ensured that in 1904 Parliament allowed continuation to Letterkenny and the change of name; the company in fact remained an independent concern, worked by the Joint Committee. Outside Letterkenny the S&LR passed over the L&LSR and then ran close by to its terminus adjacent to the latter's station; a connecting line between the two railways opened with the branch, a certain amount of traffic being exchanged including through excursions onto the Burtonport line for pilgrims to a religious site near Kilmacrenan.

When the two states came into being, the committee had to live with customs posts and timetables warned passengers that trains would not be held if examination of their luggage was not completed in the allotted time – it would be sent on later. In terms of mileage and routes the Co Donegal system was now complete, but there was plenty more history to come, the life of the system being extended by the almost complete replacement of steam-hauled passenger trains by railcars, less demanding on the track, under the energetic direction of Henry Forbes, the general manager. It was almost by accident that a railcar came into daily use, a small inspection car of 1906 being pressed into use during 1926 when the British coal miners were on strike, serving Glenties and making a daily trip to Strabane, running some 6,000 miles and proving to be a practical replacement for steam. Thereafter the fleet steadily expanded and in 1931 the Joint Committee broke new ground by being the *first* railway in the British Isles to use diesel railcars regularly. Steadily the red and cream railcars became a familiar sight, often with a *red wagon* in tow for excess luggage, and the steam fleet was substantially reduced by 1937. A typical example of Forbes' ingenuity was the small diesel locomotive *Phoenix* which in 1937 arose from the shell of an Atkinson-Walker steam locomotive which had been so unsuccessful on the Clogher Valley Railway. For the diesel cars, seemingly innumerable stopping places came into use so that services more nearly resembled a bus route.

Despite every economy, the Donegal becoming a byword for thriftiness, road competition gradually gained the ascendent. Closure started with the Glenties branch in 1947, only a few livestock, turf and bog iron ore trains continuing until total closure during 1952. Then the Derry line closed at the beginning of 1955 (but a Sunday School excursion ran six months later); all the rest closed on 1 January 1960, other than an interim goods service on the Finn Valley section for a few more weeks. The route of the replacement bus from Strabane to Letterkenny had to cross an old bridge at the border which the local councils declared unsafe for large vehicles; thus passengers had to walk across this bridge and go through customs. Fed up with typical local government indecision and muddling, the Joint Committee simply took up the rails over the bridge across the River Finn between the two countries and ran their buses across it! It was not until 1971 that the two railway companies were wound up and the Co Donegal buses replaced by those of CIE and so disappeared the last vestige of the largest narrow gauge system in the British Isles – well, not quite, for one engine and *Phoenix* rest in the Ulster Folk & Transport Museum and three other engines still exist.

THE TAIL THAT WAGGED THE DOG

There was hardly a less promising area for a railway to thrive than Co Donegal and yet the Londonderry & Lough Swilly Railway was to be one of the most prosperous of Irish railways. The north east corner of the county includes a good fertile area close to the city of Derry, with the towns of Buncrana and Letterkenny the main centres – the latter has benefited substantially from Partition, partly taking the place of the 'Maiden City' as the area's focal point. Impoverished beyond belief, the poor looking after the destitute, gentry and middle classes being absent in the extreme, depopulation of the county has been severe and people became the main export, the current number being only 40 per cent of that of 1841. A canal was planned in 1763–5 to connect the great inlets of Lough Foyle and Lough

Swilly, the eventual outcome being an Act of 1838 which authorised the draining and embanking of areas adjacent to Lough Swilly. The contractor for the reclamation works was William McCormick, an Ulster man, mentioned many times in this narrative, who with the help of others completed embankments that created good fertile lands by 1850.

Mania schemes envisaged south to north lines through the county, the Great County of Donegal Railway from Ballyshannon to Ramelton on Lough Swilly and the Great North Western Junction Railway from Sligo to Letterkenny and Derry with a branch to Ramelton and Rathmullan. The Lough Foyle & Lough Swilly Railway of 1852 was to connect Derry with Farland Point on Lough Swilly, authorised in 1853 as the L&LSR; it needed another Act in 1859 before McCormick started on the 8¾ miles of 5ft 3in gauge line. At the end of 1863, trains started from a terminus over one mile from the city centre to a small pier from which passengers could sail to other places on Lough Swilly. After leaving the Derry terminus the line crossed a main road obliquely, it being decreed that trains or wagons must not be worked across by any mechanical means, only animal power being authorised – apart from a few days in early 1864 when horses were used, the order was ignored and for another ninety years all movements were illegal! An Act of 1861 permitted a branch to Buncrana, completed by McCormick and opened in 1864, diverging at Junction (6¼ miles), leaving Farland as a branch which for a while in 1864–5 was horse-worked, the service being terminated altogether in 1866. For a while one engine worked both services, interrupting its Buncrana journeys to run to Farland and back. In 1868 Fahan replaced Farland Point when the pier was moved to the former and a spur added for transfer of goods to the lough steamers.

To get closer to the centre of Derry, the company arranged that its trains would run over the track of the Londonderry Port & Harbour Commissioners to a platform erected at the Middle Quay, close to the point where the Guild Hall was built later, starting in 1869, engines being changed to run over the tramway. With interruptions due to disagreements, the through working continued until the end of 1887. Public timetables show that Sunday trains continued to use the old terminus (although many issues did not indicate which station trains were using). In the meantime the L&LSR had changed its gauge to 3ft, the wider gauge trains ceasing on 28 March 1885; narrow gauge trains started between the Junction and Buncrana early in the next week and the whole job was completed in seven days. Thus for a while narrow gauge trains were hauled by broad gauge engines over the harbour tramway, a practice that had been totally illegal as neither party had powers to run passenger trains over the tramway. One reason for the change was the Letterkenny Railway, incorporated in 1860 after an 1855 attempt had failed; the LR intended to run from Cuttymanhill on the Londonderry to Strabane line near St Johnstown but an Act of 1863 amended the course so that it turned northwards to join the Buncrana line. Greene & King then started work but everything stopped when the money ran out in 1865. Eventually, McCrea & McFarland of Derry made a fresh start after an 1880 Act permitted a change to the narrow gauge (the same Act allowed the L&LSR to make the change), the 18½ miles of line opening in 1883, using some of the old line to Farland Point. Junction became Burnfoot Junction and then Tooban Junction in 1920, but there were years when no trains were shown to stop in public timetables.

The L&LSR showed some interest during 1884–5 in planned lines to Buncrana to Carndonagh and Letterkenny to Dunfanaghy. Burtonport on the far west coast of Co Donegal had been provided with an excellent harbour in a Government inspired attempt to alleviate the poverty of the area but it needed further action to get a railway; thus the 1896 Act was used to build two extensions of the L&LSR, both paid for by Treasury grants with the inevitable consequence that those who knew nothing of equipping a railway had the final say on expenditure, exercising parsimony to the extreme and inevitably in conflict with the working company. Pauling of London had the contract for both lines and completed the shorter one of 18 miles from Buncrana to Carndonagh in 1901. The grant was for £98,527 but excess costs of £5,297 had to be met by the L&LSR with a Baronial Guarantee, the railway having purchased the extra rolling stock, despite which there was an early row over the use of these engines elsewhere on the system. The longer line was planned with Burtonport the objective and for the sake of only some five extra miles several places were left three or four miles to the side; the proverbial crow had but 28 miles to fly over the mountain barrier but the human traveller and his chattels enjoyed (or endured) 49¾ miles of some of the wildest scenery in Ireland. The grant of £313,648 was again insufficient and the excess of £1,802 was covered by another Baronial Guarantee (this time £5,000). The Londonderry terminus, known as Graving Dock, came in for severe criticism when the L&BER was inspected in 1903, being described as 'in the nature of a goods shed and has not received BOT approval' – there is nothing to show that it ever did! It was always a dark place and had been put 'in order' in 1883, at least for goods traffic, when the dispute with the LP&HC was foreseen.

Both lines were worked at a cost up to £3–10 per mile per week, any shortage falling on the L&LSR (but any profit was to be shared!). The original engines obtained for the Letterkenny & Burtonport Extension Railway were excellent 4–6–0T locomotives but they were too small so the company then purchased four eight coupled machines, two 4–8–0 engines which were to be the only tender type on any Irish narrow gauge railway and two 4–8–4T engines, both unique wheel arrangements in the British Isles. The parsimony of the lines' designers soon showed and both were badly and unsafely worked as equipment failed and defects in building became manifest; Government enquiries were needed in 1905 and 1917, the latter resulting in the resignation of the L&LSR chairman so that new management took a hand and matters improved considerably.

Just how was the L&LSR so prosperous as a company? The answer was of course the fact that its own capital accounted for only 14½ miles of line but income came from 99 miles of railway operation, coupled with tight control of expenditure, part of the cause of the disputes with the BOW. Inevitably the system was in no shape to meet road competition and unlike the Co Donegal the L&LSR decided to take to the roads in 1929. When the bus routes became more established, passenger trains were taken off in 1931 with the exception of a solitary train each Monday and Wednesday to Carndonagh, but local roads were not ready for extra traffic making it necessary to resume services within three months. The railway was becoming even more of a liability to its owners so that the Carndonagh trains ceased in 1935, leaving Buncrana with a limited summer service; then in 1940 all remaining passenger trains to Letterkenny and Burtonport ceased and the extension closed entirely. However public transport was beginning to suffer Emergency restrictions and protests forced a resumption of a goods service as far as Gweedore in 1941 (the rest of the line had been lifted); passengers were carried from March 1943 and the reprieve lasted until 1947. Buncrana benefited by a restored full daily service in 1942 which lasted until 1948 due to the number of people then working in Derry or choosing to live outside the city for the 'Duration'. Daily goods services remained to Letterkenny and Buncrana, on which a few travelled as passengers, until total closure in the summer of 1953. The year before the company handed over its boats on Lough Swilly to a local boatman, having run them since 1923, using small motor boats in place of steamers.

Travel on the Burtonport extension had not been without its dangers when the severe gales that are so frequent along the west coast of Ireland were strong enough to derail trains. The worst was that on 30 January 1925 when coaches were derailed on the Owencarrow viaduct (near Cresslough) and four passengers lost their lives, being thrown out when their carriage turned over and lost its roof. The railway then erected an anemometer at Dunfanaghy Road which very soon recorded a gust of 112 mph!

LONDONDERRY PORT LINES

The L&ER had a siding onto a quay at Derry from an early date but it fell into disrepair to the annoyance of the bridge commissioners. With railways on either side of the Foyle, some 300 yards wide through the city, it was obvious that some form of connection was urgently required. The first bridge across the Foyle was a wooden one dating from 1790 and was replaced in 1863 by the Carlisle Bridge; this was built with two decks and by January 1868 all three existing lines, then 5ft 3in gauge, were joined, tracks across the bridge being placed at right angles to those on each bank, transfer taking place on wagon size turntables, capstans and horses providing the power. The B&NCR found it worth building a new goods depot on the west side of the river and in 1877 opened Londonderry City Goods just a short distance north of the GNR station. A third rail was laid to accommodate the L&LSR when it changed its gauge in 1885 and extra tracks were added in 1900 for the Donegal when it reached the Maiden City. The LP&HC had only broad engines, giving the unusual sight of wagons of two gauges in one train – no accident seems to have occurred as a result. The Carlisle Bridge was replaced by the Craigavon Bridge in 1933, rail being retained on the lower deck, to the great advantage of road users who were provided with a second crossing after the harbour lines were finally taken out of use in 1962.

INDUSTRIAL LINES

The early working of the coalfield around Coalisland has been mentioned and one colliery had a wooden wagonway in 1754, soon put out of use. On his canal Davis Dukart built an inclined lift in 1777 using a cradle, the first known lift rather than locks but it was soon replaced by a tramway. Later a brickworks at Dungannon used a 2ft gauge line about 1945 for a few years.

In a remote part of Co Armagh, close to Lough Neagh and a little to the north of the GNR Derry line near Annaghmore, the Irish Peat Development Co lifted turf. Initially in 1901 a horse tramway was used to convey the milled peat from the factory to the nearby River Blackwater for shipment by barge but from 1907 some 8 miles of 3ft gauge lines served the factory with the special interest of using *electric* locomotives. They were supplied by a Belfast firm (Hugh J. Scott) and were most basic with home made 'sheds' (for the want of a better description of the driver's cab), taking power from an overhead line carried on *wooden* poles at about 10ft high by a conventional trolley arm mounted outside the cab. However from 1954 a couple of diesel locomotives were used until production ceased about 1965.

Two other lines of 2ft gauge were associated with turf collection and processing, both in Co Donegal. The oldest was a short one near Fintown worked by the Donegal Peat Development Co which had only a short life but the other, started by the Turf Development Co near Glenties in 1939 was, in company with the Clonsast Bog at Portarlington, the foundation of Bord na Mona which took over in 1946 and has since kept the Glenties bog going.

When Bord Solathair an Leictreachais (Electricity Supply Board) built a dam for a hydro electric plant near Ballyshannon in 1946–7 it used a small contractors line of 2ft 6in gauge. Another short-lived line was located at Glenfarne on the SL&NCR when timber was felled on the Glenfarne Hall estate by a Belfast firm, Lees & Nixon. The 2ft gauge line, installed in 1919, connected the felling areas and saw mills with the station to the south and at times there were some six miles of 'permanent' line in use as well as temporary tracks, being in fact a miniature version of the great timber tramways of Australia. Using a couple of war-surplus locomotives, the venture lasted only some twelve months or so, although there had been about 300 employees Not far away on the coast of Co Sligo close to the Sligo and Bundoran road there lies Mullaghmore harbour, built from about 1822 to 1842 and of interest to historians for it was promoted by none other than Lord Palmerston (1784–1865) who owned much of the land hereabouts and loved it deeply; it is quite certain that a tramway with iron rails was used to carry the building stone down from the nearby hills. A century later another enterprise came to use the harbour when the Barium Consolidated Co, an English concern, commenced the mining of barytes in Gleniff, 7 miles to the east, using a 2ft gauge line, with sections of 18in line in the quarries. Part way there was a cleansing mill with two levels of track so that the ore could be tipped out at the top and collected when processed at the bottom; to connect the two there was a remarkably steep incline alongside the plant. Two factors brought about an untimely end in 1930–1, one being the collapse in the Great Depression of the tin mining consortium which controlled the company, the other action by the Irish Government which required 51 per cent control of foreign companies operating in Ireland, so antagonising the directors that they ceased production immediately despite so much expenditure and dashed all hopes of a new prosperity in the area.

PRESERVATION

After the County Donegal closed a Dr Cox of New Jersey purchased four engines and some rolling stock with the idea of setting up a narrow gauge pleasure line in the United States but they were never taken away, the coaches disintegrating, the engines vandalised. However in 1971 the North West of Ireland Railway Society was set up to build a line in Londonderry, initially using the former Donegal station as the headquarters but now established on the opposite bank of the Foyle. A couple of miles of track exists on the bed of the former GNR line in the Foyle Valley Riverside Park and public services are provided by a CDRJC railcar dating from 1934. A couple of the narrow gauge 2–6–4T locomotives have fortunately found their way to this site and several other items of rolling stock are to hand, hopefully to be put into working order before too long. In Co Donegal work has recently started on a project to revive a short length of the Glenties branch near its terminus and a small·museum in the town contains memorabilia of railway days. There is also some work in hand in the vicinity of Donegal town intended to bring to life the spirit of the narrow gauge.

The Peatlands Park near Annaghmore is being developed as a country park using much of the area formerly worked by the Irish Peat Development Co. It proved impossible to reinstate the original railway so a new circular line of a couple of miles, using a little of the former railway, was completed in 1988. Two diesel locomotives remaining from the turf-cutting days have been restored to working order and each summer run round the system with open coaches, often full of children on school outings.

CHAPTER VIII

Belfast and the North East

The nearest approach to a large area of high population density in Ireland away from Dublin is the Lagan valley of Ulster with a succession of towns westward from Belfast which has dominated the province once it became industrialised, founded on linen and shipbuilding. Previously the city was but an obscure village where the Lagan meets the tides, with a ford guarded by a castle founded in 1177; the name derives from *Beal Feirste*, the ford of the sandbank. Indeed the place was of so little importance that Belfast Lough was then known as Carrickfergus Bay, although it had been granted a Charter in 1613. There were about 25,000 in Belfast in 1800, its first industry, cotton, having given way to linen and already it was becoming more like an English manufacturing town. Growth continued, the city's population having increased to 76,000 in 1841 with successive census figures being 110,000, 122,000 and 175,000 in 1871, reaching 393,000 in 1911 and contrary to the depopulation of so many other towns. The increase then became more gradual, rising to 416,000 in 1961, but now a decline has set in. Shipbuilding was started about 150 years ago, by Wm Dargan, followed by more general engineering, developments unique in Ireland on such a scale for almost all materials had to be imported but it was the large local source of labour that enabled hard-headed Ulster businessmen to draw in British capital. Belfast was late in gaining city status, not granted until 1888.

New town projects have changed the situation in recent years but in 1911 Lurgan had 11,800, Lisburn 12,400 and Portadown 11,700, all places in the Lagan valley which had expanded since the Famine, two and threefold. Lisburn has continued to expand so that it is now home to some 27,500 and Portadown has 50 per cent more, the whole area being developed as Craigavon. Around Belfast there lie Holywood (4,000), Bangor (7,800) and Newtownards (9,600) in Co Down and Carrickfergus (4,600), Larne (8,000) and Ballymena (11,900) in Co Antrim (1911 figures), all having expanded since 1841. Bangor has developed into one of Ireland's premier coastal resorts and its population now exceeds 25,000and all the others have enlarged, a distinct contrast to most of the rest of Ireland. Other places of importance are Coleraine (7,800), Downpatrick (3,200), Ballymoney (3,100) and Limavady (2,700) in 1911, not overlooking Portrush, another holiday resort (4,000); of these places Ballymoney is the one which has expanded the least. Many of the other smaller places have diminished in the rush to find work in expanding Belfast.

Most of the area drains into the River Bann, divided by Lough Neagh into Upper and Lower portions. Thus the Mountains of Mourne and the higher ground of Co Armagh feed the Upper Bann while further north the tablelands of Co Antrim and the Sperrins force the Lower Bann northwards to an estuary near Coleraine. The north east coast along the North Channel is bounded by the heights of Antrim, leaving little space for much more than a very scenic coast road, culminating in the grandeur of the geological curiosity of the Giant's Causeway east of Portrush. Within this area there were deposits of iron ore and bauxite, worked sufficiently to attract railways and to establish an aluminium smelter at Larne, but otherwise quarrying was a major industry and farming is well established in the broader fertile valley areas. There are numerous peaks which exceed 1,500ft, many becoming familiar to locomotive enthusiasts as they were a useful source of names.

The Lagan Canal, long in the making from 1753, which started from the River Lagan a couple of miles upstream from Belfast did not reach Lisburn until 1763 nor Lough Neagh, 26 miles in all, until 1794. Like the Newry Canal this one could take barges of 14ft 6in beam and trading continued until 1951. Elsewhere there was 3 miles 'cut' from Limavady to Lough Foyle dating from 1827 and the Bann was made navigable between 1847 and 1859, comprising 32 miles from Coleraine to Lough Neagh which is still partly used, but navigable portions of the Upper Bann and the River Blackwater were abandoned in 1954.

THE ULSTER RAILWAY

Unlike the route from Dublin to Cork, that to Belfast was built up by three of the companies that formed the GNR, the 1825 attempt to build a through line, the Leinster & Ulster Railway, having failed. Trade between Dublin and Belfast was diminishing when the introduction of steam-powered ships made both places more accessible from Britain, causing enough concern for a revival of plans in 1835. However it was the industry of the Lagan valley that really attracted the businessmen of Belfast who were more interested in serving the further Belfast hinterland of Armagh and Enniskillen than a

Dublin line, seen by many as too large a project for the times. Thus the Ulster Railway of 1836, the second public railway authorised in Ireland, was to build a line of 36 miles from Belfast to Armagh and because there was no statute prescribing the gauge, tracks were laid to one of 6ft 2in; in fact they were guided by the 1836 Commission which informed the UR directors that this was the preferred width. The first section to Lisburn opened on 12 August 1839 with a station at Dunmurry, the Belfast terminus being in Glengall Place (now Great Victoria Street) and reasonably central. Immediately the company incurred the wrath of the Belfast Presbytery when it was seen that trains would run on Sundays – they claimed that vice would inevitably increase, blind to the fact that unlike the highway there were no public houses on the line and one clergyman even proclaimed that he would 'rather join a company for theft and murder than the Ulster Railway Co since it would be sending souls to the devil at the rate of 6d a piece', going on to say that 'every sound of the Railway whistle is answered by a shout in Hell'!

Dargan continued the line onwards to Portadown, trains reaching Lurgan on 18 November 1841 and a temporary terminus at Seagoe on 31 January 1842, the nature of the ground delaying completion into Portadown (25 miles) until 12 September 1842. First and Second Class passengers had the luxury of covered carriages but the luckless Thirds had to find a space within the goods wagons! It was not until 1841 that an open Third Class carriage was added to each train and unbelievably to present-day minds it was 1857 before the company ceased this practice.

The Ulster started with a single line; when Parliament passed a fresh Act in 1845 permitting extension to Armagh the company was warned that it would have to use whatever gauge would be decreed by the expected Gauges Act (see Chapter 1) and so when doubling took place between Belfast and Portadown a second track of the new gauge was first put down and used by goods trains from January 1847, passengers remaining on the original track while second platforms were built at stations; normal double line working on the new gauge came into force later that year. The cost of gauge alteration was shared, at Parliamentary direction, with the D&DR, D&BJR, D&ER and N&ER but it took years for the Ulster to collect the sums due, the last-named holding out until 1856.

There have been many changes to stations between Belfast and Portadown, being listed in Table 3, including some built for a rail motor service as far as Lisburn in competition with Belfast's new electric trams. Remarkably, Moira still has its 1841 buildings. At Portadown the original station was replaced in 1848 by a new one half a mile further on but that in turn was displaced in 1863 by a return to the original site.

With increasing traffic and its status as the main line between Ireland's largest centres, there was need for steady improvement, Portadown being enlarged in 1901 when the number of platforms was increased to four. At Belfast the old UR engine shed and works were moved out to a large new shed at Adelaide in 1911, alongside a new marshalling yard opened in 1909, the ground vacated alongside the terminus being used to enlarge the Grosvenor Road goods depot, first opened in 1874. More recently Portadown station was yet again resited, returning to the 1848 position in 1970 and being known as Craigavon West for some years; Lurgan was similarly Craigavon East. The Belfast terminus, Victoria Street by 1854 (Great being added in 1856) was replaced by Belfast Central on 26 April 1976, the adjacent Grosvenor Road goods depot having closed in 1965.

The premier trains of the GNR were naturally those between the two capitals and the greatest improvement came in 1947 when the customs stops were eliminated, checks taking place at each terminus, allowing the introduction of non-stop running, notable as the first in Ireland to exceed 100 miles (although seven such runs had been recorded previously for special workings). The service was given a special name 'Enterprise Express' and started on 11 August 1947 with all seats bookable in advance. Success ensured that a second express ran each day during 1848, but the morning down run to Belfast had to make a brief stop at Dundalk to pick up an Imperial customs officer. Bravely an attempt was made to provide a through Belfast and Cork service when on 2 October 1950 one each way ran throughout, lasting as a complete train until 27 June 1953, after which a solitary carriage provided the facility until it ceased on 19 September 1953. Nowadays the Dublin and Belfast service is worked jointly by the two railway authorities and currently has six daily through trains (three on Sunday) – as part of the upgrading now taking place four new General Motors diesel locomotives have been allocated to this service.

THE BANBRIDGE LINES

The map suggests that Banbridge on the main highway from Dublin to Belfast should have been selected as the route of any railway connecting the two – it nearly was as earlier recounted. Banbridge, a linen and manufacturing town of 6,100 persons, gained a railway quite early, an Act of 1853 incorporating the Banbridge, Newry, Dublin & Belfast Junction Railway, the title making up for the shortness of the line, 6¾ miles, Scarva being chosen for the junction. Built by Dargan, it was worked by the D&BJR from opening in 1859, having adopted the more meaningful title of Banbridge Junction Railway in 1856.

To provide a direct line to Belfast an Act of 1858 created the Belfast, Lisburn & Banbridge Railway which would build a line of 15¼ miles northwards to meet the UR near Lisburn. Construction was delayed by the failure of the first contractor, Killeen, being completed by Greene & King and opened in 1863 after a prolonged dispute with the UR over working arrangements and the junction at Knockmore. The UR wanted a siding connection to avoid facing points but the BOT insisted on a full double line junction. Despite installing platforms and a turntable the local company had to accept the fact that trains ran through to Belfast – apparently the facilities provided at the junction were never used! It was a steeply graded line, with a 1 in 57 section near Hillsborough, the steepest on the GNR. At Banbridge the station was a little to the east of the BJR platform, a junction being installed soon after opening when presumably the Scarva trains ran into the new station.

The Banbridge Extension Railway of 1860 planned a line eastwards from that town to Castlewellan, with tramway branches to Rathfriland (then with 2,200 people), Dundrum and Newcastle, leading to conflict with the proposed Downpatrick & Newry Railway which also planned to serve the area. Both got Acts in 1861, the BER being allowed to build only as far as Ballyroney, with a branch to Rathfriland, never built. The Moore Bros started to build the line but were replaced by Bagnell who stopped work when the railway was bankrupted in 1865. Eventually the 8 miles of unfinished line were purchased by the GNR in 1877 and completed by McCrea & McFarland, opening in late 1880 but Ballyroney was not a sensible place for a line to end. When powers were granted in 1900 to continue eastwards, the B&CDR countered by getting powers to build westward from Newcastle to Castlewellan where it was agreed that the station would be jointly owned and operated. The GNR was granted running powers into Newcastle and the B&CDR had reciprocal powers to Ballyroney; the former were invaluable and well used but the latter were of no practical worth. When opened in 1906 after completion by Fisher & LeFanu, the new line joined the B&CDR main line just outside Newcastle station, giving the seaside resort a second route from Belfast but 46 miles compared with 38. Until then the GNR had worked one service from Belfast to Banbridge and the other from Scarva to Ballyroney but the latter became a shuttle to Banbridge with the Belfast trains running to Newcastle.

The 1933 strike finished the Scarva and Banbridge service but it was restored in late 1934 when a railbus was put to work, calling at additional wayside stopping places. Competition from UTA buses once wartime restrictions were lifted finished services between Scarva, Banbridge and Newcastle during 1955, to be followed by the rest from Knockmore

Junction a year later, leaving a short length to serve Newforge siding for a few more years until about 1961.

ANTRIM BRANCH

The Dublin & Antrim Junction Railway of 1861 was intended to give access to the northern coast of Ireland by avoiding Belfast but construction was delayed by the failure of the first contractor, Greene & King, it being left to Treadwell to hand it over to the UR which was to work it. The branch of 18³/₄ miles, opened during 1871, diverged from the Dublin and Belfast main line at Knockmore Junction and turned north to run fairly close to Lough Neagh, which can be seen at places, to join the Northern Counties Londonderry line at Antrim. Traffic was never heavy but excursion trains between the wars from GNR stations to Portrush used the branch and, during the summer months, a through Dublin and Portrush coach (slipped at Lisburn on the down journey from about 1910 until 1939) ran that way.

In August 1918 a siding was added at Aldergrove where a new aerodrome was constructed, being 3 miles long and taking a course round the northern perimeter but after the work was finished it was removed. In 1940 the airfield was greatly expanded and a new branch was added, diverging a mile north of Crumlin at Siding Junction and terminating 2¹/₄ miles away at Gortnagallon; this time both passenger and goods were handled, thousands of workers coming from Belfast or Antrim and beyond, using four special workings at the height of activities. The line was ready in May 1942 and remained in use until the summer of 1945, when the users of the base, an American air force division, returned home. The railway was ignored when the airfield was developed as Northern Ireland's prime airport, a great opportunity being lost when for the want of an extra half-mile of entry road the new 1960 terminal buildings could have been built alongside the railway. In addition World War II hugely increased traffic over the branch, such that it was necessary to add a crossing loop at Aldergrove in 1943 to handle the extra trains, mainly troop movements.

After 1945 the pre-war calm returned and the end of passenger services came in 1960 but the line lingered on for it was the only means of transferring stock between the two parts of the UTA railway system. With the closure of the Derry Road in 1965 CIE trains were diverted to run to Lisburn and then over the branch to reach the Maiden City. Events were to change the fortunes of the GNR Antrim branch when the Belfast Central line was revived so that a basic service was resumed and stations reopened in 1974; it was stated at the time that a new station to serve Aldergrove airport was to be built at Millar's Bridge (25 miles from Belfast) but nothing transpired. A separate line into Lisburn was provided to eliminate Knockmore Junction, coming into use on 30 May 1977, and the passing loops were realigned to permit fast running on the straight track so that Londonderry trains could be diverted from their long-established route in order to run into Belfast Central. When Londonderry trains return to the old NCC route out of Belfast in 1997 the Antrim branch will have no purpose other than purely local; even the IR goods trains bound for Derry may well run via Belfast to avoid reversal at Lisburn.

For some years about 1983 there were expectations that lignite from a new source close to Lough Neagh would be taken by rail directly to Ballylumford power station near Larne; to avoid reversal at Antrim a direct loop was planned but so far nothing has materialised.

GOLFERS AND FISH

The coastal side of Co Down was served by the Belfast & County Down Railway formed in 1845, its rivals, the Grand County Down Railway (Downpatrick to Belfast with a branch to Moira to the north and to Banbridge, Newry and Warrenpoint to the south) and the Belfast & Holywood Atmospheric Railway both failing. Obtaining its Act in 1846, the plan was to form a junction with the UR and serve Comber and Downpatrick, with branches to Donaghadee and Holywood. Dargan was the contractor for the line southwards to Comber and Newtownards (12¼ miles) and trains started in 1850 from the Belfast terminus on the east side of the Lagan, adjacent to the Queen's Bridge; there was no connection with the UR.

Fresh powers of 1855 revived the plans so that the Moore Bros built onwards to reach Ballynahinch during 1858, left on a branch of 3½ miles when the main line was completed to Downpatrick (26¾ miles) in 1859. Donaghadee (22¼ miles) had to wait until 1861 for its trains after T. Edwards had built the extension with a new station at Newtownards, the original then closing. The Admiralty having made its recommendation, the Treasury financed a fine harbour at Donaghadee which was completed in 1863, although a track from the station to it was not ready until 1870; across the North Channel in Wigtownshire the harbour at Portpatrick was similarly rebuilt to establish the short sea crossing of 20 miles as the mail and packet route from Scotland to Ireland. However it was not the best choice and after storms in 1865 rendered Portpatrick unsuitable, the Government decided to support the Stranraer and Larne crossing, leaving the Co Down with a hefty loan raised to build the Donaghadee line. The Treasury then granted a similar loan over 35 years at a lower rate of interest to recompense the railway. Despite the problems of Portpatrick, a steamer company was set up but soon it was conceded that the Scottish harbour was too difficult to use.

It needed a separate company to carry the line southwards, the Downpatrick & Newry Railway being incorporated in 1861 to build 31 miles, shortened in 1866 as the Downpatrick, Dundrum & Newcastle Railway. Built by Connor & Olley, the DD&NR was worked by the Co Down until absorbed in 1881, having opened in 1869 to Newcastle. The Allport Commission recommended a line to the fishing village of Ardglass and accordingly the B&CDR was sanctioned to build the Downpatrick, Killough & Ardglass Railway in 1890. Getting a free grant of £29,980 and a 3 per cent Baronial Guarantee of £17,000 and using its own labour, the County Down disturbed the ground only to lay the track at minimum expense, clearly aware that there were no rich pickings. Services on the 7¾ mile branch started during 1892 and soon afterwards a loop to avoid reversal at Downpatrick, also built by direct labour, came into use, having an exchange platform at the south end; the practice developed whereby Downpatrick passengers often had to change from a main line into the branch train to reach the town.

Newcastle was boosted as a holiday resort by the Co Down and the company provided a five floor hotel of 120 rooms, the Slieve Donard, in 1898, spending nearly £100,000 in the process but in 1966 it was sold by UTA. With the entry of GNR trains in 1906 the station was completely rebuilt, its somewhat incongruous red brick building dominated by a massive clock tower with a steeple and small turrets at each corner. As early as 1892 a special train was put on, Saturday only and usually leaving Belfast at noon, taking 50 minutes or so non stop (although for a few years part went to Ardglass), slipping a coach for Donaghadee at Comber. The Co Down's royal coach was later converted to a first class saloon and became that used by golfers, hence the train's unofficial title The Golfer's Express.

For one week each year from 1928 until 1936 a special station existed at Glass Moss crossing, 1½ miles east of Comber; the Royal Automobile Club Tourist Trophy Race was run over a 13½ miles course through Dundonald, Newtownards and Comber, practice runs leading up to 'Race Saturday'. The railway crossed the course four times, three bridges and a level crossing. Well aware of the traffic potential with vast numbers of supporters travelling to the area, the Co Down collaborated by interrupting its service to Donaghadee; on each side of the crossing a platform was erected and a shuttle service worked, through passengers using a special footbridge over the race circuit, but racegoers could book to Glass Moss. The railway also built a grandstand at Comber but all came to an end when a crash killed nine spectators.

The Co Down became a successful railway and to deal with increasing traffic in the Belfast area had to double the line from Belfast as far as Knock in 1889 and on to Comber in 1893. The company was not unaware of the need to use the roads as feeder routes, starting as early as 1903 with a traction engine and wagons to provide a goods service from the Ards peninsula to Newtownards; a bus service was started in 1916 connecting Newcastle with Kilkeel but the company could not meet the competition of no less than 27 operators that ran throughout the area by 1927. That year the railway recommenced road services in a small way but in 1935 had to surrender everything to the NIRTB. Several halts were opened in 1925–34 to meet bus competition but for many places the road distance from Belfast was shorter than the rail, Newtownards being 3½ miles less, Donaghadee 2½, Ballynahinch 6½, Downpatrick 5 and Newcastle 7½ and the wonder is that the railway lasted so long. It did not take long for UTA to finish most of the system off, closing everything between Belfast and Newcastle and the branches in two bites during 1950; no longer was it possible to bounce across Co Down in a six-wheeler, the main stay of the railway's coaching stock.

BANGOR AND BACK FOR A BOB

First intentions of the Co Down were to reach Bangor by a branch from Conlig on the Donaghadee line, the coast route being confined to a 4½ mile level stretch to Holywood; the purely passenger potential of the latter would have given the proposed atmospheric system a good chance, rather like the Dalkey line, for a few years as it would not have had the complications or length of the South Devon Railway between Exeter and Newton Abbot. Built by Dargan the line to Holywood opened in 1848, parting from the Comber line at Ballymacarrett, a half mile out, each having a separate track into its own platform at the terminus, known as Queens Quay from 1854. The Co Down still expected to approach Bangor from the south as mentioned above, the Donaghadee line being only some three miles distant but it would have made a 20 miles journey instead of 12. Eastwards from Holywood there is quite a climb and perhaps that deterred the original promoters, for plans to use an easier course along the coast were frustrated by a local landowner. At the time the B&CDR was too impoverished to undertake an extension and it was left to the Belfast, Holywood & Bangor Railway to get an Act in 1860, the Co Down then abandoning its powers to reach Bangor.

The BH&BR was the protégé of J.E.C. Koch of the London Financial Association and he engaged the Edwards Brothers to build the 7¾ mile extension which started a few chains to the west of the existing Holywood

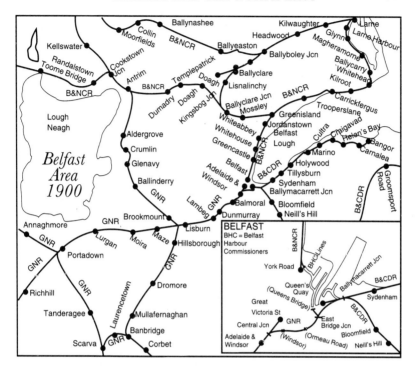

station but it was a slow job and not completed until 1865. When opened ownership of the line into Belfast passed to the BH&BR but until it obtained its own rolling stock in 1866 it was worked by the Co Down. Koch formed the Belfast & Bangor Railway & Land Co in an attempt to raise capital to develop Bangor but he succumbed with the bank crashes of 1866. One perceptive B&CDR shareholder was heard to condemn the sale of the Holywood branch, saying 'Surely you could not sell your right eye?' By an Act of 1873 the BH&BR was to be leased by the Co Down but the owners failed to maintain the line to the standard required by the lease so it was relinquished in 1876. However in 1884 the BH&BR was absorbed by the B&CDR and later that year the two stations at Queens Quay were amalgamated, being completely rebuilt in 1910–14 into a fine terminus. A branch from the Newtownards Road tramway of the Belfast Street Tramway Co was built in 1894 by the railway, horse-worked until purchased by Belfast Corporation and electrified in 1905; the tram line ran into the station itself.

Originally single track throughout, the line was doubled as far as Holywood in 1875, the remainder being done in stages, Carnalea to Bangor in 1898, Helen's Bay to Carnalea in 1899, Holywood to Craigavad in 1900 and Craigavad to Helen's Bay in 1902. Suburban traffic became heavy with vast numbers travelling into the offices and workshops of Belfast so that the County Down was issuing more season tickets than any other Irish Railway and the Bangor line could justly claim to be Ireland's busiest but excursionists also became numerous and travelled at a cheap rate – Bangor and back for a bob! To give such travellers variety the Co Down became a steamboat operator in 1893, eventually having three vessels running from Belfast to Bangor each summer, making excursions to places as far apart as Portrush and Ardglass. All came to an end in 1915 when the last vessel was requisitioned. When extension of Belfast's electric trams out to Holywood was proposed, the County Down started a railmotor service with extra halts in 1905. Later, signalling was revised so that an automatic system, with continuous track circuiting, came into use in 1923 but it had to be modified when a rear end collision in fog at Ballymacarrett in 1945 caused 23 deaths, one of Ireland's worst railway accidents.

In 1923 an extension from Bangor along the coast to Groomsport and Donaghadee was seriously considered, together with electrification from Belfast but costs deterred further action. The Bangor line has survived the UTA closures and in 1954 became the first in the British Isles to have all its regular trains diesel worked, although steam excursions from GNR lines continued until 1965. With the closure of the connecting Belfast Central line in 1965, the Bangor line became isolated from the remainder of Ireland's railways. The service became so standardised that it was not necessary to provide a separate working timetable, staff using the public issue, every train working throughout (but there was just one empty stock run). Its isolation prompted a proposal to change the gauge to 4ft 8½in so that surplus stock could be obtained from British Railways but fortunately that did not happen – it would have been an embarrassment in view of later developments. The revival of the Belfast Central line, to be described shortly, reconnected the Bangor line to the rest of the system and its trains last used Queens Quay on 10 April 1976, being diverted into the new station. Perhaps electrification will come to this line one day for it remains busy with as many as 27 trains daily passing through Belfast, about half terminating at Lisburn, the remainder running on to Portadown, apart from one which turns round at Crumlin on the Antrim line.

ANY MORE FOR THE STEAMER?

The north side of Belfast is bounded by the high ground of Cavehill and a continuous line of hills which leave a narrow strip along the north shore of Belfast Lough. Such an obstruction caused much debate about the route to be taken out of Belfast to reach Antrim and Ballymena, some proposers seeking to use the UR for part of the way. A prospectus of 1836 headed *The North-Eastern Railway* chose a route northward out of Belfast and up over the gap in the hills to reach Antrim and Ballymena, adding a branch to Carrickfergus. By 1844 there was sufficient confidence to form the Belfast & Ballymena Railway, authorised in 1845 to build out to Ballymena and Carrickfergus, with a short branch to Randalstown in Co Antrim. Dargan set to work later that year and built a single line of railway which opened throughout on 12 April 1848, Carrickfergus being 9¹/₂ miles from the Belfast terminus which became York Road in 1854 (for the moment the Ballymena line is left aside). The line was doubled as far as Greencastle in 1862 and Carrickfergus Junction (Greenisland from 1894) in 1863, but it was not until 1897 that the work was completed through to Carrickfergus.

A separate company, the Carrickfergus Harbour Junction Railway, was formed in 1882 to serve both the Old Pier and the new West Pier with about one mile of lines, but in fact it was built by J. Hegarty under terms of the 1883 Act, complete with a Baronial Guarantee of £6,500, opening in 1887 and worked by the B&NCR.

An 1846 report in favour of the Larne and Stranraer crossing was ignored by the Government which chose to develop Donaghadee and Portpatrick as earlier mentioned. This did not deter supporters of the longer but more sheltered passage who in 1860 obtained an Act to form the Carrickfergus & Larne Railway, 14³/₄ miles of single line built by Edwards Bros and completed on 1 October 1862. The extension started a half mile west of the 1848 Carrickfergus station which was then replaced, the old course being used later by the CHJR. There is a tunnel of 157 yards near Whitehead where the line runs alongside Belfast Lough before cutting across the base of Islandmagee, a peninsula which encloses the greater part of Larne Lough. A steamer was obtained and started its crossings to Stranraer when the line opened, but the losses were much greater than expected and sailing ceased on 1 January 1864, the last mile of railway becoming unused apart from the odd coal train. However it was kept in repair in the hope of better days which did indeed come when sailings resumed on 1 July 1872 and the route has never looked back. At Larne Harbour narrow gauge trains of the Ballymena & Larne Railway shared the station from 1878, the two gauges running side by side until the latter ceased in 1950.

The Larne line has developed into a suburban route but its dual status remains as the Irish portion of the journey between Belfast and Scotland. A limited service is maintained on the line for container traffic, using former passenger stock as flat wagons. The sea crossing is busier than ever, heavily used by road vehicles, thus ensuring its survival; in fact it has been described as a 'floating motorway!' Whitehead has changed out of all proportion as a residential area and a resort; it did not get a mention in the 1871 census! The first station lay at the west end of the tunnel, the second at the other end and that of 1877 was enlarged in 1907 by the addition of excursion platforms, such was the success of the railway's efforts and large sums spent to attract tourists, such as building the cliff path out to Black Head, the promenade and landing stage; even the beach had to be created, by bringing in sand from Portrush! Sadly many of the works have fallen into decay, UTA ceasing to have an interest in 1961. In 1909 the railway purchased the Laharna Hotel at Larne, for use by steamer passengers and tourists, which lasted in railway ownership until sold in 1966; for many years it had the reputation of being the best accommodation for tourists in Ulster.

York Road had only one platform until enlargement started in 1875, reaching its maximum in 1897. It was another station into which the street tramway entered, laid in 1894 and electrified in 1905. The Midland Hotel (originally the Station Hotel) dated from the same period and was connected to the station. In 1926 the tracks in the station area were resignalled, using colour lights, the first in Ireland and doubtless a trial before wider use on the LMS. Extensive bomb damage during World War II in 1941 was only partly patched up and it was not until 1975 that a full rebuilding was undertaken. The Northern Counties naturally looked after its stock at Belfast where 37 engines were built between 1870 and 1942, together with carriages and wagons.

The double line was extended from Carrickfergus, first to Kilroot and then Whitehead during 1929; altering the tunnel was avoided by laying the new up line round the seaward side of the small headland. Larne Harbour station was rebuilt in 1967–8 in modern style, losing its Victorian grandeur. At Larne Town it was necessary to relocate the line and station in 1974 to make way for a new road. Following diversion of the Londonderry trains in 1978 the Larne service ran in isolation until reconnected to the rest of the system by the opening of the 'Cross Harbour Link' in 1994, as later described.

One of the largest plants in Northern Ireland was built by Courtaulds to process synthetic fibre, the NCC adding a signal cabin for the new sidings and a halt for workers in 1946, but the inwards coal traffic ceased in 1967. The company had used a pair of Peckett saddle tanks, new in 1948–50, but neither was saved by preservationists when sold for scrap in 1968.

Motorway construction was responsible for a late use of steam on the Larne line when all else was non-steam. To give road access alongside Belfast Lough into the city everything in the course of the motorway was pushed aside, needing relocation of the railway's workshops, and a vast amount of spoil to reclaim the foreshore. It came from Magheramourne and the UTA seized the contract for its delivery, constructing a third track for its discharge. Thus the last commercial use of steam in the British Isles attracted attention far and wide and from early 1966 until May 1970 no less than 7,600 trains, each carrying 600 tons of rock, ran – with an engine at each end. Only the 2–6–4T 'Jeeps' (new from Derby in 1946–51) were available and just about every movement must have been photographed or filmed.

Events in Belfast have changed the travel habits of the populace along the north side of Belfast Lough so that York Road became mainly a rush hour station but throughout the day there has been plenty of traffic between local stations – York Road suffered from the shift southwards of business and shops and the area is largely derelict and totally uninviting, but times have changed.

A RAILWAY LOST AND FOUND

With its three unconnected railway termini Belfast faced the same problem as Dublin; many of the difficulties were similar, in particular the raising of finance, but unlike Dublin the plans of more than a century ago were never completed by their originators, a London-based finance organisation. Two early schemes failed, one being a tramway connection from the UR to the docks, only the Belfast Central Railway getting an Act in 1864 for a central station on Victoria Street and connections to all three companies, a further Act of 1865 allowing the construction of tramways on quays on the east of the River Lagan. Until then only the B&NCR had any connection with BHC tracks at Dufferin Dock Junction, dating from 1855. Another Act of 1868 gave powers, never used, to make a second bridge over the Lagan and a curve to allow direct running from Queens Quay to York Road.

The financiers, the Imperial Credit Company of London (which had an interest at various times in several small railways, all of which were heavily over-capitalised and in debt) appointed their manager, J.D. Thornton, as contractor but he made little progress. J.W. Kelly took over, building the line from the junction with the UR at Ulster (later Central) Junction around the south side of the city area to East Bridge Junction (1¾ miles) near Maysfields where it split to serve Queen's Bridge (2) on the west bank and join the Co Down (2½) on the east bank at Ballymacarrett Junction and continue on to give access to the Abercorn Basin. Goods and coal traffic started during 1874 and passengers from Ulster Junction to Queen's Bridge in 1878 but it was already too late to be of much use as the horse trams of the Belfast Street Tramways had served the area since 1872, nor did BCR trains run into Great Victoria Street, which could have been reached by reversal and running powers. The goods extension from Queen's Bridge to Donegall

Quay Junction with BHC tracks was opened in 1876, horse-worked with a level crossing over East Bridge Street, replaced by a subway in 1880; its limited clearance meant that locomotives working through it had to have shortened chimneys. Other than the bridge over the Lagan, the Belfast Central lines were all double track.

In a move of wild speculation the BCR put forward plans for 3ft gauge lines in 1880 to reach the western suburbs of Belfast and in 1881 extended the idea as the Ballyclare, Ligoniel & Belfast Junction Railway and added, for good measure a line to Holywood, with a third rail on existing lines where needed, but no capital was ever raised.

The GNR took over the Belfast Central railway in 1885 and immediately stopped the passenger trains, but the line was useful to the GNR which added a large cattle depot and lairage at Maysfields in 1914. Apart from special permission for a weekly passenger train during the summer months of 1895, it was to be many years before the later well-known through excursions to Bangor started about 1921; a through carriage from Dublin to Bangor ran until 1939. With the decline of UTA goods traffic the line was singled in 1964, but closure took place the next year, making way for massive roadworks with a new crossing of the Lagan. The line was left derelict and never abandoned; indeed it was contended that closure was illegal, a claim not contested by UTA!

Belfast was the Irish port for two cross-channel railway steamer routes, both docking at Donegall Quay on the Co Antrim side of the river. That from Fleetwood started in 1840 and from 1870 was jointly worked by the LNWR and Lancashire & Yorkshire Railway. The other was provided by the Midland Railway, initially from Morecambe in 1851, then from Barrow in 1867 until the new railway port at Heysham started operations in 1904. Both routes were combined into one from Heysham in 1928, being equipped with new vessels. Changing traffic levels twenty years ago finished this service, the last sailing being that of 6 April 1975.

The Belfast harbour lines were purely goods lines with the exception of very limited use about 1930 when on summer Saturdays a passenger service connecting at Donegall Quay with the Heysham steamers was tried. After little use from 1966 BHC lines were closed in 1969–70.

Reuse of the Central line was investigated during 1967, resulting in the laying down of double track throughout and a new bridge over the Lagan to connect the Portadown and Bangor lines with a new Central station and another at Botanic nearer Central Junction. In association the Bangor line was resignalled and on 12 April 1976 its trains were diverted over the rebuilt line to the new station, followed by those of the Portadown line 14 days later, but it was not for two years that Londonderry trains made use of the

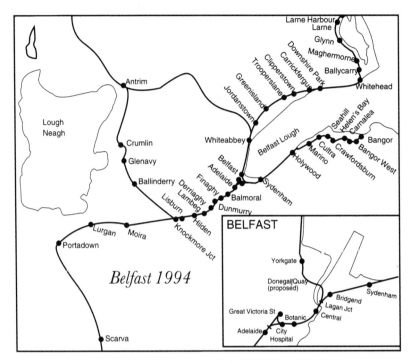

Belfast 1994

modern-style station with its four platforms of 800ft length. Short journeys from the inner Portadown line stations diminished, a reaction to the closure of Great Victoria Street, connecting buses on such a short journey being far from popular. In 1986 a further station opened on the rebuilt line at City Hospital near the former Central Junction.

The isolation of the Larne service has ended by building an entirely new line through areas of Belfast which had been cleared of old buildings and docks. NIR prepared plans for the 'Cross Harbour Link' as long ago as 1978, expecting work to start in 1980 but the project was cancelled by Westminster in 1979. Fortunately the scheme was revived and completed in 1994, its course being shown on the 1994 Belfast area map. At the northern end a new station, Yorkgate, was opened as a temporary terminus on 17 October 1992, allowing immediate closure of York Road; full opening took place on 28 November 1994, Larne trains diverging from the Bangor line at Lagan Junction. Timetables have been recast to give additional cross Belfast journeys and later Derry trains will return to their traditional route. Regrettably financial restrictions have forced the building of only a single line viaduct, although there will be a loop at the site of Donegall Quay, where a station is planned, hopefully to be opened in 1997. West of Belfast

TABLE 3
SUBURBAN STATIONS PORTADOWN – BANGOR AND LARNE
A = mileage from Belfast central; B = mileage from original termini.

(a) BELFAST CENTRAL – PORTADOWN

A	B	Station	Opened	Closed	Remarks
–	–	Queen's Bridge	1878	1885	Terminus of BCR service (2 miles from Ulster Junction)
0	–	Belfast Central	1976	OPEN	
–	–	Ormeau	1878	1885	BCR station (1 mile from Ulster Junction)
–	–	Botanic Road	1878	1885	BCR station ($^1/_2$ mile from Ulster Junction); soon became Windsor
$0^3/_4$	–	Botanic	1976	OPEN	
$1^1/_4$	–	City Hospital	1986	OPEN	
–	0	Belfast	1839	1976	Original terminus; Victoria Street added by 1854; Great Victoria Street from 1856. To be reopened
–	$0^1/_2$	Ulster Junction	1878	1885	Sometimes Central Junction
$2^1/_4$	$1^1/_2$	Adelaide & Windsor	1899	OPEN	Adelaide from 1936
3	$2^1/_4$	Balmoral	1858	OPEN	Closed for a while until 1863
$3^3/_4$	3	Finaghy	1907	OPEN	
$4^3/_4$	4	Dunmurry	1839	OPEN	
$5^3/_4$	5	Derriaghy	1907	OPEN	Closed 1953–6
$6^3/_4$	6	Lambeg	1878*	OPEN	
$7^1/_4$	$6^1/_2$	Hilden	1907	OPEN	
$8^1/_4$	$7^1/_2$	Lisburn	1839	OPEN	
$9^1/_2$	$8^3/_4$	Knockmore	1974	OPEN	
–	9	Knockmore Junction	1933	1934	
–	10	Maze Platform	1898	1974	
–	$12^1/_2$	Broomhedge	1935	1953	
–	$13^1/_2$	Damhead	1935	1973	
$15^1/_4$	$14^1/_2$	Moira	1841	OPEN	
–	17*	Pritchard's Bridge	1841	1844	
$20^3/_4$	20	Lurgan	1841	OPEN	
22	$21^1/_4$	Goodyear	1970	1983	Factory platform
–	$23^1/_4$	Seagoe	1841	1842	Temporary terminus
–	25	Portadown	1842	1848	Resited; reverted to this site in 1863 and resited again 1970
			1863	1870	
$26^1/_4$	$25^1/_2$	Portadown	1848	1863	Resited in 1863
			1970	OPEN	

(b) BELFAST CENTRAL – BANGOR

A	B	Station	Opened	Closed	Remarks
0	–	Belfast Central	1976	OPEN	
$0^3/_4$	–	Bridgend	1977	OPEN	Replaced Ballymacarrett
–	0	Belfast	1848	1976	Original terminus, Queen Quay added by 1854
–	$0^3/_4$	Ballymacarrett	1905	1977	
$1^3/_4$	$1^1/_4$	Victoria Park	1905	1988	
$2^1/_4$	$1^3/_4$	Ballymisert	1851	OPEN	Sydenham from 1856

A	B	Station	Opened	Closed	Remarks
–	2¼	Glenmachen	1861	?	Closed by 1873
–	2½	Tillysburn	1880	1945	Second station
–	2¾	Tillysburn	1848	1880	First station possibly closed by 1877
–	3	Kinnegar	1905	1957	
4¾	4¼	Holywood	1865	OPEN	Second station
–	4½	Holywood	1848	1865	Original terminus
5¾	5¼	Marino	1870*	OPEN	Closed 1957–60
6¼	5¾	Cultra	1865	OPEN	Closed 1957–78
–	6½	Craigavad	1865	1961	Closed 1957–60
8	7½	Seahill	1966	OPEN	
9¼	8¾	Clandeboye	1865	OPEN	Helen's Bay from 1885
10	9½	Crawfordsburn	1965	OPEN	
10¾	10¼	Carnalea	1873*	OPEN	
11¼	10¾	Bangor West	1929	OPEN	
12¼	11¾	Bangor	1865	OPEN	

(c) BELFAST CENTRAL – LARNE

A	B	Station	Opened	Closed	Remarks
0	–	Belfast Central	1976	OPEN	
0¾	–	Donegall Quay	–	–	Planned to open in 1997
1¼	–	Yorkgate	1992	OPEN	Replaced York Road
–	0	Belfast	1848	1992	York Road added by 1854
–	2½	Grencastle	1848	1916	
–	2¾	Whitehouse	1848	1906	Resited
–	3¼	Whitehouse	1906	1954	
5¼	4¼	Whiteabbey	1848	OPEN	
–	4¾	Bleach Green Halt	1925	1977	
6¼	5¼	Jordanstown	1861	OPEN	NI Polytechnic added 1974
7¾	6¾	Carrickfergus Junction	1848	OPEN	Greenisland from 1894
9	8	Troopers Lane	1848	OPEN	
–	8¾	Mount	1925	1972	Closed 1930 until about 1941
10¼	9¼	Clipperstown	1925	OPEN	
10½	9½	Carrickfergus	1848	1862	Resited
10½	9½	Carrickfergus	1862	OPEN	
–	10	Barn	1925	1977	Closed 1930 until about 1941
11½	10½	Downshire Park	1925	OPEN	later Downshire
–	11	Eden	1925	1977	
–	11½	Kilroot	1862	1977	
–	13¾	Whitehead	1863	1864	Resited
–	14	Whitehead	1864	1877	Resited
15¾	14¾	Whitehead	1877	OPEN	Excursion platforms added 1907
17½	16½	Ballycarry	1862	OPEN	
20¾	19¾	Ballylig	1862	OPEN	Maghermorne from about 1865
22½	21½	Glynn	1864	OPEN	
24¼	23¼	Larne	1862	OPEN	Resited on deviation 1974
25¼	24¼	Larne Harbour	1862	OPEN	No service 1864–72

* Distance or date approximate.

Central work is well in hand during 1995 to restore Great Victoria Street to use, a new curve giving access from the Bangor and Larne lines in addition to the original route from Portadown; it is fortunate that motorway plans of thirty years ago failed, allowing recovery of the closed GNR terminus. Apart from some rush hour trains the reopened terminus will be a reversing point for through suburban journeys.

It has taken well over a century for the vision of the Belfast Central Railway to materialise but now NIR has a service of value to its passengers, the immediate response being an increase by 10 per cent in travellers on the Larne line who can now reach the central parts of the city more easily. The name of William Dargan has appeared many times in this narrative and now the Cross Harbour bridge, opened by Her Majesty, Queen Elizabeth II, is named after him in recognition of his works throughout Ireland. The bridge is in fact a viaduct, only a small part actually being over water, but its total length of 4,675ft makes it by far the longest in Ireland.

TO THE NORTH COAST

Early railway planners intended to reach the north coast from a Dublin and Belfast route passing through Armagh and so in 1846 the Dublin, Belfast & Coleraine Junction Railway was incorporated, having 'seen off' the rival Armagh, Coleraine & Portrush Railway scheme. The 70 miles of line from Armagh were to pass through Dungannon, Cookstown, Magherafelt and Coleraine to Portrush with a branch from Magherafelt to Randalstown (11 miles) which explains how the B&BR came to have a branch to that place when its main line to Ballymena opened the same day as its Carrickfergus line – it was of no value when the DB&CJR expired in 1849. Another branch of the defunct company was to reach Ballymoney, to be extended to by the Belfast & Ballymena, Londonderry & Coleraine Railway (a curious blend of two other companies' titles) to Ballymena. When these schemes failed, the Ballymena, Ballymoney, Coleraine & Portrush Junction Railway was formed in 1853 to fill the gap existing in the route to Londonderry. William Dargan was the contractor, taking shares in payment, making him virtually sole owner, the line opening on 4 December 1855 from a new station at Ballymena which replaced the B&BR terminus. Portrush (67 miles from Belfast) was no more than a small fishing village but a branch to the harbour was added in 1866. The town's site on a headland with a beach either side encouraged its development into one of Ireland's premier resorts and in 1881 the B&NCR took a lease of the major hotel, The Antrim Arms, already well established; outright purchase followed in 1902 but in 1966 the hotel was sold by UTA. Portrush station was enlarged in 1892 and became noted for its fine buildings, executed in a mock-Tudor style. Coastal steamer services also called at Portrush for many years and the town was a popular destination for excursions by sea or rail – indeed it is still a place for a family day out.

Originally the route was single throughout but doubling as far as Ballymena took place in stages, from Carrickfergus Junction (Greenisland) to Ballyclare & Doagh in 1875, thence to Dunadry in 1872, through to Cookstown Junction in 1877 and finally to Ballymena in 1878. The need for reversal at Greenisland remained despite an Act of 1878 which authorised a direct line from Jordanstown to join the main line near Mossley, this scheme being abandoned in 1882. It was decided instead to fit the rolling stock with the automatic vacuum brake, a move which allowed faster running and so overcome in part the slowness imposed by reversal. Such a hindrance could not be tolerated indefinitely but it was not until 1927 that a new plan was adopted; this time the loop was to start north of Whiteabbey and join the old line near Mossley, being authorised in 1928 and undertaken as unemployment relief, work starting in 1931. The steeply inclined line with a ruling gradient of 1 in 76, built with double track, included a major concrete viaduct over Valentine's Glen and diverged at Bleach Green Junction, 4³/₄ miles from Belfast. At the other end the old main line had to be lowered to suit the new alignment and from the new junction back to Greenisland was singled, being thereafter known as the 'back line'. Thus there was a saving of 2³/₄ miles and a new improved service was put on, using new locomotives and coaches for the best trains. After a ceremonial opening by the Governor of Northern Ireland, the Duke of Abercorn, on 17 January 1934, the full service started five days later. The almost redundant parts of the old main line was retained until through Larne and Londonderry coaches were withdrawn on 9 September 1961, closure taking place on 1 October 1963.

Most of the intermediate stations have closed, starting as early as 1920 and on the Portrush branch winter services ceased from 1960, being restored in 1968 when the new University of Ulster opened near Coleraine, coupled with the addition of two new halts, University in 1968 and Dhu Varren in 1969, and the reopening of Portstewart (closed 1964) in 1968 (but lasting only until 1988) to cater for student travelling. The great change was the diversion of main line trains to run from Antrim via Lisburn into Belfast Central in 1978 with the closure of the old main line from Bleach Green Junction to Antrim. However there were demands for the restoration of trains and so an experimental service started on 1 September 1980 with reopened stations at Monkstown, Mossley and Templepatrick but it was so poorly patronised that it ceased on 21 February 1981.

With the building of the Cross Harbour Link, the old mainline to

Antrim, little-used, although it has been invaluable for diversions on a few occasions, is being renovated as a single line with crossing places at Kingsmoss and Templepatrick. The double line from Antrim to Ballymena was converted to single in 1990, a loop being installed at Magherabeg, 6 miles north of Antrim. Further north the former loop at Killagan was reinstated during 1994.

ALONG THE COAST TO DERRY

The Portrush line did not cross the River Bann, astride which Coleraine stands, although the greater part of the town lies on the east bank. Westwards the intervening area to Londonderry was to be served by the Londonderry & Coleraine Railway, a long time in gestation and building. A relief map will show why a railway route between Belfast and Derry had to be so much longer than any road; west of the Bann there is plenty of uninhabitable high ground where the present-day main road (A6) traverses the Glenshane Pass between Maghera and Dungiven at some 800ft. Thus there was never any sensible prospect of a shorter railway for the 75 miles between the two cities.

The L&CR, and its sister the L&ER, was a London company, the cause of most of its problems. With great enthusiasm its promoters set out to reclaim most of the east side of Lough Foyle by building an embankment of 15 miles between Coolkeeragh, where the river widens into the lough, and Magilligan Point, believing that the sale of the newly-created land would pay for both embankment and railway. The BOT was averse, pointing out that such a coastal line would be far from any population, that it would take time for settlement on the new lands and that there was in any case little traffic between Derry and Coleraine; despite this the company obtained its first Act in 1845. Bromhead & Hemming got the contract for all the works but progressed so slowly that in desperation the company turned to McCormick in 1850; even he achieved only partial completion of the reclamation works. The railway required little engineering, being almost level throughout, but there were two tunnels on the coast, Castlerock of 667 yards and Downhill of 301 yards; they were the first completed in Ireland, although not the first through which trains passed, that honour passing to Kilpatrick tunnel in Co Cork. The single line railway was opened from Derry to Newtownlimavady (shortened to Limavady in 1870) on 29 December 1852, goods having already started, followed by the remainder from Newtown Junction (Limavady Junction from 1876) to Coleraine on 18 July 1853. Both termini were called Waterside and both were adjacent to the solitary bridge at each town; at Coleraine Waterside was the name of the road over the river bridge.

The L&CR had a second branch, $4^1/2$ miles between Magilligan and Magilligan Point built without Parliamentary powers as the land was given free. The line appeared in *Bradshaw* first in July 1855 and then only until the October issue and the time taken, 40 minutes, seems to make it certain that horses provided the motive power. From the point there was a steamer connection to Greencastle on the Co Donegal shore of Lough Foyle. Magilligan Point is of interest geographically as the base line for the first Irish survey was set out nearby. The B&NCR considered a revival of the branch in 1894 at a time when ocean liners called in Lough Foyle, served by tenders from Moville on the Donegal shore. Magilligan was visualised as a replacement, to become a northern version of Cobh but opposition by the Admiralty and others destroyed all hopes despite an Act of 1895 permitting building of the branch.

At Coleraine there were demands for a link by means of a bridge across the River Bann but the L&CR had other ideas, getting an Act in 1853 to build a line along the valley of the Bann to Castledawson, there to join the Cookstown extension of the B&BR; to modern eyes it seems ridiculous that Parliament should authorise this on the same day as the BBC&PR but that railway did not plan to cross the Bann, nor did it serve the same area. McCormick was to build the line, the first sod was turned and after that nothing more happened. It was left to the BBC&PJR to get powers for a bridge, with an opening span, in 1859, a nominally separate company, the Belfast & Londonderry Junction Railway, being incorporated. The new line, $3/4$ miles long, diverged from the Portrush line north of Coleraine station and replaced the final $1/2$ mile of the L&CR line which closed when the bridge came into use on 19 November 1860, after a ceremonial opening four days earlier. A through line now existed between Belfast and Derry and the B&BR set about expansion by absorbing both the Portrush and L&CR lines, retitling itself the Belfast & Northern Counties Railway in 1860; of the former the BBC&PJR was taken over in 1861 and the L&CR was leased that year, being absorbed in 1871. The latter company had proved to be financially disastrous, being heavily indebted to the PWLC and to McCormick who in turn had been ruined by his involvement

Portrush as a port did not meet expectations so Coleraine merchants improved their harbour in 1884 and an Act of 1889 permitted a short branch on the east bank which curved sharply away from the river bridge approach, being opened in 1892. It was well used until 1963, being abandoned in 1966.

The Bann bridge of 1860 was an eyesore and not a few travellers were apprehensive about crossing it. Replacement was necessary by 1900 but it was not until 1914 that powers were obtained; the new course eased the curvature of the approach from the Derry side and lay a little to the north, being opened on 21 March 1924. As before there had to be a lifting span and with mechanised equipment, opening, passage of a vessel and closing could be done in under ten minutes. Further west at Ballykelly, signalling history was made in 1943 when a runaway at the adjacent Royal Air Force airfield needed extension to take the largest bombers and could only do so by crossing the railway! Special signalling had to be provided and there had to be close cooperation between the signalman in a new cabin and the airfield control tower at what was probably the only place worldwide where trains crossed an airfield.

The Derry line beyond Coleraine has been something of a remote arm and its single track is now reduced to a basic railway. For a few years until about 1940 the NCC catered for the sparse local traffic by using a bus with Howden-Meredith patent wheels which made extra stops at level crossings. At Londonderry the terminus was resited after the original had been damaged by a bomb in 1975, some 10 chains nearer the Craigavon Bridge, the old site becoming the goods yard for CIE container traffic. The new station opened on 24 February 1980. Present plans envisage replacement of the sole passing loop between Coleraine and Derry at Castlerock by one near Ballykelly to make the two sections more equal (presently 6 and 28 miles, to be 20 and 14).

NORTHERN COUNTIES BRANCHES

The plans of the BCR to reach Ballyclare rekindled a scheme of 1874, extensive traffic from the paper mills in the town, centre of that trade in Ireland, being an attraction, Acts of 1881 and 1882 allowing the B&NCR to build a branch. The unrecorded contractor worked quickly so that the 3½ miles of single track, which diverged one mile west of Ballyclare Junction station at Kingsbog Junction, opened in 1884. Traffic never came up to expectations and trains ceased during 1938 but the line was reopened as a siding in 1940 to serve an army depot at Ballyclare, lasting until 1950.

A major branch of the B&NCR served the south east corner of Co Londonderry, although its terminus at Cookstown was in Co Tyrone. In the hope of making the branch to Randalstown worthwhile, it was extended 27 miles by Act of 1853. Dargan, who had the contract, started work in 1855 and despite two major bridges, one over the Maine near Randalstown and the other across the Bann at Toome, it was ready for an opening in late 1856. The Cookstown line earned very poor receipts and was blamed soon after opening for a reduction in B&BR dividends; at one meeting the vice-chairman remarked 'perhaps if they travelled free and got their dinners, they would travel'. In 1879 the GNR became a competitor for Cookstown traffic but neither had any advantage in distance for Belfast passengers. The branch remained a backwater but it had its interest in being the haunt of most of the last of the von-Borries compounds which had been so successful on the Northern Counties. Passenger trains ceased in 1950 and goods from Magherafelt to Cookstown in 1955, the remainder finishing in 1959, having been retained solely for traffic from the Derry Central line.

Draperstown, with 500 souls, felt the need for railway connection, Magherafelt being the nearest station. The Draperstown Railway obtained its Act in 1878 for a 6½ miles branch to start at Draperstown Junction, 1¼ miles west of Magherafelt. Built by J. & W. Grainger and opened in 1883, the railway was worked by the B&NCR but it never made a profit and as the BOW had not been paid its loan interest it forced the sale of the line in 1895 to the B&NCR. Passenger trains ceased in 1930, the first NCC broad gauge line to lose them, but goods survived until 1950.

The Derry Central Railway, authorised in 1875, in part revived the aspirations of the abortive Dublin, Belfast & Coleraine Junction Railway by building a 29¼ miles line from Magherafelt to Macfin, having junctions with its working company, the B&NCR, at each end. Although a Baronial Guarantee of £45,000 was arranged, lack of capital delayed completion by C.M. Holland of Liverpool until 1880, trains running between Magherafelt and Coleraine, the latter station being enlarged that year to accommodate them.

Despite the prosperity of the area with its farming and linen trade the line did not pay, so forcing the company to sell out when the BOW took possession in 1901 for non-payment of interest, handing the company to Northern Counties. The line became a useful but restricted alternative to the main line through Ballymena and was at times used as a route for excursions to Portrush. The wonder is that the passenger service lasted so long for it did not cease until 1950, closing totally northwards from Kilrea, the rest remaining for a daily goods which primarily served a linen factory at Upperlands until it ceased in 1959. The factory was at the end of a half mile branch from the station and became well known for, apart from its excellent linen, a 2ft gauge horse tramway laid down in 1900 which connected together various parts of the works.

Dungiven was another plantation town, about the same size as Draperstown, lying in the middle of Co Derry. The northern end of the branch to Limavady was built by the L&CR as described and it was extended by the Limavady & Dungiven Railway, authorised in 1878. Capital was, as so often, the problem and recourse to a BOW loan was necessary before McCrea & McFarland could build the new railway.

Opened in 1883, the ever-mounting interest debt resulted in the BOW taking possession of the L&DR in 1907 and its sale to the Northern Counties for £2,000 although it had cost nearly £100,000 to build! Passenger trains ceased to run beyond Limavady at the beginning of 1933 but goods continued until 1950; at the same time the passenger service to Limavady ceased, followed by total closure in 1955.

NORTHERN COUNTIES NARROW GAUGE

It was iron ore that attracted narrow gauge lines to mid-Antrim, first extracted in 1861 and by 1869 some 50,000 tons being exported from various ports on the Co Antrim coast, the absence of coal inhibiting local smelting. Major sources were found to the north east of Ballymena and for a decade ore was carted down to the B&NCR. The first line, the Ballymena, Cushendall & Red Bay Railway, was authorised in 1872 but the first in operation served upper Glenariff. Thus the Glenariff Iron Ore & Harbour Co built a direct line to the coast over private land, dropping no less than 610ft in 4 miles, mostly at 1 in 40, to a pier at Red Bay. Sadly, soon after opening in 1873 the outcrop of ore proved insufficient and in 1875 mining ceased. A planned extension inland to reach Cargan would have involved 3 miles of steeply graded line with a tunnel and reached 900ft but the Glenariff Railway & Harbour Co of 1880 managed to run just one train, not for ore but to show off the proprietor's plans, all to no avail. Many assets were sold in March 1885, the two Stephenson 2–4–0T engines, new in 1872 and the first 3ft gauge in Ireland, passing to the L&LSR; the track was left in place in the hope of revival but in 1890 much of it was purloined, making it the second 'stolen railway' of Ireland!

Mining became extensive in Glenravel in 1866–75, mostly destined for Barrow-in-Furness. One attempt to ease its transport was made in 1872 when the Wire Tramway Co Ltd of London completed the Antrim Wire Tramway Co's line from Cargan to the coast near Red Bay pier but it was a failure. The BC&RBR built by James Connor first carried ore from Cargan in early 1875, cargoes being transhipped by the B&NCR at Ballymena. Extension in 1876 enabled ore to flow downwards from the Evishcrow mine near Parkmore and Retreat (16¼ miles from Ballymena) was reached later that year, the line crossing the 1,000ft contour, the summit being at Essathohan siding at 1,045ft and the highest point on any Irish railway. Several mines were served, some on separate branches owned by the mining companies, and the company had its own broad gauge wagons running on the B&NCR, using a stage at Ballymena for transhipment. The remaining 6 miles to the coast, with a drop of over 1,000ft, were never built. One plan envisaged three reversals reminiscent of an Andean railway and another would use a direct incline with 3 miles of 1 in 21! In 1884 Parliament approved the building of a roadside tramway from Retreat down to Cushendall but like the earlier plans nothing was done. Equally, nothing was achieved by plans to reach other mining areas in the Braid valley to the south of the Cushendall line, nor by a survey of another route to reach the coast at Carnlough, a Bill of 1879 being withdrawn.

Near Retreat there existed about 1872–3 a small mineral line reaching mines on the slopes of Trostan (1,817ft) lying to the north of the Cushendall line. Of unknown gauge (but perhaps 2ft), the tramway climbed to about 1,250ft in the first mile and seems to have continued even higher to about 1,400ft; it was certainly the highest of all Antrim mineral lines.

A period of depressed trade destroyed the Cushendall line's prosperity so it was sold to the Northern Counties in 1884. The new owner decided to run a passenger service which started during 1886 as far as Knockanally, extended in 1888 to Parkmore. The real reason for the existence of the line had long gone when the LMS(NCC) withdrew the passenger service in 1930 and goods in 1937, leaving only creamery traffic from Rathkenny which lingered on until total closure of the line in 1940.

The second narrow gauge line at Ballymena connected that town with Larne but the original promoters deposited plans for a direct Larne & Antrim Railway in 1872, but while in Parliament the Bill was replaced by one for the narrow gauge Larne & Ballyclare Railway to serve the well-established paper mill at the latter town. Looking further afield there was the prospect of ore traffic from mines lying on a route to Ballymena and so the Ballymena & Larne Railway replaced the Antrim proposal in 1874. Dixon of Celbridge built the line so that Larne to Ballyclare paper mill opened for goods in 1877 followed by the Ballymena line from Ballyclare Junction (renamed Ballyboley Junction in 1889) in 1878 when passenger services also commenced. The terminus at Ballymena was close to the B&NCR goods station, the original B&BR station, at Harryville but convenient to no one, so an Act of 1878 allowed he B&LR to use the widened embankment of the older railway to gain access to Ballymena passenger station (25¼ miles from Larne) and the Cushendall line. Butler & Fry completed the line which opened to all traffic in 1880, the B&LR gaining some through iron ore haulage, but never as much as expected. The same Act allowed an extension from Ballyclare to Doagh (13½ miles from Larne), also built by Butler & Fry and opened in 1884.

Expansion of the B&LR was several times proposed, the Ballymena & Portglenone Railway of 1879 obtaining powers to serve the latter 10 miles away on the banks of the Bann. This was expanded into the Londonderry &

Larne Railway in 1881 to reach the Maiden City through the sparsely-inhabited hilly moorland country earlier mentioned; the approach to Derry was to have been over a river crossing of 44 spans but the scheme never gained Parliamentary approval. Part of the original project surfaced again in 1885 as a proposed roadside tramway from Ballymena to Abhoghill, a couple of miles west of the former.

As B&LR receipts declined, it came as a welcome relief when the B&NCR took over in 1889. Harryville station was no longer used by passenger trains from the beginning of 1890 (timetables had not shown *two* stations at all) with the exception of the first morning departure until 1916. Under new owners various improvements were made, including new engines which were von-Borries compounds, having unlike their broad gauge counterparts outside cylinders. Trains connecting with the steamers at Larne were put on and it became convenient to use the narrow gauge, changing at Ballymena for stations further north. As late as 1928 the NCC built four *corridor* bogies with *lavatories*, the only such stock on any Irish narrow gauge line, for the expresses but they were really too late for the 1933 strike finished all passengers services. The section from Larne to the harbour had already lost its passenger trains, in 1932, so that work on rebuilding the station could proceed unhindered. The main line from Ballyboley was closed in 1940 and the last part of the Doagh branch beyond the paper mill siding was closed during 1944. When the paper mill ceased production, that was the end, services terminating in the summer of 1950.

Coal was extracted from a small field in the vicinity of Ballycastle on the Antrim coast from a very early date, being sent mainly to Dublin, from the small harbour constructed with locally-quarried stone; to carry it a short 300 yards narrow gauge tramway with wooden rails was laid, being mentioned in Irish House of Commons records in 1743 and was very possibly the *first* railed transport in Ireland. The Northern Counties considered in 1863–4 supporting the Belfast, Ballymoney & Ballycastle Junction Railway but one shareholder remarked that 'you might as well throw your money into the sea as give it to the Ballycastle Company' – events were to prove him right. Nevertheless the Ballycastle Railway was incorporated in 1875 to build a single track 3ft gauge line to the town of some 2,000 persons which has developed into a modest seaside resort. James Connor started the job but the line was completed by the Ballymena contractors Butler and Fry and opened in 1880; the 16 miles of line started from the B&NCR station at Ballymoney. There was a covered way (hardly a tunnel) at Capecastle (66 yards). Always impecunious the Ballycastle was unable to meet the costs arising from the 1889 Regulation of Railways Act and *never* fitted automatic brakes to its stock! Rising costs drove the company to its end, closing in

1924, even earlier than that oddity the Listowel & Ballybunion.

The new Northern Ireland Government declined to help or take over the line so the Northern Counties was induced to buy the line, paying no more than £12,500 for £104,000 expended in capital; trains resumed later in 1924, replacement rolling stock being transferred from the Ballymena lines but legal ownership did not change until a year later. The new owners reduced the line to basics and in its more economical form the Ballycastle lasted far longer than the other Northern Counties narrow gauge lines, keeping a Sunday service as well, total closure taking place during 1950.

TWO TRAMWAYS

Portstewart was left aside by the Portrush line, the first attempt to cover the 2 miles from the town to the station in 1861 being abortive. The rising prosperity of Portrush encouraged revival of the plan in 1871 as the Cromore & Portstewart Tramway but it was not until 1880 that the Portstewart Tramway Co was formed, being constructed by Butler & Fry and opened in the summer of 1882. Running entirely on the public road, tramcars drawn by Kitson steam tram engines connected with Portrush line services. Financially unsuccessful, the company went into liquidation in 1892, being purchased by the B&NCR in 1897 but it was an early casualty, closing during 1926. The original tram engines of 1882–3 have survived in preservation, although No 1 is not now in Ireland.

Not far from the Portstewart line lay the pioneer electric tramway of the British Isles, the Giant's Causeway, Portrush & Bush Valley Railway & Tramway Co, the 1880 successor to the Portrush & Giant's Causeway Tramway of 1878, promoted by the Ulster Tramways Co Ltd (which became the Counties Down & Antrim (Steam) Tramway Ltd, its other planned line being one to Ardglass). Backed by the Traill family, then well known in Co Antrim, the 1880 company planned an extension from Bushmills to Dervock on the Ballycastle Railway, hence the choice of the 3ft gauge. Very courageously electric traction was adopted, making use of a waterfall near Bushmills to generate the power, the first hydro electric plant for traction in the British Isles, but there was also a steam plant at Portrush to augment supply.

Opened on 29 January 1883 from Portrush to Bushmills, 6 miles, P. & W. McClellan of Glasgow building the tramway, the track was laid on the seaward side of the road to Bushmills with the 250 volts dc conductor rail on the north side. The seven loops were all on inclines so that cars in one direction could coast through, those going the other way drawing power! However the ½ mile of street line at Portrush made it necessary to use steam tram engines, battery power proving impracticable. Services were initially steam-worked throughout, although a special opening ceremonial run for the Lord Lieutenant on 28 September was electrically worked, only just managing to get all the way through. The BOT inspector obviously had to be convinced of the safety of the live rail – one of the Traills promptly sat on it, thus satisfying Her Majesty's representative but afterwards admitted that 'it was damned painful but he was not going to let the inspector know that!' Eventually the equipment was coaxed into working order and from late 1883 a full electric service ran, being extended in mid-1887 for a further 2 miles to the Causeway Hotel, leaving tourists another mile to walk to their destination, that extraordinary rock formation that has been such a popular spectacle for a couple of centuries.

The live rail system was condemned in 1895 when a cyclist was fatally injured so it was replaced by an overhead line which came into use on 26 July 1899, being extended to the Portrush terminus outside the Northern Counties station, although steam was used for another couple of decades to assist at the busiest times. Initially there had been some non-passenger traffic, mainly limestone carried over a short extension to Portrush harbour (sharing as mixed gauge a portion of the B&NCR harbour branch) which survived only until 1887; a small amount of other goods was handled until 1890/1. Naturally traffic was highly seasonal, not running in some winters but its uniqueness made the journey a 'must' when in the area. However with forces stationed in the area during World War II, it was necessary to run a winter service from 1940. After nearly seventy years renovations were imperative but costs made that impossible so that the last trams ran on Friday, 30 September 1949, a few years too soon for any preservation attempt.

INDUSTRIAL AND OTHER LINES

Not unexpectedly there were several small lines in Ulster for industrial purposes, more so than the rest of Ireland. Indeed one, the Cavehill Railway in Belfast, was not only the first to be authorised in Ulster but was the third in the whole of Ireland when incorporated in 1832. Its purpose was to connect a quarry on the south side of Cavehill to the north west of Belfast with quays at the head of Belfast Lough, and began operation in July 1840, its 4 miles of double track lasting until February 1896. Apart from a cable incline near the quarry, the line (4ft 9in gauge, or thereabouts) was horse-worked.

Carnlough lies 15 miles north of Larne on the Antrim Coast Road and has long been a place of quarrying, its earliest cargo of limestone being despatched to Scotland in August 1854. The first line, of 4ft 8½in gauge, needed a cable-worked incline to reach the quarry a mile inland with a second incline to upper working areas. A second quarry was opened out about 1890, some 2 miles to the south of the harbour, served by a 3ft 6in gauge line which lasted until 1922. There were also sidings about the quarries of 1ft 8in and 2ft 4in. In the mid-fifties the railway was thoroughly overhauled but all activities ceased a few year later, the harbour now sheltering pleasure craft.

The BHC had several lines, some narrow gauge, laid down, some possibly as early as 1860, to aid reclamation work at the head of Belfast Lough and seem to have lasted until 1900. Another large contract using a railway was the building of a reservoir in the Silent Valley, Co Down, on the south side of the Mourne Mountains and north of Kilkeel, for the Belfast Water Commissioners. The contractor, S. Pearson, started work in 1923 and used several 4ft 8½in gauge engines on the five miles of line from the coast at Annalong until work was completed ten years later. Another contract line was used by R. Faris from 1930 until 1939 when he supplied stone from Carnanee quarry on the west bank of the Bann for the building of a new breakwater at the mouth of the river at the behest of the Coleraine Harbour Commissioners. When the Government of Northern Ireland carried out further improvement works on the Bann navigation they used a small 2ft gauge line from 1937 and three years later Harbour & General Works Ltd of Coleraine used a short railway for a similar contract. About 1921 there was said to be a short line serving Ballycastle harbour, about which nothing has come to light. Further west on the Derry side of Lough Foyle the NI Ministry of Agriculture carried out some work on the Black Braes embankment about 1955, using a 2ft gauge line and closer to the city itself the Admiralty built a short pier at Lisahally which also had a 2ft gauge line until about 1953.

Industrial systems were rare in Ireland and one of the best examples was that installed by the British Aluminium Co at Larne in 1900 at its bauxite plant just to the north of the harbour, its 3ft gauge sidings being connected to the NCC narrow gauge and indeed it outlasted the latter, not being closed until 1960. For a couple of years 1910 to 1912 the Sulphate of Ammonia Co Ltd used a 2ft gauge well tank at its Larne plant. Not far away at Magheramorne, the British Portland Cement Manufacturers Ltd had a quarry served by a 2ft gauge system which survived until 1947; sidings at Magheramorne station were shunted from 1915 until 1935 by a Hudswell, Clarke fireless engine, unique in Ireland.

In Belfast the well-known shipbuilders Harland & Wolff not unexpectedly had a number of sidings around their yards on Queen's Island; their first shunter was a small English Electric battery locomotive. The firm also built a few diesel locomotives, one of which was used by the LMS at Heysham Harbour for a few years; production was small and most locomotives were either used in their yards or by the NCC and County Down, or both, but a shunter was supplied to Sudan in 1935 and two larger machines were sent to Argentina in 1938–9 and power equipment was supplied to Canada and New South Wales in 1937–9. Another Belfast firm, Gardner Edwards Diesel Railcar Co, built a railcar in 1933 for Columbia which ran trials on the Ballymena and Larne section of the NCC, the only diesel to work on any of those narrow gauge lines.

Quarrying and limestone production accounted for a number of small lines in Co Antrim in addition to those so far mentioned. Those known to have had their own engine power were Carnduff near Larne (Howden Bros), Glenarm (Eglinton Lime Co), Roughfort (James Boyd & Sons) and Craighahulliar (Portrush Columnar Basalt Co). Others were situated at Colinward near Whitewell, Black Hill near Belfast, Knocknadona near Lisburn, Kellswater, Irish Hill Mines near Ballyclare (for bauxite), Kilcoan on Islandmagee, Ballintoy and Craig Park near Bushmills, the second, third, fifth, sixth and seventh having incline planes. In Co Down there were incline planes at Newcastle and Scrabo near Newtownards.

Several brickworks around Belfast and one at Carrickfergus had small tramways, none with engines. Elsewhere the Northern Sand & Brick Co of Toome had a small 2ft gauge system from 1945 until 1948 but quite a different product was carried on the tramways of the United Kingdom Peat Moss Litter Co who worked near the River Bann, having a 3ft gauge line north of Castledawson and a couple of 2ft gauge lines near Portglenone.

PLEASURE LINES AND PRESERVATION

It has been quite normal for local government to provide zoos and pleasure gardens but for a transport department to manage such is extraordinary. Belfast Corporation became the owners of Bellevue Park when the local Cavehill & Whitewell Tramway was acquired in 1911 (becoming part of the Belfast Corporation electric street tramways system) and its operation and development was retained by the transport department. Later in 1933 a 15in gauge pleasure line was built, well known for obtaining a German-built steam engine *The Bug* from the Romney, Hythe & Dymchurch Railway in Kent; unused after 1950 this engine was returned to its original line. During World War II the army installed a small tramway in the grounds of Shane's Castle, near Randalstown; no doubt it disappeared soon afterwards but in its place Lord O'Neill built an extensive pleasure railway which started operations on 30 April 1971, using second hand 3ft gauge steam and diesel locomotives. The line was 1½ miles long, connecting the main car park, its station being named Antrim, and the castle itself with a halt called Millburn, but sadly this line closed down during October 1993. It was a proper commercial venture and in no way a preserved line, although its stock qualified for inclusion in lists of preserved items.

In Co Down at Downpatrick use of part of the former B&CDR has enabled the Downpatrick & Ardglass Railway, formed in 1984, to lay down some track, build workshops and gather locomotives and rolling stock. A short length from the former loop platform was ready for use in 1989 but the grand opening took place on 7 May 1990. Eventually the line is expected to be some 6 miles long with a line into Downpatrick town. Ardglass remains a hope for the more distant future.

At Whitehead the Railway Preservation Society of Ireland houses much of its collection of locomotives and rolling stock. For many years the society has run steam-hauled special trains throughout Ireland, many trips taking place on both days of a weekend. More recently the Ulster Folk & Transport Museum has been installed at Cultra on the Bangor line, where the halt was especially reopened in 1978. The wide range of exhibits comprises steam locomotives, such as GSR 4-6-0 No 800 *Maeve*, railcars, carriages and wagons, as well as a large collection of memorabilia and artefacts, housed in a specially-constructed gallery built in 1993. Its turntable, around which the locomotives stand, is connected directly to the down track of Bangor line. Recently a small 9½in gauge miniature railway has been installed in the safari park outside Ballymoney.

RAILS AGAIN IN BELFAST STREETS?

Rails may yet return to the streets of Belfast where electric trams and trolley-buses last ran in 1954 and 1968 respectively, leaving Ireland without electric passenger transport until the DART services started in Dublin during 1984. In 1988 a plan was published for a light rail suburban system which envisaged conversion of the Bangor line, with a resurrection of the former County Down as far as Dundonald, from the Queens Quay area, extended into the city streets to the City Hall and on to the Adelaide area. The latter could be extended as a second stage further west to Andersonstown and as a final stage there could be a new route northwards to Greencastle, there having an interchange station with the NIR line to Larne. The target date is 2004 when NIR would have to replace a part of its diesel train fleet.

A TUNNEL TO IRELAND

The plans of the 'All Red Route' which included a tunnel under the North Channel have been mentioned. There were earlier schemes, the first in 1868 planning a single bore to start on the Antrim coast near Cushendall and head for Scotland's Mull of Kintyre with its lowest point some 5 miles off the Antrim coast. The second scheme, dating from 1901, was more thoroughly thought-out, the emergence of electric traction making it a more practical idea. Put forward by the International Engineering Congress held in Glasgow, three routes were assessed:

(a)   Antrim coast to Mull of Kintyre ($12^1/_2$ miles),
(b)   Larne or Donaghadee to Wigtownshire (23 miles),
(c)   Howth to Holyhead (62 miles).

The last was rejected due to length and the first because of the remoteness of Kintyre; depth of both (more than 400ft) was another adverse factor. The favoured route had the problems of Beaufort's Deep, seven miles off the Scottish coast and extending for some 30 miles with depths of 600–900ft so the tunnel was to pass round its north end. The projected course was to start near Carrickfergus, leave the Antrim coast near Whitehead and reach the Scottish coast north of Portpatrick and emerge about five miles short of Stranraer; it would have been $51^1/_2$ miles long, 34 in tunnel (25 under water), and have involved grades of 1 in 75, with a minimum depth of 150ft below the sea floor. It was expected to take ten to twelve years to construct and result in a journey time of one hour between Belfast and Stranraer. Electric fans were to provide ventilation.

The scheme for this tunnel briefly came to the fore during 1934 but perhaps it was seen by the politicians as unemployment relief work rather than of value to the Northern Counties which could hardly have given serious consideration to the idea.

Appendix One

OPENING AND CLOSING DATES OF RAILWAYS & TRAMWAYS

Dates in **heavy** type indicate non–passenger events (where known separate dates of opening to **goods** are shown). After closure to regular traffic some branches continued to be used for special traffic (as mentioned in the text) until Taken Out Of Use, a term used here to indicate total closure. The date given for closure is, unless otherwise stated, the first day on which there were no services. or the line was no longer available for use.

Dublin stations are given by their pre–1966 suffix and others by their most recent name.

CHAPTER 2 – DUBLIN

	Opened	Closed Passenger	Closed Goods	Taken out of use	Notes
Gauge 4–8¹/₂ (converted to 5–3 by 30 Jun 1857)					
Westland Row – Dun Laoghaire	17 Dec 1834	OPEN	OPEN	OPEN	2/1
Dun Laoghaire (extension)	13 May 1837	OPEN	OPEN	OPEN	2/1
Dun Laoghaire – Dalkey	29 Mar 1844	OPEN	OPEN	OPEN	2/2
Gauge 5–3					
Carlisle Pier	23 Dec 1859	10 Oct 1980	–	10 Oct 1980	
Dalkey – Shanganagh Junction	10 Jul 1854	OPEN	OPEN	OPEN	2/3
Harcourt Street (extension)	7 Feb 1859	1 Jan 1959	**2 Mar 1925**	1 Jan 1959	
Harcourt Road Junction – Shanganagh	10 Jul 1854	1 Jan 1959	**2 Mar 1925**	1 Jan 1959	2/3
Shanganagh Junction – Bray	10 Jul 1854	OPEN	OPEN	OPEN	2/1, 2/3
Bray – Wicklow Junction	30 Dec 1855	OPEN	OPEN	OPEN	2/4
Wicklow Junction – Wicklow	30 Dec 1855	1 Nov 1976	9 Sep 1976	1 Nov 1976	2/5
Wicklow harbour extension	**23 Nov 1869**	–	?	?	2/6
Wicklow quay line	**11 Jul 1906**	–	**1922**	**1922**	
Wicklow– Rathdrum	20 Aug 1861	OPEN	OPEN	OPEN	
Kingsbridge – Cherryville Jct	4 Aug 1846	OPEN	OPEN	OPEN	
Sallins – Colbinstown	22 Jun 1885	27 Jan 1947	**10 Mar 1947**	**1 Apr 1959**	
Colbinstown – Baltinglass	1 Sep 1885	27 Jan 1947	**10 Mar 1947**	**1 Apr 1959**	
Baltinglass – Tullow	1 Jun 1886	27 Jan 1947	**10 Mar 1947**	**1 Apr 1959**	
Curragh siding	17 Apr 1856	7 Mar 1977	–	7 Mar 1977	2/7
Broadstone – Liffey Junction	28 Jun 1847	18 Jan 1937	**10 Jul 1944**	**10 Jul 1944**	2/8
Liffey Jct – Drumcondra Jct	**1 Mar 1864** 1 Dec 1877	OPEN	OPEN	OPEN	
Drumcondra Jct – Newcomen Jct	**1 Mar 1864** 3 Sep 1877	2 Apr 1973	OPEN	OPEN	2/9
Newcomen Jct – West Road Jct	**1 Mar 1864** 3 Sep 1877	Nov 1922	OPEN	OPEN	
West Road Jct MGWR goods depot – North Wall	**1 Mar 1864**	–	OPEN	OPEN	2/10
Spencer Dock branch (CDSP)	**15 Sep 1873**	–	?	?	
Liffey Jct – Enfield	28 Jun 1847	OPEN	OPEN	OPEN	
Enfield – Hill of Down	6 Dec 1847	OPEN	OPEN	OPEN	
Hill of Down – Mullingar	2 Oct 1848	OPEN	OPEN	OPEN	

Nesbitt Jct – Edenderry	9 Apr 1877	1 Jun 1931	**1 Sep 1932**	**1 Apr 1963**	
Amiens Street (extension)	29 Nov 1844	OPEN	OPEN	OPEN	2/1
Dublin – Howth Junction	24 May 1844	OPEN	OPEN	OPEN	2/1
Howth Junction – Drogheda	24 May 1844	OPEN	OPEN	OPEN	
Howth Junction – Howth	30 Jul 1846	OPEN	**2 Dec 1974**	OPEN	2/1
Howth (extension)	30 May 1847	OPEN	**2 Dec 1974**	OPEN	2/1
Drogheda – Navan	15 Feb 1850	14 Apr 1958	OPEN	OPEN	
Navan – Kingscourt Jct	11 Jul 1853	14 Apr 1958	OPEN	OPEN	
Kingscourt Jct – Kells	11 Jul 1853	14 Apr 1958	**1 Apr 1963**	**1 Apr 1963**	2/11
Kells – Oldcastle	17 Mar 1863	14 Apr 1958	**1 Apr 1963**	**1 Apr 1963**	
Clonsilla – Navan	29 Aug 1862	27 Jan 1947	**12 Jun 1961**	**1 Apr 1963**	
Navan – Navan Junction	15 Dec 1862	27 Jan 1947	**12 Jun 1961**	**1 Apr 1963**	
Kilmessan – Trim	**15 Dec 1863**	27 Jan 1947	**10 Mar 1947**	**1 Sep 1954**	
	26 Feb 1864				
Trim – Athboy	**21 Jan 1864**	27 Jan 1947	**10 Mar 1947**	**1 Sep 1954**	
	26 Feb 1864				
Kingscourt Jct – Kilmainham Wood	1 Nov 1872	27 Jan 1947	OPEN	OPEN	
Kilmainham Wood – Kingscourt	1 Nov 1875	27 Jan 1947	OPEN	OPEN	
Islandbridge Junction –					
Drumcondra Junction	3 Sep 1877	OPEN	OPEN	OPEN	2/12
West Road Jct – North Wall	3 Sep 1877	Nov 1922	OPEN	OPEN	
East Wall Jct – Church Rd Jct	1 Dec 1877	17 Jan 1921	OPEN	OPEN	
Church Road Jct – The Point	**6 Jul 1886**	–	OPEN	OPEN	2/13
Westland Row – Amiens Street	12 Dec 1890	OPEN	OPEN	OPEN	2/1
Amiens Street – jct with GNR	12 Dec 1890	OPEN	OPEN	OPEN	2/1
Amiens Street– Newcomen Jct	2 Jun 1892	2 Apr 1973	OPEN	OPEN	2/9
Drumcondra Junction –					
North Strand Junction	1 Apr 1901	OPEN	OPEN	OPEN	
North Strand Junction –					
Church Road Junction	1 Apr 1901	Nov 1922	OPEN	OPEN	
North Strand Junction –					
Amiens Street	1 Dec 1906	OPEN	OPEN	OPEN	2/14
Terenure – Blessington	1 Aug 1888	1 Jan 1933	**1 Jan 1933**	1 Jan 1933	
Blessington – Poulaphouca	1 May 1895	30 Sep 1927	**30 Sep 1927**	30 Sep 1927	
Sutton – Summit	17 Jun 1901	1 Jun 1959	–	1 Jun 1959	
Summit – Howth	1 Aug 1901	1 Jun 1959	–	1 Jun 1959	
Gauge 3–0 (converted to 3–6 and 5–3 as indicated in notes)					
Conyngham Road – Chapelizod	1 Jun 1881	29 Jan 1925	–	29 Jan 1925	2/15
Chapelizod – Palmerstown	Nov 1881	29 Jan 1925	–	29 Jan 1925	2/15
Palmerstown – Lucan	20 Feb 1883	29 Jan 1925	–	29 Jan 1925	2/15
Lucan – Dodsborough	1890	29 Jan 1925	–	29 Jan 1925	2/16
Dodsborough – Leixlip	1890	30 Oct 1897	–	30 Oct 1897	

2/1 Electrified 23 Jul 1984 .

2/2 Worked atmospherically until 12 Apr 1854; regauged and reopened 10 Oct 1855.

2/3 Major deviations 1915 (see text).

2/4 Major deviations 1876, 1879, 1888 and 1917 (see map on page 59).

2/5 Closed passengers 1893; reopened to passengers 10 Mar 1969.

2/6 Line appears to have been taken out of use about 1930.

2/7 Provided for race traffic (date given is that when reported ready for use).

2/8 Since 1864 non–passenger traffic has been confined to livestock (the line remained in use for access to the locomotive shed which closed on 8 Apr 1961).

2/9 Passenger use ceased 18 Jan 1937 and resumed 12 Sep 1961 (but still used for diversions).

2/10 Absorbed into North Wall goods area (as a sundries depot).

2/11 Reopened as far as Tara mines (^{1}/2 mile) **29 Jun 1977** for mineral traffic.

2/12 Junction at Drumcondra/Glasnevin closed 30 Nov 1906; new junction installed (but in opposite direction) 22 Nov 1936 (used by diverted passenger trains from 18 Jan 1937).

2/13 Now used only by departmental traffic.

2/14 New Junctions at Ossory Road 2 Apr 1973 and Suburban Junction 9 Aug 1981.

2/15 Regauged to 3– 6 and electrified 8 Mar 1896 (as Dulin & Lucan Electric Railway); converted to 5– 3 electric as part of DUTC system 14 May 1928 to Chapelizod and 27 May 1928 to Lucan (closed 13 Apr 1940).

2/16 Regauged to 3– 6 and electrified 1909 as extension of D&LER.

CHAPTER 3 – WATERFORD AND THE SOUTH EAST

Opened	Closed Passenger	Closed Goods	Taken out of use	Notes
Gauge 5–3				
Rathdrum – Avoca	18 Jul 1863	OPEN	OPEN	OPEN	3/1
Avoca – Enniscorthy	16 Nov 1863	OPEN	OPEN	OPEN
Woodenbridge Jct – Aughrim	22 May 1865	24 Apr 1944	1 May **1953**	**1 May 1953**
Aughrim – Shillelagh	22 May 1865	24 Apr 1944	**24 Apr 1944**	24 Apr 1944	3/2
Enniscorthy – Wexford	17 Aug 1872	OPEN	OPEN	OPEN
Wexford goods extension	**10 Jun 1873**	–	–	–	3/3
Wexford (extension)	Aug 1874	OPEN	OPEN	OPEN	3/4
Cherryville Jct – Maryborough	26 Jun 1847	OPEN	OPEN	OPEN
Maryborough – Ballybrophy	1 Sep 1847	OPEN	OPEN	OPEN
Cherryville Jct – Carlow	4 Aug 1846	OPEN	OPEN	OPEN
Athy–Ballylinen	**24 Sep 1918**	–	**1 Apr 1963**	**1 Apr 1963**	3/5
Ballylinan – Wolfhill	**24 Sep 1918**	–	**12 Jul 1930**	**12 Jul 1930**	3/6
Carlow – Bagenalstown	24 Jul 1848	OPEN	OPEN	OPEN
Bagenalstown – Kilkenny	14 Nov 1850	OPEN	OPEN	OPEN	3/7
Lavistown curve	UNDER CONSTRUCTION			
Maryborough – Abbeyleix	**1 May 1867**	1 Jan 1963	**1 Jan 1963**	1 Jan 1963	3/8
	15 May 1867			
Abbeyleix – Kilkenny	1 Mar 1865	1 Jan 1963	**1 Jan 1963**	1 Jan 1963	3/9
Conibery Jct – Mountmellick	2 Mar 1885	27 Jan 1947	**27 Jan 1947**	**1 Jan 1963**
Castlecomer Jct – Castlecomer	15 Sep 1919	26 Jan 1931	**1 Jan 1963**	**1 Jan 1963**
	25 Apr 1921			
Castlecomer – Deerpark Coll.	**19 Oct 1920**	–	**1 Jan 1963**	**1 Jan 1963**
Kilkenny – Thomastown	12 May 1848	OPEN	OPEN	OPEN
Thomastown – Jerpoint Hill	29 May 1850	OPEN	OPEN	OPEN
Jerpoint Hill – Dunkitt	21 May 1853	OPEN	OPEN	OPEN
Clonmel – Fiddown	15 Apr 1853	OPEN	OPEN	OPEN
Fiddown – Dunkitt	23 Aug 1853	OPEN	OPEN	OPEN
Dunkitt – Waterford	11 Sep 1854	OPEN	OPEN	OPEN
Waterford new station	29 Aug 1864	OPEN	OPEN	OPEN
Waterford North Wharf ext.	**26 May 1883**	Absorbed into 1904 lines		
Mallow – Fermoy	17 May 1860	27 Mar 1967	**27 Mar 1967**	27 Mar 1967
Fermoy – Lismore	1 Oct 1872	27 Mar 1967	**27 Mar 1967**	27 Mar 1967
Fermoy – Mitchelstown	23 Mar 1891	27 Jan 1947	**27 Jan 1947**	**1 Dec 1953**
Lismore – Grace Dieu Jct	12 Aug 1878	25 Mar 1967	25 Mar 1967	25 Mar 1967	3/10
Ballinacourty factory branch	**3 Apr 1970**	–	**28 Jul 1982**	**21 Nov 1993**	3/10
Grace Dieu Jct – Waterford South	12 Aug 1878	31 Jan 1908	**9 Sep 1976**	**9 Sep 1976**
Grace Dieu Junction –				
Suir Bridge Junction	30 Aug 1906	25 Mar 1967	**28 Jul 1982**	**21 Nov 1993**	3/10
Waterford Manor – Tramore	7 Sep 1853	1 Jan 1961	**1 Jan 1961**	1 Jan 1961
Bagenalstown – Borris	11 Dec 1858	2 Feb 1931	**27 Jan 1947**	**1 Apr 1963**	3/11
Borris – Ballywilliam	17 Mar 1862	2 Feb 1931	**27 Jan 1947**	**1 Apr 1963**	3/11
Ballywilliam – Palace East	26 Oct 1870	2 Feb 1931	**27 Jan 1947**	**1 Apr 1963**	3/11

	Opened	Closed	Closed	Taken out	Notes
Palace East – Macmine	26 Oct 1870	1 Apr 1963	**1 Apr 1963**	1 Apr 1963	3/11
Macmine – Macmine Junction	1 Apr 1873	1 Apr 1963	**1 Apr 1963**	1 Apr 1963	3/11
Palace East – New Ross	19 Sep 1887	1 Apr 1963	**1 Apr 1963**	**1 Apr 1963**	
New Ross – Abbey Junction	**15 Feb 1904**	1 Apr 1963	**6 Sep 1976**	OPEN	
	27 Apr 1904				
Wexford – Rosslare Pier	24 Jun 1882	OPEN	**2 Jun 1978**	OPEN	3/12
Rosslare Harbour extension	30 Aug 1906	14 Sep 1989	**2 Jun 1978**	–	3/13
Waterford North – Abbey Jct	**15 Feb 1904**	OPEN	OPEN	OPEN	
	27 Apr 1904				
Abbey Jct – Wellington Bridge	1 Aug 1906	OPEN	OPEN	OPEN	
Wellington Bridge – Killinick	1 Aug 1906	OPEN	**Oct 1979**	OPEN	
Killinick – Rosslare Strand	30 Aug 1906	OPEN	**Oct 1979**	OPEN	
Killinick – Felthouse Jct	1 Aug 1906	1 Jul 1910	**28 May 1911**	**28 May 1911**	
Gauge 3–6					
Avoca mines – Arklow harbour	?	–	**Jul 1874**	?	3/14

3/1 Rathdrum was a temporary terminus 1 mile north of the later station.

3/2 No trains from date given and line closed **20 Apr 1945;** Exemption Order not applicable until 1 May 1953.

3/3 Absorbed by later extension to Wexford North and Wexford South.

3/4 Sanctioned 13 Aug 1874.

3/5 Part retained as a siding ($1/2$ mile) at Athy for access to a factory.

3/6 Closure date is that for last entry in lists of GSR speed restrictions.

3/7 Separate line into Kilkenny until junction was installed at Lavistown 9 Jun 1979

3/8 Reopened as a siding from Portlaoise to Coolnamona ($2^1/4$ miles) late **Sep 1965.**

3/9 Closed 31 Aug 1866; reopened **1 May 1867** (goods) and 15 May 1867 (passenger).

3/10 Deviation at Carroll's Cross 7 Nov 1909; part reopened **3 Apr 1970** for minerals, etc. with new line to Ballinacourty; traffic ceased 28 Jul 1982; line effectively closed 21 Nov 1993 on conversion to a siding.

3/11 Closed between Bagenalstown and Ballywilliam 1 Jan 1864; reopened Bagenalstown – Borris 5 Sep 1870 and Borris – Ballywilliam 26 Oct 1870; closed Bagenalstown – Macmine Junction 30 Sep 1873; reopened throughout 9 Feb 1874.

3/12 Closed 16 May 1889 (apart from a few cattle trains, etc); reopened 6 Aug 1894 as far as Kilrane and Jun 1895 to Rosslare Pier.

3/13 Pier extended 15 chains and became Rosslare Harbour 30 Aug 1906; pier became sidings only from 14 Sep 1989.

3/14 Hodgson's tramway; in use before **1861** and not used after **Jul 1874.**

CHAPTER 4 – LIMERICK AND THE GOLDEN VALE

	Opened	Closed Passenger	Closed Goods	Taken out of use	Notes
Gauge 5–3					
Ballybrophy – Thurles	13 Mar 1848	OPEN	OPEN	OPEN	
Thurles – Limerick Junction	3 Jul 1848	OPEN	OPEN	OPEN	
Limerick Junction – Mallow	19 Mar 1849	OPEN	OPEN	OPEN	
Ballybrophy – Roscrea	19 Oct 1857	OPEN	OPEN	OPEN	
Roscrea – Birr	8 Mar 1858	1 Jan 1963	**1 Jan 1963**	1 Jan 1963	
Birr – Portumna	5 Nov 1868	29 Nov 1878	**29 Nov 1878**	29 Nov 1878	
Portumna goods extension	**5 Nov 1868**	–	**29 Nov 1878**	**29 Nov 1878**	
Roscrea – Nenagh	5 Oct 1863	OPEN	OPEN	OPEN	
Nenagh – Birdhill	1 Jun 1864	OPEN	OPEN	OPEN	
Silvermines mineral branch	**30 Dec 1966**	–	**29 Oct 1993**	**29 Oct 1993**	4/1
Goolds Cross – Cashel	19 Dec 1904	27 Jan 1947	**27 Jan 1947**	**1 Sep 1954**	
Limerick (extension)	1857	OPEN	OPEN	OPEN	4/2
Limerick – Tipperary	**24 Apr 1848**	OPEN	OPEN	OPEN	
	9 May 1848				

Limerick market branch	**7 Jan 1864**	–	**1940**	**1940**	4/3
Limerick Junction east curve	**16 Oct 1967**	OPEN	OPEN	OPEN	4/4
16 Sep 1968					
'Keane's Points' –					
Limerick Junction	3 Jul 1848	OPEN	OPEN	OPEN	
Tipperary – Clonmel	1 May 1852	OPEN	OPEN	OPEN	
Killonan – Castleconnell	28 Aug 1858	OPEN	OPEN	OPEN	
Castleconnell – Birdhill	23 Jul 1860	OPEN	OPEN	OPEN	
Birdhill – Killaloe	12 Apr 1862	17 Jul 1931	**24 Apr 1944**	**1 Jun 1953**	
Killaloe – R. Shannon pier	?	–	?	?	4/5
Killaloe passenger extension	1894	17 Jul 1931	**24 Apr 1944**	**1 Jun 1953**	4/5
Clonmel – Fethard	23 Jun 1879	9 Sep 1963	**27 Mar 1967**	**27 Mar 1967**	
Fethard – Thurles Junction	1 Jul 1880	9 Sep 1963	**27 Mar 1967**	**27 Mar 1967**	
Limerick 'Check' – Foynes Jct	12 Jul 1856	1910	OPEN	OPEN	4/6
Limerick station – Foynes Jct	1 May 1863	4 Feb 1963	**29 Sep 1975**	**29 Sep 1975**	
Foynes Jct – Ballingrane	12 Jul 1856	4 Feb 1963	OPEN	OPEN	
Castlemungret cement factory	1 Oct 1957	–	OPEN	OPEN	
Ballingrane – Askeaton	12 May 1857	4 Feb 1963	OPEN	OPEN	
Askeaton – Foynes	28 Apr 1858	4 Feb 1963	OPEN	OPEN	
Patrickswell – Charleville Jct	1 Aug 1862	31 Dec 1934	**27 Mar 1967**	**27 Mar 1967**	
	1 Sep 1862				
Charleville north curve	**1897**	–	?	?	4/7
Ballingrane – Newcastle West	1 Jan 1867	4 Feb 1963	**3 Nov 1975**	**3 Nov 1975**	
Newcastle West – Listowel	20 Dec 1880	4 Feb 1963	**4 Dec 1972**	**3 Nov 1975**	
Listowel – Abbeydorney	20 Dec 1880	4 Feb 1963	**10 Jan 1977**	**10 Jan 1977**	
Abbeydorney – Tralee	20 Dec 1880	4 Feb 1963	**2 Jun 1978**	**2 Jun 1978**	
Tralee connection	**1882**	4 Feb 1963	**2 Jun 1978**	**2 Jun 1978**	4/8
GS&WR/W&LR	1901				
Tralee – Fenit	5 Jul 1887	31 Dec 1934	**2 Jun 1978**	**2 Jun 1978**	
Ennis Jct – Longpavement	26 Mar 1859	OPEN	**18 Dec 1978**	OPEN	4/9
Longpavement – Clarecastle	17 Jan 1859	OPEN	**18 Dec 1978**	OPEN	4/9
Clarecastle – Ennis	20 Jun 1859	OPEN	**18 Dec 1978**	OPEN	4/9
Gauge 3–0					
Ennis – Milltown Malbay	2 Jul 1887	1 Feb 1961	**1 Feb 1961**	1 Feb 1961	
Milltown Malbay – Moyasta Jct	**7 Nov 1892**	1 Feb 1961	**1 Feb 1961**	1 Feb 1961	4/10
	23 Dec 1892				
Kilrush – Kilkee	**11 May 1892**	1 Feb 1961	**1 Feb 1961**	1 Feb 1961	4/11
	13 Aug 1892				
Kilrush – Cappagh Quay	**11 May 1892**	1 Oct 1916	**1 Feb 1961**	**1 Feb 1961**	
	13 Aug 1892				
Tralee GS&WR – T&DLR	**31 Mar 1891**	–	**10 Mar 1947**	**1 Jul 1953**	
Tralee – Dingle	31 Mar 1891	17 Apr 1939	**10 Mar 1947**	**1 Jul 1953**	
Dingle pier extension	**31 Mar 1891**	–	?	?	4/12
Castlegregory branch	31 Mar 1891	17 Apr 1939	**17 Apr 1939**	17 Apr 1939	
Gauge Monorail					
Listowel – Ballybunion	29 Feb 1888	14 Oct 1924	**14 Oct 1924**	14 Oct 1924.	

4/1 Date given is that of last train – line not yet formally abandoned.

4/2 Extension of 25 chains from 1848 terminus (in use about Oct 1857 but not inspected until Sep 1858).

4/3 Retained until **1950** as a siding to a bus depot (branch shortened about **1930**).

4/4 Occasional passenger trains from 30 Jun 1968.

4/5 Date not known but not ready in 1874. probably in use by 1883; passenger extension used 34 chains of this line (inspection report dated 20 Jun 1894 and likely to have come into use on 9 Jul 1894).

4/6 Extensive alterations at Limerick sanctioned 26 Aug 1910 (when passenger trains were diverted from this curve).

4/7 Inspected **1 May 1897** and passed; used until about **1906** (junction removed 1912).

4/8 Ready Oct 1882; sanctioned 2 Feb 1883; little used until 1901.

4/9 Passenger service withdrawn 5 Apr 1976 but excursions occasionally ran and unadvertised services were provided until timetabled services resumed in 1993.

4/10 Both curves at north end of Moyasta Junction opened on this date.

4/11 South curve at Moyasta Junction not normally used by passenger trains from 1916 until diesel railcars used it from 17 Mar 1952.

4/12 Last use not known.

CHAPTER 5 – CORK AND THE SOUTH WEST

Gauge 5–3

	Opened	Closed Passenger	Closed Goods	Taken out of use	Notes
Mallow – Cork	20 Oct 1849	OPEN	OPEN	OPEN	5/1
Cork (extension)	3 Dec 1855	OPEN	OPEN	OPEN	5/2
Connecting line to Grattan Hill Junction	**Dec 1868** 1 Jan 1876	2 Feb 1893	**2 Feb 1893**	replaced	5/3
Replacement connecting line to Tivoli Junction	2 Feb 1893	OPEN	OPEN	OPEN	
Cork Summerhill (extension)	30 Dec 1861	2 Feb 1893	**Dec 1868**	2 Feb 1893	
Bruin Lodge – Grattan Hill Jct	1 Oct 1860	2 Feb 1893	**Dec 1868**	2 Feb 1893	
Grattan Hill Jct – Tivoli Jct	1 Oct 1860	2 Feb 1893	**2 Feb 1893**	2 Feb 1893	
Tivoli Jct – Dunkettle	1 Oct 1860	OPEN	OPEN	OPEN	
Dunkettle – Cobh Junction	10 Nov 1859	OPEN	OPEN	OPEN	
Cobh Junction – Cobh	10 Mar 1862	OPEN	OPEN	OPEN	5/4
Cobh Junction – Midleton	10 Nov 1859	4 Feb 1963	**2 Jun 1978**	OPEN	5/5
Midleton – Killeagh	27 Feb 1860	4 Feb 1963	**2 Jun 1978**	OPEN	5/5
Killeagh – Youghal	23 May 1860	4 Feb 1963	**2 Jun 1978**	OPEN	5/5
Cork – Ballinhassig	8 Dec 1851	1 Apr 1961	**1 Apr 1961**	1 Apr 1961	
Ballinhassig – Bandon	30 Jul 1849 **8 Dec 1851**	1 Apr 1961	**1 Apr 1961**	1 Apr 1961	
Bandon – Dunmanway	12 Jun 1866	1 Apr 1961	**1 Apr 1961**	1 Apr 1961	
Dunmanway – Skibbereen	23 Jul 1877	1 Apr 1961	**1 Apr 1961**	1 Apr 1961	
Skibbereen – Baltimore	2 May 1893	1 Apr 1961	**1 Apr 1961**	1 Apr 1961	
Baltimore pier extension	**1916**	–	1 Apr **1961**	**1 Apr 1961**	
Kinsale Junction – Kinsale	27 Jun 1863	3 Aug 1931	3 Aug 1931	3 Aug 1931	
Clonakilty Jct – Clonakilty	28 Aug 1886	1 Apr 1961	**1 Apr 1961**	1 Apr 1961	
Ballinascarthy – Timoleague	22 Sep 1890	24 Feb 1947	**1 Apr 1961**	**1 Apr 1961**	
Timoleague – Courtamacsherry	May 1891	24 Feb 1947	1 Apr 1961	1 Apr 1961	5/6
Drimoleague Jct – Bantry	**1 Jul 1881** 4 Jul 1881	1 Apr 1961	**1 Apr 1961**	1 Apr 1961	5/7
Bantry extension	22 Oct 1892	1 Apr 1961	**1 Apr 1961**	1 Apr 1961	
Bantry pier extension	**22 Oct 1892**	?	1 Apr **1961**	**1 Apr 1961**	5/8
Cork – Ballyphehane Junction	27 Sep 1879	2 Mar 1925	**2 Mar 1925**	**2 Mar 1925**	5/9
Ballyphehane Jct – Macroom	12 May 1866	1 Jul 1935	**10 Mar 1947**	**1 Dec 1953**	
Cork City Railways	**1 Jan 1912**	–	12 Apr 1976	12 Apr 1976	5/10
Killarney Jct – Millstreet	16 Apr 1853	OPEN	OPEN	OPEN	
Millstreet – Freemount	25 May 1853	OPEN	OPEN	OPEN	5/11
Freemount – Killarney	15 Jul 1853	OPEN	OPEN	OPEN	
Tralee Junction – Tralee	18 Jul 1859 **24 Aug 1859**	OPEN	OPEN	OPEN	
Banteer – Newmarket	1 Apr 1889	27 Jan 1947	**2 Feb 1963**	**2 Feb 1963**	5/12
Headford Junction – Kenmare	4 Sep 1893	1 Jan 1960	**1 Jan 1960**	1 Jan 1960	
Farranfore – Killorglin	15 Jan 1885	1 Feb 1960	**1 Feb 1960**	1 Feb 1960	
Killorglin – Valentia Harbour	12 Aug 1893	1 Feb 1960	**1 Feb 1960**	1 Feb 1960	

Gortatlea – Castleisland	30 Aug 1875	24 Feb 1947	**10 Jan 1977**	**10 Jan 1977**	5/13
Gauge 5– 3 (converted to 3–0 29 Oct 1900)					
Cork – Passage	8 Jun 1850	12 Sep 1932	**12 Sep 1932**	12 Sep 1932	5/14
Gauge 3–0					
Passage – Monkstown	1 Aug 1902	12 Sep 1932	**12 Sep 1932**	12 Sep 1932	
Monkstown – Carrighaline	15 Jun 1903	1 Jun 1932	**1 Jun 1932**	1 Jun 1932	
Carrighaline – Crosshaven	1 Jun 1904	1 Jun 1932	**1 Jun 1932**	1 Jun 1932	
Skibbereen – Schull	9 Sep 1886	27 Jan 1947	**27 Jan 1947**	**1 Jun 1953**	5/15
Schull pier extension	**1 Oct 1893**	–	?	?	5/16
Cork – Blarney	8 Aug 1887	31 Dec 1934	**31 Dec 1934**	31 Dec 1934	
Coachford Jct – Coachford	18 Mar 1888	31 Dec 1934	**31 Dec 1934**	31 Dec 1934	
St. Annes – Donoughmore	6 May 1893	31 Dec 1934	**31 Dec 1934**	31 Dec 1934	

5/1 Temporary terminus at Cork (Victoria) but better known as Blackpool.

5/2 Temporary terminus at Cork goods depot; permanent terminus opened 28 Jul 1856.

5/3 Goods diverted from Summerhill **Dec 1868**; mail traffic commenced to use the line from 3 Jan 1869.

5/4 There is now no non–passenger traffic beyond Marino Point.

5/5 Not taken out of use but no traffic at time of writing.

5/6 Exact day of opening not certain but possibly 23 May 1891.

5/7 Original Bantry terminus abandoned when extension opened.

5/8 Goods only to the pier originally, but passenger use was approved on 1 Jan 1909 by BOT letter.

5/9 Junction at Ballyphehane removed 12 Sep 1879 and restored for passenger use 2 Mar 1925 (there was a siding connection from Apr **1918** and used until **1920**); line continued in use for delivery of fuel to a GSR bus depot until 1946.

5/10 A passenger service was provided during the summer of 1914 only.

5/11 Freemount was a temporary terminus.

5/12 Regular goods suspended **27 Jan 1947**, resumed **1 Jun 1956**.

5/13 Regular goods suspended **10 Mar 1947**, resumed **7 Jan 1957**.

5/14 Original terminus Cork (Victoria Road) replaced 6 Feb 1873 by Cork (Albert Street).

5/15 All services suspended 6 Apr 1887 until 2 Jan 1888.

5/16 Last use not known; land sold 1941.

CHAPTER 6 – THE MIDLANDS AND FAR WEST

	Opened	Closed Passenger	Closed Goods	Taken out of use	Notes
Gauge 5–3					
Mullingar – Athlone (East Jct)	1 Aug 1851	18 May 1987	**2 Nov 1987**	OPEN	
Athlone (East Jct) – Galway	1 Aug 1851	OPEN	OPEN	OPEN	
Galway harbour branch	**1858**	–	**1960**	**1960**	6/1
Portarlington – Tullamore	2 Oct 1854	OPEN	OPEN	OPEN	6/2
Tullamore – Athlone	3 Oct 1859	OPEN	OPEN	OPEN	6/2
Athlone (GS&WR) – Athlone East Junction (MGWR)	1860	OPEN	OPEN	OPEN	6/3
Clara & Banagher Junction – Banagher	29 May 1884	24 Feb 1947	**1 Jan 1963**	**1 Jan 1963**	
Streamstown – Clara	1 Apr 1863	27 Jan 1947	**27 Jan 1947**	**1 Jul 1965**	
Attymon Junction – Loughrea	1 Dec 1890	3 Nov 1975	**3 Nov 1975**	3 Nov 1975	
Galway – Oughterard	1 Jan 1895	29 Apr 1935	**29 Apr 1935**	29 Apr 1935	
Oughterard – Clifden	1 Jul 1895	29 Apr 1935	**29 Apr 1935**	29 Apr 1935	
Athlone – Roscommon	13 Feb 1860 **12 Mar 1860**	OPEN	OPEN	OPEN	
Roscommon – Castlerea	15 Nov 1860	OPEN	OPEN	OPEN	
Castlerea – Ballyhaunis	9 Sep 1861	OPEN	OPEN	OPEN	
Ballyhaunis – Claremorris	19 May 1862	OPEN	OPEN	OPEN	
Claremorris – Castlebar	17 Dec 1862	OPEN	OPEN	OPEN	

Castlebar – Westport	29 Jan 1866	OPEN	OPEN	OPEN	
Manulla Junction – Foxford	1 May 1868	OPEN	OPEN	OPEN	
Foxford – Ballina	19 May 1873	OPEN	OPEN	OPEN	
Ballina – Killala	2 Jan 1893	1 Oct 1931	**2 Jul 1934**	**2 Jul 1934**	
Westport – Westport Quay	**19 Nov 1873**	14 Sep 1912	**1 Mar 1943**	**1977**	
	1 Oct 1874				
Claremorris – Ballinrobe	1 Nov 1892	1 Jan 1960	**1 Jan 1960**	1 Jan 1960	
Westport – Newport	1 Feb 1894	1 Oct 1937	**1 Oct 1937**	1 Oct 1937	6/4
Newport – Mallaranny	1 Aug 1894	1 Oct 1937	**1 Oct 1937**	1 Oct 1937	6/4
Mallaranny – Achill	13 May 1895	1 Oct 1937	**1 Oct 1937**	1 Oct 1937	6/4
Mullingar – Longford	8 Nov 1855	OPEN	OPEN	OPEN	
	1 Jan 1856				
Longford – Sligo	3 Dec 1862	OPEN	OPEN	OPEN	
	17 Dec 1862				
Sligo station extension	1864	OPEN	–	OPEN	6/5
Sligo quay branch	**17 Dec 1862**	–	OPEN	OPEN	
Kilfree Jct – Ballaghaderreen	1 Nov 1874	2 Feb 1963	**2 Feb 1963**	2 Feb 1963	6/6
Inny Junction – Cavan	8 Jul 1856	27 Jan 1947	**1 Jan 1960**	1 Jan 1960	6/7
Crossdoney – Killeshandra	1 Jun 1886	27 Jan 1947	**27 Jan 1947**	**1 Mar 1955**	
Ennis – Athenry	15 Sep 1869	5 Apr 1976	**18 Dec 1978**	OPEN	
	15 Oct 1869				
Athenry – Tuam	27 Sep 1860	5 Apr 1976	**18 Dec 1978**	OPEN	
Tuam – Claremorris	30 Apr 1894	5 Apr 1976	**18 Dec 1978**	OPEN	
Claremorris W&LR – MGWR	1 Oct 1895	5 Apr 1976	**18 Dec 1978**	OPEN	
Claremorris – Collooney Jct	1 Oct 1895	17 Jun 1963	**3 Nov 1975**	**3 Nov 1975**	
Collooney W&LR – SL&NCR	1 Oct 1895	?	1944	1 Oct 1957	6/8
Gauge 3–0					
Dromod – Belturbet	**17 Oct 1887**	1 Apr 1959	**1 Apr 1959**	1 Apr 1959	
	24 Oct 1887				
Ballinamore – Arigna	2 May 1888	1 Apr 1959	**1 Apr 1959**	1 Apr 1959	
Arigna – Derreenavoghy	**2 Jun 1920**	–	**1 Apr 1959**	**1 Apr 1959**	
Derreenavoghy – Aughabehy	**2 Jun 1920**	–	**1930**	**1930**	

6/1 Use of harbour branch intermittent.
6/2 Tullamore station left on a spur in 1859; resited on main line 1 Oct 1865.
6/3 Exchange of wagons began in **Oct 1860** and passengers soon afterwards.
6/4 Deviation at Newport opened 7 Mar 1896; line closed 1 Jan 1935 but reopened 20 Apr 1936.
6/5 Use sanctioned 29 Jan 1864.
6/6 Branch closed 1 Jan 1876, reopened 24 Mar 1876.
6/7 Cavan station continued to be served by GNRB trains until 14 Oct 1957.
6/8 Line sanctioned for passenger use 13 Jul 1896.

CHAPTER 7 – DUNDALK TO DONEGAL

	Opened	Closed Passenger	Closed Goods	Taken out of use	Notes
Gauge 5–3					
Drogheda – Newfoundwell	11 May 1853	OPEN	OPEN	OPEN	7/1
Newfoundwell – Dundalk	15 Feb 1849	OPEN	OPEN	OPEN	7/1
Dundalk – Wellington Inn	31 Jul 1850	OPEN	OPEN	OPEN	7/1
Wellington Inn – Bessbrook	10 Jun 1852	OPEN	OPEN	OPEN	7/1
Bessbrook – Portadown	6 Jan 1852	OPEN	OPEN	OPEN	
Drogheda Cement Factory	**Apr 1938**	–	OPEN	OPEN	7/2
Dromin Junction – Ardee	1 Aug 1896	3 Jun 1934	**3 Nov 1975**	**3 Nov 1975**	
Dundalk – Castleblayney	15 Feb 1849	14 Oct 1957	**1 Jan 1960**	**1 Jan 1960**	
Castleblayney – Ballybay	17 Jul 1854	14 Oct 1957	**1 Jan 1960**	**1 Jan 1960**	

Ballybay – Newbliss	14 Aug 1855	14 Oct 1957	**1 Jan 1960**	**1 Jan 1960**		
Newbliss – Clones	7 Jul 1858	14 Oct 1957	**1 Jan 1960**	**1 Jan 1960**		
Clones – Lisnaskea	7 Jul 1858	1 Oct 1957	**1 Oct 1957**	1 Oct 1957		
Lisnaskea – Lisbellaw	16 Aug 1858	1 Oct 1957	**1 Oct 1957**	1 Oct 1957		
Lisbellaw – Enniskillen	15 Feb 1859	**1 Oct 1957**	**1 Oct 1957**	1 Oct 1957		
Inniskeen – Carrickmacross	31 Jul 1886	10 Mar 1947	**1 Jan 1960**	**1 Jan 1960**		
Shantona Jct – Cootehill	18 Oct 1860	10 Mar 1947	**10 Mar 1947**	**20 Jun 1955**		
Dundalk West Junction – East Junction	15 Feb 1849 1 May 1873	1 Jan 1952	**1 Jan 1952**	1 Jan 1952		
Dundalk South – East Junction	**1874**	–	**31 Mar 1995**	**31 Mar 1995**		
Dundalk East Junction – Barrack Street	**15 Feb 1849** 1 May 1873	1 Jan 1952	**31 Mar 1995**	**31 Mar 1995**		
Barrack Street – Windmill Road Junction	1 May 1873	1 Jan 1952	?	?	7/3	
Windmill Road Jct – Greenore	1 May 1873	1 Jan 1952	**1 Jan 1952**	1 Jan 1952		
Georges Quay branch	**1873**	–	?	?	7/3	
Greenore – Newry (Bridge St)	1 Aug 1876	1 Jan 1952	**1 Jan 1952**	1 Jan 1952		
Newry (Bridge St) – Newry (King Street Junction)	**1 Feb 1877** 1 Jul 1880	1 Jan 1952	**1 Jan 1952**	1 Jan 1952		
Goraghwood – Newry (Edward Street)	Mar 1854	4 Jan 1965	**4 Jan 1965**	4 Jan 1965		
Newry (Albert Basin) branch	**1854**	–	**4 Jan 1965**	**4 Jan 1965**	7/4	
Newry (Edward Street) – Newry (Dublin Bridge)	2 Sep 1861	4 Jan 1965	**4 Jan 1965**	4 Jan 1965		
Newry (Dublin Bridge) – Kilmorey Street Junction	28 May 1861	4 Jan 1965	**4 Jan 1965**	4 Jan 1965		
Newry – Warrenpoint	28 May 1849 **16 Jul 1849**	4 Jan 1965	**4 Jan 1965**	4 Jan 1965	7/5	
Goraghwood – Markethill	25 Aug 1864	1 Feb 1933	**2 May 1955**	**2 May 1955**		
Markethill – Armagh	25 Aug 1864	1 Feb 1933	**1 Feb 1933**	1 Feb 1933	7/6	
Armagh – jct with Ulster Rly	13 Feb 1865	1 Feb 1933	**1 Feb 1933**	1 Feb 1933	7/6	
Portadown – Armagh	1 Mar 1848	1 Oct 1957	**1 Oct 1957**	1 Oct 1957	7/7	
Armagh – Glaslough	25 May 1858 **Jul 1858**	1 Oct 1957	**1 Oct 1957**	1 Oct 1957		
Glaslough – Monaghan	25 May 1858 **Jul 1858**	1 Oct 1957	**31 May 1958**	**3 May 1958**	7/8	
Monaghan – Clones	2 Mar 1863 **Jun 1863**	14 Oct 1957	**1 Jan 1960**	**1 Jan 1960**	7/8	
Clones – Cavan	7 Apr 1862	14 Oct 1957	**1 Jan 1960**	**1 Jan 1960**		
Ballyhaise – Belturbet	29 Jun 1885	14 Oct 1957	**1 Apr 1959**	1 Apr 1959		
Armagh – Keady	31 May 1909	1 Jan 1932	**1 Oct 1957**	**1 Oct 1957**		
Keady – Castleblayney	10 Nov 1910	2 Apr 1923	**2 Apr 1923**	2 Apr 1923		
Enniskillen – Belcoo	**12 Feb 1879** 18 Mar 1879	1 Oct 1957	**1 Oct 1957**	1 Oct 1957	7/9	
Belcoo – Glenfarne	1 Jan 1880	1 Oct 1957	**1 Oct 1957**	1 Oct 1957		
Glenfarne – Manorhamilton	1 Dec 1880	1 Oct 1957	**1 Oct 1957**	1 Oct 1957		
Manorhamilton – Collooney	1 Sep 1881	1 Oct 1957	**1 Oct 1957**	1 Oct 1957		
Collooney – Carrignagat Jct	1 Jul 1882	1 Oct 1957	**1 Oct 1957**	1 Oct 1957		
Enniskillen – Dromore Road	19 Aug 1854	1 Oct 1957	**1 Oct 1957**	1 Oct 1957		
Dromore Road – Fintona Jct	14 Jan 1854	1 Oct 1957	**1 Oct 1957**	1 Oct 1957		
Fintona – Omagh	15 Jun 1853	1 Oct 1957	**1 Oct 1957**	1 Oct 1957		
Bundoran Jct – Bundoran	13 Jun 1866	1 Oct 1957	**1 Oct 1957**	1 Oct 1957		
Bundoran Jct north curve	1894	1 Oct 1957	**1 Oct 1957**	1 Oct 1957	7/10	
Portadown Jct – Dungannon	5 Apr 1858	15 Feb 1965	**15 Feb 1965**	15 Feb 1965	7/11	
Dungannon – Omagh	2 Sep 1861	15 Feb 1965	**15 Feb 1965**	15 Feb 1965	7/12	

Dungannon Jct – Coalisland	28 Jul 1879	16 Jan 1956	**4 Jan 1965**	4 Jan 1965	
Coalisland – Cookstown	28 Jul 1879	16 Jan 1956	**5 Oct 1959**	5 Oct 1959	
Omagh market branch	**Jun 1862**	–	**15 Feb 1965**	15 Feb 1965	
Omagh – Newtownstewart	13 Sep 1852	15 Feb 1965	**15 Feb 1965**	15 Feb 1965	
Newtownstewart – Strabane	9 May 1852	15 Feb 1965	**15 Feb 1965**	15 Feb 1965	
Strabane – Londonderry	19 Apr 1847	15 Feb 1965	**15 Feb 1965**	15 Feb 1965	
Londonderry (extension)	18 Apr 1850	15 Feb 1965	**15 Feb 1965**	15 Feb 1965	
Londonderry port lines	Jan 1868	–	**31 Aug 1962**	31 Aug 1962	7/13
Gauge 5–3 (converted to 3–0 as indicated in the notes)					
Strabane – Stranorlar	7 Sep 1863	1 Jan 1960	**1 Jan 1960**	1 Jan 1960	7/14
Londonderry – Tooban Jct	31 Dec 1863	6 Sep 1948	**10 Aug 1953**	**10 Aug 1953**	7/15
Tooban Jct – 'Burt'	31 Dec 1863	3 Jun 1940	**10 Aug 1953**	**10 Aug 1953**	7/16
'Burt' – Farland Point	31 Dec 1863	Jun 1866	**Jun 1866**	Jun 1866	
Tooban Jct – Buncrana	8 Sep 1864	6 Sep 1948	**10 Aug 1953**	**10 Aug 1953**	7/15
Gauge 3–0					
Bessbrook – Newry	1 Oct 1885	10 Jan 1948	**10 Jan 1948**	10 Jan 1948	
Tynan – Maguiresbridge	2 May 1887	1 Jan 1942	**1 Jan 1942**	1 Jan 1942	
Victoria Bridge – Castlederg	4 Jul 1884	17 Apr 1933	**17 Apr 1933**	17 Apr 1933	
Londonderry – Strabane	**1 Aug 1900**	1 Jan 1955	**1 Jan 1955**	1 Jan 1955	
	6 Aug 1900				
Strabane new station (DR)	16 Jul 1894	1 Jan 1960	**1 Jan 1960**	1 Jan 1960	7/17
Strabane – Letterkenny	1 Jan 1909	1 Jan 1960	**1 Jan 1960**	1 Jan 1960	7/18
Stranorlar – Glenties	3 Jun 1895	3 Dec 1947	**3 Dec 1947**	3 Dec 1952	
Stranorlar – Lough Eske	25 Apr 1882	1 Jan 1960	**1 Jan 1960**	1 Jan 1960	
Lough Eske – Donegal	16 Sep 1889	1 Jan 1960	**1 Jan 1960**	1 Jan 1960	
Donegal – Killybegs	18 Aug 1893	1 Jan 1960	**1 Jan 1960**	1 Jan 1960	
Donegal – Ballyshannon	21 Sep 1905	1 Jan 1960	**1 Jan 1960**	1 Jan 1960	
Buncrana – Carndonagh	1 Jul 1901	2 Dec 1935	**2 Dec 1935**	2 Dec 1935	
'Burt' – Letterkenny	30 Jun 1883	3 Jun 1940	**10 Aug 1953**	**10 Aug 1953**	7/19
Letterkenny – Gweedore	9 Mar 1903	3 Jun 1940	**3 Jun 1940**	6 Jan 1947	7/20
Gweedore – Burtonport	9 Mar 1903	3 Jun 1940	**3 Jun 1940**	3 Jun 1940	7/20

7/1 Temporary viaduct (Boyne Viaduct) at Drogheda; permanent viaduct completed and taken into use 5 Apr 1855; Newfoundwell and Wellington Inn were temporary termini.

7/2 Retained only as sidings.

7/3 Used by GNRB after closure of DN&GR to an unspecified date.

7/4 Partly replaced in 1861 by Town of Newry Connecting Railway.

7/5 Original NW&RR terminus at Kilmorey Street closed to passengers when connecting line opened 28 May 1861 (but remained in use as a goods depot until about 1900); line shortened at Warrenpoint (by 7 chains) during 1891 (Inspector's report dated 9 May 1891).

7/6 Originally a temporary terminus before extension to join UR.

7/7 Line retained to Brownstown Siding until 4 Jan 1965.

7/8 Original terminus at Monaghan abandoned because extension to Clones diverged 1/4 mile to north.

7/9 SL&NCR trains commenced to use the GNR station at Enniskillen in 1883 (sanctioned 15 Jan 1883).

7/10 Sanctioned 3 Apr 1894 but details of first use not available; last use 9 Sep 1957.

7/11 Junction at Portadown not sanctioned until 4 Jul 1858.

7/12 Extension from the temporary terminus at Dungannon.

7/13 L&LSR passenger trains used Middle Quay on LPHC lines instead of Graving Dock from 1 Jan 1869 to about 31 Dec 1884 and from 1 Jul 1885 to 31 Dec 1887 (except on Sundays); gauge mixed 1885 where necessary and tracks extended in 1900 to connect with narrow gauge Strabane – Londonderry line.

7/14 Line diverted to new station when gauge was altered to 3–0 16 Jul 1894; some goods trains continued until **6 Feb 1960** (or a few days later).

7/15 Gauge altered to 3–0 28 Mar 1885; limited passenger accommodation provided on goods trains until closure.

7/16 Line closed Jun 1866; gauge altered to 3–0 30 June 1883 and line reopened; passenger service withdrawn 4 Apr 1931 and resumed 21 Jun 1931; limited passenger accommodation provided on goods trains from Mar 1943 until closure.

7/17 Trains diverted from GNR station alongside; goods continued until **6 Feb 1960** (or a few days later).

7/18 Included connecting line at Letterkenny to L&LSR.

7/19 Passenger services withdrawn 4 Apr 1931 and resumed 21 Jun 1931; limited passenger accommodation provided on goods trains from Mar 1943 until closure.

7/20 Passenger service withdrawn 4 Apr 1931 and resumed 21 Jun 1931; some goods ran until **Jul 1940;** goods resumed from Letterkenny to Gweedore **3 Feb 1941** with limited passenger accommodation from Mar 1943; specials continued until **Jun 1947.**

CHAPTER 8 – BELFAST AND NORTH EAST

	Opened	Closed Passenger	Closed Goods	Taken out of use	Note
Gauge 6–2 (converted to 5–3 May 1847)					
Belfast (Great Victoria St.) –					
Central Junction	12 Aug 1839	26 Apr 1976	**4 Jan 1965**	26 Apr 1976	
Central Junction – Lurgan	12 Aug 1839	OPEN	OPEN	OPEN	
Lurgan – Seagoe	31 Jan 1842	OPEN	OPEN	OPEN	8/1
Seagoe – Portadown	12 Sep 1842	OPEN	OPEN	OPEN	8/2
Gauge 5–3					
Knockmore Junction – Antrim	13 Nov 1871	OPEN	OPEN	OPEN	8/3
Gortnagallon branch	May 1012	1945	**1945**	1945	8/4
Knockmore Jct – Banbridge	13 Jul 1863	29 Apr 1956	**29 Apr 1956**	29 Apr 1956	8/5
	21 Sep 1863				
Scarva – Banbridge	23 Mar 1859	2 May 1955	**2 May 1955**	2 May 1955	8/6
Banbridge – Ballyroney	13 Dec 1880	2 May 1955	**2 May 1955**	2 May 1955	
Ballyroney – Newcastle	24 Mar 1906	2 May 1955	**2 May 1955**	2 May 1955	
Belfast (Queens Quay) – Holywood	2 Aug 1848	OPEN	**24 Apr 1950**	OPEN	8/7
Holywood – Bangor	18 May 1865	OPEN	**24 Apr 1950**	OPEN	
Belfast (Queens Quay) –					
Newtownards	6 May 1850	24 Apr 1950	**24 Apr 1950**	24 Apr 1950	
Newtownards – Donaghadee	3 Jun 1861	24 Apr 1950	**24 Apr 1950**	24 Apr 1950	8/8
Donaghadee harbour branch	**Mar 1870**	–	**24 Apr 1950**	24 Apr 1950	8/9
Comber – Ballynahinch	10 Sep 1858	16 Jan 1950	**16 Jan 1950**	16 Jan 1950	
Ballynahinch Junction –					
Downpatrick	23 Mar 1859	16 Jan 1950	**16 Jan 1950**	16 Jan 1950	
Downpatrick – Newcastle	25 Mar 1869	16 Jan 1950	**16 Jan 1950**	16 Jan 1950	
Downpatrick loop	24 Sep 1892	16 Jan 1950	**16 Jan 1950**	16 Jan 1950	
Ardglass Jct – Ardglass	**27 May 1892**	16 Jan 1950	**16 Jan 1950**	16 Jan 1950	
	8 Jul 1892				
Ardglass harbour branch	**31 May 1892**	–	?	?	8/10
Belfast (York Road) –	11 Apr 1848	OPEN	4 Jan 1965	OPEN	8/11,
Carrickfergus					8/12
Carrickfergus harbour lines	**Jan 1887**	–	1957	1957	
Carrickfergus – Larne Harbour	1 Oct 1862	OPEN	**4 Jan 1965**	OPEN	8/13
Bleach Green Jct – Monkstown	22 Jan 1934	21 Jan 1981	**4 Jan 1965**	OPEN	8/14
Greenisland – Monkstown	11 Apr 1848	9 Sep 1961	?	1 Oct 1963	
Monkstown – Antrim	11 Ayr 1848	21 Jan 1981	**4 Jan 1965**	OPEN	8/14
Kingsbog Jct – Ballyclare	3 Nov 1884	1 Jan 1938	**2 May 1938**	**3 Jul 1950**	8/15
Antrim – Ballymena	11 Apr 1848	OPEN	OPEN	OPEN	
Ballymena extension	7 Nov 1855	OPEN	OPEN	OPEN	
Ballymena – Coleraine	7 Nov 1855	OPEN	OPEN	OPEN	
Coleraine – Portrush	7 Nov 1855	OPEN	**1954**	OPEN	
Portrush harbour branch	Mar 1866	–	?	?	
Cookstown Jct – Randalstown	11 Apr 1848	28 Aug 1950	**5 Oct 1959**	5 Oct 1959	
Randalstown – Magherafelt	10 Nov 1856	28 Aug 1950	**5 Oct 1959**	5 Oct 1959	

Magherafelt – Cookstown	10 Nov 1856	28 Aug 1950	**2 May 1955**	2 May 1955	
Draperstown Jct – Draperstown	20 Jul 1883	1 Oct 1930	**3 Jul 1950**	**3 Jul 1950**	
Magherafelt – Kilrea	19 Feb 1880	28 Aug 1950	**5 Oct 1959**	5 Oct 1959	
Kilrea – Macfin	19 Feb 1880	28 Aug 1950	**28 Aug 1950**	28 Aug 1950	
Coleraine connecting line	19 Nov 1860	OPEN	OPEN	OPEN	8/16
Coleraine harbour branch	**1 Jan 1892**	–	**30 Sep 1966**	**30 Sep 1966**	
Coleraine – Limavady Junction	18 Jul 1853	OPEN	OPEN	OPEN	8/16
Limavady Jct – Londonderry 20 Dec 1852	**29 Sep 1852**	OPEN	OPEN	OPEN	
Londonderry new station	24 Feb 1980	OPEN	–	OPEN	
Magilligan branch	Jul 1855	Oct 1855	–	Oct 1855	8/17
Limavady Jct – Limavady 20 Dec 1852	**29 Sep 1852**	3 Jul 1950	**2 May 1955**	2 May 1955	
Limavady – Dungiven	4 Jul 1883	1 Jan 1933	**3 Jul 1950**	**3 Jul 1950**	
Central Jct – East Bridge Jct 5 Aug 1878	**9 Aug 1874**	30 Nov 1885	**4 Jan 1964**	**31 Jul 1965**	8/18
East Bridge Junction – Ballymacarrett Junction	**9 Aug 1874**	–	**4 Jan 1964**	**31 Jul 1965**	8/18
Abercorn basin branch	**9 Aug 1874**	–	**4 Jan 1964**	**31 Jul 1965**	
East Bridge Jct – Queen's Bridge 5 Aug 1878	**12 Jun 1876**	30 Nov 1885	**3 Jun 1963**	**3 Jun 1963**	
Queen's Bridge – Donegall Quay Junction	**12 Jun 1876** Belfast harbour lines:–	–	**3 Jun 1963**	**3 Jun 1963**	
(Co. Down side)	?	–	**1969**	**1969**	8/19
(Co. Antrim side)	1855	–	**1969**	**1970**	8/19
Dufferin Dock Jct – York Rd	**Jun 1855**	–	**1969**	**1969**	8/20
Central Jct – Belfast Central	26 Apr 1976	OPEN	–	OPEN	8/21
Belfast Central – Ballymacarrett Junction	12 Apr 1976	OPEN	–	OPEN	8/21
Lagan Jct – Yorkgate	28 Nov 1994	OPEN	–	OPEN	8/22
Yorkgate – (York Road jct)	17 Oct 1992	OPEN	–	OPEN	
Gauge 3–0					
Larne Harbour – Larne 24 Aug 1878	**1 Sep 1877**	1 Jun 1932	**3 Jul 1950**	**3 Jul 1950**	
Larne – Ballyclare 24 Aug 1878	**1 Sep 1877**	1 Feb 1933	**3 Jul 1950**	**3 Jul 1950**	
Ballyclare – Doagh	**8 Feb 1884** **1 May 1884**	1 Oct 1930	**15 Jun 1944**	**15 Jun 1944**	
Ballyboley Jct – Ballymena	24 Aug 1878	1 Feb 1933	**2 Jun 1940**	**2 Jun 1940**	
Ballymena connecting line	22 Sep 1880	1 Feb 1933	**2 Jun 1940**	**2 Jun 1940**	
Ballymena – Rathkenny 5 Apr 1886	**26 Mar 1875**	1 Oct 1930	**2 Jun 1940**	**2 Jun 1940**	
Rathkenny – Knockanally 5 Apr 1886	**26 Mar 1875**	1 Oct 1930	**10 Apr 1937**	**10 Apr 1937**	
Knockanally – Cargan 27 Aug 1888	**26 Mar 1875**	1 Oct 1930	**10 Apr 1937**	**10 Apr 1937**	
Cargan – Parkmore 27 Aug 1888	**8 Oct 1876**	1 Oct 1930	**10 Apr 1937**	**10 Apr 1937**	
Parkmore – Retreat	**8 Oct 1876**	–	**10 Apr 1937**	**10 Apr 1937**	
Ballymoney – Ballycastle	18 Oct 1880	3 Jul 1950	**3 Jul 1950**	3 Jul 1950	8/23
Portstewart tramway	28 Jun 1882	31 Jan 1926	–	31 Jan 1926	
Portrush – Bushmills	29 Jan 1883	30 Sep 1949	**1890–1**	30 Sep 1949	
Portrush harbour extension	**1883**	–	**1 Jun 1887**	**1 Jun 1887**	8/24
Bushmills – Giant's Causeway	1 Jul 1887	30 Sep 1949	–	30 Sep 1949	

Great Southern & Western Railway (including Geasehill Extension stock)
Midland Great Western Railway,
Cork, Bandon & South Coast Railway (including Bantry Bay Extension).

The Great Southern Railway and the Dublin & South Eastern Railway (including City of Dublin Junction Railways and New Ross & Waterford Extension Railways) were incorporated into the Great Southern Railways on 1 January 1925 (SR&O 1925 No. 1). A secondary amalgamation took place on 2 March 1925 (SR&O 1925 No. 4) when the Great Southern Railways and the Bantry Extension Railway combined. The remaining railways were absorbed in a series of Great Southern Railways Absorbtion Schemes during 1925:–

No. 1 (SR&O 1925 No. 5)	Clonakilty Extension Railway,
	Cork, Blackrock & Passage Railway,
	Cork & Macroom Direct Railway,
	Dublin & Kingstown Railway,
	Waterford & Tramore Railway.
No. 2 (SR&O 1925 No. 6)	Baltimore Extension Railway,
	Cork City Railways.
No. 3 (SR&O 1925 No. 7)	Tralee & Fenit Railway.
No. 4 (SR&O 1925 No. 8)	Athenry & Tuam Extension to Claremorris Railway,
	Ballinascarthy & Timoleague Junction Light Railway,
	Ballinrobe & Claremorris light Railway,
	Cavan & Leitrim Railway,
	Cork & Muskerry Light Railways,
	Donoughmore Extension Light Railway,
	Loughrea & Attymon Light Railway,
	West Carbery Tramways & Light Railways (Schull & Skibbereen Light Railway),
	South Clare Railways,
	Timoleague & Courtmacsherry Extension Light Railway,
	Tralee & Dingle Light Railway,
	West Clare Railway.

All the above orders were dated 3 March 1925.
No. 5 (SR&O 1925 No. 59)   Southern Railway.
This order was issued on 18 November 1925. The outstanding colliery lines (Castlecomer, Wolfhill and Arigna) were not absorbed until 1929.
(SR&O = Statutory Rules & Orders)

Appendix Four

The following lines were listed in a GSR minute (25 January 1931) which decreed that they were to be maintained only for the remaining life of the track:-

ex-GS&WR	Tullow, Wolfhill, Castlecomer, Bagenalstown - Palace East, Mountmellick, Birr, Cashel, Mitchelstown, Newmarket, Kenmare, Castleisland.
ex-MGWR	Edenderry, Ballaghadereen, Loughrea, Clifden, Ballinrobe, Killala, Achill.
ex-D&SER	Aughrim.
ex-CB&SCR	Kinsale, Clonakilty, Skibbereen - Baltimore.
ex-C&MDR	Cork - Macroom.
ex-T&CLR	Ballinascarthy - Courtmacsherry.
ex-C&LR	Ballinamore - Arigna.
ex-C&MLR	Cork - Blarney/Coachford/Donoughmore.
ex-CB&PR	Cork - Crosshaven.
ex-S&SLR	Skibbereen - Schull.
ex-T&DLR	Tralee - Dingle/Castlegregory.
ex-WCR	Ennis - Kilkee/Kilrush.

It will be noted that all narrow gauge lines, other then Dromod - Belturbet, were to close.

Appendix Five

The GSR submitted a list of lines to be closed, totalling 861³/₄ miles out of the system mileage of 2,340. The lines were:

ex–GS&WR	Tullow, Cobh Junction – Youghal, Bagenalstown – Palace East, Cashel, Mitchelstown, Newmarket, Thurles – Clonmel, Patrickswell – Charleville, Birr, Castleisland, Banagher, Mountmellick, Killaloe, Fenit, Valentia, Kenmare, Foynes, Castlecomer, Claremorris – Collooney.
ex–MGWR	Kingscourt, Athboy, Edenderry, Ballinrobe, Loughrea, Ballaghadereen, Killeshandra, Cavan, Streamstown – Clara, Claremorris – Westport/Ballina
ex–D&SER	Shillelagh, Macmine Junction – Waterford

ex–CB&SCR	Cork – Bantry, Clonakilty, Drimoleague Junction – Baltimore.
ex–C&MDR	Cork – Macroom
ex–T&CLR	Ballinascarthy – Courtmacsherry.
ex–W&TR	Waterford – Tramore.
ex–C&LR	Dromod – Belturbet, Ballinamore – Arigna.
ex–S&SLR	Skibbereen – Schull.
ex–T&DLR	Tralee – Dingle/Castlegregory.
ex–WCR	Ennis – Kilkee/Kilrush.

Appendix Six

SUSPENSIONS AND RESTORATIONS OF SERVICES 1939–1950

As the fuel situation became more difficult the following notice was issued to the Irish press and published on 22 August 1941:-

The Great Southern Railways Company regrets to announce to the travelling public that its train services are considerably disorganised owing to the extremely inferior quality of coal being supplied, the use of which renders the company's locomotives unreliable in service. No better quality of coal is available at the present time.

Every possible step is being taken to secure improvement, but the public is notified that late arrival of trains cannot be avoided until supplies of better coal are available. Intending passengers are asked to appreciate the Company's difficulties, and to understand that the delays are entirely outside the Company's control.

As the situation worsened the Minister for Industry and Commerce in Dublin issued to the GSR on 19 November 1941 certain directions in the operation of railways. There were to be no increases in passenger services and the greatest possible speed in loading and unloading wagons was to be exercised with only one day free of demurrage for firms using their own staff allowed, the GSR being empowered to use their own staff to load or unload at the firm's expense if the day was exceeded. It was directed that all railway and road vehicles were to be used for the following traffics, in order of priority:–

1. Livestock being sent to and from markets or fairs or for shipment.
2. Beet, sugar and beet pulp.
3. Grain and products of grain in covered wagons.
4. Coal.
5. Turf and cut timber for fuel.
6. Petroleum products and industrial alcohol.

7. Milk, cream, returned empty milk and cream containers, dressed meat, cooked meat, fish and live and dead poultry.
8. Eggs.
9. Butter.

The following curtailments, suspensions and restorations of services took place in 1939–1950 (GSR/CIE unless otherwise stated):–

Sep 1939	GNR through Dun Laoghaire coach taken off (never restored).
1 Jan 1940	Foynes passenger service to cease (postponed).
3 Jun 1940	L&LSR passenger service Tooban Junction – Burtonport terminated; goods from Letterkenny to Burtonport terminated.
1 Feb 1941	Direct road lorry services ceased (replaced by combined rail and road distribution).
3 Feb 1941	L&LSR goods service resumed from Letterkenny to Gweedore.
10 Feb 1941	Bus services drastically reduced.
1 Jul 1941	GSR announced 25% cut in services.
12 Jul 1941	Tullow to close (postponed).
13 Jul 1941	Sunday trains on main lines ceased. Restaurant and buffet cars withdrawn. Newspaper trains suspended. Boat trains no longer provided between Westland Row and Kingsbridge (no booked passenger trains Glasnevin Junction – Islandbridge Junction).
14 Sep 1941	Sunday trains from Cork to Cobh and Youghal ceased.
8 Oct 1941	Severe curtailments of passenger services with most lines reduced to one train each way. Passenger services to Kingscourt, Athboy and Streamstown – Clara suspended.
	Trains ceased to call at Clonsilla, Lucan (North), Leixlip, Kilcock, Ferns Lock, Moyvalley and Clonhugh.
	Night mail trains suspended (mails carried by goods trains).
27 Oct 1941	Through Dublin locals with GNR participation commenced.
7 Dec 1941	Dublin suburban Sunday trains ceased.
1 Jan 1942	CVR all services terminated.
5 Jan 1942	Dining cars restored to Cork, Galway and Wexford.
29 Jun 1942	Slight improvement to main line services with separate Cork and Waterford/Limerick departures and arrivals at Kingsbridge and separate Galway and Sligo trains.
	Through GSR/GNR workings at Dublin ceased.
	Clonsilla, Leixlip, Kilcock, Ferns Lock, Moyvalley, Clonhugh reopened to passengers.
15 Feb 1943	Horseleap – Streamstown closed to goods (Horseleap served from Clara).
Mar 1943	L&LSR limited passenger accommodation provided on trains to Letterkenny and Gweedore.
12 Jul 1943	Additional trains to Wexford and Limerick. Mayo train separate from Galway train.
	Kingscourt passenger service resumed.
	Special Sunday service Dublin to Bray for summer weeks.
22 Nov 1943	Horseleap served from Streamstown instead of Clara.
15 Apr 1944	Permits issued for persons with priority needs to travel by overnight perishable trains between Dublin and Cork.

24 Apr 1944	Severe curtailments:–
	Passenger trains, unless totally suspended, Monday and Thursday only (with exceptions of Dublin suburban, Cork – Cobh/Youghal, Cork – Mallow, Limerick – Nenagh, Limerick – Ennis, Wexford Rosslare Harbour which retained weekday services).
	Dining cars withdrawn.
	Goods trains Monday, Tuesday, Thursday, Friday (with a few exceptions).
	Passenger services suspended – Tullow, Kingscourt, Cavan, Macmine – Waterford.
	All services suspended – Bagenalstown – Palace East, Mountmellick, Killaloe, Cashel, Mitchelstown, Newmarket, Fenit, Killeshandra, Shillelagh, Horseleap – Clara, Skibbereen – Schull.
	Stations closed – Clondalkin, Lucan South.
6 May 1944	Skibbereen – Baltimore reduced to one return Saturday evening only.
12 Jun 1944	Hill of Howth tramway (GNR) service suspended.
17 Jul 1944	Passenger trains on Tuesday and Saturday in addition to Monday and Thursday.
25 Sep 1944	Hill of Howth tramway (GNR) service resumed.
6 Jul 1945	Friday passenger trains resumed.
8 Jul 1945	Sunday passenger trains for summer Westland Row – Bray, Cork – Cobh/Youghal, Waterford – Tramore.
15 Aug 1945	Passenger trains restored on Wednesday to give Monday to Saturday services.
10 Dec 1945	Suspended passenger services resumed:– Tullow, Mountmellick, Cashel, Mitchelstown, Newmarket, Cavan, Killeshandra, Kingscourt, Athboy, Macmine Junction – Waterford, Skibbereen – Schull.
	Goods resumed Bagenalstown – Palace East, Fenit, Streamstown – Clara.
	Stations reopened – Clondalkin, Lucan South
14 Jan 1946	Restaurant car services restored.
4 Nov 1946	Suspended passenger service restored Streamstown – Clara.
6 Jan 1947	L&LSR all services terminated Letterkenny – Gweedore (but specials continued until June 1947).
20 Jan 1947	All Sunday trains ceased. Restricted weekday services on main lines and several lines Wednesday trains suspended.
	Passenger services from Clondalkin and Lucan South withdrawn.
27 Jan 1947	Passenger services suspended:– Tullow, Kingscourt, Athboy, Cavan, Macmine Junction – Waterford.
	Goods services suspended:– Fenit, Bagenalstown – Palace East.
	All services suspended:– Cashel, Mountmellick, Mitchelstown, Newmarket, Ballaghadereen, Streamstown – Clara, Skibbereen – Schull.
17 Feb 1947	Tuesday passenger trains suspended on lines without Wednesday trains.
	All livestock trains suspended.
	Goods trains restricted to three days per week (but in one direction

	on Monday, Wednesday and Friday, returning on Tuesday, Thursday and Saturday).
24 Feb 1947	All passenger services suspended with exception of limited suburban services Dublin – Bray and Greystones, Cork – Cobh, Cork – Mallow, limerick – Nenagh, Waterford – Tramore. Limited accommodation provided on mail trains and overnight perishables from Dublin to Cork (also overnight perishables to Athlone soon afterwards).
10 Mar 1947	Goods services suspended on following lines:– Tullow, Banagher, Castleisland, Kingscourt, Athboy, Cavan, Ballinrobe, Skibbereen – Baltimore, Clonakilty, Courtmacsherry, Macroom, Dingle, Loughrea, Ballinrobe, Birr, Thurles – Clonmel, Macmine Junction – Waterford. GNR passengers services on Belturbet, Carrickmacross and Cootehil branches suspended.
24 May 1947	Passenger services resumed on Monday, Tuesday, Thursday, Saturday on main lines and branches which had a service up to 24 February 1947 with exception of Birr, Loughrea and Clonakilty, but were restored to Ballaghadereen. Goods services restored:– Birr, Thurles – Clonmel, Ballaghadereen, Loughrea, Ballinrobe, Macmine Junction – Waterford, Skibbereen – Baltimore.
2 Jun 1947	GNR passenger service to Belturbet restored.
3 Jun 1947	Goods service to Cavan restored.
15 Jun 1947	Sunday services restored Dublin – Bray and Greystones, Cork Cobh/Youghal, Waterford – Tramore, Wexford – Rosslare Harbour.
16 Jun 1947	Passenger services resumed on Wednesday and Friday and on Birr and Loughrea branches.
23 Jun 1947	All services resumed on Clonakilty branch.
30 Jun 1947	Goods service to Kingscourt resumed.
5 Jul 1947	Passenger service (Saturday only) resumed Skibbereen – Baltimore (weekday service not restored until 31 May 1948).
30 Sep 1947	Goods restored to Banagher and Fenit branches.
1 Oct 1947	Goods (wagon load only) restored to Courtmacsherry branch.
10 Nov 1947	The following stations closed to passengers:– Hazlehatch, Straffan, Clonsilla, Leixlip, Maynooth, Kilcock, Ferns Lock, Enfield, Hill of Down, Killucan.
3 Dec 1947	CDRJC services, except limited use for turf, livestock and ore trains, from Stranorlar to Glenties terminated.
10 Jan 1948	All services on B&NT ceased.
6 Sep 1948	L&LSR passenger service Londonderry to Buncrana terminated.
30 Sep 1949	GCP&BVR&T services terminated.
2 Oct 1950	Through boat train Dun Laoghaire – Kingsbridge restored

Appendix Seven

MILNE REPORT 1948

This report listed proposed CIE action in respect of the following branches:–

(i) Lines with all services being considered for closure:–
Ballinrobe, Kenmare, Ballaghadereen, Loughrea, Birr, Tramore, Clonakilty, Skibbereen – Baltimore, Cavan & Leitrim, West Clare.

(ii) Lines without passenger services being considered for closure:–
Courtmacsherry, Banagher, Kingscourt, Athboy.

(iii) Lines with only special services being considered for closure:–
Bagenalstown – Palace East, Newmarket, Streamstown – Clara, Macroom, Mitchelstown, Castleisland, Mountmellick, Tullow.

(iv) Lines closed for which Abandonment Orders had been submitted:–
Killaloe, Killeshandra, Cashel, Shillelagh, Skibbereen – Schull, Dingle.

Appendix Eight

STATIONS, HALTS AND OTHER STOPPING PLACES

Space within the text has prevented a mention of every station on each of Ireland's railway routes and individual dates of use. Apart from the permanent stations and halts there were many other stopping places, some not even having a nameboard, for purely local use, not being advertised and existing for undetermined periods in several instances. In the following lists stations underlined were added after the line was opened and minor stopping places are given in italics. Places and distances entirely within brackets are non passenger locations. Several stations had name changes, strokes indicating successive names, but where a second part was simply discarded it is shown with brackets, eg. Goolds Cross & Cashel became Goolds Cross. Timetables and official documents have shown much inconsistency over names, such that junction stations are sometimes shown as XX Junction or just XX, even in concurrent issues.

Stations in use at the time of writing can be established by consulting Maps numbers 6, 16 and 17.

Mileages (to the nearest $1/4$ mile) run from the first named station or junction.

* indicates distance not to hand or not certain.

Lines forming the GSR

For stations between Dublin and Greystones see Table 2. Dublin (Harcourt Street) 0, Kilcool/Kilcoole $19^3/_4$, <u>Newcastle</u> $22^1/_2$, Killoughter $25^1/_2$, <u>Wicklow</u> $27^3/_4$, Wicklow (Murragh) $28^3/_4$, <u>Rathnew</u> $29^3/_4$, Glenealy $32^3/_4$ later $33^1/_4$, Kilcommon 36, Rathdrum $37^1/_4$, Ovoca/Avoca $42^3/_4$, <u>Woodenbridge Junction</u> $44^3/_4$, Arklow 49, <u>Inch</u> $53^1/_2$, Gorey $59^1/_2$, <u>Camolin</u> 67, Ferns $69^3/_4$, Enniscorthy $77^1/_2$, Edermine Ferry 81, <u>Macmine Junction</u> $83^1/_4$, Killurin 86, Wexford $92^1/_4$ later $92^3/_4$.

Woodenbridge Junction 0, Aughrim $4^1/_2$, <u>Ballinglen</u> 9, Tinahely 12, Shillelagh $16^1/_2$.

Macmine Junction 0, Macmine $^1/_2$, Sparrowsland $2^3/_4$, <u>Chapel</u> $6^1/_2$, Palace East $10^1/_2$, <u>Rathgarogue</u> $13^1/_4$, New Ross $18^3/_4$, Aylwardstown/Glenmore (& Aylwardstown) $24^3/_4$, Waterford North 34.

Dublin (Kingsbridge) 0, (Islandbridge Junction $^3/_4$), *Inchicore* $1^3/_4$, <u>Cherry Orchard</u> 3, Clondalkin $4^1/_2$, Lucan $6^1/_2$, Hazlehatch & Celbridge 10, <u>Straffan</u> 13, Sallins/Sallins & Naas 18, Newbridge/Droiched Nua $25^1/_2$, Curragh Main Line $27^1/_2$, <u>Curragh Siding</u> $27^3/_4$, Kildare 30, (Cherryville Junction $32^1/_2$), Monasterevan $36^1/_2$, Portarlington $41^3/_4$, Mayborough/Portlaoise 51, <u>Mountrath & Castletown</u> $59^1/_2$, Borris & Roscrea/ Roscrea & Parsonstown Junction/Ballybrophy $66^3/_4$, <u>Knockahaw/Lisduff</u> $72^1/_2$, Templemore $78^3/_4$, Thurles $87^3/_4$, (Thurles Junction $87^3/_4$), <u>Goold's Cross (& Cashel)</u> 95, Dundrum $99^1/_2$, (Kyle Crossing $106^1/_4$), Limerick Junction 107, <u>Emly</u> $113^1/_2$, Knocklong 117, Kilmallock 124, (Charleville Junction 128), Charlevill/Rathluric $129^1/_4$, Buttevant (& Doneraile) $137^1/_4$, Mallow $144^1/_2$, <u>Mallow South</u> $145^1/_4$, (Killarney Junction $145^1/_4$), <u>Mourne Abbey</u> $148^1/_4$, <u>Rathduff</u> $154^1/_4$, <u>Blarney</u> $159^1/_4$, Cork (Victoria) 164, Cork $165^1/_4$, Tivoli $166^3/_4$, Dunkettle 168, Island Bridge/Little Island $169^3/_4$, <u>Queenstown Junction</u>/Cobh Junction/Glounthaune 171, Foty/Fota $171^1/_4$, Carrigaloe 174, Monkstown Ferry/Rushbrooke (sometimes called Wheeler's Dock), $175^1/_2$, Queenstown/ Cobh $176^1/_2$; Carrigtwohill 174, Midleton $177^3/_4$, Mogeely $182^3/_4$, Killeagh $185^1/_2$, Youghal 192.

(Islandbridge Junction 0), (Glasnevin Junction $2^1/_2$), Glasnevin 3, Drumcondra $3^3/_4$, (North Strand Road Junction $4^1/_4$), Dublin (Amiens Street) $4^3/_4$ and (Church Road Junction $4^3/_4$), North Wall $5^1/_4$.

Sallins 0, Naas 2, Harristown $7^3/_4$, Dunlavin 14, Colbinstown 17, Grange Con $19^3/_4$, Baltinglass $24^1/_4$, Rathvilley $28^3/_4$, Tullow $34^3/_4$.

(Cherryville Junction 0), <u>Kildangan</u> 4, Athy $12^1/_4$, Magheny $18^1/_2$, Carlow $23^1/_2$, Milford $27^3/_4$, Bagenalstown $33^1/_2$, Gowran $41^3/_4$, (Lavistown Junction $46^1/_2$), Kilkenny $49^1/_2$.

Athy 0, (Ballylinan $4^1/_2$), (Wolfhill Collieries 10).

Bagenalstown 0, Goresbridge $4^3/_4$, Borris $7^3/_4$, <u>Glynn</u> $16^3/_4$, Ballywilliam $20^3/_4$, Palace East $24^1/_4$.

Portarlington 0, Geashill $8^3/_4$, Tullamore $15^1/_2$ later $16^1/_4$, Clara $22^3/_4$, (Clara & Banagher Junction $24^1/_4$), <u>Prospect</u>/Ballycumber $26^1/_2$, <u>Doon</u>/Ballinahoun 33, Athlone $38^3/_4$, (Athlone East Junction 39).

(Clara & Banagher Junction 0), Belmont (& Cloghan) $11^1/_2$, Banagher $17^3/_4$.

Maryborough 0, (Conibery Junction $^3/_4$), Abbeyleix $9^3/_4$, Attanagh $14^3/_4$, Ballyragget $17^3/_4$, (Castlecomer Junction $24^1/_2$), Kilkenny $28^1/_2$, <u>Lavistown</u> $30^3/_4$, <u>Dunbell</u> 33, Bennetsbridge $34^1/_4$, <u>Newhouse</u> 37, Thomastown 39, Jerpoint Hill 40, Ballyhale $43^1/_4$, Mullinavit $51^3/_4$, Kilmacow $54^3/_4$, Dunkitt $56^3/_4$,

(Newrath Junction 60).

(Conibery Junction 0), Mountmellick 6³/₄.

(Castlecomer Junction 0), <u>Corbetstown</u> 3, Castlecomer 7¹/₂, (Deerpark Colliery 9³/₄).

Ballybrophy 0, Roscrea 10¹/₄, Cloghjordan 20¹/₄, Nenagh 29¹/₂, (Silvermines Junction 35¹/₄), <u>Shallee</u> 36, Birdhill 42¹/₂, Castleconnell 47, <u>Nenagh Road</u>/Lisnagry 48³/₄, <u>Grange</u>/Annacotty 50¹/₂, Killonan 52¹/₂.

Roscrea 0, <u>Brosna</u> 5, Parsonstown/Birr 12; Parsontown/Birr 0, Portumna 12.

Birdhill 0, Killaloe 2¹/₂ later 3.

(Thurles Junction 0), Horse & Jockey 4¹/₄, Laffan's Bridge 8¹/₄, Farranalean 12³/₄, Fethard 15³/₄, <u>Powerstown</u> 23³/₄, Clonmel 24¹/₄.

Limerick 0, 1st station ¹/₄, (Limerick Check ¹/₂), (Ennis Junction 1), Killonan 4¹/₄, <u>Boher</u> 7¹/₂, <u>Dromkleen</u> 11¹/₂, Pallas 14, Olla 18¹/₂, (Milltown Crossing 21¹/₂), (Keane's Points 21³/₄), Limerick Junction 22; (Milltown Crossing 21¹/₂), (Kyle Crossing 22); Tipperary 24³/₄, Bansha 29¹/₂, Cahir 38¹/₂, Clonmel 49¹/₂, Kilsheelan 55³/₄, Carrick-on-Suir 63, Fiddown (& Portlaw) 67¹/₄, <u>Grange</u> 70, Dunkitt 75¹/₂, (Newrath Junction 76), (Suir Bridge Junction 76³/₄), Waterford 77 later 77¹/₄.

(Charleville Junction 0), Bruree 4³/₄, <u>Rosstemple</u> 8³/₄, Croom 12³/₄, Patrick's Well 17³/₄.

Mallow 0, <u>Castletownroche</u> 7, <u>Ballyhooley</u> 11³/₄ Fermoy 16³/₄, Fermoy (WD&LR station) 17, Clondulane 19¹/₂, Ballyduff 25³/₄, Tallow Road 29¹/₄, Lismore 32, Cappoquin 36, Cappagh 40¹/₄, Dungarvan 46¹/₄, (divergence of Ballinacourty branch 49¹/₂), Durrow (& Stradbally) 53¹/₄, Kilmacthomas 60¹/₄, <u>Carroll's Cross</u> 64¹/₄, Kilmeadan 68³/₄, (Grace Dieu Junction 73¹/₂), Waterford South 75 and (Suir Bridge Junction 75).

Waterford North 0, (Abbey Junction ¹/₂), <u>Kilmokea</u> 6, Campile 8, Ballyculane 13¹/₄, Wellington Bridge 17¹/₄, Duncormick 24, Bridgetown 28, Killinick 31³/₄, Rosslare Strand 34³/₄ ; Killinck 0, (Felthouse Junction 2).

Wexford North 0, <u>South Wexford</u>/Wexford South ³/₄, (Felthouse Junction 4¹/₄), Rosslare/Rosslare Strand 6¹/₄, Ballygeary/Rosslare Harbour/Kilrane 8³/₄, <u>Ballygeary</u>/Rosslare Harbour (Mainland) 9¹/₄, Rosslare Pier 9³/₄, Rosslare Harbour/Rosslare Harbour (Pier) 10.

Fermoy 0, Glanworth 4¹/₂, <u>Ballindangan</u> 8¹/₂, <u>Brigown</u> 11¹/₂, Mitchelstown 11³/₄.

(Killarney Junction 0), <u>Lombardstown</u> 5¹/₂, Kanturk/Banteer 10³/₄, <u>Rathcool</u> 15, Millstreet 19, <u>Shinnagh</u>/Shinnagh & Rathmore/Rathmore 25¹/₂, Freemount 28, <u>Headford</u> 32¹/₄, <u>Headford Junction</u> 32³/₄, (Tralee Junction 39¹/₂), Killarney 40, <u>Fitzgerald Platform</u> 40¹/₄, <u>Ballybrack</u> 46³/₄, Farranfore Junction 50¹/₄, <u>Gortatlea</u> 54¹/₄, Tralee 61¹/₂.

Banteer 0, Kanturk 3³/₄, Newmarket 8³/₄.

Headford Junction 0, Loo Bridge 6¹/₄, Morley's Bridge 9³/₄, Kilgarvan 13¹/₄, Kenmare 19³/₄.

Farranfore Junction 0, Molahiffe 1³/₄, Castlemaine 6¹/₂, <u>Milltown</u> 7³/₄, Killorglin 12¹/₂, Carragh Lake 16, <u>Dooks</u> 18¹/₄, Glenbigh 19³/₄, Mountain Stage 23³/₄, Kells 30¹/₂, Cahirciveen 36³/₄, Valentia Harbour 39¹/₄.

Gortalea 0, Castleisland 4¹/₂.

Limerick 0, (Foynes Junction ¹/₂), <u>Fort Etna</u> 6, Patrick's Well 6³/₄, <u>Kilgobbin</u> 9¹/₄, Adare 10¹/₂, Rathkeale/Ballingrane Junction 16³/₄, Askeaton 20¹/₄, Foynes 26¹/₄.

(Limerick Check 0), (Foynes Junction) $^1/_2$.

Ballingrane Junction 0, Rathkeale $1^3/_4$, Ardagh $7^1/_4$, Newcastle West 12, Barnagh 18, Devon Road $22^3/_4$, Abbeyfeale 26, Kilmorna 28, Listowel $35^1/_4$, Lixnaw $41^3/_4$, Abbeydorney $36^3/_4$, Ardfert 50, Tralee $54^3/_4$.

Tralee 0, Spa $4^1/_4$, Kilfenora $6^1/_4$, Fenit 8.

Limerick 0, (Ennis Junction 1), Longpavement 4, Cratloe $9^3/_4$, Sixmilebridge 13, Ballycar & Newmarket $16^3/_4$, Ardsolus & Quin $19^3/_4$, Clarecastle $22^3/_4$, Ennis $24^3/_4$, Crusheen $32^1/_2$, Tubber $36^3/_4$, Gort $42^1/_4$, Ardrahan 49, Craughwell (& Loughrea) 55, Athenry $60^1/_2$, Ballyglunnin 70, Tuam 76, Castlegrove $80^3/_4$, Milltown 85, Ballindine $88^3/_4$, Claremorris 93, Claremorris (MGWR) $93^1/_4$, Kiltimagh $102^3/_4$, Swinford $110^1/_2$, Charlestown $117^1/_2$, Curry $120^1/_4$, Tubbercurry 124, Carrowmore 129, Leny $134^1/_2$, Collooney 139, (Collooney Junction $139^1/_2$); (connecting line to SL&NCR $^1/_4$).

Waterford (Manor) 0, Tramore $7^1/_2$.

Cork city line $^3/_4$ from Glanmire Road to Albert Quay

Cork (Albert Quay) 0, (Ballyphehane Junction 1), Waterfall $6^3/_4$, Ballinhassig (& Kinsale Road) 10, <u>Junction</u>/Kinsale Junction/Crossbary $13^1/_4$, Upton & Brinny/Upton & Innishannon $15^1/_4$, Innishannon Road $17^3/_4$, <u>West Cork Junction</u> $19^1/_2$, Bandon 20 later $19^3/_4$, <u>Bandon West</u> $20^1/_2$, <u>Castlebernard</u> $21^3/_4$, <u>Clonakilty Junction</u> 24, Desert $27^3/_4$, Enniskeen $29^1/_2$, <u>Ballineen & Enniskeen</u> 30, Ballineen $30^3/_4$, *<u>Manch (or Ballyboy Fair Field)</u>* $34^1/_4$, Dunmanway $37^3/_4$, <u>Knuckbue</u> 42, Drimoleague Junction $45^3/_4$ later $45^1/_2$, <u>Madore</u> 49, Skibbereen $53^1/_2$, Creagh $57^3/_4$, Baltimore $61^1/_4$.

Kinsale Junction 0, <u>Ballymartle</u> $3^3/_4$, Farrangalway $7^3/_4$, Kinsale $10^3/_4$.

Clonakilty Junction 0, Ballinascarthy $5^1/_2$, Clonakilty $8^1/_4$.

Ballinascarthy 0, <u>Skeaf</u> $2^1/_2$, Timoleague 6, Courtmacsherry $8^1/_2$.

Drimoleague Junction 0, <u>Augherville</u> 5, Durrus Road $6^1/_2$, Bantry $11^3/_4$ later $12^1/_2$, Bantry Pier $12^3/_4$.

Skibbereen 0, Newcourt $2^3/_4$, Church Cross 4, Hollyhill $5^1/_2$, Kilcoe $6^1/_2$, Crooked Bridge $7^1/_4$, Ballydehob $9^1/_2$, Woodlands 12, Schull $14^1/_4$, (Schull pier $14^3/_4$).

Cork (Capwell) 0, (Ballyphehane $^3/_4$), <u>Bishopstown</u> 3, Ballincollig $6^1/_2$, Killumney $9^1/_2$. Kilcrea $12^3/_4$, Crookstown Road $16^3/_4$, Dooniskay 21, Macroom $24^1/_2$.

Cork (Albert Street) 0, *<u>Cork Show Yard Half</u>*, *<u>Athletic Ground Half</u>*, (point of 1873 deviation $1^1/_4$), Blackrock 2, *<u>Ballynure</u> (private)* *, Douglas/Rochestown $3^3/_4$, Passage $6^1/_4$, Glenbrook $7^1/_4$, Monkstown $8^1/_4$, Rafeen $9^3/_4$, Carrigaline $11^1/_2$, *<u>Hoddersfield</u> (private)* *, Crosshaven 16.

Cork (Western Road) 0, <u>Gaol Cross</u> $^3/_4$, <u>Victoria</u> 1, <u>Exhibition Halt</u> $1^1/_4$, Carrigrohane $3^1/_2$, <u>Leemount</u> 4, Heely's Bridge 5, Junction/Coachford Junction $6^1/_4$, Tower Bridge 7, St. Anne's $7^1/_4$, Blarney $8^3/_4$.

Coachford Junction 0, Cloghroe $1^1/_2$, <u>Gurteen</u> $3^1/_4$, Dripsey 5, Kilmurry $6^1/_4$, Peake 8, Coachford $9^1/_4$.

St. Anne's 0, <u>Burnt Mill</u> $1^3/_4$, *<u>Gurth</u>* 3, Fox's Bridge 4, <u>Knockane</u> 5, Firmount 7, Donoughmore $8^1/_2$.

(Tralee GS&WR yard 0), Tralee T&DLR $^1/_4$.

Tralee 0, Basin 1, Blennerville $2^1/_4$, *<u>Tonavane</u>* $3^1/_4$, Curraheen $5^1/_2$, Derrymore $7^1/_2$, Camp Junction/ Castlegregory Junction $9^3/_4$, *Camp* $11^1/_4$, *Glenagalt Bridge/Glounagalt Bridge* 14, *<u>Glenmore</u>* 16, Emalough $17^3/_4$, Annascaul $20^3/_4$, *<u>Ballinasare</u>/Ballinosare* 23, *<u>Puck Island</u>* $24^1/_4$, Garrynadure $24^3/_4$, Lispole $26^1/_2$, *<u>Ballinsteenig</u>/Ballinasteenig* 28, Dingle 31, (Dingle Pier $31^1/_2$).

Castlegregory Junction 0, *Deelis* 2^1/$_2$, *Aughacasla* 4^1/$_4$, Castlegregory 6^1/$_4$.

Ennis 0, _Lifford_ 1^3/$_4$, _Ruan/Ruane_ 6^3/$_4$, Corofin 8^3/$_4$, _Roxton_ 9^3/$_4$, _Willbrook_ 11^3/$_4$, _Clouna_ 14, _Monreal_ 15^3/$_4$, Ennistymon 18^1/$_2$, _Workhouse_ 19^1/$_2$, Lahinch 20^3/$_4$, _Hanrahan's Bridge_ 22^1/$_4$, _Rineen_ 25, Milltown Malbay 27, _Annagh No. 2_ 29^1/$_2$, Quilty 31, Kilmurray 32^1/$_2$, Craggaknock 43^1/$_2$. _Tully Cross_ *, Doonbeg 37^3/$_4$, _Shragh_ 39^3/$_4$, Moyasta Junction 43, Blackweir 45^1/$_4$, Kilkee 47^3/$_4$.

Moyasta Junction 0, Kilrush 3^3/$_4$, Cappagh Pier 4^3/$_4$.

Dublin (Amiens Street) 0, (Newcomen Junction ^{1}/$_4$), (Glasnevin Junction 2^3/$_4$), Liffey Junction 3^1/$_2$, (Church Road Junction 0), (West Road Junction ^{1}/$_4$), (Newcomen Junction ^{1}/$_2$) ; (North Wall MGWR 0), (West Road Junction ^{1}/$_2$).

Dublin (Broadstone) 0, _Liffey Junction_ 1^1/$_2$, Reilly's Bridge 2, _Broombridge_ 2, _Ashtown_ 3, _Castlenock_ & _Granard_ _Bridge_ 4, Blanchardstown 4^1/$_2$, _Coolmine_ 5, Clonsilla 7, Lucan/Leixlip Confey 9, Coldblow & Louisa Bridge/Leixlip/Leixlip Louisa Bridge 11^1/$_4$, Maynooth 15, Kilcock 19^3/$_4$ later 20, Ferns Lock 20^3/$_4$, Enfield 26^1/$_2$, (Nesbit Junction 27^3/$_4$), Moyvalley 30^1/$_4$, Kinnegad/Hill of Down 35^3/$_4$, Killucan 41^3/$_4$, Mullingar 50^1/$_4$, _Newbrook_ 51^1/$_2$, Castletown 58^1/$_4$, Streamstown 61^3/$_4$, Moate 68^1/$_2$, (Athlone East Junction 77^3/$_4$), Athlone 78, _Thomastown_/Carrowduff 85, Ballinasloe 91^3/$_4$, Woodlawn 101^1/$_2$, _Attymon_ _Junction_/Attymon 107^1/$_4$, Athenry 113^1/$_2$, Oranmore 121^1/$_2$, (junction for Clifden branch 126^1/$_2$), Galway 126^3/$_4$.

Clonsilla 0, Dunboyne 3^1/$_4$, _Fairyhouse_ 5^1/$_2$, Batterstown 8^3/$_4$, Drumree 11^3/$_4$, Kilmessan 17^1/$_4$, Bective 20^1/$_4$, Navan 23, _Navan Junction_ 23^1/$_2$, _Proudstown Park_ 26, Gibbstown 27^1/$_4$, Wilkinstown 30, _Castletown_ 32^3/$_4$, Nobber 36^1/$_4$, Kilmainham Wood 39, Kingscourt 43^1/$_2$.

Kilmessan 0, Trim 5^1/$_2$, Athboy 12^1/$_4$.

(Nesbit Junction 0), Carbury 6, Edenderry 9^1/$_2$.

Mullingar 0, Clonhugh 6^1/$_4$, Multyfarnham 7^1/$_4$, _Cavan Junction_/Inny Junction 10^3/$_4$, _Street_/Street & Rathown 13, Edgeworthstown/Mostrim 17^1/$_2$, Longford 26, _Newtownforbes_ 29^3/$_4$, Dromod 37, _Drumsna_ 42^3/$_4$, Carrick-on-Shannon 47^1/$_2$. Boyle 56^1/$_4$, _Kilfree Junction_ 62^1/$_4$, Ballymote 70^1/$_4$, Collooney 77^1/$_2$, (Collooney Junction 77^3/$_4$), (Carringnagat Junction 78^1/$_2$), Ballysodare 79^1/$_2$, Sligo 83^1/$_2$ later 84; (Sligo Quay 85).

Inny Junction 0, Float 3^3/$_4$, Ballywillan 9^1/$_4$, _Drumhawnagh_/Drumhawna 15^1/$_4$, Crossdoney 20^1/$_2$, Cavan 24^3/$_4$.

Crossdoney 0, Arva Road 2^1/$_4$, Killeshandra 7.

Kilfree Junction 0, _Island Road_ 4^3/$_4$, Edmondstown 6^3/$_4$, Ballaghaderreen 9^1/$_2$.

Streamstown 0, Horseleap 3, Clara 7^1/$_4$.

Athlone 0, Kiltoom 5^1/$_2$, _Nine Mile Bridge_ 9, Knockcroghery 12, Ballymurry 14^3/$_4$, Roscommon 18^1/$_4$, Donamon 23^3/$_4$, _Ballymoe_ 29^1/$_2$, Castlerea 34^1/$_2$, _Ballinlough_ 40^3/$_4$, Ballyhaunis 46, _Bekan_ 50^3/$_4$, Claremorris 56^3/$_4$, Balla 64^1/$_4$, _Manulla Junction_ 68, Castlebar 71^3/$_4$, _Islandeady_ 77, Westport 83, Newport 90^3/$_4$, Mallarany 101^1/$_4$, Achill 109^1/$_2$.

Westport 0, Westport Quay 1^3/$_4$.

Claremorris 0, Hollymount 7^1/$_4$, Ballinrobe 12^1/$_2$.

Manulla Junction 0, _Ballyvary_ 4^1/$_2$, Foxford 11, Ballina 20^1/$_4$, Killala 28^1/$_4$.

Attymon Junction 0, Dunsandle 4, Loughrea 9.

(Galway 0), Moycullen 8, _Ross_ 12^1/$_2$, Oughterard 17, Maam Cross 27, _Recess hotel_ _platform_ 35^1/$_4$, Recess 36^1/$_2$, _Ballynahinch_ 41^3/$_4$, Clifden 49^1/$_2$.

Dromod 0, _Dereen_ 2^1/$_4$, _Clooncahir_ 4^3/$_4$, Mohill 5^1/$_2$, _Rosharry_ 7 later 7^1/$_2$, _Adoon_ 10,

Fenagh 12¹/₂, *Lawderdale* 14, Ballinamore 16, <u>*Corgan*</u> 17³/₄, *Garadice* 19¹/₄, <u>*Killyran*</u> 21, Bawnboy Road & Templeport/ Bawnboy Road 23, *Ballyheady* 24¹/₂, Ballyconnell 27¹/₄, <u>*Killywilly*</u> 29¹/₂, *Tomkin Road* 30, Belturbet 33¹/₂

Ballinamore 0, Ballyduff 3¹/₄, *Cornabrone* 6, *Annadale* 7³/₄ <u>*Driney*</u> 8, *Kiltubrid* 8³/₄, *Creagh* 10¹/₄ Drumshambo 12¹/₄, Arigna 14³/₄, (Derreenavoghy 16¹/₄), (Aughabehy 19).

Lines forming the GNR

For stations Dublin (Amiens St) - Howth see Table 2

Dublin (Amiens Street) 0, Baldoyle 5¹/₄, Portmarnock 6³/₄, Malahide 9, Donabate 11¹/₂, Rusk, Lusk/Rush & Lusk 14, <u>Baldungan</u> 16, <u>Skerries Golf Club Halt</u> 17¹/₄, Skerries 18, *Ardyillan (Private)* 20¹/₂, Balbriggan 21³/₄, <u>Gormanstown</u> 24, <u>Mosney</u> 25³/₄, Laytown/Laytown & Bettystown 27¹/₄, Bettystown 28¹/₂, Drogheda 31¹/₂ later 31³/₄, Newfoundwell 32¹/₂, <u>Dunleer</u> 41³/₄, <u>Dromin Junction</u> 43³/₄, <u>Castlebellingham</u> 47¹/₄, (Dundalk South Junction 53¹/₂), Dundalk Junction 54, <u>Dundalk (Junction)</u> 54¹/₂, Plaster/Mount Pleasant (& Jonesborough) 58, <u>Adavoyle</u> 62¹/₂, Wellington Inn 64¹/₄, <u>Newry (Main Line)</u>/Bessbrook & (Newry Main Line)/Newry 69¹/₄, Mullaglass/Newry (Armagh Road) 70¹/₂, Goraghwood 72, <u>*Knockarney*</u> 73¹/₂, <u>*Aughteranter*</u> 76, Poyntzpass 77, <u>*Acton*</u> 78, Scarva 79¹/₂, Madden's Bridge/Tanderagee (& Gilford) 82, (Portadown Junction 87¹/₄), Portadown 87¹/₂, (Knockmore Junction 103¹/₂), (Ulster or Central Junction 112), Belfast (Great Victoria Street) 112¹/₂ ; (for stations between Poratdown and Belfast see Table 3.

(East Wall Junction 0), (Church Road Junction ¹/₂).

Drogheda 0, <u>Duleek</u> 4³/₄, <u>Loughter</u> 8¹/₂, <u>Beauparc</u> 11³/₄, *Factory Crossing* 16¹/₄, Navan 16³/₄, <u>Navan Junction</u> 17, *Newgate Crossing* 18³/₄, *Ardbraccan Crossing* 20, *Castlemartin Crossing* 21¹/₂, *Phoenixtown Crossing* 22¹/₄, <u>Ballybeg</u> 23, Kells 26¹/₂, Virginia Road 33, Oldcastle 39.

Dromin Junction 0, Ardee 4³/₄.

(Dundalk South Junction 0), (Dundalk East Junction ¹/₄).

Warrenpoint 0, Narrow Water (& Green Island) 1¹/₄, Newry Kilmorey Street 5³/₄, Newry (Dublin Bridge) 6, (King Street Junction 6¹/₂), Newry (Edward Street) 6³/₄, Goraghwood 10, <u>Ballydogherty</u> 14, Loughgilly/Glen Anne 16, Markethill 18³/₄, Hamilton's Bawn 22³/₄, Armagh 26¹/₂ later 27¹/₂.

(King Street Junction 0), (junction with DN&GR ¹/₄).

Scarva 0, *Martin's Bridge* 1¹/₄, *Kernan* 2*, *Drumhork Cross* 3¹/₂, *Uprichard's Cross* 3³/₄ Laurencetown 4, *Chapel Row Cross* 4¹/₄, *Hazelbank Cross* 4¹/₂, Lenaderg 5, *Millmount Cross* 6¹/₄, Banbridge 6³/₄.

(Knockmore Junction 0), *Newport* 2, Hillsborough 3, *Ballygowan* 5, *Magherabeg* 7, Dromore 8³/₄, *Ashfield* 102, Mullafernaghan 11³/₄, Banbridge 15¹/₂, <u>Corbet</u> 18¹/₂, *Poland's Bridge* 20¹/₂, Katesbridge 22¹/₂, Ballyroney 24¹/₂, *Drumdonald* 26¹/₄, <u>Ballyward</u> 28, *Savage's Bridge* 31, Castlewellan 33.

(Knockmore Junction 0), Brookmount 2, *Brookhill* 3¹/₄, *Meeting House* 4¹/₂, Ballinderry 5¹/₂, *Legatiriff* 6³/₄, Glenavy 8³/₄, Crumlin 11¹/₄, *Millar's Bridge* 15, Antrim 18³/₄.

Dundalk Junction *(2nd station)* 0, (Dundalk West Junction ¹/₂), *Carrickallen* 2, <u>Kellybridge</u> 4, Inniskeen 7¹/₄, *Lannatt* 7³/₄, <u>Blackstaff</u> 9¹/₂, Culloville 12, *Drumgoose* 13, *Annadrumman* 14¹/₂, *Carrigartha* 15, Castleblayney 18, *Doohamlet* 20¹/₂, *Knockmaddy* 23¹/₄, Ballybay 24³/₄, *Shantona Junction* 26¹/₄, *Lislynchahon* 27¹/₂,

Monaghan Road $29^1/2$, _Killygraggy (2)_ 31, _Dromate_ 33, _Drumshannon_ 33, Newbliss 35, _Laeger_ $37^1/2$, Clones $39^1/4$, _Clonmaulin_ $41^1/4$, Newtownbutler $44^1/2$, _Lisnanock_ $46^1/2$, _Sallaghy_ 48, _Keady_ $48^1/2$, _Augherlurcher_ $49^1/2$, _Killynamph_ $49^3/4$, _Castlebalfour_ $50^1/2$, _Barnhill_ 51, Lisnaskea $51^3/4$, _Lisnagole_ $52^1/2$, _Aughernaskew_ 53, Maguiresbridge $53^3/4$, _Kilnashambally_ $54^1/4$, _Coolane_ 55, Lisbellaw 57, _Ballylucas_ $59^3/4$, Enniskillen 62, _Drumclay_ $62^1/4$ _Gortaloughan_ $64^1/4$, _Drumcullion_ $65^3/4$, Ballinmallard $67^1/2$, _Drumcunnis_ 67, Lowtherstown Road/Irvinestown Road/Bundoran Junction 70, _Loughterush_ $70^3/4$, Trillick $71^1/2$, _Shanmullagh_ $73^1/4$ _Galbally_ $74^1/4$, Dromore Road $75^1/4$, _Lissandeden_ 77, _Racrane_ $80^3/4$, Fintona Junction 81, _Togher_ $82^1/4$, _Kiltamnagh_ 83, _Edergole Upper_ $84^1/2$, _Culmore_ $85^3/4$, Omagh $87^3/4$.

(Dundalk West Junction 0), (Dundalk East Junction $^1/2$), (Windmill Road Jct $1^1/2$), (Barrack St. $1^1/2$).

Inniskeen 0, _Essexford_ $3^1/2$, Carrickmacross $6^3/4$.

Armagh 0, Irish Street 1, Milford $2^1/2$, _Ballyards_ 4, _Tassagh_ $6^1/4$, Keady 8, _Carnagh_ $11^3/4$, Creaghanroe 14, Castleblayney 18.

(Shantona Junction 0), Rockcorry $3^1/2$, Cootehill $7^1/2$.

Bundoran Junction 0, _Tague's Crossing_ *, Irvinestown 4, _Johnston's Crossing_ *, _Castlearchdale_ *, _Crowe's Crossing_ *, Kesh 8, Pettigo $13^1/4$, _Castlecaldwell_ $20^1/2$, _Magherameenagh_ 23, Belleek $25^1/2$, Ballyshannon $29^1/2$, Bundoran $33^3/4$.

Fintona Junction 0, Fintona $^3/4$.

(Portadown Junction 0), Richhill $5^1/4$, _Retreat_ $6^1/4$, Armagh $9^3/4$, _Killylea_ $14^1/4$, Tynan Caledon & Middletown/Tynan & Caledon $16^3/4$, Glaslough $20^3/4$, Monaghan $25^3/4$ later 26, Smithborough $32^1/4$, Clones $38^1/2$, _Redhills_ $45^1/2$. Belturbet Junction/Ballyhaise $47^1/2$, _Loreto College_ 52, Cavan $53^3/4$.

Ballyhaise 0, Belturbet $4^1/4$.

(Portadown Junction 0), _Annakeera_ $1^1/2$, Annaghmore $5^3/4$, _Derrycoose_ $6^1/2$, _Verner's Bridge_ $8^1/2$, Trew & Moy $10^1/4$, _Shaw's_ $13^1/2$, Dungannon $13^3/4$ later $14^1/2$, _Junction_ 15, _Donaghmore_ $17^1/4$ _Mullafurtherland_ $18^3/4$, _Reynold's_ $19^1/2$, _Brimmage's_ 20, Pomeroy $23^1/2$, _Carrickmore_ $28^1/2$, _Rollingford_ $30^3/4$, _Sixmilecross_ 32, Beragh 34, _Tattykeeran_ 36, _Edenderry_ $38^1/4$, _Garvagh No. 1_ $38^3/4$, _Garvagh No. 2_ $39^1/4$, (Omagh Market branch junction $40^1/4$), Omagh 41 later $40^3/4$, Mountjoy $44^1/2$, Newtownstewart $50^1/2$, Victoria Bridge $55^1/4$, Sion Mills $56^3/4$, (original junction of Finn Valley Railway 60), Strabane $60^1/4$, _Porthall_ $63^1/2$, _Carrickmore_ 65, St. Johnstown $67^1/2$, Carrigans 69, Londonderry 74 later Foyle Road $74^3/4$.

(Dungannon Junction o), _Old Engine_ $2^1/4$, Coalisland 5, _Annagher_ 6, _Listnastrain_ 7, Stewartstown $8^1/4$, _Grange Crossing_ * _Killymean Golf Links_ *, Cookstown 14.

(Omagh Market branch junction 0), (Omagh Market $^1/2$).

Sligo, Leitrim & Northern Counties Railway

Enniskillen 0, _Mullaghy_ 3, Florencecourt $5^1/4$, _Abohill_ $8^1/4$, Belcoo/Belcoo & Blacklion 12, Glenfarne $17^1/4$, _Kilmackerill_ $21^1/2$, Manorhamilton 25, _Lisgorman_ $29^1/2$, Dromahir $33^1/4$, _Ballintogher_ $36^1/4$, _Ballygawley_ $39^3/4$, Collooney $41^1/2$, (Carrignagat Junction $42^3/4$).

Dundalk, Newry & Greenore Railway

(Windmill Road Junction 0), Dundalk Quay Street $^1/4$, _Bellurgan Point_ $2^1/2$, Bellurgan $3^3/4$, _Annaloughan_ $5^1/4$, _Gyles Quay_ $6^1/4$, Bush 9, _Crossalaney_ $10^1/4$, (junction with Newry line $12^1/2$), Greenore $12^3/4$.

Newry Bridge Street (and junction with GNR) 0, Omeath $6^3/_4$, _White's Crossing_ *, Carlingford $11^1/_4$, _Dunstable's Crossing_ *, (junction with Dundalk line $13^3/_4$).

Belfast & County Down Railway

Belfast Queens Quay to Bangor - see Table 3.

(Ballymacarrett Junction 0), Fraser Street Halt $^1/_4$, Bloomfield 1, Neill's Hill $1^3/_4$, Knock/Nock & Belmont/Knock $2^1/_4$, Dundonald $4^1/_2$, Comber $7^1/_2$, Ballygowan $11^1/_2$, Shepherd's Bridge Halt $13^1/_4$, Saintfield $14^3/_4$, Ballynahinch Junction $17^1/_4$, Crossgar $20^3/_4$, King's Bridge Halt $23^1/_4$, (Downpatrick north junction $25^3/_4$), (junction $26^1/_4$), Downpatrick $26^1/_2$.

(Downpatrick north junction $25^3/_4$), Downpatrick Loop $26^1/_4$, Tullymurry 29 later $29^1/_2$, Ballykinlar Halt $30^1/_2$, Dundrum $32^3/_4$, (junction with Castlewellan line $36^1/_4$), Newcastle $36^1/_2$.

Comber 0, Newtownards $5^1/_2$ later 5, Conlig $7^1/_2$, Groomsport & Bangor/Groomsport Road/Ballygrainey $9^3/_4$, Ballyfotheeley $11^3/_4$, Millisle Road $13^3/_4$, Donaghadee $14^3/_4$, (Donaghadee harbour $15^1/_4$).

Ballynahinch Junction 0, Ballynahinch $3^1/_2$.

Downpatrick (junction) 0, Downpatrick Loop $^1/_2$, Race Course Platform 1, Ballynoe $3^1/_2$, Bright Halt $4^3/_4$, Killough $6^3/_4$, Coney Island Halt 7, Ardglass 8, (Ardglass harbour $8^1/_2$).

(Newcastle junction 0), Castlewellan $3^1/_2$.

Northern Counties Committee

Belfast (York Road) 0, (harbour line junction $^1/_4$), (Bleach Green Junction $4^3/_4$), Monkstown (and junction with old main line) 6, Mossley 7, Ballynure Road/Ballyclare Junction $8^1/_4$, (Kingsbog Junction 9), Ballyrobert Halt $9^3/_4$, Ballypallady/Ballyclare & Doagh/Doagh $10^3/_4$, Templepatrick 14, Dunadry 16, Muckamore Halt $17^3/_4$, Antrim $19^1/_4$, Oriel Park Racecourse $20^1/_2$, Drumsough Junction/Cookstown Junction/Drumsough $22^1/_2$, _Andraid_ 26*, Kellswater $26^3/_4$, Ballymena $30^1/_2$ later 31, Cullybackey 34, Glarryford $38^3/_4$, Bellaghy/ Killagan 41, Dunloy $43^3/_4$, Ballymoney 51, Macfin 54 later $54^1/_2$, Coleraine $59^1/_4$, _Barmouth_ 64, Castlerock 65, Downhill $66^1/_2$, _Umbra_ 68, Magilligan $69^1/_2$. Bellerena $72^1/_2$, Newton Junction/Limavady Junction $77^1/_4$, Ballykelly $79^1/_4$, Carrickhue $80^1/_4$, _Faughanvale_ $81^3/_4$, Willsborough/Muff/Eglinton $85^1/_4$, Culmore 88, Lissahaly $88^1/_4$, Londonderry (Waterside) $92^1/_2$ (add $2^1/_4$ miles for pre 1934 distances and $1^1/_4$ miles for 1994 distances from Belfast Central).

Belfast - Larne Harbour - see Table 3.

Greenisland 0 - Monkstown 2, Mossley $2^3/_4$ (old main line).

(Kingsbog Junction 0), Kings Moss Halt $^1/_2$ Lisnalinchy $1^1/_2$, _Lisnalinch Race Course_ 2, Ballyclare $3^1/_2$.

Cookstown Junction 0, Randalstown 2, Randalstown Camp $2^1/_4$, Staffordstown 8 later $7^1/_2$, Toome Bridge $11^1/_2$, Castledawson $15^3/_4$, Magherafelt 18, (Draperstown Junction $19^1/_4$), Moneymore $24^1/_4$, Cookstown 29.

(Draperstown Junction 0), Desertmartin $1^3/_4$, Draperstown $6^1/_2$.

Magherafelt 0, Knockloughrim 4, Maghera 7, Upperlands $9^1/_2$, Tamlaght 13, Kilrea 16, Garvagh $21^1/_2$, Moneycarrie $22^3/_4$, Arghadowey 25, Curragh Bridge $26^3/_4$, Macfin $29^1/_4$.

Coleraine 0, (Coleraine harbour $^1/_4$ later $^1/_2$).

Coleraine 0, University $1^1/_4$, Portstewart/Cromore 3, Dhu Varren $5^1/_4$ Portrush

5³/₄.

Magilligan 0, *Drummond**, *Magilligan Point* 4¹/₂.

Limavady Junction 0, Broighter ¹/₂, Limavady 3¹/₄, Ardmore 6, Drumsarn 8¹/₂, Derryork 10³/₄, Dungiven 13¹/₂.

Larne Harbour 0, Larne 1, Kilwaughter 4, Ballygowan/Headwood 6¹/₄, Ballyclare Junction/Ballyboley Junction 7³/₄, Ballyeaston 10, Ballynashee 12, Collin 15¹/₄, Moorfields 17¹/₂, Kells 20¹/₂, Ballymena 24³/₄ later 25¹/₄, Ballygarvey 28, Ballycloghan 29¹/₄, Rathkenny 31¹/₄, Clough Road 32, Knockanally/ Martinstown 33¹/₂, Carrowcowan/Cross Roads 35, Cargan 36¹/₂, Parkmore 38³/₄, (Retreat 41¹/₂).

Ballyboley Junction 0, Ballynure 2, Ballyclare 3³/₄, Doagh 6.

Ballymoney 0, Dervock 4¹/₂ Stranocum 6³/₄, Gracehill 8¹/₂, Armoy 10¹/₄, Capecastle 13, Ballycastle 16.

Portstewart station 0, Portstewart town 2.

Londonderry & Lough Swilly Railway

Londonderry (Graving Dock) 0, (*Pennyburn* ¹/₄), Gallagh Road 2, Harrity's Road 2³/₄, Bridge End 3³/₄, Burnfoot 5¹/₄, Junction/Burnfoot Junction/Tooban Junction 6¹/₄, Inch Road 7, Lamberton's Halt 7³/₄, Fahan 9¹/₄, Beach Halt 10¹/₂, Golf Platform/Lisfannon Links 11, Buncranna 12¹/₄, Ballymegan 14¹/₄, Kinnego Halt 15³/₄, Drumfries 18, Meendoran Halt 21¹/₂, Clonmany 23, Ballyliffan 24¹/₂, Rashenny 26¹/₄, Carndoagh Halt 28, Carndonagh 30¹/₄.

Tooban Junction 0, Trady 1¹/₄, (divergence 2 to Farland Point 2¹/₄), Carrowen 3, Newtowncunningham/ Newtoncunningham 6³/₄, Sallybrook 10¹/₂, Manorcunningham 12¹/₄, Pluck 14¹/₄, Letterkenny 18¹/₄, Old Town 19, New Mills 22¹/₄, Foxhall 23³/₄, Churchill 27¹/₄, Kilmacrenan 31, Barnes Halt 33¹/₄, Cresslough 39¹/₄, Dunfanaghy Road 40¹/₄, Falcarragh 47¹/₄, Cashelnagore 50¹/₄, Gweedore 56¹/₄, Crolly 59³/₄, Kincasslagh Road 65¹/₄, Loughmeela/Dungloe Road (Loughmeela)/Dungloe (Loughmeela)/Dungloe 66³/₄, Burtonport 68¹/₄.

County Donegal Railways Joint Committee

Londonderry (Victoria Road) 0, New Buildings 2³/₄, Desertone Halt 5, Cullion 6¹/₄, Donemena 8¹/₄, Ballyheather 10, Ballymagorry 11³/₄, Strabane 14¹/₂, Clady 18¹/₂, Castlefinn 20¹/₂, Lisscooly 22¹/₂, Killygordan 24¹/₄, Cavan Halt 26¹/₂, Town Bridge Halt 27³/₄, Stranorlar 28¹/₄, Carrickmagrath/Meenglas 30³/₄, Derg Bridge 36¹/₄, Barrack Bridge/Barnesmore 40¹/₄, Druminin/Lough Eske 42¹/₄, Clar Bridge 44¹/₄, Donegal 46¹/₄, Killymard 48¹/₄, Mountcharles 50¹/₄, Doorin Road 52, Mullanboy 53¹/₂, Inver 54¹/₂, Port 56¹/₄, Dunkineely 58¹/₂, Bruckless 60³/₄, Ardara Road 63, Killybegs 65¹/₄. *(Additional railcar stops at County Gates (Strabane – Stranorlar), Quinn's Crossing, No. 3 Gates, Lough Gates, Dunnion's Crossing, Townawilly Crossing, Harvey's Hill (Stranorlar – Donegal), Drimark Hill, No. 18 Gates, No. 20 Gates, No. 22 Gates, Spamount, No. 30 Gates (Donegal – Killybegs)).*

Strabane 0, Lifford ¹/₂, Ballindrait 2³/₄, Coolaghey 4³/₄, Raphoe 6¹/₂, Convoy 9, Cornagillagh 11, Glenmacquin 13³/₄, Letterkenny 19¹/₄. *(Additional railcar stops at No. 53 Gates, Killen's Gate Signal, No. 56 Gates, No. 62 Gates).*

Stranorlar 0, Ballybofey ¹/₂ Glenmore 4, Cloghan 6³/₄, Elaghtagh 9, Glassagh 11¹/₂, Ballinamore 13³/₄, Fintown 16, Shallogans 21, Glenties 24. *(Additional railcar stops at Double Gates, Cronadun Bridge, No. 36 Gates, Ballast Pit, Brennan's Gates, No. 38*

Gates).
Donegal 0, Hospital $^1/_2$ Drumbar $1^1/_2$, Laghey $3^1/_4$, Bridgetown 5, Ballintra 7, Dromore 8, Rossnawlagh $10^1/_4$, Friary Bridge $10^1/_2$, Coolmore 11, Creevy $12^3/_4$, Ballyshannon $15^1/_2$. *(Additional railcar stops at No. 41 Gates, Drumorry Bridge, Dorrian's Bridge, Corker Crossing, McCann's Crossing, Kildoney Crossing, Gillen's Crossing).*

Castlederg & Victoria Bridge Tramway
Victoria Bridge 0, <u>*Glen*</u> *, *Stonewalls* $1^3/_4$, *Fyfin* $2^3/_4$, *Crew* $4^1/_4$, *Spamount* $5^3/_4$, Castlederg $7^1/_4$.

Clogher Valley Railway
Tynan 0, *Caledon* 1, *Kilsampson* $1^1/_2$, *Ramaket* 3, *Curlagh/Emyvale Road* $4^1/_4$, *Cumber* $5^1/_4$, *Glenkeen* $6^1/_4$, *Crilly* 7, *Glencrew* $8^1/_4$, Aughnacloy $9^1/_2$, *Stormhill* $10^1/_2$, *Tullyvan* $11^3/_4$, Ballygawley $13^1/_2$, *Lisodart* $14^1/_2$, *Annaghilla* $15^1/_2$, *Roughan* $16^3/_4$, Augher $18^1/_2$, *Summerhill/Farrenetra* $19^1/_4$, Clogher 20, *Carryclogher* 21, *Findermore* 22, *Ballagh* $23^1/_4$, *Kiltermon* $25^1/_4$, <u>*Ballyvadden*</u> $26^1/_2$, Fivemiletown $27^1/_2$, *Cranbrooke* $28^1/_2$, *Tattynuckle* $28^3/_4$, *Corralongford,* $29^1/_2$ *Killarbran* $30^1/_4$, *Claraghy* 31, Colebrook $31^1/_2$, *Stonepark* $31^1/_2$, <u>*Skeoge*</u> $32^3/_4$, Brookeborough $33^1/_2$, *Aghavea* $34^3/_4$, *Maguiresbridge Town/Maguiresbridge Fair Green* $36^1/_2$, Maguiresbridge 37.

Giant's Causeway, Portrush & Bush Valley Railway & Tramway
Portrush NCC station 0, Portrush depot $^1/_2$, Bushmills 6, Giant's Causeway 8.

Bessbrook & Newry Tramway
Newry 0, *Craigmore* $1^1/_2$, *Millvale* 2, *Maytown/Maytown & Mullaglass/Mullaglass & Derramore* $2^1/_2$, Bessbrook 3.

Dublin & Lucan Steam Tramway/Electric Railway
Dublin (Parkgate Street) 0, *Islandbridge* *, *Capelizod* *, *St. Lawrence* *, *Palmerstown* *, *Cursis' Stream* *, *Ballydowd* *, *Lucan* 7, *Dodsborough* $7^1/_2$, *Leixlip* 9. *(principal stopping places only.)*

Dublin & Blessington Steam Tramway
Terenure, Kimmage Road, Templeogue Depot, Templeogue Bridge, Templeogue Mill, Balrothery, Stubb's Lane, Tallaght, Clondalkin Road, The Common, Fox's Lane, Fortunestown Lane, Jobstown, Mount Siskin Road, Embankment, Mahon's Lane, Old Saggart Road, Kenny's, Glenaraneen, Crooksling, Brittas, The Lamb (for Kilbride), Tinode Post Office, Hempstown, Slate Quarries Road (for Kilteel), Cross Chapel (for Rathmore), Redlane, Blessington, Corner of Naas Road, Baltiboys Road, Burgage Lane, Featherbed Lane, Ballymore Road, Poulaphouca (timetables were very specific that trams would stop at only these places and no other).

Listowel & Ballybunion Railway
Listowel 0, Liselton/Lisselton $4^3/_4$, <u>Francis Road Halt</u> 7, Ballybunion $9^1/_4$.

Belfast Harbour lines
(junction with NCC 0), (Donegall Quay junction with Belfast Central line 1).

Londonderry Port & Harbour line
Middle Quay 0, (junction with L&LSR $^3/_4$).

Author's Acknowledgements

Why should an Englishman with no Irish ancestry of any sort write about Ireland's railways? Just look at the number of articles in magazines since railway publishing began that have been written by other than Irishmen, or the books that have appeared – that does not deny the great contribution by the Irish to the recording of their railway history. Like so many others your author became entranced at an early age by the articles and illustrations that had appeared in the *Railway Magazine*, especially in the May issues of the years 1936 to 1940, which his father had purchased in quantity about 1946. In those days there was not the quantity of literature on Ireland's railways and some railways had only a little written of them. Then came a chance for a first visit to Ireland, in 1951 soon after starting an Engineering Apprenticeship at Crewe Locomotive Works, when with his colleagues a Saturday visit to Dublin and Inchicore Works gave first sight of both CIE and GNR locomotives, followed by more extended visits in steam days.

It was on joining the Irish Railway Record Society that a greater volume of knowledge became available and the beginnings of friendships that have enabled the author to amass so much of the detail needed for a book in the *Regional History* series, so admirably started by its then publisher, David St John Thomas, as long ago as 1960. Thus the author came to know one who, in his time, has probably done more than anyone behind the scenes to gather together so much knowledge from prime railway source material such as minute books – I refer to the late R.N. Clements, who sadly died when the finishing touches were being put to this work. During many happy visits to his home near Dublin a great variety of aspects of Irish railway history and locomotive practice were mulled over and between us we began to understand the meaning of just a few of those perplexing minutes and inspection reports, no doubt very clear to those who wrote them a century or more ago but full of obscurity to the modern researcher. There are not enough words to express appreciation of Bob's generosity in passing on the results of his own endeavours and his, and his family's, hospitality for so many years; thankfully I was able to reciprocate by forwarding the discoveries I had made in sources in Britain. Therefore I have dedicated this work to him in grateful memory.

Many other members of the Irish Railway Record Society, past and present, have been most helpful with the supply of information – G. Beesley, D.G. Coackham, D.B. McNeil, K.A. Murray, D. Murray, H. Richards, R.C. Flewitt, T. Wall, W.E. Shepherd, J. Langford – to name but a few, and I am very grateful to the society's librarians over the years for access to the collection of so many of the non-public documents from railway sources now safely housed by the IRRS in Dublin.

The Public Record Office at Kew has been a valued source of material, especially in the MT6 and MT29 series relating to inspections of new works up to 1920, and within many other papers and files, especially from the GWR. Membership of the Railway Club of London NW1 has given the author access to many publications of the past, especially the *Railway Gazette*, a source surprisingly little used by railway historians. More recently, the establishment of the Railway Studies Collection at Newton Abbot public library has added to the supply of books and timetables for consultation. To the officers of the Railway Club and the officials at Kew and Newton Abbot the author must grant special thanks for all their trouble in making material available. Peter Kay and K. Manto of the Signalling Record Society have been very generous in passing many useful items that have come to their notice for my use.

The author is especially indebted to J. Langford and M. Davies for their kindness in allowing use of their researches into railcar and railbus stopping places, having identified and located a great many in the northern counties of Ireland.

G. Toms has been very encouraging during the process of compiling the text, drawing attention to many magazine articles and very kindly making available his researches into the quarry and whaling station tramways in the remote Belmullet peninsula of Co Mayo. W.E. Shepherd very kindly allowed a sight of his manuscript on the Midland Great Western Railway well before its publication and the use of facts of value to this text.

The Southern Education and Library Board, Irish Studies Library, Armagh and D. Fitzgerald of Armagh have been most helpful in clarifying matters relating to the Castleblayney, Keady and Armagh Railway.

Both CIE, now Irish Rail, and NIR have been very kind in answering queries and helpfully making some of the more obscure data available; special thanks are extended to M. Foley and D. Grimshaw in Dublin and Belfast respectively.

The author has been fortunate in having his draft read through by D.G. Coakham and D. Steggles who drew attention to shortcomings in presentation, encouraging redrafting to ensure a clearer text. The latter, in his capacity as librarian in charge of the Railway Studies Collection at Newton Abbot has taken a great deal of trouble to draw attention to various official documents which made it possible to provide a better background to the history of railways in Ireland.

Sources and Bibliography

Material has been gathered over some forty years starting in youthful days with the assembly of little more than basic lists of lines and their dates and the purchase of the relatively few books on Irish railways then on the market; like so many, early interest was directed at the locomotives but widened with maturity to embrace all that could be discovered when places such as the Public Record Office, Kew, and the libraries of the Irish Railway Record Society and the Railway Club became accessible. Apart from railway and government department records a whole host of books on Irish railways has been consulted for the material on both company history and the various lines.

To produce a complete list of individual sources would now be just about impossible. However the reader who desires greater detail of Ireland's railway history will find the following invaluable:–

Journal of the Irish Railway Record Society (from No. 1 (1946) and continuing);
Irish Railfans' News (1955 until 1973);
Irish Railway News (October 1993 and continuing)
Irish Railway Record Society, Dublin:
The Great Southern & Western Railway K.A. Murray & D.B. McNeill 1976
Ireland's First Railway K.A. Murray 1981
Irish Railway Record Society (London Area):
Sligo, Leitrim and Northern Counties Railway N.W. Sprinks 1970 and 1980
Irish Railways in Pictures No. 1 – The Great Northern 1976
Irish Railways in Pictures No. 2 – The Midland Great Western Line 1990
David & Charles:
The County Donegal Railways E.M. Patterson 1962
The Lough Swilly Railway E.M. Patterson 1964
The Ballycastle Railway E.M. Patterson 1965
The Canals of the North of Ireland W.A. McCutcheon 1965
The Canals of the South of Ireland V.T.H. & D.R. Delany 1966
The Cavan & Leitrim Railway P.J. Flanagan 1966
Atmospheric Railways; a Victorian Venture in silent speed C. Hadfield 1967

The Ballymena Lines E.M. Patterson 1968

Irish Passenger Steamship Services (two vols) D.B. McNeill 1969 and 1971

Railway History in Pictures – Ireland Vols 1 and 2 Alan McCutcheon 1969 and 1970;

The Runaway Train – Armagh 1889 J.R.L. Currie 1970

The Waterford & Tramore Railway H. Fayle & A.T. Newham 1971

NCC Saga R.N. Arnold 1972

The Clogher Valley Railway E.M. Patterson 1972

An Outline History of Irish Railways H.C. Casserley 1973

The Northern Counties Railway (Vols 1 and 2) J.R.L. Currie 1973 and 1974

The Dublin & South Eastern Railway W.E. Shepherd 1974

Irish Standard Gauge Railways T. Middlemass 1981

The Irish Narrow Gauge Railway J.D.C.A. Prideaux 1981

Irish Steam O.S. Nock 1981

The Belfast & County Down Railway E.M. Patterson 1982

Oakwood Press:

The Dundalk Newry & Greenore Railway D.S.M. Barrie 1957

The Belfast & County Down Railway E.N. Patterson 1958

The Great Northern Railway E.N. Patterson 1962

The Dublin & Blessington Steam Tramway H. Fayle & A.T. Newham 1963

The Giant's Causeway Tramway J.H. Guigan 1964

The Dublin and Lucan Tramway A.T. Newham 1964

The Schull and Skibbereen Tramway A.T. Newham 1964

The Listowel & Ballybunion Railway A.T. Newham 1967 and 1989

The Cork and Muskerry Light Railway A.T. Newham 1968

Steam over Belfast Lough R.M. Arnold 1969

The Cork Blackrock & Passage Railway A.T. Newham 1970;

Private and Untimetabled Railway Stations G. Croughton, R.W. Kidner and A. Young 1982

Belfast Transport Museum:

Ulster Tramways and Light Railways D.B. McNeill 1956

Standard Gauge Railways in Northern Ireland R.G. Morton 1962

Coastal Passenger Steamers and Inland Navigations in the South of Ireland D.B. McNeill 1965

Coastal Passenger Steamers and Inland Navigations in the North of Ireland D.B. McNeill 1965

Longmans, Green & Co. Ltd.:

A History of Railways in Ireland J.C. Conroy 1928

Dublin:

The Great Northern Railway (Ireland) Past, Present and Future K.A. Murray 1944

The Railway Gazette:

Fifty Years of Railway Life J. Tatlow 1920 and 1948
Greenlake Publications:
The Narrow Gauge Railways of Ireland H. Fayle 1946
Blackstaff Press:
The Golden Years of the Great Northern Railway (two parts) R.M. Arnold 1976 and
    1980
The County Down R.M. Arnold 1981
The Belfast & County Down Museum Trust:
Twenty-Five Years Gone R.J.A. Pue 1975
Goose & Son:
British Locomotive Builders J.W. Lowe 1975 and supplement 1988
Railway Executive Northern Counties Committee:
Centenary of the Opening of the Belfast and Ballymena Railway: 1948
Ian Allan Ltd:
Narrow Gauge Album P.B. Whitehouse 1956
Light Railways W.J.K. Davies 1964
Irish Railway Album C.P. Boocock 1968
Irish Railways Since 1916 M.H.C. Baker 1972
Bradford Barton:
The Railways of the Republic of Ireland M.H.C. Baker 1975
The Tralee & Dingle Railway D.G. Rowlands 1977
Irish Railways in the Heyday of Steam H.C. Casserley
The Londonderry & Lough Swilly Railway J.I.C. Boyd
Locomotive Publishing Co:
The Tralee & Dingle Light Railway P.B. Whitehouse & A.J. Powell 1958
Melledgen Press:
A Gazetteer of the Railway Contractors and Engineers of Ireland 1833–1914 L.
    Poplewell 1987
Transport Research Associates:
Irish Railways Today B. Pender & H. Richards 1967
Transport in Ireland 1880–1910 Patrick Flanagan 1969
Track Diagrams Mallow – Rosslare H. Richards 1970
The Baronial Lines of the MGWR Padraig O'Cuimin 1972
Signal Press:
Locomotives & Rolling Stock of Coras Iompair Eireann and Northern Ireland Railways
    (Doyle & Hirsch – various editions)
Railways in Ireland 1834 – 1984 Doyle & Hirsch 1983
Railway Lines of Coras Iompair Eireann and Northern Ireland Railways Doyle &
    Hirsch 1985
Railway News:
The War of the Gauges in Ireland 1889 pamphlet

Midland Publishing:
The Irish Narrow Gauge (two vols) T. Ferris 1993
Irish Railways in Colour T. Ferris 1992
Midland Great Western Railway W.E. Shepherd 1994
Plateway Press:
The West Clare Railway Patrick Taylor 1994
Silverlink Press:
An Illustrated History of British Railway Hotels 1838–1987 D. Carter 1990
Published by author:
Cork City Railway Stations Colm Creedon 1985
The Cork, Bandon and South Coast Railway Vols 1, 2 and 3 Colm Creedon
    1986–91;
The Cork & Macroom Direct Railway Colm Creedon 1960;
The Cork, Blackrock & Passage Railway and River Steamers 1850–1932 Colm
    Creedon 1992
Some Industrial Railways of Ireland W. McGrath 1959
Railways around County Armagh E. McKee 1990
Sealink and its Predecessors in Dublin B. Scott 1989
A History of Northern Ireland Railways W. Robb
Irish Industrial Railways (Nos. 1 and 2) I. Biscoe 1984
Files of the following periodicals have proved to be invaluable:–
*Railway Magazine, Locomotive Magazine, Railway World, Trains Illustrated, Modern
    Railways, Modern Tramway, Light Rail and Modern Tramway, Branch Line
    News, Railway Observer, Journal of the Stephenson Locomotive Society, Five Feet
    Three,*

In addition the following documents have provided valuable source information:–

Bradshaw's Railway Timetables, Bradshaw's Shareholders' Manuals, Railway Year Book, Jane's World Railways, railway timetables (public and working), railway general appendices, railway weekly notices and operating instructions, etc,

Index